NUTRITION & HEALTH IN THE BIBLE

Kathleen O'Bannon, CNC
Larry Richards, General Editor

THOMAS NELSON
Since 1798

NASHVILLE DALLAS MEXICO CITY RIO DE JANEIRO BEIJING

Nutrition & Health in the Bible
The Bible Smart Guide™ Series

Published in Nashville, Tennessee, by Thomas Nelson. Thomas Nelson is a trademark of Thomas Nelson, Inc.

Originally published by Starburst Publishers under the title *Health & Nutrition: God's Word for the Biblically-Inept.* Now revised and updated.

This book is intended for educational purposes only. Neither the publisher nor the author intends this book to be used for diagnosing or prescribing in any way. If you have any medical or health problems, see your doctor or the appropriate health-care practitioner. If you have spiritual concerns, consult with your pastor or a counselor specializing in this area.

Thomas Nelson, Inc. titles may be purchased in bulk for educational, business, fundraising, or sales promotional use. For information, please e-mail SpecialMarkets@ThomasNelson.com.

To the best of its ability, GRQ, Inc., has strived to find the source of all material. If there has been an oversight, please contact us, and we will make any correction deemed necessary in future printings. We also declare that to the best of our knowledge all material (quoted or not) contained herein is accurate, and we shall not be held liable for the same.

General Editor: Larry Richards
Managing Editor: Lila Empson
Scripture Editor: Deborah Wiseman
Assistant Editor: Amy Clark
Design: Diane Whisner

ISBN 13: 978-1-4185-1003-9

Printed in the United States of America
10 11 RRD 9 8 7 6 5 4 3

Introduction

Welcome to *Nutrition & Health in the Bible—The Smart Guide to the Bible™*. The Bible contains a lot of information on health, nutrition, foods, cooking, and even cures for many recently discovered health problems (also called diseases at one time or another). Who would have thought that 2,000 to 5,000 years ago the inspired writers of the Bible would know that we were going to do this book? There is a vast amount of information in the Bible that corresponds to health and medical information just published.

To Gain Your Confidence

Nutrition & Health in the Bible—The Smart Guide to the Bible™ is a unique book. In it I have compared modern scientific research with what the Bible has to say on topics like food, exercise, and keeping healthy. Scientists and theologians can make things so complicated; it's difficult to make sense of what they're saying. You can be sure that I have tried to make this material as simple as possible without sacrificing accuracy. I believe using the Bible to learn about nutrition and health should be useful and exciting!

We all know that the Bible was written in the area of the world that is called the Mediterranean. Yes, that's right, the Bible is the first Mediterranean diet book. By "diet" I don't mean weight loss; I mean your daily food, your daily regimen of eating, your food lifestyle. Many of the foods that are now being touted as healthy—foods like olive oil, yogurt, whole grains, fish, millet, and bitter herbs—were all part of the Bible lifestyle, the original Mediterranean diet.

Why Use the Bible to Learn About Nutrition and Health?

One New Testament writer put it this way: "All Scripture is given by inspiration of God, and is profitable for doctrine, for reproof, for correction, for instruction in righteousness, that the man of God may be complete, thoroughly equipped for every good work" (2 Timothy 3:16–17 NKJV). This tells me that the Bible should be used as a guide for life and living. No matter what your life needs are, the Bible can guide you. I have found this to be especially true in the area of nutrition and health, and as you read this book, I think you will find the same.

How Is This Book Organized?

As you study *Nutrition & Health*, keep in mind the two main divisions: "Smart Guide to Nutrition" and "God's Word on Good Health." "Smart Guide to Nutrition" is about the foods to eat and how they will help you. "God's Word on Good Health" is about healthy living. You know what I mean: exercise, weight loss, feasting, fasting, health diets, and more.

Nutrition & Health—The Smart Guide to the Bible™ is a unique book. In it, I have compared modern scientific research with what the Bible has to say on topics like food, exercise, and eating disorders. Scientists and theologians can make things so complicated, it's very difficult to make any sense of what they're saying. You can be sure that I have tried to make this material as simple as possible without sacrificing accuracy. I believe using the Bible to learn about nutrition and health should be useful and exciting!

The Languages of the Bible and When It Was Written

The first books of the Bible, written about 1400 BC, and most of the Old Testament, which was completed about 400 BC, were written in Hebrew. However, parts of the books of Daniel and Ezra were written in Aramaic, a related language spoken by most Near Eastern peoples from about 600 BC onward. The people of Jesus's day also spoke Aramaic in everyday situations but studied the Bible in their ancient tongue, Hebrew. About one hundred years before Christ, the Old Testament was translated into Greek, because most people throughout the Roman Empire spoke Greek.

The New Testament was written in the Greek spoken by ordinary people. This meant that the New Testament was easy for all people throughout the Roman Empire to understand, so the message of Jesus spread quickly. All of the New Testament books were written between about AD 40 and AD 95.

Because the Old and New Testament books were recognized as holy, first by Jews and then by Christians, they were copied accurately and carefully preserved. Much later, chapter and verse divisions were added to the Bible to make it easier to find and remember the location of specific teachings. The many Bible translations we now have all try to express the original words of God in ways that people today can understand his message.

What's Amazing About the Bible?

1. The Bible is like no other book. It was written over a span of some 1,500 years. It is a collection of sixty-six different books by a number of different authors. Yet the Bible is one book, with a single story to tell!

2. The first book of the Bible was written in Hebrew some 3,400 years ago, and the last book was written in Greek about 1,900 years ago. Yet the Bible we read in English today is essentially the same as when its words were first written. Uncertainties about Greek words take up no more than a half page in the Greek New Testament—and not one uncertainty affects any basic Bible teaching. Our English Bibles give a reliable and trustworthy account of what was originally written in Hebrew and Greek thousands of years ago!

3. The Bible contains predictions about the future which have come true! Hundreds of predictions have been fulfilled—centuries after they were written. There is only one way this was possible. God knew what would happen ahead of time, and he guided the Bible writers when they wrote their predictions down!

A Word About Words

There are several interchangeable terms: *Scripture, Scriptures, Word, Word of God, God's Word,* etc. All of these mean the same thing and come under the broad heading "the Bible." I will use each at various points throughout the book.

One Final Tip

God gave us the Bible so that by reading it we would enjoy fuller, more healthy lives. Before jumping into the Bible, ask God to help you learn whatever he wants to teach you. With prayerful study of the Scriptures, your life is bound to change for the better! Along with the psalmist, let me urge you to "taste and see that the LORD is good" (Psalm 34:8 NKJV).

About the Author

Kathleen O'Bannon is a Certified Nutrition Consultant, speaker, healer, and author of eight books, including *The Anger Cure, The World's Oldest Health Plan, Sprouts,* and *Whole Food for Seniors.* Kathleen has appeared on thousands of radio and television shows in Canada and the U.S., promoting healthy living and natural foods cooking. Her motto is: Eat Right—Feel Right!

Kathleen divides her time between the U.S. and Nigeria where she works tirelessly with the Bishop Mark Wokocha Foundation HIV/AIDS, skills testing, and poverty abatement programs. She is the formulator of natural supplements and can be reached through www.healthaliveproducts.com or www.kathleenobannon.com.

About the General Editor

Dr. Larry Richards is a native of Michigan who now lives in Raleigh, North Carolina. He was converted while in the Navy in the 1950s. Larry has taught and written Sunday school curriculum for every age group, from nursery through adult. He has published more than two hundred books, and his books have been translated into some twenty-six languages. His wife, Sue, is also an author. They both enjoy teaching Bible studies as well as fishing and playing golf.

Understanding the Bible Is Easy with These Tools

To understand God's Word you need easy-to-use study tools right where you need them—at your fingertips. The Smart Guide to the Bible™ series puts valuable resources adjacent to the text to save you both time and effort.

Every page features handy sidebars filled with icons and helpful information: cross references for additional insights, definitions of key words and concepts, brief commentaries from experts on the topic, points to ponder, evidence of God at work, the big picture of how passages fit into the context of the entire Bible, practical tips for applying biblical truths to every area of your life, and plenty of maps, charts, and illustrations. A wrap-up of each passage, combined with study questions, concludes each chapter.

These helpful tools show you what to watch for. Look them over to become familiar with them, and then turn to chapter 1 with complete confidence: You are about to increase your knowledge of God's Word!

Study Helps

The thought-bubble icon alerts you to commentary you might find particularly thought-provoking, challenging, or encouraging. You'll want to take a moment to reflect on it and consider the implications for your life.

Don't miss this point! The exclamation-point icon draws your attention to a key point in the text and emphasizes important biblical truths and facts.

death on the cross
Colossians 1:21–22

Many see Boaz as a type of Jesus Christ. To win back what we human beings lost through sin and spiritual death, Jesus had to become human (i.e., he had to become a true kinsman), and he had to be willing to pay the penalty for our sins. With his death on the cross, Jesus paid the penalty and won freedom and eternal life for us.

The additional Bible verses add scriptural support for the passage you just read and help you better understand the underlined text. (Think of it as an instant reference resource!)

How does what you just read apply to your life? The heart icon indicates that you're about to find out! These practical tips speak to your mind, heart, body, and soul, and offer clear guidelines for living a righteous and joy-filled life, establishing priorities, maintaining healthy relationships, persevering through challenges, and more.

This icon reveals how God is truly all-knowing and all-powerful. The hourglass icon points to a specific example of the prediction of an event or the fulfillment of a prediction. See how some of what God has said would come to pass already has!

What are some of the great things God has done? The traffic-sign icon shows you how God has used miracles, special acts, promises, and covenants throughout history to draw people to him.

Health and nutrition are important in caring for the body God gave you. The harvest icon gives you facts and advice on how to achieve and maintain good health in your life and in the lives of those you love.

Since God created marriage, there's no better person to turn to for advice. The double-ring icon points out biblical insights and tips for strengthening your marriage.

The Bible is filled with wisdom about raising a godly family and enjoying your spiritual family in Christ. The family icon gives you ideas for building up your home and helping your family grow close and strong.

Isle of Patmos
a small island in the Mediterranean Sea

something significant had occurred, he wrote down the substance of what he saw. This is the practice John followed when he recorded Revelation on the **Isle of Patmos.**

What does that word really mean, especially as it relates to this passage? Important, misunderstood, or infrequently used words are set in **bold type** in your text so you can immediately glance at the margin for definitions. This valuable feature lets you better understand the meaning of the entire passage without having to stop to check other references.

the big picture

Joshua

Led by Joshua, the Israelites crossed the Jordan River and invaded Canaan (see Illustration #8). In a series of military campaigns the Israelites defeated several coalition armies raised by the inhabitants of Canaan. With organized resistance put down, Joshua divided the land among the twelve Israelite

How does what you read fit in with the greater biblical story? The highlighted big picture summarizes the passage under discussion.

what others say

David Breese

Nothing is clearer in the Word of God than the fact that God wants us to understand himself and his working in the lives of men.[5]

It can be helpful to know what others say on the topic, and the highlighted quotation introduces another voice in the discussion. This resource enables you to read other opinions and perspectives.

Maps, charts, and illustrations pictorially represent ancient artifacts and show where and how stories and events took place. They enable you to better understand important empires, learn your way around villages and temples, see where major battles occurred, and follow the journeys of God's people. You'll find these graphics let you do more than study God's Word—they let you *experience* it.

Chapters at a Glance

Part One
SMART GUIDE TO NUTRITION

Chapter 1: The Bible Diet

Chapter Highlights:
- **Whole Grains—The Good Grains**
- **Vegetables and Your Heart**
- **Benefits of Omega-3 Fatty Acids**

Let's Get Started

Are you trying to find the "perfect diet" that will bring you extreme health, great energy, and freedom from many common **diseases**? Perhaps you have read books, articles in newspapers, and entire magazines devoted to health and are still no closer to a healthy diet than before you began your search. Is your head swirling with facts that don't mean anything to you? Well, you can just relax. The Bible has the answer. Yep! God has outlined the perfect diet for you and your family in the Bible. Chapter 1 is an overview of the foods found in the "Bible diet." Each chapter that follows in Part One, Smart Guide to Nutrition, will open up to you a simple, easy-to-follow lifestyle plan that will show you the way to be as healthy as you can be. This lifestyle plan comes from the diet outlined in the Bible; that's why we call it the "Bible diet"!

created
Genesis 1:21, 27; Ephesians 2:10; Colossians 1:16

man and woman
Genesis 1:27

diseases
condition in the body resulting from various causes, such as infection, genetic defect, or environmental stress, and characterized by an identifiable group of signs or symptoms

created
to cause to exist

God Creates

GENESIS 1:1 *In the beginning God created the heavens and the earth.* (NKJV)

In Old Testament times the Hebrew verb for <u>**created**</u> was used only when referring to divine activity, not human activity. Only God could create. It is fitting that the very first chapter in the Bible, Genesis 1, gives the account of Creation and outlines the foods that God created for us to eat.

Food First—Then Man and Woman

After God had created the earth and sky, light and darkness, water, dry ground, vegetation of seed-bearing plants and trees, birds, sea creatures, livestock, creatures that move along the ground, and wild animals, God created the first <u>man and woman</u>—Adam and Eve. God created a garden in the east—in Eden—for them to live and be

Tree
Genesis 2:9

Tree of the Knowledge of Good and Evil
a tree in Eden that signified the ability to know good and evil by personal experience

together in (see Illustration #1). Adam and Eve were allowed to eat of all the plants and trees except for the **Tree of the Knowledge of Good and Evil.** In other words, the first humans had a wide variety of foods to choose from.

Many people look at this passage from Genesis and think we were created to eat only fruits, nuts, and vegetables (which includes grains). These people are called vegans; they do not eat any animal products, including honey and dairy products, nor do they wear leather or use any animal products. This is a popular lifestyle that many young people are now choosing, but it is not scriptural. We will learn in chapter 11 about clean and unclean foods and that with the New Covenant all foods are to be considered clean. It is no longer necessary to follow a specific food rule from the Old Testament. However, we are obligated to eat what is healthiest for our specific bodily needs. If eating certain foods makes you ill or causes allergic reactions, then it is wise to not eat those foods. You have the choice to eat them or not.

In these times of stressful lifestyles, rushing around, breathing in pollution, and so many new antibiotic-resistant health problems, it is best to eat the diet that keeps you the healthiest. It could be based on your blood type, your metabolic type, or trial and error. One thing is certain; you are obligated to take care of your body to better serve God.

what others say

Billy Graham

Human history began at Eden where God planted a garden and made man for his eternal fellowship.[1]

Forbidden Fruit?

GENESIS 2:15–16 ***Then the LORD God took the man and put him in the garden of Eden to tend and keep it. And the LORD God commanded the man, saying, "Of every tree of the garden you may freely eat." (NKJV)***

All of the food in the Garden of Eden was available for Adam and Eve, except the fruit of one tree. God forbade them from eating of the Tree of the Knowledge of Good and Evil. We do not know what the tree was or what the "fruit" of it was, but we do know that the fruit of disobeying God was a curse on Adam and Eve that can still be felt today.

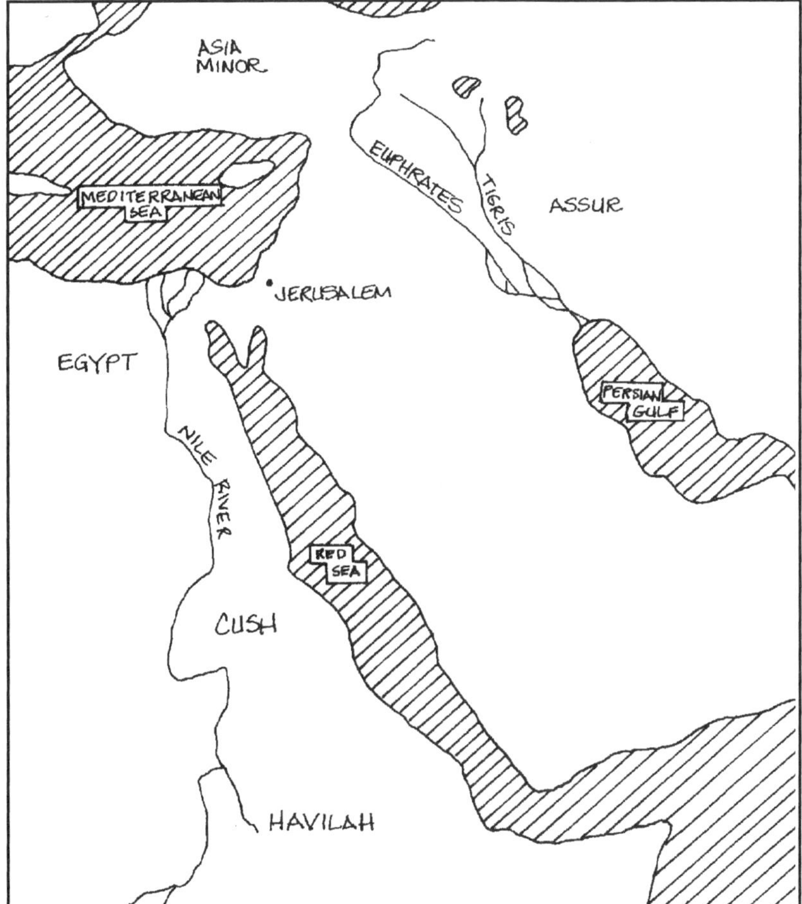

Illustration #1
Map of Eden—Genesis places Eden in this area, probably at the head of the Persian Gulf. Four streams are named, but only two of them are known today, the Hiddekel (Tigris) and Euphrates.

Lots and Lots of Water

Many generations after Adam and Eve, Noah was born. God told Noah to save a male and a female of each kind of living creature and to put them into an **ark**, which he was to build according to God's instructions. He was to include his wife, his sons, and his sons' wives. He was also to include all the food they would need for the voyage. After the Flood, when the water started to recede, God talked to Noah again and gave him some new instructions on what to eat.

Hiddekel (Tigris) and Euphrates
Genesis 2:14

Noah
Genesis 6:9–22

ark
a large, floating vessel

Gotta Have My Meat!

meat
Genesis 27:7, 9; Deuteronomy 12:15

grains
small hard seeds produced by grasses

proteins
the basic element of all plant and animal tissues

GENESIS 9:2–3 *And the fear of you and the dread of you shall be on every beast of the earth, on every bird of the air, on all that move on the earth, and on all the fish of the sea. They are given into your hand. Every moving thing that lives shall be food for you. I have given you all things, even as the green herbs. (NKJV)*

Since Genesis 9, man has been allowed to eat the meat of all animals. For many years before the Flood, man ate only plant foods such as vegetables, fruits, **grains**, beans, and nuts and seeds. But in Genesis 9 God added meat and all other animal products to man's diet. This changed man from just a gatherer to a hunter/farmer/fisherman. This was good news for hunters and farmers; man was now allowed to eat meat from all different animals and fish. So meat was made as important in their diets as vegetables.

When you think about it, there are some similarities between the development of man's diet (in Genesis) and the development of a baby's diet. The first food a baby should eat is mother's milk, then fruits and vegetables, which can include beans, followed later by grains, and last, meat is added.

Only the Right Foods

A wide variety of foods is essential for a healthy body and mind. A healthy diet contains fresh fruits (this includes olives and avocados as they are considered fruits), fresh vegetables and dried beans, whole grains, nuts and seeds, and animal **proteins**. They are the foods that are now proven by science and medicine to be the most healthy, the most healing, the most nourishing, and essential for a vital, fulfilled, and healthy life.

Work the Fields

PSALM 104:14 *He causes the grass to grow for the cattle, and vegetation for the service of man, that he may bring forth food from the earth. (NKJV)*

God taught man to cultivate the plants he made for them to eat, and man became a farmer. Before the Flood, food was found by foraging and digging. But with the advent of farming, after the Flood, man was able to grow the plants he preferred in the quantities necessary to feed himself, his family, and perhaps his neighbors. Man was becoming civilized; he was fending for himself.

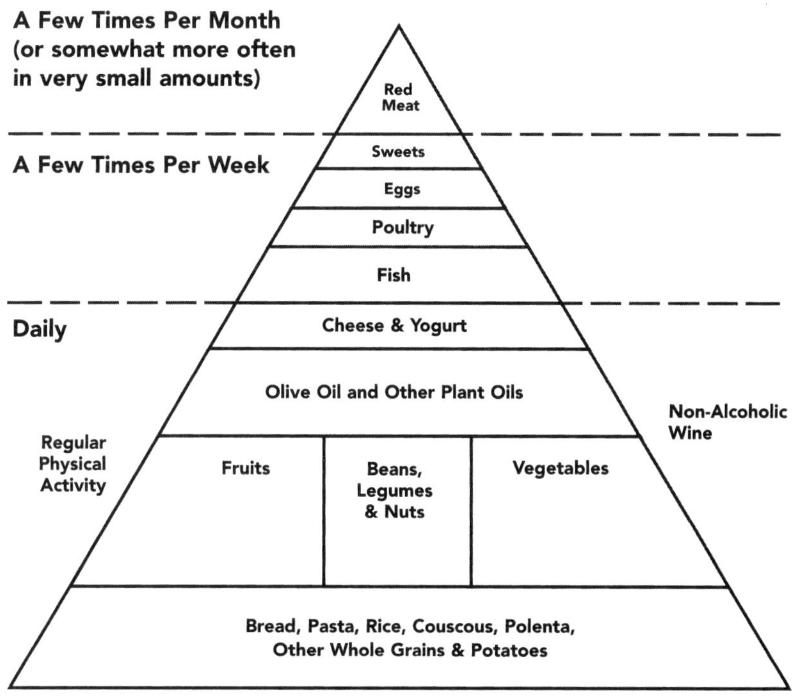

SOURCE: http://oldwayspt.org/index.php

Illustration #2
The Mediterranean Diet Pyramid—From just a glance at this pyramid, you can see we should all eat whole grain breads, pasta, rice, potatoes, polenta, bulgur, and other grains as well as fruits and vegetables. But we should rarely eat red meat, candy, cake, ice cream, and pie.

The Mediterranean Diet / The Bible Diet

The **diet** people followed in **Bible times** is still being eaten today in the **Mediterranean region** of the world (see Appendix B). It has been touted as the healthiest diet and is called either the "Mediterranean diet" or the "Bible diet," which is understandable because the Mediterranean area is where most of the events in the Bible took place. The Bible diet is derived from two biblical sources: specific instructions of what to eat, and general information about the foods available in Bible times. It is simple to follow, and the rewards are great. The Mediterranean diet pyramid (see Illustration #2) is a visual picture of which foods should be in your diet and how much you should eat of each. The more space a particular group of foods takes up, the more you should eat from that group. By just looking at this graph, you can plan a diet every day that will be

diet
the usual food and drink of a person or animal

Bible times
from approximately 1500 BC to AD 50

Mediterranean region
area bordering the Mediterranean Sea

complex carbohydrates
sugar and starches found in whole grains, fruits, and some vegetables

insulin
a hormone produced by your pancreas that regulates the metabolism of sugar in your body

healthy and complete. It will enable you to follow all the dietary guidelines of the Bible.

Do not try a new diet on your own. Always discuss any program with your doctor, especially if you are a diabetic, have a heart condition, or have high blood pressure.

Chew It Up!

The most important thing to remember when you switch to a higher-fiber diet is that chewing starts digestion. Each time you chew grains until they are fully chewed, you are aiding your digestion and reducing your need for larger quantities of food. Saliva contains the enzyme "salivary amylase," which digests starch. The more you chew each mouthful of starch, the easier it will be to digest it. The chewing also starts all the processes of digestion going in your stomach, pancreas, intestines, and so on.

Fiber and Diabetes

For years fiber has been used to reduce the risks and symptoms of diabetes. When I worked as a nutritionist in a Toronto clinic we used a specific diet of 80 percent **complex carbohydrates**, 10 percent fat, and 10 percent protein to help people with diabetes. Most of the patients reduced their **insulin**, and some didn't need insulin at all when they followed the high-fiber diet.

New research is showing that following a diet like the Mediterranean diet can help to reduce the risk of cancer, Alzheimer's disease, strokes, and also reduce the risk of obstructions in blood vessels in the elderly as well as increase longevity and improve quality of life.[2]

Mediterranean Diet and Cancer

An article published in the journal *Cancer Epidemiology, Biomarkers and Prevention* in 2000 concluded that following a Mediterranean diet with its emphasis on low consumption of red meat and high consumption of fruits and vegetables can reduce the incidents of colorectal cancer by 25 percent; breast cancer by 15 percent; and prostate, pancreas, and endometrial cancers by 10 percent. If you have a family tendency to any of these cancers, you owe it to yourself and your family to consume at least the recommended servings of fresh fruits and vegetables.[3]

Mediterranean Diet and Alzheimer's Disease

The Taub Institute for Research in Alzheimer's Disease and the Aging Brain did a study published in 2006 showing that following the Mediterranean diet daily and accurately could reduce the risk of Alzheimer's disease up to 60 percent and also reduce the risk of other brain-related problems thought to be part of old age.[4]

In the Mediterranean area people eat cheese and yogurt almost daily. The yogurt and cheese are often from goat's or sheep's milk and are generally not as fat- or sugar-laden as the cheese and yogurt eaten by most North Americans. When looking at the food pyramid you can see that Mediterranean people eat very little red meat, and that allows them to eat more cheese and yogurt than people who eat mostly red and/or fatty meats. A healthy Mediterranean diet does not include fast-food burgers and fries! It does include fresh vegetables at every meal and fresh fruits, lots more than most North Americans now eat. You might even say that when following the foods and lifestyle of the Bible region, the Mediterranean, you will have an emphasis on vegetables, especially fresh raw ones and dark green leafy ones. Eating at least five to ten servings of vegetables a day is really the key to a healthy and long life.

what others say

Reginald Cherry, M. D.

> A great interest has arisen in medical and health circles today about the foods that have been eaten for centuries in the lands of the Bible. The diet of Middle Eastern people is of particular interest. One name given to this group of foods that prevent disease and help to cure diseases is the "Mediterranean Diet." This is very similar to the one described in Genesis.[5]

Grains, Grains, Grains

The foundation, or base, of the Mediterranean diet is grains. It is the widest section of the pyramid but not necessarily the largest (see

spelt
an ancient form of grain from the wheat family

millet
a high-protein grain of small yellow or brown seeds

triticale
a blended grain of rye and wheat

kamut
an ancient grain found in the pyramids

quinoa
a grain native to Central and South America

Illustration #2). This means that grains should be the base or foundation of a daily diet. The grains available today are wheat, rye, barley, oats, **spelt**, rice, **millet**, **triticale**, **kamut**, buckwheat, amaranth, **quinoa**, and sometimes corn. The suggested amount to eat daily is two to eleven servings. One serving is considered to be one piece of bread, so a sandwich would be two servings of grains. If you also ate another serving of grain for lunch or dinner, like rice or barley, you would meet the minimum daily requirement. Many people decide to eat the grains as snacks. Things like whole grain pretzels, crackers, and toast are great sources of grains.

A Grain Is a Grain

Grains are not all equal. For example, millet, amaranth, and quinoa have less starch or carbohydrates and are higher in protein than the other grains mentioned, making them easier to digest and easier on your blood sugar. Most of the pasta in the Mediterranean region is made from durum flour. Durum is a kind of wheat that is often used to replace Western wheat because it is easier to digest and has had less hybridization over the years so it is often more natural and is perfect for making pasta. Spelt is an ancient grain that is similar to wheat and was not commonly used for thousands of years, so it, too, has not been hybridized or overcultivated. There are many people who are sensitive to wheat who can safely eat whole grain products made from durum or spelt. Please consult your doctor if you are allergic to wheat before you try eating these other wheatlike grains.

Gluten

Gluten is the protein found in wheat, rye, barley, and oats. Gluten is known to cause several kinds of health problems, including celiac disease, dermatitis herpetiformis (a gluten-induced skin sensitivity), and some kinds of autism. Some people find that gluten causes them to have bloating, gas, and other digestive disturbances that can be rectified by taking digestive enzymes. Generally, buckwheat, millet, rice, amaranth, and quinoa can be used in place of gluten grains. If you are a person with any of the health problems related to gluten, please consult your doctor before trying any of these other grains, as there may be other reasons to avoid grains than just gluten.

Spelt

Spelt is an ancient grain that is mentioned in the Bible and is one of the ingredients in Ezekiel's bread.

Spelt, *Triticum spelta*, is an ancient and distant cousin to modern wheat, *Triticum aestivum*. Spelt, along with barley, is one of the oldest of cultivated grains. Spelt is a more flavorful grain than wheat and is often described as having a nutty flavor. In Italy it is known as *farro*; in Germany it is called *dinkle*. In Roman times it was called *farrum*.

Grains

Each of us should eat three to eleven servings of potatoes, bread, pasta, couscous, polenta, bulgur, or other whole grains each day.

Give Us This Day Our Daily Bread . . .

bread
Ezekiel 4:9

daily bread
Matthew 6:11; Luke 11:3

Lord's Prayer
Matthew 6:9–13

encouraged
Luke 18:1–8

refined
Coarse ingredients have been removed.

PROVERBS 30:8 ***Give me neither poverty nor riches—feed me with the food allotted to me.*** **(*NKJV*)**

In Bible times the basic grain was barley. It was made into a round, heavy, full-bodied loaf that was baked fresh every day. This was the "daily bread" that Jesus mentioned in what we call the Lord's Prayer. Much of the bread eaten in Bible times was made of barley and emmer wheat. Emmer wheat is similar to the spelt we have available today.

Daily bread was very important to all people living in the Middle East. Jesus encouraged all people to pray for their daily bread and trust God for it rather than rely on the government of Rome to provide it.

Daily bread was so important for the Israelites that they preferred it over riches. Daily bread was distributed in Roman times to Roman citizens. A recently excavated pyramid showed that workers were paid in "daily bread" while building the pyramids around 2575 BC in the Giza Plateau, Egypt (see Appendix B).[6]

Whole Grains—The Good Grains

Because only whole grains were available in Bible times, it is obvious that we are supposed to eat whole grains, not **refined** ones.

fiber
the indigestible part of plants

nutrients
substances needed by plants and animals for life and health

carbohydrates
substances in plant-based foods that contain carbon, hydrogen, and oxygen

starch
a carbohydrate found in plants

B complex vitamins
needed for health of hair, nails, nerves, skin, liver, mouth, and eyes; found in plant and animal sources

Whole grains contain protein (differing amounts for each type of grain), **fiber**, **nutrients**, and **carbohydrates** or **starch**. Whole grains have the nutrients that God intended people to eat when he made food. When grains like rice, wheat, barley, and spelt are refined, much of the fiber is lost as well as most of the **B complex vitamins**. Fiber and B complex vitamins play important roles in the digestion of the starch in these grains.

Brown or White?

Who decided that white was better? I have read many references that say how years ago the wealthy had the more-refined grains, and the peasants had the cruder, unrefined grains. Who do you think was healthier? I suspect the peasants were.

As a comparison I checked with the USDA National Nutrient Database for Standard Reference, Release 18 (2005), and made a chart. Look at the differences in protein and fiber between the whole grains and the refined grains. It wasn't clear if the wheat flour and rice were enriched because it didn't specify. I chose wheat, rice, and barley because they are the most common grains that we eat in North America and the grains that are most commonly refined. In each selection there is a large difference in some areas, especially fiber, calcium, magnesium, potassium, zinc, and selenium, all nutrients that we need daily.

Comparisons of Three Grains per 100g

Food	Kcal	Protein	Fat	Carbs	Fiber	Ca	Mg	Fe	K	Na	Zn	Se
Wheat flour (white, refined)	361	11.98	1.66	72.53	2.4	15	25	4.41	100	2	0.85	39.7
Wheat flour (whole)	339	13.70	1.87	72.57	12.2	34	138	3.88	405	5	2.93	70.7
Rice, white	130	2.69	0.28	28.17	0.4	10	12	1.20	35	1	0.49	7.5
Rice, brown	111	2.58	.090	22.96	1.8	10	43	0.42	43	5	0.63	9.8
Barley, pearl	352	9.91	1.16	77.72	15.6	29	79	2.50	280	9	2.13	37.7
Barley, whole	354	12.48	2.30	73.48	17.3	33	133	3.60	452	12	2.77	37.7

Key: Kcal=calories (kilocalories); Protein, Fat, Carbohydrates, Fiber, Ca=Calcium in mg (milligrams); Mg=magnesium in mg; Fe=iron in mg; K=potassium in mg; Na=sodium in mg; Zn=zinc in mg; Se=selenium in mcg (micrograms)

what others say

Don Colbert, M.D.

Roman gladiators were sometimes called *hordearii*, which means "barley eaters," because the grain was added to their diet to give them bursts of strength before their contests. Barley is considered to be one of three balanced starches (rice and potatoes being the other two) that are rich in complex carbohydrates and fuel the body with a steady flow of energy.[7]

legumes
seeds of plant, also called beans

vitamins
substances required in small quantities for life and health

minerals
nonliving elements that are essential to the functioning of the human body

The Largest Food Group of the Pyramid

The next section up from the base of the pyramid is the group comprised of fruits, beans and other **legumes**, and vegetables (see Illustration #2). This is the largest section of the Mediterranean pyramid because it is the group of foods that you should eat the most of each and every day.

Dried beans such as navy, kidney, turtle, lima, pinto, and others are really the seeds of the same kinds of plants that produce the green and yellow beans we eat as fresh vegetables. Yellow beans produce a black seed that is used in black bean soup. When the green or yellow beans are left to grow until the green or yellow part is dried out, the seed inside is harvested as a dried bean. It can be used as the seed to plant and grow more beans the following year, or it can be soaked, cooked, and eaten as food.

Powerhouses of Nutrients

GENESIS 1:12 ***And the earth brought forth grass, the herb that yields seed according to its kind, and the tree that yields fruit, whose seed is in itself according to its kind. And God saw that it was good.*** *(NKJV)*

The foods in this largest section of the pyramid, the ones that should be eaten most during the day, are also the same foods God created for the first people on earth. Grains, fruits, beans, nuts and seeds, and vegetables contain **vitamins**, **minerals**, proteins, carbohydrates, fiber, essential fatty acids, and amino acids. These are the powerhouses of health, vitality, and well-being. The concentrated vital nutrients in these foods should be eaten in abundance every day. This group of foods comprises all the foods mentioned in Genesis

1:29: "God said, 'See, I have given you every herb that yields seed which is on the face of all the earth, and every tree whose fruit yields seed; to you it shall be for food'" (NKJV).

RDI, RDA, DRI, Not Too Confusing

The Department of Agriculture in the United States has published the nutrients essential for health since 1941. Of course as we learn more, the nutrients have changed, the amounts have changed, and, in some cases, the required amount has increased. The Mediterranean food pyramid shows the foods to eat and how much of each category of food to eat, but it doesn't tell why. The RDI, RDA, and DRI reveal that. These stand for Recommended Daily Intake, Recommended Daily (or dietary) Allowance, and Dietary Reference Intake (which also includes UL [Upper Limits] for each nutrient). Chapter 20 has made this easy for you. We have listed the RDA and then given some foods containing the nutrient so you can see how to increase your intake of vegetables and fruits to obtain at least the RDA.

The best way to eat more fresh vegetables and fruits is to eat them as snacks. Snack on carrots, cucumbers, radishes, mango, celery, melon, broccoli, red and green bell peppers—the list of snacks is endless. Try having half an apple and six or eight natural almonds or walnuts or three to four whole grain crackers with natural cheese and some lettuce or cucumber slices for a between-meal snack for more energy and vitality. Celery or lettuce spread with peanut, almond, or pistachio butter is a terrific snack that even the pickiest children generally love; you will too. Unsweetened yogurt with chopped fresh veggies and fresh mint is a fabulous cooling and refreshing snack.

What About Nutritional Supplements?

Nutritional supplements are designed to *supplement* your food intake, not take the place of it. In most of the research done on the importance of vegetables and fruits to health, basic nutritional supplements like multivitamins and multiminerals were taken into consideration, and although those who took supplements were healthier, it was generally noted that those people also ate the most servings of fresh vegetables and fruits. You cannot live a healthy, disease-reduced life without eating vegetables and fruits.

Vegetables and Your Heart

We have all heard that vegetables are good for us, but we never heard exactly why they were good for us. Research published in 2001 of an ongoing study showed that for every serving of vegetables, especially dark green leafy ones, and fruits a day, the risk for coronary heart disease goes down 4 percent to 6 percent. Increasing your servings of fresh vegetables and fruits to at least six servings daily can reduce your risk of coronary heart disease from 5 percent to 20 percent. This was especially true for those vegetables and fruits highest in potassium and vitamin C, which lowered blood pressure as well as other risks for coronary heart disease (CHD).[8]

Research published in 2006 in the *Journal of Nutrition* showed that mice fed a diet of green and yellow vegetables reduced their aortic atherosclerosis by 38 percent. Their total cholesterol levels were reduced as well as the low-density lipoprotein levels (LDL). LDL is currently thought to be the form of cholesterol that is dangerous because it can clog the arteries, making it difficult for adequate blood flow through the body and increasing the risk of a stroke or vascular incident because of blood clots being lodged in the narrowed arteries.[9]

So your mother was correct: Eat your vegetables!

what others say

Kenneth Cooper, M.D.

The Mediterranean diet is characterized by an abundance of plant foods such as fruits, vegetables, breads, cereals, potatoes, beans, nuts, and seeds. Fresh fruit is the typical daily dessert and olive oil is the principal source of fat.[10]

Julian Whitaker, M.D.

You should eat plenty of citrus fruits, because they supply you with lots of vitamin C . . . And green leafy vegetables provide the important vitamin E.[11]

Vegetables and Fruits

Eat vegetables at every meal and as snacks; always eat at least one serving of raw vegetables and one serving of fruit each day.

The United States Department of Agriculture used to recommend

oil
Leviticus 2:4

anointing
Exodus 30:26

anointing
putting oil on

that all people eat at least five half-cup servings of vegetables and fruit a day and one serving must be raw. This is the minimum amount of these foods that you need to stay alive, think properly, be alert, heal wounds, grow, maintain proper body weight, and have enough energy to live healthily and be able to exercise daily.[12]

Every year as more research comes out on the importance of eating vegetables and fruits, the recommended amount keeps increasing. In 2006 the recommended amounts were eight to ten servings. This would mean that a small can of mixed vegetable juice would qualify as one serving, a salad meal might contain three or four half-cup servings of different vegetables, therefore constituting three to four servings, and when fresh fruit is added for dessert, you might be eating five servings at that meal alone. If you also have snacks of veggies and fruits during the day, it is easy to eat that amount of food, eight to ten half-cup servings of vegetables and fruits. And by the way, potato chips and French fries do *not* count as anything; sure, they might have started as potatoes, but they are not considered "food."

Five to Keep Alive!

For many years the U.S. Department of Agriculture has promoted various programs trying to convince people to eat at least five half-cup servings of vegetables and fruits. In January of 2006 the *Lancet* published a study showing that eating at least five servings of vegetables and fruits daily can reduce the incidence of stroke by up to 75 percent. That in itself is enough reason to eat your veggies! The more servings of vegetables you have every day, the better you will feel, so try to eat more than the old recommendation of five half-cup servings.[13]

Olive Oil

LEVITICUS 24:2 ***Command the children of Israel that they bring to you pure oil of pressed olives for the light, to make the lamps burn continually.*** *(NKJV)*

In Bible times the oil in olives was used for heating, as lamp fuel, in cooking and baking, for **anointing** and for healing. Olive oil is part of the Mediterranean diet (see Illustration #2) because olives grow in abundance in the **Middle East**, Italy, Greece, and Spain. Olive oil is high in monounsaturated fatty acids. This "good fat" has been shown to help reduce the "bad **fat**" or bad **cholesterol** that sticks to the arteries and may cause many different diseases. The olive oil section of the pyramid shows that it is to be used as the main fat or oil in the diet. This should replace the saturated fats that come mainly from animal sources and the **polyunsaturated fats** that are found in a highly processed form in manufactured bakery products such as crackers and sweet rolls, and some other processed and packaged foods, creating dangerous trans fats.

offerings
Leviticus 2:1

Middle East
the area from Libya east to Afghanistan

fat
an oily solid or semisolid that is the main part of many animal tissues

cholesterol
a necessary component of cells manufactured by all creatures with backbones

polyunsaturated fats
come from vegetable sources

Oil in the Grain Offering

Oil was so important that God commanded it be used for the consecration of priests—the ceremony included anointing with oil and was part of the **grain offerings**. The grain offerings were made with grain or bread and olive oil to symbolize devotion to God. Offerings were important because without an offering, an Israelite was not allowed to approach God.

Olive Oil

In biblical times, the people used olive oil every day for preparing their meals, and we should do the same today.

> **what others say**
>
> **Kenneth Cooper, M.D.**
>
> It is possible that natural **antioxidants** in olive oil help prevent **oxidation** of "bad" **LDL cholesterol**, the major, underlying cause of **atherosclerosis**, or clogging of the arteries.[14]

grain offerings
grains mixed with oil and presented to God

antioxidants
any substance that inhibits or blocks harmful reactions with oxygen

oxidation
combining with oxygen

LDL cholesterol
low density lipoprotein or "bad" cholesterol

atherosclerosis
when fatty substances cling to arteries

A Bull and Two Rams?

EXODUS 29:2–3 ***[Take] unleavened bread, unleavened cakes mixed with oil, and unleavened wafers anointed with oil (you shall make them of wheat flour). You shall put them in one basket and bring them in the basket, with the bull and the two rams.*** (NKJV)

Fine flour and oil were presented to those men who were chosen to become priests, along with a bull and two rams. Imagine the importance of olive oil if cakes mixed with oil, and wafers (or crackers) spread with oil, held the same importance as a bull and two rams.

calcium
mineral essential for bone, teeth, and organ health

I'll Give You My Oil for Your . . .

Jeremiah 41:8 ***But ten men were found among them who said to Ishmael, "Do not kill us, for we have treasures of wheat, barley, oil, and honey in the field." So he desisted and did not kill them among their brethren.*** *(NKJV)*

Oil was so important that it was a major export product of the time. Ancient Greece was one of the largest producers of olive oil. One of the reasons it was important to their economy was olive trees could grow and thrive in rocky soil, which could produce very few other crops. They were also known to live for a long time. Olive production began when a tree was about five years old and was at the height of production between forty and fifty years old. Oil was essential for life because it was used for cooking, lighting, cosmetics, and medicine. Because of its value, the men in Jeremiah 41:8 were able to convince Ishmael to spare their lives when he was thinking about killing them. And why? They knew of a valuable supply of oil hidden in a field. So valuable was this oil, as well as the other foods they mention, that their lives were spared for the sake of obtaining them.

Dairy in the Diet

The next section of foods is even smaller: cheese and yogurt (see Illustration #2). Cheese and yogurt are already partially broken down, which makes them easier to digest than milk. In Bible times most people did not drink mugs or cups of milk, and neither do most people living in the Mediterranean region today. Small quantities of cheese and yogurt can be consumed daily. Of all the available proteins, cheese and yogurt are the best choice for small amounts of daily protein.

There is not the emphasis on drinking milk in the Mediterranean region as there is in North America. Milk is touted as a good source of **calcium**, but dark green leafy vegetables, whole grains, almonds, broccoli, and fish with bones like sardines, anchovies, or salmon are all good sources of calcium. So when you eat a varied diet rich in vegetables and these other sources of calcium, it isn't as essential to drink glasses of milk.

Whey? Never Heard of It

Genesis 18:8 ***So he took butter and milk and the calf which he had prepared, and set it before them; and he stood by them under the tree as they ate.*** *(NKJV)*

whey
liquid part of milk containing most of the B vitamins and some protein

Butter is made by setting cream out overnight to sour slightly, then churning it so the butterfat comes together to make butter, leaving some bits of butter and the soured milk that is left, which contains the **whey**, or liquid. The resulting liquid is also called buttermilk. Buttermilk has been used for centuries as medicine and as a cooling refreshing drink in the summer.

Cheese is made from milk. Some form of acid is used to curd it, then the curds are cooked, strained, and pressed to remove most of the whey. If the cheese is to be an aged cheese like cheddar, it is set in a cool clean place to age. Cottage cheese used to be made naturally like this, but in modern times it is mostly done fast with chemicals unless you are using organic cottage cheese or some local farm/dairy where they still make cottage cheese the natural way. Once the curds form and they are cooked, the process stops there and cream is added to make creamed cottage cheese. It is not pressed or aged, but the whey is generally removed from the curds before the cream is added. Many Europeans drink whey and claim it is helpful for weight loss.

Whey protein is now one of the most fashionable protein powders used in meal-replacement powders or drinks.

Cheese

Cheese is used in the Mediterranean diet as part of a meal or snack. Many cheeses are added to vegetable dishes. Cheese can be made from full-fat milk, which is about 4 percent butterfat, or some imported from France even contain 35 percent butterfat. Cheeses like mozzarella are often made from skimmed milk and have very little butterfat in them. If you are eating cheese as your main protein, then you will want to have regular-fat cheese; 4 percent is fine. If you are adding cheese to a meal that has other fat in it, then you will want to use a lower-fat type of cheese. (See chapter 6 for more information on milk and cheese.)

fermented
made to sour using acid, bacteria, or enzymes

kefir
a fermented milk product

Yogurt

ISAIAH 7:22 ***So it shall be, from the abundance of milk they give, that he will eat curds; for curds and honey everyone will eat who is left in the land.*** *(NKJV)*

Yogurt was eaten in Bible times because it is already fermented, so to speak, and it keeps without much refrigeration, so it was easier to transport.

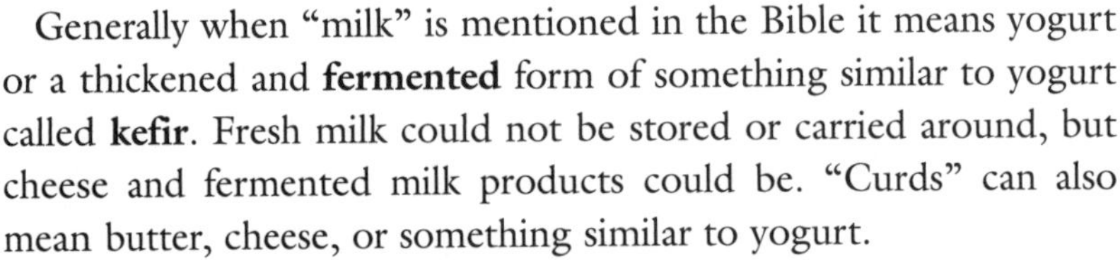

what others say

Pamela Smith

Keep power snacks available wherever you are—in your car, your desk drawer, your briefcase, a purse, or a diaper bag. They can be as simple as fresh fruit or a box of raisins with low-fat cheese or yogurt.[15]

Cheese and Yogurt

Eating cheese and/or yogurt provides nutrients for health.

Generally when "milk" is mentioned in the Bible it means yogurt or a thickened and **fermented** form of something similar to yogurt called **kefir**. Fresh milk could not be stored or carried around, but cheese and fermented milk products could be. "Curds" can also mean butter, cheese, or something similar to yogurt.

The following chart of dairy products compares the calories, protein, fats, calcium, magnesium, iron, potassium, sodium, and zinc in some common dairy foods. For example, when you look at the cow's milk as compared to the goat's milk, you will see small differences in protein and fats, and a huge difference in potassium. If you are a person who needs more potassium, goat's milk might be a better choice for you on a regular basis. Processed cheddar-type cheese, also called American or Canadian cheese, has more than twice the amount of sodium as real or unprocessed cheddar. Please read the labels on all packaged foods that you purchase to check for these nutrients.

Comparisons of Dairy Products per 100 g

Food	Kcal	Protein	Fat	Ca	Mg	Fe	K	Na	Zn
Milk, whole	60	3.22	3.25	113	10	0.03	143	40	.04
Milk, 1%	42	3.37	0.97	119	11	0.03	150	44	0.42
Milk, goat	69	3.56	4.14	134	14	0.05	204	50	0.30
Yogurt, whole	61	3.43	3.25	121	12	0.05	155	46	0.89
Yogurt, low-fat	63	5.25	1.55	183	17	0.08	234	70	0.89
Cheddar	403	24.90	33.14	721	28	0.68	98	621	3.11
Cheddar, processed American	240	15.60	14.10	529	33	0.20	330	1587	2.36
Feta	264	14.21	21.28	493	19	0.65	62	1116	2.88
Blue	353	21.40	28.74	528	23	0.31	256	1395	2.66
Edam	357	24.99	27.80	731	30	0.44	188	965	3.75
Brie	334	20.75	27.68	184	20	0.50	152	629	2.38
Camembert	300	19.80	24.26	388	20	0.33	187	842	2.38
Goat, hard	452	30.52	35.59	895	54	1.88	48	346	1.59
Goat, semisoft	364	21.58	29.84	298	29	1.62	158	515	0.66

Fish, Not a Snake

> MATTHEW 7:9–10 ***Or what man is there among you who, if his son asks for bread, will give him a stone? Or if he asks for a fish, will he give him a serpent?*** (NKJV)

Jesus considered bread and fish good gifts for children. In the Bible, snakes are often used as symbols for evil. For example, in Genesis 3 Eve was tempted by a snake (or serpent), which triggered the fall of man. Obviously a decent father would not want to give his son a snake. However, he would want to give his son bread and fish, the very foods that Jesus multiplied for feeding the multitudes.

fall of man
Genesis 3

fish
Genesis 1:26, 28

fall of man
sin is introduced

Fish is a staple protein food in the Mediterranean diet (see Illustration #2) just as it was in Jesus's time. This is why it has its own section in the Mediterranean diet pyramid. Fish is high in protein, relatively low in saturated fats, and contains omega-3 essential fatty acids or EFAs.

When it comes to heart health, we are hearing more and more about the benefits of this particular type of polyunsaturated fatty acid, the omega-3 fatty acids. The most common omega-3 fatty acids are eicosa-pentaenoic (EPA), docosahexaenoic (DHA), and alpha-linolenic (ALA) acids. EPA and DHA are found in fatty fish such as salmon, white tuna, mackerel, rainbow trout, herring, halibut, and sardines. ALA is more commonly found in soybean oil, walnuts, and flaxseeds or flaxseed oil. The American Heart Association has recommended that healthy adults eat at least two servings of fish per week to boost their omega-3 fatty acid intake. Eating two to four ounces of these fish will generally provide about one gram of omega-3 fatty acids.

Benefits of Omega-3 Fatty Acids

- Reduce inflammation
- Help prevent blood from clotting and sticking to artery walls
- Help to lower the risk for blocked blood vessels and heart attacks
- Prevent hardening of the arteries
- Decrease the risk of sudden death and abnormal heart rates
- Decrease triglyceride levels
- Improve overall heart health
- Lower blood pressure
- Slow the development of dementia

what others say

Jordan Rubin

Since salmon caught in the wild are a richer source of omega-3 fats, protein, potassium, vitamins, and minerals, purchase fresh salmon and other fish from your local fish market or health food store that is labeled "Alaskan" or wild-caught.[16]

Fish

Fish can be eaten daily in 4- to 5- ounce servings.

What's a Vegetarian?

There are many kinds of vegetarians. All vegetarians eat vegetables, fruits, grains, and nuts and seeds. *Lacto-ovo vegetarians* eat dairy products and eggs, *lacto vegetarians* eat dairy products but not eggs, *ovo vegetarians* eat eggs but not dairy products. *Vegans* do not eat animal products, which is to say they do not eat meat, dairy products, or eggs.

metaphor
a word or phrase that symbolizes something else, as in "a mighty fortress is our God"

Which Came First: The Chicken or the Egg?

> ISAIAH 10:14 ***My hand has found like a nest the riches of the people, and as one gathers eggs that are left, I have gathered all the earth; and there was no one who moved his wing, nor opened his mouth with even a peep.*** *(NKJV)*

In this passage, God is quoting an Assyrian king, who boastfully claims full credit for Assyria's victories when they were actually all God's doing. God seems to be using egg-gathering as a **metaphor** for political triumph. It would have been an effective metaphor because the Israelites and Romans kept chickens for their eggs and their meat, and they gathered the eggs of chickens that were allowed to wander around.

Poultry and eggs are in the section of foods that are recommended to be eaten a few times per week (see Illustration #2). This would mean that once a week you might have eggs for breakfast, an egg sandwich for lunch, and chicken once for lunch and once for dinner.

The Mediterranean diet is one of the tried-and-true lifestyles and eating programs that have been found to promote good health. Vegetables and grains comprise the largest portions of foods each day; therefore, a variety of different proteins can be eaten. The suggested amount is about four ounces, the size of a deck of cards. When you consider eating eggs, fish, cheese, peas and beans, nuts and seeds, chicken, lamb, and small amounts of red meat as your protein, this means that you would only want to have eggs a few times a week. If you are a person who doesn't want to eat beef, lamb, or chicken, then eating eggs more frequently would be fine. It is essential to eat some protein every day, especially if you do heavy physical work, work out in a gym, play sports, or are recovering from an illness or surgery.

Law
Nehemiah 8:18

read
Exodus 24:7

Nehemiah
Nehemiah 8:9

Trumpets
Hebrews 29:1

Law
the Law of Moses; the Ten Commandments and other Old Testament laws

Feast of Trumpets
an assembly on a day of rest commemorated with trumpet blasts and sacrifices; later called Rosh Hashanah

sweet
containing or derived from sugar or honey

what others say

Maureen Salaman

Eggs are mentioned in various parts of the Scriptures, and it is common knowledge that they were eaten in Old and New Testament times when available.[17]

ON Target	OFF Target
Broiled, poached, baked, stewed fish	Breaded or deep-fried fish, composition fish sticks

A Sweet and Joyful Feast

NEHEMIAH 8:10 ***Then he said to them, "Go your way, eat the fat, drink the sweet, and send portions to those for whom nothing is prepared; for this day is holy to our LORD. Do not sorrow, for the joy of the LORD is your strength."*** *(NKJV)*

Ezra, the priest commissioned to teach the **Law**, had been in Babylon for years; he returned to Judah to read the Law. This was such an important occasion that women and children were allowed to be there. Ezra praised God and read the Law, which took from daybreak to noon, and afterward Nehemiah the governor declared the beginning of the **Feast of Trumpets**. He also instructed the Israelites to share the feast with those who had nothing prepared so that they too would be able to share the food and joy of the Lord that came from reading the Law.

Sweets for the Sweet

Sweets are to be eaten on special occasions only, like the Feast of Trumpets Nehemiah opened. We are not supposed to eat sweets every day (see Illustration #2), whether it is **sweet** foods or sweet drinks. By "sweets" I mean those foods that have been sweetened with honey, sugar, or artificial sweeteners. Naturally sweet fruits and vegetables (like carrots) are to be eaten daily. Sugar contains no nutrients. Yet the average American eats more than 42 teaspoons of sugar a day.

ON Target	OFF Target
Eating naturally sweet fruits and vegetables	Eating artificially sweetened foods on a daily basis

what others say

Dr. Mary Ruth Swope

When we eat large amounts of concentrated sweet foods (the sugars and starches in the form of candies, baked desserts, ice cream, pancakes with syrup, biscuits with honey) the body is put under great stress.[18]

Daily Sweets

Many of us have overdeveloped our sweet tooth, but we need to remember that sweets must not be eaten daily, because sweets can harm our bodies. Sweets are to be eaten on special occasions only.

That Meat Again

GENESIS 27:9 ***Go now to the flock and bring me from there two choice kids of the goats, and I will make savory food from them for your father, such as he loves.*** *(NKJV)*

Eventually God allowed people to eat meat, so it became part of many special occasions like feasts, celebrations, weddings, and other important gatherings. Isaac was fond of roasted goat and other meat, so his wife, Rebekah, sent their son Jacob out to get a couple of goats for his father. The meal came just before Isaac, who was dying, gave his blessing to Jacob—a very special occasion.

The Few-Times-Per-Month Food

Of all the foods found in the Mediterranean diet, red meat is the only one listed as a food that should be eaten in small amounts, like a few times per month (see Illustration #2). Beef, lamb, mutton, goat, and venison are the main red meats we eat today that were also eaten in Bible times. Many people eat pork as well, which the Israelites did not eat. Most people in Bible times ate meat during special feasts or **Passover**.

Passover
Exodus 12:11

Passover
a Jewish festival commemorating the Exodus of the Israelites

It's reasonable to estimate they ate red meat a few times per month, which is exactly what the Mediterranean diet recommends. The main difference is that North Americans also eat pork in the form of roasts, ham, bacon, and hot dogs, and in Bible times Israelites did not eat any pork or pork products. Many cultures of the world do not eat red meat.

condiment
a seasoning for food like mustard or catsup

Much research has been published over the years as to the dangers of eating red meat. Most of the studies show that red meat cooked so that the melting fat hits the heat source and splashes back up on the meat is the most dangerous red meat to eat. This kind of cooking produces so-called carcinogens, cancer-causing particles.[19]

Research also shows that processed red meats and frequent consumption of meats that have the burned fats can contribute to high blood pressure, prostate cancers in blacks, and stomach and esophageal cancers.[20] Much research has also been published showing that some of the nutrients in red meat can be useful for good heart health and weight loss like the amino acid l-carnitine and conjugated linoleic acid (CLA) respectively. It isn't the meat but the fat and processing that cause the problems (see chapter 9).

If you are following a modified Mediterranean diet and want to eat red meat weekly, there is no problem as long as it is not fatty meat like higher-fat burgers, broiled over an open flame, or overcooked until it is no longer pink inside.

what others say

Dr. Mary Ruth Swope

The dietary lifestyle you choose will affect your body performance, body size, resistance to disease, and your life expectancy. If you're sick and tired of feeling sick and tired, only YOU can effect the remedy. There is no magic solution.[21]

Meat

Eat small amounts of meat and large amounts of vegetables.

ON Target	OFF Target
Meat as a **condiment**	Meat as the main component of a meal

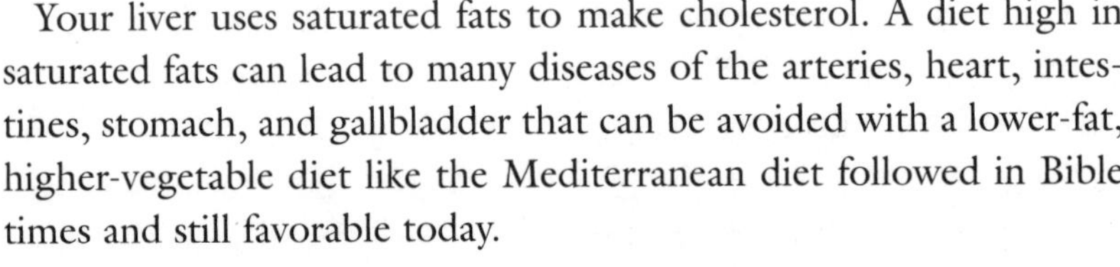
Your liver uses saturated fats to make cholesterol. A diet high in saturated fats can lead to many diseases of the arteries, heart, intestines, stomach, and gallbladder that can be avoided with a lower-fat, higher-vegetable diet like the Mediterranean diet followed in Bible times and still favorable today.

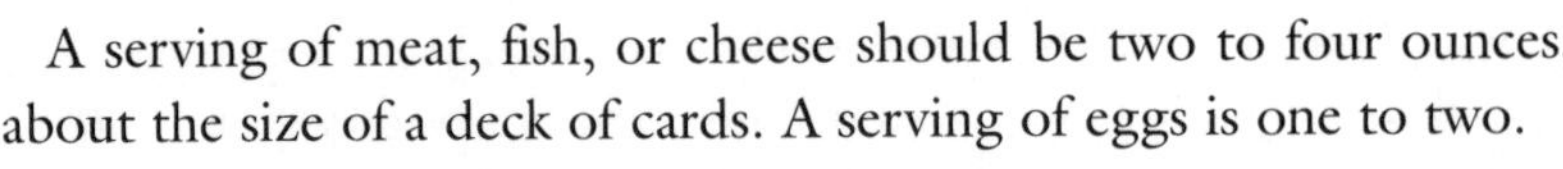
A serving of meat, fish, or cheese should be two to four ounces, about the size of a deck of cards. A serving of eggs is one to two.

Chapter Wrap-Up

- God created two kinds of foods for man to eat: plant foods and animal foods.
- Before the Flood man was to be a vegetarian; after the Flood he could eat animal products. (Genesis 1–6)
- The Mediterranean diet is the same as the Bible diet. (Genesis 1)
- Medical doctors, scientists, nutritionists, and many health-care practitioners agree that the healthiest diet consists of a foundation of whole grains, lots of fruits and vegetables, smaller amounts of dairy products and fish, and minute amounts of fats, sweets, and red meats.
- The foods that the Bible tells us to eat in large quantities are the healthiest for us. The foods that the Bible tells us to eat on special occasions or with discernment are less healthy for us but still useful if eaten in moderation.

Study Questions

1. Which foods did God give us to eat in the Garden of Eden? Are they still available today and where?
2. Which foods did God allow man to eat after the Flood? Name some occasions when they were eaten in Bible times. When do you eat them?
3. How can we know which foods to eat? Do you ever eat foods more often than recommended? Which ones and why?
4. What is the Mediterranean diet pyramid? What are its eight food groups?
5. Of all the foods God gave us to eat, which do you eat daily and which do you never eat? Why? According to the Mediterranean pyramid, what foods should you be eating the most of?
6. Of all the foods God gave us, which should we eat sparingly? Why?

Chapter 2: The Foundation of the Bible Diet

Chapter Highlights:
- Two Kinds of Fiber
- Wheat—Grain #1
- Barley in the Bible
- Fed on Bread
- Some Whole Grain Brands

Let's Get Started

Grains have always been the foundation of a healthy diet, in Bible times and in our times. This means every day you should eat something made with grains, just as the Israelites did. It does not mean grains are the largest part of a healthy diet; they are actually the second largest part (see Illustration #3).

In this chapter you will see how and why it is essential to eat grains every day, which kinds are best for you and why, and how to prepare them so they can be added to your diet with grace and ease.

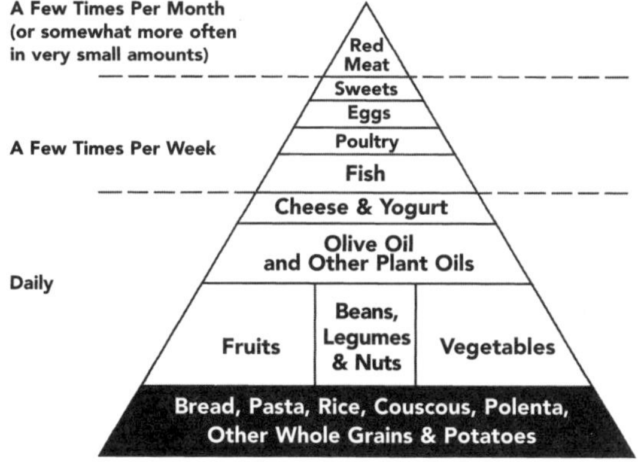

Illustration #3
The Grains Section—The darkened section of this pyramid represents how much of your diet should be devoted to grains.

A Grainy Dream

> GENESIS 41:22 ***Also I saw in my dream, and suddenly seven heads came up on one stalk, full and good.*** (NKJV)

Pharaoh dreamed of seven good heads of grain and asked Joseph, the young Hebrew, what this meant. Joseph, who was gifted with dream interpretation, answered that it meant there would be seven years of great abundance in the land of Egypt. Because grains were a very important part of the lives of all people in the Mediterranean region, it is not surprising that the pharaoh would have grains in his dream, and that Joseph would be able to understand the significance of grains in a dream. Grains held an important part in the everyday

staff of life
a staple or necessary food, especially bread

durum wheat
the kind of wheat used in most pastas

buckwheat
the four-cornered seed of a plant in the rhubarb family

hybridized
different strains of grains mixed together or cross-bred

kamut
a variety of wheat found in the pyramids of Egypt

quinoa
a grain used by the Aztecs

amaranth
a very high-protein seed of a plant that grows in many different areas of the world

lives of the people, which is why we call grains, and bread made from grains, the **staff of life**—the very foundation of a healthy diet.

This Grain, That Grain, Every Kind of Grain!

There is a large variety of grains, each with a distinct flavor and use. The most basic and universally available grain in the West is wheat. Hard wheat or winter wheat is used for making bread and thickening. Soft wheat or spring wheat is used for pastries, cakes, pies, muffins, and quick breads. Other common grains are rice, barley, rye, millet, corn, triticale, **durum wheat**, oats, spelt (a kind of wheat), **buckwheat**, and corn. Many ancient grains are becoming popular because they have a heartier taste and are higher in nutrients than the **hybridized** grains used in North America. The most popular are **kamut**, **quinoa**, and **amaranth**.

God provided us with bread for our health and healing, but today we must be careful to choose the correct bread. Look for barley bread, whole wheat bread, and breads containing spelt and millet. Breads containing millet and spelt can help ease premenstrual cramps and heal wounds. Barley bread can help our bodies to lower cholesterol, improve digestion, and reduce cancer risk. Whole wheat bread provides us with B complex vitamins, phosphorous, iron, and vitamin E, which protect against heart disease and cancer. Also, the fiber in whole wheat bread can help protect against colon cancer.

Modern and Ancient Grains

Modern Grains	Ancient Grains Rediscovered
Barley	Amaranth
Buckwheat	Barley
Corn	Kamut
Durum Wheat	Quinoa
Hard Wheat	Spelt (a kind of wheat)
Millet	
Oats	
Rice	
Rye	
Soft Wheat	
Triticale	

Can't Do That!

LUKE 6:1–2 *Now it happened on the second Sabbath after the first that He went through the grainfields. And His disciples plucked the heads of grain and ate them, rubbing them in their hands. And some of the Pharisees said to them, "Why are you doing what is not lawful to do on the Sabbath?"* (NKJV)

In Jesus's day, many people ate grain right out of the field, while it was still **green**. Just like you can have fresh or green lima beans and dried lima beans, you can also have fresh or green grains and dried grains. Usually we eat them dried. In fact, grain is always dried before it is ground into flour. Jesus and his disciples got in trouble for eating the grains, not because they were in somebody else's field (they were allowed to **glean** in those days), but because they were picking grains on the Sabbath, which was considered work, and that was not allowed on the **Sabbath**. The grains had nothing to do with it.

green
fresh, not dried

glean
to pick up grains that were left behind by the harvesters

Sabbath
seventh day of the week; a day set aside for rest and worship

what others say

Don Colbert, M.D.

Other grains mentioned in the Bible besides wheat and barley are millet and rye. Millet is mentioned only once in the Scriptures.[1]

Eat 'Em Every Day

Grains are good sources of protein, carbohydrates, and fiber only if they are whole grains. Whole grains have not been polished or "refined" to remove any of the nutritional part of the grain. The outer layer of most grains—wheat, rice, and barley especially—contains the B vitamins essential for digesting the starch or carbohydrates in the grain. The fiber is roughage that is essential for healthy intestines and good digestion. God made grains to contain a high amount of nutrients so that they could be the foundation of a healthy diet.

It's the Fiber!

Intake of whole grains has been shown to be paramount in helping to reduce the risk of type 2 diabetes in both children and adults.

A study published in the *European Journal of Clinical Nutrition* in 2004 concluded that eating three servings of whole grain products daily reduced the incidence of type 2 diabetes. They concluded that the intact fibers were responsible for this. However, when they added bran fiber to an ordinary diet, it did not reduce the risk of type 2 diabetes. The conclusion to this study of the literature is that only whole grains, because of their soluble fiber, along with additional legumes and fruits, were responsible for reducing the incidence of type 2 diabetes.[2] Whole grains are useful in reducing serum homocysteine and C-reactive protein, two types of inflammation often thought to contribute to cardiovascular disease.[3] Barley fiber is known to reduce cholesterol, and in May 2006 the FDA approved of this as a medical claim for barley.

Two Kinds of Fiber

Whole grains, legumes, fruits, and vegetables all contain fiber that is essential in a healthy diet. There are two kinds of fibers—soluble and insoluble.

1. ***Soluble fiber:*** Gums, pectins, and mucilages are the gummy parts of food that slow its passage through the digestive system. They are found in whole grains, dried beans (legumes), and some fruits like apples and vegetables like okra.
2. ***Insoluble fiber:*** Cellulose, hemicellulose, and lignin are not soluble in water and increase bulk in the stool and regulate bowel movements. They are found in whole grains, some vegetables, and wheat bran.

Fiber in Your Grains

Grain	Amount	Fiber in Grams
Whole wheat bread	2 slices	6.0
Buckwheat (Kasha), cooked	1 cup	9.6
All-Bran cereal	1/2 cup	10.6
Oatmeal (not instant)	3/4 cup	7.7
Ry-Krisp	3 single	2.3
Popcorn (unseasoned)	1 cup	1.0
Brown rice, cooked	1 cup	5.5
Whole wheat spaghetti, cooked	1 cup	5.6

Look for the Stamp

The Whole Grains Council places a stamp on many whole grain products that tells if it has 100 percent whole grain or the percentage of whole grains so consumers can be proactive in adding whole grains to their lifestyle and make sure they eat up to forty-eight grams of whole grains a day.

bran
outer fiber covering grains

phytoestrogens
plant-based hormonal substances

cardiovascular
having to do with the heart and circulatory systems

Will the Real Whole Grain Please Stand Up?

White flour and white flour products are not whole grains. White rice is not a whole grain. They are refined, or stripped of most nutrients, and processed to remove all the fiber. Often, wheat flour is even bleached to make it look whiter.

> **what others say**
>
> **Don Colbert, M.D.**
>
> The conclusion we can draw is this: Choose whole-grain products! If the label on these products does not read "whole wheat" or "whole grain," you should assume that the product is made completely or partially with refined flour.[4]
>
> **Cheryl Townsley**
>
> White flour has been robbed of its color, taste, smell, and nutrition. Not even cockroaches will eat white-flour based products. Twenty-six essential nutrients, plus the **bran**, have been removed from wheat to produce white flour. Four of the removed nutrients are returned (in a chemical form) to produce "enriched" flour. What an enriching process![5]

Grains

God's whole grains contain fiber. Eat at least three to eleven servings of whole grain products a day.

Whole Grains to Protect You

What is there about whole grains that makes them such powerhouses of nutrition and health? They contain antioxidants and **phytoestrogens** that are known to protect you against many chronic diseases including cancer and **cardiovascular** disease.[6] Whole grains

carcinogens
substances that are capable of causing cancerous changes in your body

ephah
3/5 bushel, a biblical unit of measurement

groats
unmilled, unpolished whole grains

wheat
an edible grass

help to protect you against cancer by binding to **carcinogens** and removing them from your body.[7]

Roasting on an Open Fire . . .

1 SAMUEL 17:17 ***Then Jesse said to his son David, "Take now for your brothers an ephah of this dried grain and these ten loaves, and run to your brothers at the camp."*** *(NKJV)*

Many grains will cook faster and have a nutty taste if they are roasted first. This might be why Jesse sent roasted grains to the soldiers; they would take less time to cook and they could even eat them roasted as soon as they got them. During the Vietnam War many Vietnamese soldiers were found with roasted rice in their pockets. Often, this was all the food they had. Rice, wheat, barley, and buckwheat are often roasted or toasted in a heavy pan over a medium-low heat before water is added to cook them. If whole wheat bread flour is roasted this way before it is used as a thickening agent or in gravy, it will take less time to thicken and taste fully cooked.

During Bible times, the only grains people had were whole grains. Grain refinement had not been invented yet. They often roasted grain whole before eating it as a snack. When grains were ripe, they either roasted them or cooked them in a liquid just as you do when you eat whole oats, wheat **groats**, or whole barley. People of the Bible also made them into flour to make flour products such as bread and flat breads, just the same as we do today.

I often dry-roast barley and/or brown rice before I cook it for a sweeter, nuttier taste. This can make a dish of barley or rice, which might be bland by itself, taste rich. If you cook the roasted grains in a flavored broth such as vegetable or chicken broth, instead of water, it will turn these grains into a dish fit for a king.

Wheat—Grain #1

Wheat is the most common grain used in the West, so we will start with it. There are many kinds of wheat: winter wheat, spring wheat, hard wheat, soft wheat, and emmer wheat, just to name a few. There are also several ancient grains that are in the wheat family but are not the same as the wheat we use today. These are spelt and kamut.

toxins
poisons that harm your body

what others say

Jordan Rubin

High-fiber diets cut down on that transit time, so food has less time to putrefy in the colon, and toxins are quickly flushed out of the system.[8]

Fiber Sweeps You Clean

Wheat, barley, and rice fiber are all also called "bran." When you eat whole grains you are eating the natural bran or fiber that God created to be part of a healthy diet. Fiber has at least two roles in your health:

1. It binds undesirable **toxins** and chemicals to itself and removes them from your body.
2. It acts like a broom and sweeps out unwanted materials from your intestines or bowels.

Your body needs fiber, bran, and B complex vitamins to digest the starch or carbohydrates in wheat. Fiber, bran, and B complex vitamins are already a part of whole wheat, but are refined out of white flour, which makes white flour products very difficult to digest. For example, your body needs B complex vitamins to digest the starch in wheat. If you were to eat, say, a whole grain piece of bread, within the bread are all the B complex vitamins you need to digest it. On the other hand, if you were to choose a piece of bread made from white flour, your body is forced to rob B vitamins from somewhere else in your body, causing a stress. The result may be that you become deficient in B vitamins, which could cause health problems either directly related to this lack of B vitamins or to the stress your body goes through when robbing B vitamins from elsewhere.

Whole wheat contains protein, carbohydrates, fiber, calcium, phosphorus, iron, potassium, magnesium, zinc, copper, selenium, folate, phytic acid, saturated fat, monounsaturated fat, polyunsaturated fat, and the vitamins B_1, B_2, B_3, B_6, C, E.

If you eat refined white-flour products, replace the B vitamins with ⅛ teaspoon nutritional yeast and replace the fiber with ½ teaspoon wheat or rice bran to avoid nutritional deficiencies.

barley
2 Kings 7:1, 16;
2 Chronicles 2:10, 15

spelt
an edible grass

husk or hull
the outer layer of fiber

abbess
female head of a convent

Spelt

Spelt is an ancient grain that was known to the Romans as "farrum" and has been traced as far back as 5000 BC in the area we now call Iran. It is also called "farro" and "dinkle." Spelt has a nutty taste that gives it a stronger presence in baked goods. Many people who are sensitive to wheat can often eat whole grain spelt products with no reaction. Because spelt retains its **husk or hull**, it is also more resistant to disease and pollution than wheat, which has been bred to lose its husks. This also means that it requires fewer pesticides and other chemicals. Purity Foods reintroduced spelt to the West in 1987, and it has become very popular since.

Spelt was used extensively as medicine by Hildegard von Bingen, or Saint Hildegard as she is often called. Hildegard was an **abbess** who lived from 1098 to 1179.

> what others say
>
> **Hildegard von Bingen**
>
> The spelt is the best of grains. It is rich and nourishing and milder than other grain. It produces a strong body and healthy blood to those who eat it and it makes the spirit of man light and cheerful.[9]

Barley in the Bible

Barley	Scripture
Barley in the Field	Exodus 9:31 • Deuteronomy 8:8 • Ruth 1:22; 2:23; 3:2 • 2 Samuel 21:9 • 1 Chronicles 11:13 • Job 31:40 • Isaiah 28:25 • Joel 1:11
Barley in Measures	Leviticus 27:16 • Numbers 5:15 • Ruth 2:17, 23; 3:2, 15, 17 • 2 Samuel 17:28 • 1 Kings 4:28 • 2 Kings 7:1, 16, 18 • 2 Chronicles 2:10, 15 • Jeremiah 41:8 • Ezekiel 45:13 • Hosea 3:2 • Revelation 6:6
Barley Products	Judges 7:13 • 2 Kings 4:42 • 2 Chronicles 27:5 • Ezekiel 4:9, 12; 13:19 • John 6:9, 13

Barley in the Bible

REVELATION 6:6 ***And I heard a voice in the midst of the four living creatures saying, "A quart of wheat for a denarius, and three quarts of barley for a denarius; and do not harm the oil and the wine."*** *(NKJV)*

Barley is one of the most-mentioned whole grains in the Bible. It was considered a "lowly" grain and fit for non-royalty. This is why it was used by Elisha and Jesus; they dealt with the common man. Wheat was worth a lot more money than barley, about three times as much.

While barley was not valued as highly as whole wheat, we know barley's great value today. It helps to lower our risk of heart disease and cancer. Barley stops heart disease in these two ways: it prevents the dangerous LDL cholesterol from sticking to our artery walls, and it prevents tiny blood clots from forming. Barley fights cancers, because barley contains cancer-fighting selenium and vitamin E.

Elisha
2 Kings 4:42–44

loaves
Matthew 14:15–20;
Mark 6:35–44;
Luke 9:12–17;
John 6:9–13

barley
a cereal grass

what others say

Dr. Mary Ruth Swope

Since barley was very possibly the first cereal grain known to man, it should come as no surprise that God built it so nutritionally perfect. The nutrient profile of barley is just about perfect. Nearly everything the human system needs is present in ideal proportions.[10]

Barley Bread Multiplies

JOHN 6:9–11 ***"There is a lad here who has five barley loaves and two small fish, but what are they among so many?" Then Jesus said, "Make the people sit down." Now there was much grass in the place. So the men sat down, in number about five thousand. And Jesus took the loaves, and when He had given thanks He distributed them to the disciples, and the disciples to those sitting down; and likewise of the fish, as much as they wanted.*** *(NKJV)*

Elisha and Jesus both multiply a few loaves of barley bread to feed large numbers of people (see Illustration #4). There are four times listed in the Bible when Jesus multiplies loaves of bread to feed the crowds, but only one of them, John 6:9–13, mentions that the loaves of bread are made of barley. The people who followed Jesus were common people, not royalty. Their bread would have been the kind that took the least expense to make and was, therefore, the least processed. The less grains are changed from their original form, the better they are for health, and the closer they are to the food God created for us to eat.

Barley Water

Barley water is an old-fashioned remedy for diarrhea, constipation, and an upset stomach. Generally it is called "lemon barley water" or "ginger barley water" and often is called "barley gripe water." Barley protects against heart disease and cancer. In addition, it tastes great.

Four Healthy Ways to Eat Barley

Barley as:	Health Benefits:
Loaves or cakes	Great for people who can't eat wheat
Crackers	Do not usually contain wheat Often used as teething biscuits for babies
Soup	Full meal Whole grains in a form kids like
Water	Great cure for gas and diarrhea in babies

Illustration #4
Jesus Multiplies Bread—Jesus took the loaves of barley, gave thanks, and distributed them to the people.

Barley is often in baby-teething crackers and is almost always in vegetarian soup. Mushroom-and-barley soup is a real comfort food (see recipe in chapter 19). Made in twenty minutes, the barley will be firm and still in the form of the grain itself. If barley is left to simmer on low for an hour or more (make sure there is enough water for this before you try it), the barley will begin to absorb the water or other liquid and swell. Some of the creamy goodness of the barley will become a great base for the soup. Cooked overnight or throughout the day in a slow cooker of some type, barley soup will be an easy and hearty meal. Barley-and-mushroom or barley-and-vegetable soup is a great way to introduce whole grain barley into your diet.

millet
Ezekiel 4:9; 27:17

millet
an edible grass

gluten
a protein found in wheat, rye, barley, and oats; the elastic substance in flour

> **what others say**
>
> **Don Colbert, M.D.**
>
> In some areas of the Middle East, barley has been called the "medicine for the heart." It contains fiber that can lower the risk of heart disease by reducing artery-clogging LDL (bad) cholesterol. This same high fiber content keeps a person regular, relieving constipation and warding off a variety of digestive problems.[11]

Millet, Low Starch and High Protein

Millet is mentioned in the Bible only twice. Small and round, this grain is often used to feed songbirds. For a grain, millet is low in starch and high in protein. It contains no **gluten**, so it is very difficult to be made into a loaf of bread on its own. Millet is very good cooked into a porridge and eaten for breakfast. It can also be eaten as a cooked grain at meals in place of rice. I often use it in soups because it opens up or explodes in the pot when it is boiled, and this makes for nice thickening.

> **what others say**
>
> **Reginald Cherry, M.D.**
>
> Millet and spelt can help to ease premenstrual discomfort and to speed healing in wounds.[12]

The Case of the Missing Rice

Grasses and cereals are mentioned in the Bible, but rice is not mentioned by name. We know that people in Bible times had rice, however, because there are recipes using rice that were published around the time of Jesus.

pilafs
rice dishes cooked with beans, or meat, or shellfish

risottos
rice dishes cooked in broth and flavored with vegetables or cheese

Rice Is a Grain

Brown rice or unpolished rice is a whole grain. White rice of any kind—polished, enriched, fortified, or instant—is still not a whole grain. Whole-rice or brown-rice flour is whole grain flour. White-rice flour is not. This means that most ethnic restaurants that serve rice (for example: Chinese, Japanese, Greek, Italian, Mexican, East and West Indian, Spanish, Portuguese, and African restaurants) are not serving whole grain rice.

In restaurants, read the menu and ask questions if you want whole grain rice. Ask the server if the restaurant offers brown, unpolished rice. Look for brown, unpolished rice on your grocery shelves. Don't neglect rice, since rice plays a prominent role in the Mediterranean diet and in your health. Besides, rice can be enjoyed in many wonderful ways, from rice **pilafs**, **risottos**, and cold rice salads, to thick soups and stews.

Rice Pasta

Rice pasta is very popular in oriental cooking. Alas, it is not whole grain or brown rice. However, health food stores and health food sections of large supermarkets often have brown-rice pasta available. It is generally considered an "allergy" product because people who are allergic to wheat or gluten can often eat rice products, as they do not contain gluten.

The White and Brown of It

White rice of all kinds takes less time to cook than brown or whole grain rice. This makes it almost impossible to gradually introduce brown rice in with white rice, unless you plan ahead. By precooking brown rice and adding it to the final stage of cooking white rice, you can introduce brown rice to your family slowly. Once you develop a taste for whole grains and their rich, nutty flavors, you won't have to be concerned with this; you will be able to serve brown rice on its own!

Roasted Grain—Brown Rice

JOSHUA 5:11 ***And they ate of the produce of the land on the day after the Passover, unleavened bread and parched grain, on the very same day.*** *(NKJV)*

Roasted grain was very popular in Bible times because it was partially cooked by the roasting, and people could eat it without any further cooking. It also had more taste than non-roasted grains. Roasting grains before cooking is done in many different recipes using brown rice, barley, or wheat. Brown rice is excellent when it is roasted before adding water or liquid to cook it. Try roasting it over medium heat in a heavy pan until it begins to give off a nutty smell. Stir it frequently. It can also be roasted in a small amount of olive oil or clarified butter until it browns or roasts. Then add the required amount of liquid for cooking. Popped corn might be considered the modern version of roasted grains.

A baked brown-rice pudding, with roasted rice, dried fruit, and roasted nuts, is a wonderful dessert, whether it is made with dairy, soy, or rice milk. Often, roasting the rice first shortens the cooking time.

Fed on Bread

ACTS 2:42 ***And they continued steadfastly in the apostles' doctrine and fellowship, in the breaking of bread, and in prayers.*** *(NKJV)*

In the Bible, the word *bread* and the word *food* are practically interchangeable. That's how important bread was in these ancient times. Breaking bread together was almost a necessity of hospitality in Bible times, and still is in the Middle East. Whole grain flour products, like breads and crackers, are an easy way to eat whole grains. Bread is the most popular way to eat wheat, the grain of choice for North Americans. As long as the bread is made of whole grains, it is nutritious. Whole grain bagels, muffins, pita bread, pasta, biscuits, cookies, crackers, tortillas, and even pretzels are available in most grocery stores and health food stores. Look for whole grain mixes to make cakes, quick breads, pancakes, and waffles. Whole grain bread can also be made in bread machines, and there are many natural whole grain bread mixes available.

Illustration #5
The Last Supper—Jesus and his disciples most likely ate whole grain, unleavened bread on the evening before the Crucifixion.

what others say

Maureen Salaman

When we talk about "our daily bread," that is the correct name for it. In biblical times, people ate bread at every meal, mainly barley bread for the poor and wheat bread for the wealthy.[13]

In Bible times bread was the main part of every meal. This bread was much coarser than the bread we have today. The grains were ground with stone grinding wheels, and very fine flour was reserved for wealthy people. The common man ate a heavy bread made of coarsely ground grains. Every day was bread-breaking day in Bible times. The barley or wheat flour was mixed with water and salt, shaped into loaves, and then baked. At the Last Supper, Jesus described the breaking of the unleavened bread of Passover as a symbol of himself, and early Christians remembered Jesus's words in a ceremony called "breaking of bread" (see Illustration #5). The breads that contain cooked whole grains or coarsely ground grains are much healthier than breads made of just flour. Bread made from branless flour is generally not considered a whole grain product.

"Whole grain," "whole wheat," and "made with only whole grains" are the phrases to look for on the labels of bakery products. If the label says "wheat flour," "unbleached wheat flour," or anything other than "whole grain" or "whole wheat," chances are the product is not entirely made of whole grains.

daily bread
Matthew 6:11

fine flour
Leviticus 2:1–7

breaking of bread
Acts 2:42

Many food companies would like you to think that their breads, rolls, and crackers are entirely made of whole grains, or that their products are made from the entire grain. This is not always the case. Many products advertise that they contain whole grains, and they do. But they are made from refined wheat flour with very few whole grains added. This is not a whole grain product! Please read the labels before you buy a product.

Jesus Told Me to Do It, So I'm Gonna Do It

ACTS 20:11 ***Now when he had come up, had broken bread and eaten, and talked a long while, even till daybreak, he departed. (NKJV)***

The disciples were always breaking bread as Jesus had shown them to do (see Illustration #5); it is called the Lord's Supper now. Even Paul performed this remembrance act in Troas. While he was talking, or giving the sermon, one of the people listening, Eutychus, sank into a deep sleep, fell out of the third-story window, and died. Paul came out and hugged him, and he was raised from the dead. Then Paul went upstairs again, performed the Lord's Supper, and talked until daylight. Presumably nobody else fell out of the window.

Can't Stand the White Stuff

Whole grain pasta is the easiest way to introduce whole grain products to your family. Whole wheat, spelt, durum wheat, buckwheat, rice, and mixed-grain pastas are available in health food stores and many grocery stores. I especially like the spelt pastas that are made by Purity Foods and sold under the name VitaSpelt. Many companies make whole grain pastas; just read the label. Even a pasta product that is only partially made up of whole grain is better than one that has no whole grains in it at all. Once you and your family get used to the taste of whole grains and whole grain pastas, you will not be able to eat the white stuff again. Now that you have read this information on how important whole grains are, please consider changing to a whole grain diet.

Lord's Supper
1 Corinthians 11:20

Troas
Acts 20:5–7

Eutychus
Acts 20:9

worrying
Luke 12:22–23

If you or your family has trouble wanting to eat the very heavy, natural, whole grain bread that is the most healthful, which is also the most similar to the bread eaten in Bible times, start slow. Start by eating bread that contains some whole grains. When you have become accustomed to this, switch to a product that contains 100 percent of the grain and no refined flours.

Pasta in the Bible

Nope, there is no mention of pasta in the Bible. But there are recipes published during the time of Jesus that refer to "paste" in various dishes. This paste, which is made of flour and water, and sometimes eggs, is then rolled flat. That sounds suspiciously like pasta!

Although it is very important for your health to eat whole grains, it is also important to keep your sanity about it. If you are out to eat at a friend's house or a potluck, don't make a big scene. Just eat what is provided. It is better to eat refined grains once in a while than to offend your friends and neighbors by refusing them. Worrying about your health is not recommended either.

Some Whole Grain Brands

Here are some brand names of foods that generally are made from whole grains. Please read the label to ensure that whole grains are in the products. Also try to purchase organic grains and grain products whenever possible.

Ancient Harvest	Annie's	Arrowhead Mills
Back to Nature	Barbara's	Barilla
Bob's Red Mill	Cascadian Farms	Clif Bars
De Bowes	De Cecco	Eden Foods
Erwhon	Food for Life	Garden of Eatin'
General Mills	Gia Russa	Health Valley
Hodgson Mills	Kashi	Lotus Foods
Lundberg	Nature's Path	Newman's Own
Pacifica Natural Foods	Peace Cereal	Purity Foods
Seeds for Change	Tinkyáda	

Chapter Wrap-Up

- God made grains to contain carbohydrates, proteins, amino acids, B vitamins, vitamin E, minerals, fiber, and every good thing essential for health. (Genesis 1:11–12)
- God made whole grains, and people in Bible times, like Elisha and Jesus, ate whole grain barley bread. (1 Kings 4:42–44 and John 6:9–13)
- Wheat, spelt, barley, millet, and rice were eaten in Bible times and are still considered to be the most healthful grains today.
- Jesus told us to eat bread daily, as was the custom in those days. (Matthew 6:11)

Study Questions

1. When is the best time to eat grains? How many different times a day do you think you should eat grains?
2. Name at least five health benefits of eating whole grains.
3. Which grains were eaten in Bible times? Which ones should you eat and why?
4. What kind of bread did Elisha and Jesus multiply and why? What made bread in Bible times different from bread today?

Chapter 3: Ezekiel's Punishment: Our Health Food

Chapter Highlights:
- **It's Essential!**
- **Beans—Our Health Food**
- **Lentils: The Bible's Very First Vegetable**

Let's Get Started

The second level of the Mediterranean food pyramid has three categories. In this chapter we will start with the second level's smallest section: beans and other **legumes** (see Illustration #6). Beans and legumes played a very important role in the food supply of people in Bible times and still do today for all people the world over. "Legumes," "beans," and "pulses" all mean the same thing. They are the seeds of plants in the same families. Dried peas are also in this category.

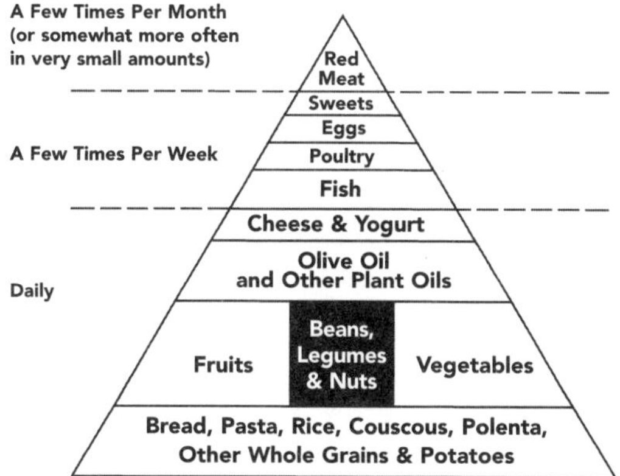

Illustration #6
Beans, Other Legumes, and Nuts Section—The darkened section of this pyramid represents how much of your diet should be devoted to beans, other legumes, and nuts.

Ezekiel's Punishment

EZEKIEL 4:9 ***Also take for yourself wheat, barley, beans, lentils, millet, and spelt; put them into one vessel, and make bread of them for yourself. During the number of days that you lie on your side, three hundred and ninety days, you shall eat it.*** *(NKJV)*

Ezekiel was of a priestly family, and he was called upon to be a prophet among the Jews who were exiled in Babylon. God told him to put the sins of the house of Israel upon himself and lie on his left side for 390 days and then to lie on his right side for 40 days. During this time he was to eat only this special food at set times with water to go with it.

legumes
plants that have edible seeds within a pod

sprouted
encouraged to grow without being in soil

pulses
another name for beans

amino acids
the building blocks of protein

essential amino acids
tryptophan, leucine, isoleucine, lysine, valine, threonine, methionine, phenylalanine

complete protein
containing all the essential amino acids in a nearly equal complement

Ezekiel Bread

Flour or bread made with a combination of wheat, barley, millet, spelt, beans, and lentils is generally called "Ezekiel bread" or "Ezekiel 4:9 Bread." Many of the specialty breads use **sprouted** grains and sprouted beans to make the flour for this bread. Most often the ingredients are ground into flour and then made into bread. Some recipes call for a combination of whole grain flours and precooked beans that are simply mixed together and then baked.

Often grains and **pulses** are sprouted and then ground, or the beans are cooked and added to the grain flours. Any combination of these ingredients is called Ezekiel bread.

what others say

Rex Russell, M.D.

Ezekiel bread has been analyzed and eaten by many people through the years. It has the complete package of essentials for health. It can be bought either as flour or bread at some natural food stores. Many people have used it during times of sickness and have given good reports.[1]

It's Essential!

All animals and plants need protein, which is made of **amino acids**. There are twenty-two known amino acids, and of these, eight are considered to be essential for humans. The **essential amino acids** cannot be made in your body as the other amino acids can; that is why it is "essential" to get them from your food. Foods that contain all the essential amino acids are sources of **complete protein**. Dairy products, all animal meats, eggs, and soybeans are the only foods that contain complete protein. Grain, beans, nuts, and seeds contain incomplete proteins.

Complementary Proteins

Since the 1970s, there has been much controversy about the nutritional value of eating foods that do not contain all the amino acids. For example, wheat and other grains are low in an amino acid called lysine. Beans, however, are high in lysine. So it was thought that the solution was simply to eat grains, like wheat or rice, at the same meal

with beans. These were called complementary proteins, since they complemented each other to make a complete protein. It was done with several combinations—beans with rice or wheat, beans with nuts or seeds, or dairy products with grains and/or beans. Ezekiel bread contains grains and beans combined to make complementary proteins. Ezekiel flour contains balanced protein, fiber, and vitamins B and E.

A Balancing Act: Amino Acids

When Frances Moore Lappé published *Diet for a Small Planet* in 1971, her theory was that the amount of available amino acids was determined by whatever was the lowest level of any of the amino acids in all the food eaten at one meal. So a lot of people actually kept track of which foods they ate and whether they had complete protein at each meal. Nutritionists now know that the amount of amino acids in each meal does not determine the amount of amino acids for the entire day. It is possible to have a high-lysine food at one meal and wheat at another and still have a balance of amino acids.

God knew that something like this would be too complicated for people to keep track of, so he allowed the Israelites to eat meat, dairy products, and eggs, and he gave them Ezekiel flour. Ezekiel flour has the perfect mix of grains and beans to make complete protein (see Illustration #7). According to the Mediterranean diet, we should eat beans and grains daily.

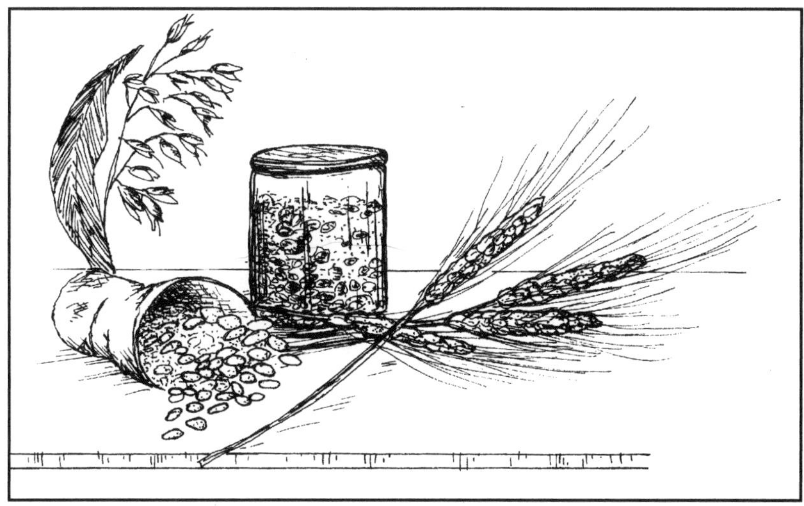

Illustration #7
Dried Beans and Grains—Beans and grains combine to form complete protein.

diverticulitis inflamed pockets in the large intestine

Beans—Our Health Food

2 SAMUEL 17:28–29 ***[They] brought beds and basins, earthen vessels and wheat, barley and flour, parched grain and beans, lentils and parched seeds, honey and curds, sheep and cheese of the herd, for David and the people who were with him to eat. For they said, "The people are hungry and weary and thirsty in the wilderness." (NKJV)***

David's friends brought him grains, beans, and dairy products—a perfect complement of proteins to keep his soldiers healthy. The only additional foods they needed were some fresh greens.

Have you been eating low-fiber foods? Have you ignored whole grains and beans? Perhaps you need to have some Ezekiel flour products to restore your health! Beans contain protein, carbohydrates, and fiber. They also contain B vitamins and are low in fat. Beans are easy to carry around dry without spoiling, and they have a variety of tastes.

what others say

Maureen Salaman

[In Bible times] grains, as well as lentils or beans were cooked in water or olive oil with onions, leeks, and garlic, or in butter and, when available, with meat or fish.[2]

Cheryl Townsley

Dried beans, split peas, lentils, and black-eyed peas are examples of legumes. They have little, if any, fat and are high in fiber. They are a complex carbohydrate high in vitamins and minerals.[3]

Beans, Lentils, or Nuts

Have at least one serving per day.

In societies where there are no refined grains, where the majority of meals and foods are high in natural plant-based fibers, there are also very low rates of degenerative diseases like heart disease, cancer, diabetes, colon cancer, and **diverticulitis**.

Where Do I Get This Fiber?

By following the Mediterranean diet and eating whole grains frequently during the day and adding in some form of high-fiber beans, legumes, or nuts, you will start getting the kind of fiber required for health. There are many companies that make whole grain and/or bean products: Eden Foods, Hains, Kashi, Westbrae, Cascadian Farm, Amy's, Garden of Eatin', Soy Deli, White Wave, Lundberg Family Farms, Barbara's Bakery, Arrowhead Mills, and Bob's Red Mill. Many of these products are sold frozen in your health food store or supermarket health food section.

Cascadian Farm, for example, makes a frozen entrée from **bulgur wheat**, lentils, **garbanzo beans**, vegetables, raisins, and seasonings. This is a great meal in itself. All you really need to add is a dark green salad.

bulgur wheat
Whole wheat that has been cooked, chopped, and dried. It is easily reconstituted by adding boiling water to it.

garbanzo beans
round beans also called "chick peas"

tofu
a compressed block of soy protein made from curded, fully cooked soy milk

body fat
also called "lipids"

Beans As Medicine

Beans have been shown to reduce serum cholesterol in many studies. Canned beans and even **tofu** are being used to reduce all **body fat** in many clinics in the United States and Canada. The old saying still stands: eat a cup of beans a day and lose a pound of weight. Beans can reduce your cholesterol and other body fats.

what others say

Pamela Smith, R.D.

Because soybeans are especially rich in phytoestrogens (containing the genistein and daidzein types), they have been studied extensively.[4]

If you are going to eat canned beans, check the sugar content. Please do not eat beans with any sugar in them, as this defeats the purpose of healthy eating. Diabetics may benefit from eating bean fiber but not if it contains sugar.

Lower Your Cholesterol

A mixed diet containing soybeans, almonds, oats, and barley was used in the dietary portfolio of cholesterol-lowering foods used in

glucose
the simple sugar that is the source for the energy in your body

GTT
used as one of the diagnostic tools for diabetes and hypoglycemia

hyperinsulinism
a high level of insulin in your body

hypoglycemia
a low level of blood sugar in your body

several studies done at the University of Toronto in Toronto, Ontario, Canada, showing that these foods, high in the ingredient beta-sitosterol, can help to lower cholesterol levels up to 20 percent if followed for a year. This particular study found that these foods in the diet lowered LDL (low-density lipoprotein) cholesterol, often called the "bad cholesterol," in similar ways to statin drugs, but with none of the side effects of the statins. This study also showed that it wasn't just one food that did it, but a mixed diet of different high-fiber foods combined with foods high in beta-sitosterol.[5] For more information on using beta-sitosterol for health, visit www.healthaliveproducts.com.

what others say

Rex Russell, M.D.

When asked how much fiber we need, I often give the admittedly earthy answer that we need only to look into our toilets. As insoluble fiber passes through the bowel, it takes fat with it into the stool. Fat floats. So floating stools are a good sign that you have enough fiber.[6]

Reginald Cherry, M.D.

Fiber is turning out to be a major factor used to lower blood sugar. Fiber has decreased insulin requirements 30 to 40 percent in type 1 diabetes. In type 2 diabetes, most patients were off insulin in 10 to 20 days in one study.[7]

GTT

In 1924 Dr. Seale Harris recognized that certain individuals secreted excessive insulin in response to eating refined carbohydrates and white flour. He even devised a special blood sugar test called the six-hour **Glucose** Tolerance Test, or **GTT**, to diagnose **hyperinsulinism** and functional **hypoglycemia**. Beans are excellent for diabetics.

Fiber is essential to your digestive processes. Digestion is less efficient in a low-fiber lifestyle.

But Beans Give Me Gas!

Beans are known for giving people gas, which happens because beans are difficult for some people to digest. There are two reasons for this. One is that the fiber in beans causes your body to work better and this creates gas at first. After you have been eating a high-fiber diet for a few days or weeks, this will not happen. The second reason is that there are two complex sugars called raffinose and stachyose in beans that some people cannot digest very well without forming gas. Generally, this is remedied by adding **kombu** to the bean-cooking water or a small amount of **asafoetida** to the food. You can also purchase Beano in most stores, which will help you digest many gas-giving foods.

Beano is made of alpha galactosidase, an enzyme that can help digest beans, whole grains, broccoli, cabbage, and other sulfur-containing foods. A product called Super Digestive Enzyme Formula contains alpha galactosidase and seven other enzymes to help improve digestion and prevent gas from eating beans and whole grains.

kombu
a sea vegetable; can be purchased in Japanese or health food stores

asafoetida
an herb from India; generally called "hing" or "yellow powder"

clean
Wash off the beans. Pick out any dirt, sticks, or hulls and remove them. Remove any discolored or broken beans.

rehydrated
Water is fully soaked up into beans.

slow simmer
using a heat low enough that the water bubbles break at a slow rate

what others say

Cheryl Townsley

If you have trouble digesting legumes, try a strip of kombu. Kombu is a sea vegetable sold in dried strips . . . in health food stores or Asian markets. A six-inch strip adds nearly one week's worth of minerals.[8]

Cooking Beans

The best way to cook beans to avoid the gas problem is to use the "quick soak" method. This will reduce the amount of complex sugars that ferment and give you gas. Start by using a stainless-steel saucepan that has a tight-fitting lid. Add three times as much water as the amount of beans you want to cook. Bring the water to a boil on high heat while you **clean** the beans. Slowly add the beans to the boiling water and boil them hard for 2 minutes. Turn off the heat, cover the beans, and let them sit until they are completely **rehydrated**. The time it takes will vary between bean sizes and could be anywhere from 1½ to 4 hours. When the beans are fully soaked and no longer look shriveled, pour out the water. Add fresh water and bring them to a boil over medium heat. Then reduce the heat to a **slow simmer** until they are fully cooked. Then add seasonings. Do not add salt, tomatoes, or other acids during the initial cooking.

soba
flat noodles made from buckwheat flour

whole wheat udon
flat noodles made from whole grain wheat flour

serotonin
a chemical found in the brain that is essential for relaxation, sleep, and concentration

Voilà! Instant meals!

Many health-conscious companies make quick lunch or snack soups or pasta meals in a cup that you just have to add boiling water to and wait 3–5 minutes. This makes it possible to have whole grains and beans ready in just a few minutes. Please look at the label of any meal-in-a-cup-type foods to be sure that they are really made of whole grains and beans. A black bean soup should really have black beans in it, but it should also have whole grain flour or pasta. If you are fond of the ramen noodles meals, please buy the ones made of whole grains like **soba** or **whole wheat udon**.

White Flour Noodles Spell Trouble

If you eat meals of white refined flour noodles, you are only asking for trouble later on. White pasta can raise your blood sugar or **serotonin** levels too high and make you sleepy. They can also strip your body of B vitamins (because B vitamins are required to digest the starch in pasta and grains) by using up your B vitamins and not replacing them as there are no B vitamins in white flour pastas. This could make you feel nervous, edgy, hyper, tired, or lead to exhaustion later in the day.

Beans Under Pressure

A pressure cooker may be used to cook large beans, but not the smaller beans like mung beans or lentils. The skins on the smaller beans have a tendency to come off during cooking and clog up the air vent. I generally cook beans in a pressure cooker with an onion, garlic, carrot, bay leaf, and strip of kombu. When you use a pressure cooker the beans don't have to be soaked first, they take less time to cook as well, and they don't cause gas. If you want to cook beans in a pressure cooker, read your pressure cooker's instructions. Beans can be cooked many different ways.

Patience Is a Virtue: Slow-Cook Beans

With the exception of soybeans, it is possible to cook beans without soaking them first. Put them in a pot of water after cleaning them. Use enough water to soak the beans and to cook them. So if you are cooking one cup of beans, you will need at least 3½ to 4 cups of water. Do not add salt or **acid**. Cover the pan. Turn the heat to medium-high and bring the beans to a simmer. This should take around an hour. Turn the heat to low and let them simmer for about 4 hours. I have done this in a slow cooker overnight or during the day and found the beans to be perfectly cooked. Many ethnic recipes for cooking beans and even recipes from famous chefs do not call for soaking the beans first. It might be said, then, that not soaking the beans before cooking is the newest and the oldest trend in cooking them. Please do not add baking soda to beans at any stage of soaking or cooking. This can remove a lot of nutrients from the finished beans.

acid
lemon juice, orange juice, vinegar, tomatoes, or tomato juice

EDTA
a preservative

Beans from a Can

If you want to use canned beans, check the labels first. Make sure that there is no sugar or **EDTA** in the beans. Wash them off to remove the majority of added salt. Many health food stores have beans in jars and cans with no preservatives or additional ingredients. They often have beans that have been organically grown without chemicals as well. Canned beans with no or low salt and no sugar are good for you.

Easy Beans

Cook beans according to the recipe for regularly cooked beans and put them on a paper towel to dry them just enough to no longer be wet. Then put them in a plastic bag or covered refrigerator container in the freezer. Use them in salads, add them to soups and grain dishes, mash them and put them in sandwiches, or just keep them handy so you can eat them any time of the day. If you freeze several different types of beans, you will have lots of variety. It is especially wonderful to have black beans like this that you can defrost and make into black bean dip or add to basic soup, to give you a special black bean soup.

Illustration #8
A Bible Diet Meal—Try cooking olive oil, onion, garlic, and beans in a large pot.

ON Target	OFF Target
Eating beans and dairy daily Protein Facts: 2 tablespoons of lentils = 7.1g of protein 2 tablespoons of cheddar cheese = 7.1g of protein	Eating beans loaded with salt or fat
Eat 20–35 grams of fiber a day.	Eating refined breads and pastas

Lentils: The Bible's Very First Vegetable

GENESIS 25:34 ***And Jacob gave Esau bread and stew of lentils; then he ate and drank, arose, and went his way. Thus Esau despised his birthright.*** *(NKJV)*

Jacob bought Esau's birthright with a dinner of lentil stew. They had been fighting over who would take over when their father died. Esau had been out in the field and was very hungry, so hungry that he gave up his rightful place in the family for some lentil stew. Lentils are a kind of bean or legume. They are easy to cook and do not require soaking first. They are red, brown, or green and are shaped like a convex lens. Lentils happen to be the first vegetable mentioned in the Bible.

lentils
2 Samuel 23:11

How Much Fiber Should I Eat?

The recommendation for total fiber in the daily diet is 20 to 35 grams. This will allow for proper daily bowel movements that will

assist your body in removing the toxic waste matter excreted in your stools without the excretion of any calcium.[9] Children two years of age and up should increase their dietary fiber intake in an amount equal to or greater than their age plus 5 grams a day. For example, a three-year-old child should have at least 8 grams of fiber a day. This should continue to increase until age twenty, when the fiber intake should be 25 to 35 grams a day.[10] This includes all fiber from whole grains, beans, fruits, and vegetables. Even as much as a 6-gram increase in fiber can reduce **serum cholesterol concentrations**.[11]

Soybeans: They Didn't Have 'Em, but We Do!

Many kinds of beans were eaten in Bible times and still are eaten in the Middle East and the entire Mediterranean region. Soybeans, unfortunately, were not grown in this area during Bible times, according to Bill Shurtleff, the author of many books on tofu and soybeans and an authority on soybeans. Nowadays, there are many kinds of soybeans for your use, and they make a wonderful addition to your life.

The Complete Protein Bean

In 1979 Nevin Scrimshaw and Vernon Young of **M.I.T.** published the results of research showing that soybeans do contain complete protein.[12] They are the only beans known to contain complete protein. This means that they are balanced in amino acids and do not need to be complemented with grains, nuts, seeds, dairy products, or animal proteins. Until this discovery, it was not known why soybeans were so healthy.

> what others say
>
> **Francisco Contreras, M.D.**
>
> Soybeans contain **genistein**. This **phytochemical** has an **anti-aggregate** that won't allow small tumors to attach themselves to **capillaries**. In this way, the tumors can't get nutrients and, consequently, they can't **metastasize**.[13]

Soybeans Are Important Seeds

GENESIS 1:12 ***And the earth brought forth grass, the herb that yields seed according to its kind, and the tree that yields fruit,***

serum cholesterol concentrations
amount of cholesterol in your blood

M.I.T.
Massachusetts Institute of Technology

genistein
one of the phytonutrients in soybeans

phytochemical/phytonutrient
plant-based chemical or nutrient

anti-aggregate
against clumping together tumors: a growth arising from existing tissue, but growing independently

capillaries
one of the minute blood vessels that connect the arteries and veins

metastasize
transmitted from one site to another within the body

isoflavones
plant-based hormones

phytoestrogen
plant-based estrogen, a hormone necessary for women and men

whose seed is in itself according to its kind. And God saw that it was good. (NKJV)

Soybeans are the seeds of the soy plant. They are used as food and for oil in North America and throughout the world and have many other industrial uses that make them a valuable cash crop. Soybeans are also very healthy to use as a regular food. Some form of soybean can be eaten daily.

Soybeans Contain Phytoestrogens

Isoflavones have been in the news lately because they are the newest form of plant-based hormones. Genistein is an isoflavone found in soybeans that is especially beneficial to men and women because it contains **phytoestrogen**. Phytoestrogens have been shown to be effective in both protecting against and treating prostate cancer[14] and in preventing the symptoms of menopause such as hot flashes, memory loss, and night sweats.

what others say

Pamela Smith, R.D.

I suggest including 45 mg of isoflavones in your diet each day. You could get this from just a half cup of edamame, two ounces of tempeh, three ounces of tofu, or two cups of soymilk; it doesn't require massive amounts. One study showed a 40 percent reduction in hot flashes from this "dose."[15]

Phyto-What?

Oftentimes, there are undesirable side effects with synthetic estrogen pills and creams. These generally do not occur with plant-based estrogens in your diet. Phytoestrogens have been proven useful in offering protection against breast, bowel, prostate, and other cancers, cardiovascular disease, brain function, alcohol abuse, osteoporosis, as well as menopausal symptoms.[16]

Soybeans and Beta-sitosterols

Sprouted soybeans are an excellent source of beta-sitosterols, also called sterols. Sterols have been researched for more than thirty years for their immune-boosting properties. Research published in 2004 in the journal *Lipids in Health and Disease* shows that sterols from plants, including nuts, seeds, and soybeans can not only lower cholesterol levels, but also shows that plant sterols possess anti-cancer, anti-inflammatory, **anti-atherogenicity**, and **anti-oxidation** activity.[17] The best soybeans are non-GMO and/or organic; this ensures that they will not contain genetically modified materials that have not been fully researched as to safety.

It is the high-soybean diet in the East that is deemed responsible for the low level of menopausal symptoms in Asian women, who traditionally eat a high-soybean, high-fiber diet.

Women with PMS (generally including the symptoms of bloating, crankiness, headaches, fatigue, or water retention directly before menstruation) or women who are entering menopause (the actual stoppage of the menstrual flow), or the years before actual menopause called perimenopause (characterized by many symptoms including weight gain, craving for sugars, salt, or fats, fatigue, hot flashes, memory loss, and irritability) find that including soy products in their lifestyle can reduce some of these symptoms. Although there are many creams and supplements in the health food store or pharmacy for these conditions, it is best to seek the advice of a medical professional before using anything stronger than eating foods high in phytoestrogens like soybeans.

Women with **PMS**, **perimenopause**, or actual **menopause** should eat some soybean products daily to ease their symptoms.

How Do You Like Your Soybeans?

Soybeans are eaten as beans in a side dish or as baked beans, the traditional ways of eating any dried beans. I prefer to eat soybeans in the form of tofu, **tempeh**, soyburgers, or tempeh burgers. I also drink soy protein and soy milk–based shakes that are high in isoflavones, especially genistein.

A diet high in soybeans and avocados was very useful in reducing the amount of **NSAIDS** used for treating symptomatic osteoarthritis of the knee and hip.[18]

anti-atherogenicity
against changes in the smooth muscles in the vascular system that play a role in atherosclerosis development

anti-oxidation
against the oxidation of fats and cholesterol, therefore creating a protective effect against DNA damage caused by oxidation

PMS
"premenstrual syndrome," characterized by bloating, crankiness, headaches, fatigue, or water retention before menstruation

perimenopause
the time leading up to the end of the menses when there may be some symptoms like fatigue and weight gain, but there still is menstruation

menopause
the time in a woman's life when menstruation stops, often characterized by hot flashes, fatigue, and weight gain due to hormonal imbalances

tempeh
a firm, generally flat, soy product made of fermented soybeans; a vegetarian source of vitamin B_{12}

NSAIDS
nonsteroidal anti-inflammatory drugs like ibuprofen or naproxen

Ezekiel's Punishment Is Our Health Food

The mixing of fibers from whole grains, beans, and lentils into what we call Ezekiel flour may have been a punishment for Ezekiel, but it is really a wonderful health food for everybody. Because there are so many modern health problems that can be directly related to a low-fiber diet, it is no wonder that people all over the world are rediscovering the special flour blend that has come to be known as Ezekiel flour. God created this special recipe for Ezekiel thousands of years ago, and now it is your special health food.

Chapter Wrap-Up

- For years there has been a controversy in the area of health foods and nutrition about eating beans and grains together to make complementary and complete protein. Ezekiel was told by God how to make grains and beans into a bread that would sustain life for a long time—more than a year, actually. This should tell scientists that God made the food, and he knows exactly how to put it together to be the most healthful. (Ezekiel 4:9)
- Make sure that when you eat beans you also eat whole grains on the same day, not necessarily at the same meal. Try various ethnic dishes that naturally mix beans or lentils and whole grains together as a way to start eating this more healthful diet.
- Beans in some form should be eaten daily as part of the Mediterranean diet. Doing so will improve your digestion and elimination, and reduce your risk for heart disease, cancers, and menopause or PMS symptoms.
- God also made soybeans, even if the Bible does not mention them or if people did not know of them in the Bible lands. They are very healthful and can be included in your diet weekly.

Study Questions

1. What is different about Ezekiel's bread recipe?
2. Why is Ezekiel's punishment our health food?
3. What are amino acids, and why do we need them?
4. What's so great about beans and lentils? Give four examples.
5. Which bean is the most healthful? Why?

Chapter 4: Daniel and His Diet for Strength

Chapter Highlights:
- **Daniel Put Vegetables to the Test**
- **Broccoli Sprouts, Cabbage, Ginkgo Biloba, and Garlic**

Let's Get Started

Believe it or not, whole grains, beans, and peas are from the vegetable family. You probably don't think of them as vegetables, but they are. There are a lot more vegetables in the vegetable kingdom than we have discussed so far—root vegetables like potatoes, beets, carrots, and sweet potatoes; bulb vegetables like onions, garlic, and kohlrabi; flowering vegetables like broccoli and cauliflower; head vegetables like cabbage and lettuce; leafy vegetables like parsley, kale, and collards; and hanging vegetables like tomatoes and peppers. There are yellow, orange, red, purple, brown, green, white, and pink vegetables. In short, vegetables are endless in tastes and varieties.

Daniel Put Vegetables to the Test

DANIEL 1:12–13 ***Please test your servants for ten days, and let them give us vegetables to eat and water to drink. Then let our appearance be examined before you, and the appearance of the young men who eat the portion of the king's delicacies; and as you see fit, so deal with your servants.*** *(NKJV)*

Daniel asked to eat vegetables in preference to the king's royal food and wine. Why do you think he did that? Because he didn't want to fit in with the Babylonians? Because he missed his regular food? The clue to this strange action is in Daniel 1:3–4.

Did They Eat Junk Food?

DANIEL 1:3–4 ***Then the king instructed Ashpenaz, the master of his eunuchs, to bring some of the children of Israel and some of the king's descendants and some of the nobles, young men in whom there was no blemish, but good-looking, gifted in all wisdom, possessing knowledge and quick to understand, who had ability to serve in the king's palace, and whom they might teach the language and literature of the Chaldeans.*** *(NKJV)*

test
Daniel 1:18–21

The young men chosen for this assignment were to be the healthiest men among the royalty and nobility, the best learners, the best of all the available young men. This was Daniel and his friends. What made them this way? You got it! Eating mostly vegetables, no wine, no rich foods, and no junk foods. Even when they were put to the test, they were ten times better in wisdom and understanding than all the magicians and astrologers in his kingdom.

what others say

Jack and Judy Hartman

Many of us who desire increased energy should follow the example of Daniel and his friends. We should turn away from the "rich dainties" that so many of us eat and eat more of the vegetables God has provided for us.[1]

Illustration #9
The Vegetables Section—The darkened section of this pyramid represents how much of your diet should be devoted to vegetables.

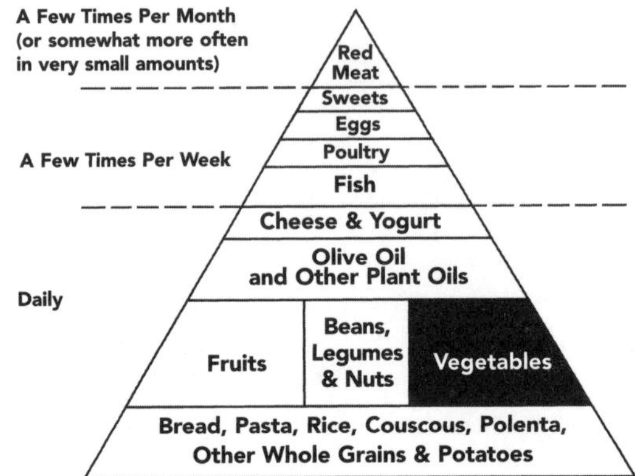

How Much Should I Eat?

If you look at the Mediterranean diet/Bible diet food pyramid section for vegetables, you will notice it is actually the largest section (see Illustration #9). This means you should eat more vegetables than any other food each day. It also means that you should eat more vegetables than fruit, grains, or animal proteins. Whew! That's a lot of vegetables! Isn't it wonderful that vegetables are also the most convenient to carry around and the least expensive to buy?

Have Some More!

real food
food in its natural, healthful state

The average North American eats only the basic seven or eight kinds of vegetables—corn, peas, potatoes, green beans, head lettuce, green peppers, cucumbers, and tomatoes. As recently as fifty years ago, the average person ate more than twenty different vegetables, which they grew and stored or preserved for the winter. Actually, a wider variety of vegetables is available to us today, in most supermarkets, than was available ten years ago. Be adventurous and try a new vegetable!

> **what others say**
>
> **Mark A. Pearson, D.O.**
>
> There is some evidence that a diet with between 5–6 servings of fruits and vegetables a day protects against cancer.[2]

A Word About Potatoes

Whole, unpeeled potatoes are **real food**. Peeled and deep-fried French fries are not. Baked potatoes are real food, potato chips are not. Homemade scalloped potatoes made from fresh potatoes that have not been peeled and are baked in a low-fat sauce are real food. Packaged, peeled, chemically treated scalloped potatoes are not real food—they are processed food stuffs.

Illustration #10
Potatoes vs. French Fries—Always make sensible choices when selecting food. Ask yourself questions like: Is it high in fats? Does it contain lots of salt? Is it filled with chemicals? If the answer is "yes" to any of these questions, make a healthier selection.

A Not-So-Well-Known Benefit of Spinach

Your mother, grandmother, and, perhaps, your second-grade teacher all told you to "eat more vegetables." Most of you grew up knowing that spinach made Popeye stronger, but do you eat spinach on a regular basis? Do you know that it can prevent macular degeneration, the most common cause of blindness in people over sixty-five?

fresh
not canned or frozen

raw
not cooked or processed (pickles and sauerkraut are processed)

enzymes
substances that start or speed up chemical reaction in your body without being consumed in the process

Fresh Is Best

Fresh vegetables are the best. **Raw** vegetables are excellent snack foods (see Illustration #11). Each day you need to eat some raw vegetables. The U.S. government says everyone should eat at least five to eight half-cup servings of vegetables, and at least one should be raw. This is actually less than the Bible diet recommends.

what others say

Jack and Judy Hartman

I believe our Creator provided fruit to cleanse our bodies and vegetables to build our bodies. As I've grown older and studied the Word of God, I've come to the conclusion that almost everyone can benefit from eating more fresh vegetables. The Word of God explains how important it is to eat fresh vegetables.[3]

Raw Vegetables Are Essential

Raw vegetables are essential for a vital life. They contain **enzymes** that are destroyed by cooking. Raw vegetables are high in vitamin C, beta-carotene, and phytochemicals. Raw vegetables, along with vegetable oils, fish, beta-carotene, vitamin E, and calcium, have been shown to be responsible for prevention of breast cancer in a study done in Italy between 1991 and 1994.[4]

Canned vegetables do not have the same nutritional impact as fresh vegetables do, mainly because they have been heated and cooked so they are deficient in enzymes. They also might be loaded with sugar, salt, or other preservatives. Canned vegetables should be your last resort.

Illustration #11
Vegetables—These are great snacks! They are easy to carry and are packed full of nutrition—just what you need to keep you going!

Frozen vegetables can be better for you in the winter if your grocery carries wilted and limp produce. Frozen veggies are picked at their peak of ripeness and **flash frozen**. Don't overcook them. Often they don't need to be cooked any more, just defrosted.

flash frozen
frozen quickly

Cooked Veggies Are Good?

There are many secrets to cooking vegetables. First of all, the fat-soluble vitamins like E and A that are in deep-yellow and -orange vegetables are rendered more available to your body if they are cooked. So that means carrots, sweet potatoes, orange yams, winter squash like hubbard, acorn, turban, butternut, and any other deep-orange-fleshed squash can be baked, steamed, or stir-fried. You will get more nutritional value if it is cooked. That is why dishes like squash soup or stuffed squash are fabulous for your health, and they taste great, too.

Foods high in calcium such as kale, collard greens, turnip greens, broccoli, and brussels sprouts should also be lightly cooked to get the calcium from them. Also, if you add some acid at the table like lemon or lime juice, you will get better breakdown and absorption of the calcium and other minerals in these dark green foods. You could even grate some lemon peel in the water under the cooking basket.

A really good stew can be made with sweet potatoes, kale, onions, garlic, and whole grains like cooked brown rice or millet, and cumin. Try cooking these ingredients in a slow cooker while you're out during the day, and you will find a really vital and exciting meal awaiting you when you return.

We have known for thirty years or more that vegetables should be cooked on a high heat to seal in the juices and nutrients. This means having the cooking pot already hot before the veggies go into it. A steamer is the best way to do this as it is a high heat and will also cook most vegetables in less time.

Boil, Boil, and Bubble

Boiling is the worst way to cook vegetables, especially if you start with cold water and bring the veggies to a boil. This overcooks them and drains most of the nutrients into the water that you end up throwing away. Now soup is a different matter. You want the nutrients in the water because you are going to eat that.

Different Temperatures

Vegetables should be baked at 375°–425°F for about an hour. Most meats should be roasted in the oven at 325°–350°F. So if you are planning on baking or roasting veggies in the oven with the meat, you will have to pre-steam them first for about five to seven minutes to get them sealed and to start the cooking process so they will all be cooked together.

The Perfect Snack

It is often easier to eat vegetables raw as snacks. Children love snacks of raw vegetables, especially if they have been included in the preparation of the snacks. I often recommend that people carry raw vegetable snacks with them to eat between meals. If you are out and about, and feel a slump in energy, don't reach for a caffeine-laden drink, reach for some raw vegetable snacks. Go to a supermarket and get a bag of salad greens and some baby carrots. You'll be surprised how much energy eating these will give you.

Peas from the Pod

I love to eat peas in the pod as a snack. They make a good substitute for candy or sugar, they are so sweet-tasting. Let your children open the peas themselves and find the surprise of what the peas look like. Did you get one that has big peas or are they really little? Is the pod bigger than the peas inside? What a thrill it is to find a pod that has some peas that are already sprouting inside. Plant these in a pot and see how peas grow. Make eating vegetables fun!

Children Need Vegetables

Research with children and nutrients used to be centered on the actual nutrients in each food like the vitamins and minerals. Now it is different. The research with children and vegetables and fruits is showing that not only are children not getting enough vegetables and fruits, but also that children as young as eleven years old have high cholesterol and triglyceride counts, which eating more vegetables can help to reduce. In the 1950s and 1960s, high cholesterol was for people over fifty. Not anymore! Due to our fast-food lifestyles and lack of nutrients from fruits and veggies, North Americans, adults and children, are suffering from many noncommunicable diseases as a direct result.

Kcal
kilocalories, a measure of energy, the amount of heat produced by metabolizing food

The World Health Organization (WHO) estimates that up to 2.6 million deaths per year around the world are directly related to low consumption of fruits and vegetables. They state that various cardiovascular diseases and cancers are the result in this lack of proper eating lifestyles. This shows all parents that they must monitor and supervise the foods their children (and other members of the family) eat if they are to obtain at least the recommended servings of three to five half-cups of vegetables a day.[5]

The World Health Organization estimates the following percentages of disease reduction from eating veggies and fruits:

- ***heart disease***—31 percent reduction
- ***ischemic stroke***—19 percent reduction
- ***stomach cancer***—19 percent reduction
- ***esophageal cancer***—20 percent reduction
- ***lung cancer***—12 percent reduction
- ***colorectal cancer***—2 percent reduction

What Is a "High-Fiber Diet"?

The general consensus is that a diet of around 35 grams of fiber a day is considered to be a normal high-fiber diet for North Americans. According to David Jenkins of the Department of Nutritional Sciences, Faculty of Medicine, at the University of Toronto, this diet would also include 30 percent fat and 1,800 **Kcal** overall.[6]

phytochemicals health-protective substances in plants

hypertension high blood pressure

Why We Need Fiber

Fiber in the form of grains and especially vegetables has been shown to prevent colon cancer, and reduce high cholesterol and high blood pressure. There is so much research out showing that the risks for all diseases go up with a diet low in vegetables, fruits, and whole grains, that anyone who ignores it is asking for trouble.[7] But that's why you are reading this book right now, to change your lifestyle to a healthier one!

Solomon Said!

Proverbs 15:17 ***Better is a dinner of herbs where love is, than a fatted calf with hatred.*** *(NKJV)*

Solomon, the writer of this section of Proverbs, points out that even a special occasion where they would serve a fattened calf was worthless if there was hatred. A special occasion was a really big deal for them. A meal of herbs (vegetables) was the general daily fare for most people in Bible times. So he is saying that even a regular meal with love is better than a feast with hatred. The important part of this verse for now is that it lets you understand that the daily fare was a meal of vegetables. Vegetables were their main food! They only ate meat on special occasions.

They're Everywhere!

All throughout the Bible there are references to vegetables, eating vegetables, and different kinds of vegetables, starting with God's creation of them. This should really be the only reason you need to eat vegetables; they are very important.

Powerhouses of Phytochemicals

Phytochemical is a big-looking word, but all it means is plant chemicals or ingredients. Often they are also called "phytonutrients," plant-based nutrients. These phytochemicals have been associated with protection from and/or treatments for chronic diseases such as heart disease, cancer, diabetes, and **hypertension**, as well as other medical conditions. The foods and herbs with the highest anticancer activity include garlic, soybeans, cabbage, ginger, and umbelliferous vegetables, sprouts, broccoli sprouts, and sprouted grasses.[8]

> **what others say**
>
> **Kenneth Cooper, M.D.**
>
> Cruciferous vegetables, notably broccoli, brussels sprouts, cauliflower, and cabbage, have been identified as strong anticancer weapons. They are also thought to be protective against other conditions including heart disease, diverticulitis, and constipation.[9]

Antioxidants: What's the Buzz?

The one phytochemical mentioned in the news more than any other is the antioxidant. There are many of them; perhaps twenty are being used in nutritional supplements right now. Cabbage, tomatoes, grape seeds, wheat germ, green tea, black tea, carrots, all dark green leafy vegetables, and all dark orange vegetables contain antioxidants. Antioxidants are shown to be preventive agents against cancer and heart disease, especially **atherosclerosis**.[10]

Peppers Fight Cancer

Research done in Mexico on the effectiveness of the antioxidant **carotenoids** beta-carotene and **xanthophylls** shows that they were able to reduce the **mutagenic** and **carcinogenic** properties of various known mutagens that they introduced. They used extracts of bell peppers, poblano peppers, serrano peppers, and jalapeño peppers, all readily available in most supermarkets—fresh, dried, or in cans.[11]

> **what others say**
>
> **Kenneth Cooper, M.D.**
>
> Beta-carotene, which is transformed into vitamin A after it enters the body, is part of the "carotenoid" family of nutrients. Their pigments are the source of the yellow, orange, and green colors in certain vegetables and fruits like carrots, cantaloupe, sweet potatoes, spinach, collard greens, and kale. High blood serum levels of beta-carotene have been linked to lower risk of cataracts, heart disease, and cancers such as rectal cancer, **melanoma**, and bladder cancer. The best way to take beta-carotene into your body is through foods high in this nutrient.[12]

atherosclerosis
the most common type of **arteriosclerosis**

arteriosclerosis
the accumulation of fatty deposits in the inner linings of the arteries

carotenoids
orange or yellow pigments converted into vitamin A in the body

xanthophylls
carotenoids

mutagenic
known to cause mutation

carcinogenic
known to induce cancerous changes

melanoma
malignant tumor on the skin

Smoking Destroys Antioxidants

Smoking cigarettes, cigars, or pipes, or inhaling secondhand smoke can deplete your body of vitamin C and beta-carotene. This is why it is very important for smokers to eat a lot of deeply colored vegetables, preferably raw, every day. Obviously, it would be better to stop smoking or to stop going to places where people smoke, but that might not always be an option for people.

what others say

Julian Whitaker, M.D.

A smoker inhales high levels of free radicals which deplete key antioxidant nutrients like vitamin C and beta-carotene.[13]

Antioxidants and Lung Function

A study that started in 1992 and followed 864 subjects into 2000 showed that the antioxidant beta-carotene protected the general population in the study from lung function decline, and the smokers in the study were protected by beta-carotene and vitamin E intake.[14]

Antioxidants and Age-Related Macular Degeneration

Since the first study on age-related macular degeneration (AMD) and dark green vegetables was published in 1994, there has been a lot of research. In 2003 a study was published saying that the specific antioxidants or carotenoids that help slow AMD are lutein and zeaxanthin. Both are found in dark green leafy vegetables. The study also recommended wearing UV protective lenses and a hat when outdoors.[15]

The study in 1994 named spinach, kale, and broccoli, which contain these carotenoids, as AMD-protective. Another study done in Canada showed that adding multivitamins and minerals and additional supplementation of the antioxidants beta-carotene, vitamins C and E, and zinc could reduce the progression of AMD.[16]

Colored Vegetables

mucous membranes
lining inside your mouth, nose, intestines, anus, and vagina

Dark-colored vegetables have the highest amounts of phytochemicals, especially beta-carotene. Winter squash generally have very dark-colored flesh and are excellent sources of beta-carotene, a vegetable source of vitamin A, essential for the health of **mucous membranes**. Vitamin A counters the effects of aging and air pollution. Dark-colored vegetables are wonderful to have as a basic winter food. Isn't it interesting how the very foods that can be stored and used over the winter are the same foods that contain the precious nutrients you need to be healthy during the winter? The darker or brighter colored a vegetable is, the better it is for you.

Winter Squash

Eating winter squash like turban, gold nugget, kabocha, hubbard, butternut, or acorn can increase your resistance to winter colds and the flu. Beta-carotene, vegetable-source vitamin A, is essential for the health of mucous membranes. It counters the effects of aging and air pollution. Kids love eating baked squash with a little salt and pepper and butter or olive oil on it. They especially love eating puréed winter squash when it is disguised as pumpkin pie or molasses and honey muffins. Baked squash can also be used as a thickener in soups, stews, and gravies if your family finds squash unacceptable as a vegetable on their plates.

I like to bake a squash in the oven and freeze the mashed or puréed pulp in the amounts I need for my favorite recipes.

Broccoli for Breakfast . . . Why Not?

"Broccoli for breakfast" was the headline of an article that appeared in Toronto's *Globe and Mail* newspaper in 1978. It was an interview with me! Yes, I did eat broccoli for breakfast, and I still do. Had some just yesterday. Breakfast is a great time to eat vegetables. I often eat steamed veggies for breakfast with a boiled egg. Sometimes I put cheese, leftover meat, or even tofu in with the veggies. I especially love potato, carrot, squash, broccoli, green peas, green beans, beets and beet tops, mustard greens, and any combination of these vegetables. When they are steamed, I add some fresh parsley or cilantro, pressed garlic, chopped onion, cumin, butter and/or olive oil, and salt and pepper. I actually mash it all up with a fork and eat it with a spoon. It is delicious! Often I add vegetables to oatmeal while it is cooking and add the fresh parsley at the end. This is more like the kind of food they ate in Bible times.

Often a typical breakfast in Bible times would consist of dark whole grain bread, olives, fresh or dried figs or raisins, cheese—sort of like the feta we have now, or a pressed cottage cheese or cream cheese—cucumbers, garlic, onions, and perhaps parsley or romaine lettuce. A meal like this will give you a really great start to the day without any sugar highs or letdowns.

Repeating Vegetables

NUMBERS 11:5 ***We remember the fish which we ate freely in Egypt, the cucumbers, the melons, the leeks, the onions, and the garlic.*** *(NKJV)*

All the vegetables the Israelites longed for in Numbers 11:5, are the ones we call the "repeating" vegetables. Many people find the taste of these vegetables coming up, hence repeating, in the gas released from the stomach for several hours after eating. Cabbage, broccoli, and green peppers are generally in this list, as well as the cucumbers, onion, and garlic mentioned (see Illustration #12). Guess what? It isn't the vegetables' fault! If you chew each mouthful really well and allow your stomach to have the necessary digestive enzymes by reducing your stress level and, perhaps, taking a digestive enzyme containing alpha-galactosidase, you will not experience this repeating from these vegetables. It is very important to eat slowly and chew well when eating any food; and these vegetables are no exception. Why do you think God gave us teeth, if not to use them when we eat?

Illustration #12
Garlic, Leeks, and Onions—These three vegetables make up part of the family of onions—the lily family.

Cucumbers

trace
very little, as in just a trace

Cucumbers have a very high water content and are eaten often, along with melons, in dry, hot areas. Eating cucumbers is a great way to keep from getting dehydrated in the desert. Cucumbers also contain calcium, iron, phosphorus, potassium, magnesium, vitamin A, and folate as well as **trace** amounts of zinc, copper, and the B vitamins.

Leeks, Onions, and Garlic

Leeks, onions, and garlic come from the same family. They have been used around the world for thousands of years for healing and for eating, and they make many ethnic dishes taste great. Include garlic and onions in your diet daily.

> **what others say**
>
> **Francisco Contreras, M.D.**
>
> Garlic is known to have therapeutical value in a wide variety of diseases. From an antibiotic (as potent as penicillin or tetracycline), anti-micotic (fungus), anti-viral, to cancer killing powers.[17]

What About the Smell?

Many people can eat raw garlic and have no body odor of garlic. The smell of garlic and onions is "set" by heat and removed by cold. When you peel, cut, or chop garlic or onions, always wash off everything—your hands, knife, and cutting board—with cold water, and they will not smell. If you wash off with hot water, you will smell like garlic or onions for several hours, or even days afterward. Eating garlic that has been heated during cooking will cause a body odor of garlic. This is why French, Italian, and other garlic-spiced cooking is known for causing the garlic odor.

Raw garlic in salad dressings or on bread generally will not give that garlic after-odor. If you want to take garlic supplements, you will want a garlic extract that is not oil-based, since heat is used to extract oils. The aged garlic extract Kyolic has been proven to promote health and have no odor. One capsule or tablet is equivalent to an entire head of garlic, and yet, there is no body or breath odor.

triglycerides
the form in which fat is stored in your body

HDL cholesterol
high-density lipoprotein, the "good" cholesterol

what others say

Rex Russell, M.D.

Garlic cloves are often used successfully to protect people from infections. It is helpful in treating asthma, diabetes, and high blood pressure. It stimulates the immune system and is also a pain killer. Population studies indicate an inverse relationship between the amount of garlic consumed and the number of cancer deaths in a given population.[18]

Stop That Bacteria!

Research done in India in 1997 and published in the U.S. in 1998 indicated that garlic inhibited the following bacteria: *Staphylo-coccus aureus*, *Salmonella typhi*, *Escherichia coli*, and *Listeria monocytogenes.* Garlic is the most effective against *E. coli.*[19] Garlic is a good preventative for people who live or work in areas where these bacteria might be present. Have you ever noticed that places where outbreaks of bacteria-related illnesses occur are almost always places where garlic is not on the menu and where the people who eat or live there don't eat garlic? When was the last time you heard of a nursing home serving garlic or handing out aged garlic extract tablets or capsules? When was the last time you ate garlic in a fast-food burger place?

Garlic: Is It Useful for Health?

There has been a lot of publicity about garlic being useless. Research was done using garlic powder, like from your kitchen, and garlic oil in a laboratory. The research indicated that these two forms of garlic did not reduce cholesterol or high blood pressure.[20] This is no surprise! Garlic has to be vital and alive to do its job! Crushed raw garlic put into capsules did significantly lower total serum cholesterol and **triglycerides** and increased the **HDL cholesterol** activity. All good results.[21]

Aged Garlic Extract

Most of the really great garlic research has been done using aged garlic extract. A recent study done at East Carolina University School of Medicine in Greenville, North Carolina, concluded that aged garlic extract reduced **platelet adhesion** by 30 percent in men with high cholesterol.[22] Aged garlic extract also had a positive effect on their blood **lipids** and blood pressure. A recent study published in the journal *Atherosclerosis* indicated that the aged garlic extract Kyolic provided protection against the onset of atherosclerosis.[23]

platelet adhesion
clumping together of the smallest particles in the blood

lipids
a type of blood fat not soluble in water

dulse
coarse edible red seaweed

Broccoli Sprouts, Cabbage, Ginkgo Biloba, and Garlic

The American Association for Cancer Research's fourth annual Frontiers in Cancer Prevention Research meeting in Baltimore, Maryland, October 2005, presented many papers on foods that prevent cancers. Here are the titles of some of the abstracts:

- "Broccoli Sprouts Relieve Gastritis in H. Pylori Patients; May Help Prevent Gastric Cancer" (#3442)
- "Broccoli Sprout Extract Protects Against Skin Cancer from UV Light" (#2597)
- "Change in Diet [adding cabbage/sauerkraut] at Any Age May Help Protect Against Breast Cancer" (#3697)
- "Possible Chemoprevention of Ovarian Cancer by the Herbal, Ginkgo Biloba" (#3654)
- "Garlic Shown to Inhibit DNA Damaging Chemical in breast Cancer" (#2543)

To read more on this and other interesting topics, go to www.aacr.org.

Sea Vegetables

There are many kinds of sea vegetables in common use. The most common is **dulse**. It is a reddish-brown color and is often sold dried in seafood markets. Generally it comes from Maine or New Brunswick, where many people eat it fresh or dried as a high mineral snack. It is very salty and should not be consumed regularly, especially if you have high blood pressure or a heart condition. The nutrients in dulse are the minerals iodine, phosphorus, bromine, rubidium, manganese, titanium, along with trace minerals, and vitamins B_6, B_{12}, C, and E.

alginates
the main, slippery part of seaweed that grabs onto toxins and expels them from the body

atrophy
waste away

Kelp or Kombu?

Deep-sea kelp, which is called kombu in Asian markets, is the highest in iodine and potassium. Kelp has over two hundred times more potassium than sodium. That is why kelp powder is often added to salt substitutes to give the salty taste with less sodium than table salt. It also contains **alginates**, which can remove toxins from your body like lead, mercury, and cadmium, and some kinds of environmental pollutants. Because kelp is so high in iodine, many people take kelp tablets to stimulate their thyroid gland. This is not a good idea unless you are directed to do so by your health-care practitioner, because taking kelp tablets in large doses can often make your thyroid **atrophy**.

Sea Vegetables in Daily Life

Sea vegetables are great to add to many foods such as soups, stews, or cereals. I often add them to cooking grains or beans to aid digestion. Rehydrated sea vegetables can be added to salads or can make a salad on their own as they do in most Asian cuisines.

You Decide

How would you rather spend your money: $1.00 for a candy bar that robs your body of calcium, B vitamins, and stimulates your adrenal glands and keeps you wired? Or $1.00 for a few baby carrots, ¼ of a red pepper, and several slices of cucumber, which would give you vitamin C, beta-carotene, potassium, calcium, and magnesium? It's up to you. God gave you a wide variety of vegetables that contain all the nutrients you need to be healthy. Do you choose health?

Chapter Wrap-Up

- Daniel and his friends refused to eat the king's food and asked for their regular meals, which consisted of vegetables. Their diet also included grains, nuts, seeds, and beans but excluded strong drink and fatty meats. (Daniel 1:3–20)
- God created a wide variety of vegetables for all people.
- Vegetables should comprise the largest group of foods you eat each day.
- Vegetables contain many health-giving properties such as fiber, vitamins, minerals, and antioxidants.
- God gave man a really easy way to tell which vegetables were good to eat by giving the deepest colors to the ones that were essential for health and vitality.
- Even when God was providing food for the Israelites, they longed for their health foods: cucumbers, leeks, onions, and garlic. (Numbers 11:5)

Study Questions

1. Why was Daniel chosen to be in the king's service?
2. What special favor did Daniel request and why?
3. What part of your diet should be vegetables?
4. Is the color of vegetables important and why?
5. Which vegetables are especially good for your health?
6. Name at least five diseases or conditions that can be improved or prevented by eating vegetables.
7. Name the best ways to get children to eat vegetables.
8. Which vegetables did the Israelites long for in the desert, and why are they healthy for you?

Chapter 5: Solomon's Garden

Chapter Highlights:
- **The Nuts on Solomon's Trees**
- **Flaxseed Oil for Health**
- **Fruit in the Mediterranean Diet**

Let's Get Started

Nuts, seeds, and fruits are the basic crops Solomon grew in his luxurious garden. All of them are amazingly portable and convenient nutrition. Isn't it also amazing that God created these essential foods to taste great! Walnuts are a marvelous Bible food that lowers cholesterol, and they were grown in Solomon's garden. In the mid-1990s grape seeds and skins became the hottest health food supplement of the day. They are filled with **proanthocyanidins**, antioxidants for health, anti-aging, and vitality. Olives—they are a fruit, you know—are one of the best sources of monounsaturated fatty acids, and they have a large section of the Mediterranean food pyramid. Olives and grapes are the health foods of the twenty-first century, just as they were in Bible times. **Flaxseeds** are not mentioned in the Bible, but flax plants are. They are one of the best sources of omega-3 essential fatty acids.

proanthocyanidins
antioxidants found in grape seeds and skins and in pine bark

flaxseeds
seeds of a plant grown for making linen from the fibrous stems

The Nuts on Solomon's Trees

SONG OF SOLOMON 6:11 ***I went down to the garden of nuts to see the verdure of the valley.*** *(NKJV)*

The nuts on Solomon's trees are in the same category as beans and other legumes in the Mediterranean diet pyramid (see Illustration #13). See chapter 3 for more information about the protein in nuts and seeds. They can be eaten daily along with dried beans and peas. Nuts and seeds also can team up with the proteins of grains and/or beans to make complete protein, which is necessary for optimum health. The only nuts that are bad for you are roasted and salted ones, or ones that are rancid due to improper storage.

Illustration #13
The Nuts Section—The darkened section of this pyramid represents how much of your diet should be devoted to nuts.

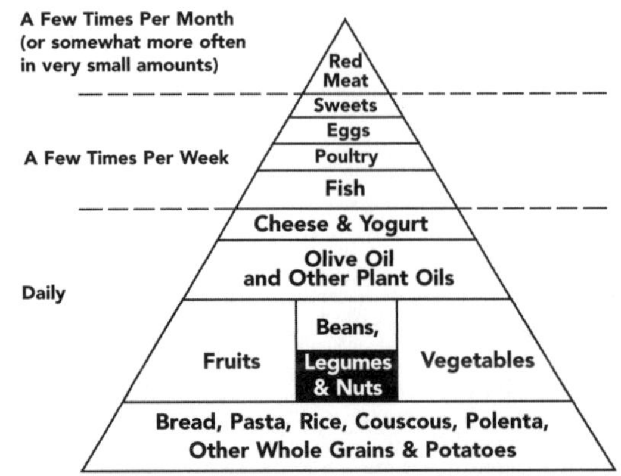

Walnuts, almonds, and pistachios were the most common nuts grown in Bible lands, and you can be sure they were in Solomon's garden. Walnuts are the nuts that Solomon went down to his garden to see, according to F. Nigel Hepper in the *Baker Encyclopedia of Bible Plants.*

Walnuts Are Healthful

Walnuts have long been used in cookies, sweet rolls, and candies. Today's research indicates that walnuts are useful as part of a low-fat diet, to reduce **LDL cholesterol** and increase **HDL cholesterol.**[1]

According to the Bible diet, we should eat nuts every day, particularly walnuts and almonds, because of their ability to lower our "bad" cholesterol. In addition, nuts are so filling that you may find you lose your desire for high-fat junk foods and large portions.

almonds
Exodus 37:19–20; Numbers 17:1–9

famine
Genesis 42–50

LDL cholesterol
low-density lipoprotein, the bad cholesterol

HDL cholesterol
high-density lipoprotein, the good cholesterol

The Best Products of the Land

GENESIS 43:11 ***And their father Israel said to them, "If it must be so, then do this: Take some of the best fruits of the land in your vessels and carry down a present for the man—a little balm and a little honey, spices and myrrh, pistachio nuts and almonds." (NKJV)***

When Jacob wanted to impress Joseph, the Egyptian ruler, he sent pistachio nuts and almonds. Pistachio nuts didn't grow in Egypt, so it was a very special gift. There was a famine in the land of Canaan where they lived and not in Egypt, so they went to Egypt to ask to buy grains.

Scientists Work with Almonds and Walnuts

Almonds and walnuts have both been used in research to lower LDL cholesterol and total cholesterol, and to preserve higher levels of HDL cholesterol.[2] Adding almonds and/or walnuts to your diet is very helpful for reducing blood fats.

> **what others say**
>
> **Reginald Cherry, M.D.**
>
> Almonds (10 per day) or walnuts (10 per day) rank at the top of the list of acceptable nuts in the Mediterranean diet.[3]

Lots of Nutrients in Nuts

Nuts contain vitamin E, fiber, and essential fatty acids. Essential fatty acids (EFAs) are very useful for smooth skin and shiny healthy hair. Essential fatty acids are also called vitamin F. Vitamin F has been used for years to reverse an overactive thyroid, to help reverse some of the symptoms of **scleroderma**, to improve immune function, and to improve digestion. The fatty acids found in nuts are **unsaturated fatty acids** and **polyunsaturated fatty acids**, both known to be healthful.

Eating walnuts daily can reduce triglyceride levels up to 17 percent and increase HDL (high-density lipoprotein), the "good" cholesterol, by 9 percent according to a study published in the journal *Angiology*. So eating just twenty grams of walnuts daily can actually be like medicine for those with **hyperlipidemia**.[4]

Essential Fatty Acids for Health

In a study done in the early 1990s, EFAs were used to recover people with **chronic fatigue syndrome** with a 90 percent success rate.[5] EFAs have also been shown to be of use during pregnancy for the development of fetuses and for the prevention of premature births.[6] Essential fatty acids were used with patients with **chronic gastrointestinal disorders** such as **Crohn's disease**, and good response was obtained.[7] Essential fatty acid deficiencies have also been implicated in **cystic fibrosis**, **schizophrenia**, and the tendency to develop **pressure ulcers**. Essential fatty acids have been shown to increase calcium absorption by preventing the loss of calcium in urine and increasing the depositing of calcium in bones, preventing **osteoporosis**.[8]

scleroderma
a disease characterized by hardening of the skin and organs

unsaturated fatty acids
vegetable fats that are liquid at room temperature

polyunsaturated fatty acids
fat found in corn, soybean, safflower, and some fish oils; may help to reduce cholesterol

hyperlipidemia
a condition of high amounts of lipids (fats) in the blood

chronic fatigue syndrome
an illness that extends over a long period of time, extreme fatigue being one of the many symptoms

chronic gastrointestinal disorders
diseases of the intestines, stomach, mouth, and anus

Crohn's disease
ulceration and inflammation of the digestive system

cystic fibrosis
a genetic defect that affects the pancreas, sweat glands, and the entire digestive and breathing systems

schizophrenia
a mental illness of disordered thinking and emotional changes

pressure ulcers
sores caused by pressure such as bed sores

osteoporosis
porous bones

Brazil Nuts for Health

Brazil nuts are high in the mineral selenium. A selenium deficiency can often cause symptoms that are closely related to some kinds of depression. I had a friend who got off a prescription drug for depression, with her doctor's help, by eating Brazil nuts every day. She had a selenium "deficiency"–induced depression!

Selenium and Ovarian Cancer

Selenium supplementation is being recommended to women with ovarian cancer who are undergoing chemotherapy, to improve their recovery rate.[9] It seems that Brazil nuts and sunflower seeds are useful for more than just elevating mood.

Nuts and seeds can go rancid easily, making them dangerous for your health. Purchase nuts or seeds in the shell for your protection. Keep them in the refrigerator or freezer once they are shelled. Many health food stores keep their nuts and seeds refrigerated for this very reason. So be sure to look for nuts and seeds that have been kept refrigerated.

what others say

Cheryl Townsley

Seeds, along with nuts, do contain oil. If they are fresh and properly stored, the natural oils will not turn rancid. Buy nuts and seeds in whole form (versus chopped) for longer freshness. Store in the refrigerator or freezer.[10]

Nuts Make Great Snacks

Nuts make great snacks. They can be easily carried in your purse or briefcase. They go well in school lunches. Nuts are a good source of protein and the essential fatty acids so necessary for growth and health. When well chewed, they can relieve the fatigue of low blood sugar and give you a boost of energy as an afternoon snack.

The healthiest nuts and seeds are not coated with salt or oil-roasted. Dry-roasted nuts or natural unroasted and unsalted nuts are best.

Nut Butter

suppressed
subdued, lowered

lozenges
medicated discs that you suck on

Nut butters have been considered "kid food" for as long as I can remember. I hardly ever ate peanut butter, because I didn't like the way it stuck to my mouth. Commercial nut butters also have added sugar, salt, and fillers. Natural nut butter doesn't have added sugar or fillers. When I first began to eat natural nut butters as an adult, I was amazed that they didn't stick to my mouth. A lettuce and nut butter sandwich on whole grain bread is a really nutritious lunch or snack for children and adults. I like a sandwich of Maranatha's almond butter and leaf or bibb lettuce on whole wheat bread. Make sure that the nut butter you purchase has no fillers, sugars, or salt added.

what others say

Joyce Meyer

Nuts, beans, and seeds have a terrific mix of protein, fiber, vitamins, and other essential nutrients, with no saturated fat.[11]

Nothing Seedy About This

2 Samuel 17:28 . . . ***wheat, barley and flour, parched grain and beans, lentils and parched seeds.*** *(NKJV)*

Seeds grow on plants in the field or in gardens. God gave them to you for your health along with fruits, vegetables, and proteins. Choose snacks from these healthy foods. Snacks of nuts, seeds, and fruit are superior to nutrientless junk food as snacks. All seeds have unsaturated fatty acids, which are also known as vitamin F. Pumpkin seeds are known for their zinc content, which is useful for men's problems and for general healing for everyone. Low levels of zinc in your body signal that you are undernourished and likely to have a **suppressed** immune system. It may mean you get more colds and bouts of the flu than other people or that you tire more easily, or just that you are more susceptible to many diseases. Zinc and vitamin C **lozenges** have become popular for helping with colds and sore throats, and there is research showing that they both work and don't work, so it's up to you if you want to use them. Sunflower seeds are high in calcium and magnesium, and are very good for someone who wants to add these nutrients to their diet.

eicosapentaenoic acid
EPA, a PUFA (polyunsaturated fatty acid)

cardioprotective
good for the heart

soluble fiber
fiber that can be easily dissolved

insoluble fiber
fiber that is incapable of being dissolved

mucilage
one of the seven basic kinds of fiber found in food

colon
large intestine

Flaxseeds

PROVERBS 31:13 *She seeks wool and flax, and willingly works with her hands.* (NKJV)

Flaxseeds are the latest health food, and one of the oldest seeds referred to in the Bible. The Bible mentions the growing of flax for making linen. The stems were spun into threads that were woven into cloth. Some of the finest cloth in the Bible comes from flaxseeds, and the finest health food comes from flaxseeds, too. Flaxseeds grown for oilseed use (rather than for the flax fiber made into linen) contain omega-3 fatty acids.

Flaxseed Oil for Health

Flaxseed oil contains alpha-linolenic acid or ALA, which is converted into omega-3 fatty acids when eaten and can be a major vegetarian source of the omega-3 fatty acid **eicosapentaenoic acid**, generally found in fish oils and known to be **cardioprotective**.[12]

Two Kinds of Fiber

Flaxseeds contain both **soluble** and **insoluble fiber**. The soluble fiber in flaxseed is **mucilage**, a thick sticky substance. It is similar to the soluble fibers in fruit pectin, oat bran, or mustard seed. A lot of people make a morning "tea" of flaxseeds and boiling water to supply this mucilaginous fiber to their diets and prevent constipation. When I was at a health spa once, we were awakened each morning with a steaming cup of flaxseed and lemon juice tea.

The insoluble fiber in flaxseeds is similar to wheat bran and is helpful for regulating bowel movements. This part of flaxseed contains lignan and cellulose, which hold water in the stool, allowing it to move through the colon more quickly.

The National Cancer Institute included flaxseeds in a study of foods that have cancer-fighting ability. The other foods were garlic, licorice root, vegetables from the parsnip family, citrus fruits, and soybeans. All were found beneficial in fighting cancers.

Eating Flaxseeds

fruit
Isaiah 16:9–10; Daniel 4:21

bulk fiber
fiber that aids in digestion by providing bulk in the intestines

Flaxseeds can be added whole to baked goods. There are many commercial breads that contain whole flaxseeds. Just remember to chew them well for the most benefit. They can also be freshly ground in a seed mill or blender and used in baked goods, on cereals, or in protein shakes. Many companies produce flaxseeds already ground and nitrogen sealed to preserve freshness. Keep ground flaxseeds in the refrigerator or freezer.

Flaxseed bread is a great way to add these wonderful seeds to your diet. Some Roman Meal breads and cereals have flaxseeds in them.

> **what others say**
>
> **Pamela Smith**
>
> Flaxseed has the highest content of vitamin E of any known seed. It excels in complete **bulk fiber**, is easy to digest, is high in complete protein, and rich in minerals and oil.[13]

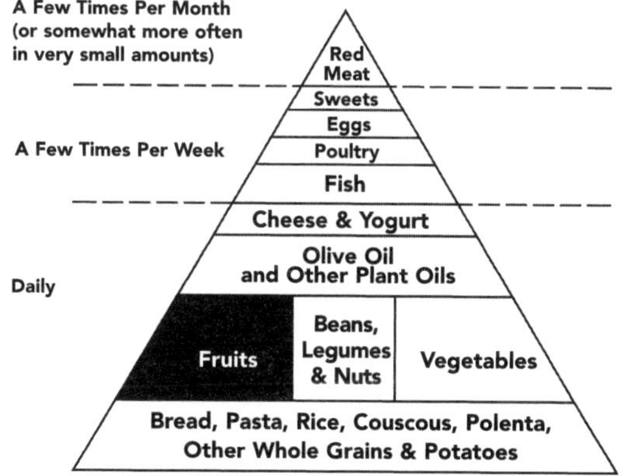

Illustration #14
The Fruit Section—The darkened section of this pyramid represents how much of your diet should be devoted to fruit.

Fruit in the Mediterranean Diet

> JEREMIAH 29:5 ***Build houses and dwell in them; plant gardens and eat their fruit.*** *(NKJV)*

Fruits are so important in the Bible or Mediterranean diet that they have their own section in the food pyramid (see Illustration #14). Some form of fruit should be eaten daily for really vibrant health. There are many kinds of fruits. Some grow on vines like grapes and kiwi. Some grow on bushes like blueberries, raspberries,

grapes
Isaiah 5:2, 4; 18:5

raisins
1 Chronicles 12:40

gooseberries, currants, and huckleberries. Some grow on the ground like strawberries. And still others grow on trees like apples, pears, oranges, bananas, mangoes, grapefruit, avocados, apricots, peaches, and plums, just to mention a few. With so many choices, it should be easy to select some fruit each day.

This Won't Hurt a Bit

cerebrovascular
pertaining to the blood vessels supplying the brain

mortality
death rate

ISAIAH 4:2 ***In that day the Branch of the LORD shall be beautiful and glorious; and the fruit of the earth shall be excellent and appealing for those of Israel who have escaped.*** *(NKJV)*

We have all heard the expression "An apple a day keeps the doctor away," but do we really believe it? Most people don't take it seriously enough to have fruit every week, let alone daily.

> **what others say**
>
> **Jim Shriner**
>
> Fruit in the morning is a good colon cleanser, so eat some every morning.[14]

Fruit and Cerebrovascular Disease

A twenty-year study of diet, lifestyle, and **cerebrovascular** disease (CVD) in Spain indicated that as the general public became more aware of the need to eat more fruits and fish and decrease wine consumption, the rates of CVD decreased measurably. In people over forty-five years of age, the decline in **mortality** by CVD decreased by 22 percent.[15] Here is an example of the saying that some fruit a day keeps the undertaker away, not just the doctor.

Grapes or Raisins?

SONG OF SOLOMON 2:5 ***Sustain me with cakes of raisins, refresh me with apples, for I am lovesick.*** *(NKJV)*

Grapes grow on vines in a vineyard. When grapes are dried in the sun, or any other way, they are called raisins. Raisins are perfect for carrying around as a fruit snack while traveling, working, or going to school. Grapes, raisins, and apples are high in fiber and natural sugars and can provide an energy boost anytime, not just when you are lovesick.

what others say

Reginald Cherry, M.D.

Grapes contain ellagic acid. This compound blocks enzymes that are necessary for cancer to grow, thus slowing the growth of tumors. Grapes also contain compounds that can prevent blood clots. Another substance in grape skins (resveratrol) prevents the deposit of cholesterol in arteries.[16]

figs
Luke 21:29

resveratrol
chemopreventive agent found in grapes and other food

mcg
micrograms, a small unit of measure

folic acid
If begun before pregnancy, 400 mcg a day in the diet of a pregnant woman can prevent neural-tube birth defects.

mg
milligram

pharyngeal cancer
cancer of the passageway extending from the nose to the voice box

flavonoids
crystalline compounds found in plants

anti-atherosclerotic
"against atherosclerosis," the most common type of hardening of the arteries

Grapes Are Great!

Scientists are working to extract **resveratrol** from grapes to use as an anticancer agent.[17] This could be very promising for those people who have cancer in their family history. There are many "health" diets that prescribe drinking grape juice or eating grapes as part of the diet. Grapes contain small amounts of protein and fiber, vitamins A and C, calcium and magnesium, phosphorus, and very small amounts of zinc, manganese, iron, and copper. One cup of grapes has about 6 **mcg** of **folic acid**, a nutrient essential for pregnant women. Raisins have high amounts of iron in them because they are concentrated. Two-thirds of a cup of raisins has 2 **mg** of iron. Natural practicing doctors generally recommend 18 mg of iron a day for optimum health. Much research has been published on the benefits of drinking wine, but resveratrol is in all grape juice. Drinking wine is not essential to get the health benefits of grapes.

Figs Are Fantastic!

MATTHEW 7:16 ***You will know them by their fruits. Do men gather grapes from thornbushes or figs from thistles?*** **(NKJV)**

Figs are high in fiber; this makes them healthful for preventing cancers of all kinds. So much research is being published these days that shows we all need to eat more fruits than we do, it is impossible to include it all here. Eating more fruits, especially high-fiber ones, can lower cholesterol, reduce blood pressure, and prevent many different types of cancers, including breast cancer.

In one study it was shown that low fruit and vegetable intake and high meat intake were directly responsible for **pharyngeal cancer**.[18] Fruits and other plant materials high in **flavonoids** are **anti-atherosclerotic** components of your diet.[19]

apoptosis
self-inflicted cell death

Cake of Figs or Raisins

1 CHRONICLES 12:40 ***Moreover those who were near to them, from as far away as Issachar and Zebulun and Naphtali, were bringing food on donkeys and camels, on mules and oxen—provisions of flour and cakes of figs and cakes of raisins, wine and oil and oxen and sheep abundantly, for there was joy in Israel. (NKJV)***

Figs and raisins have been pressed into cakes or strung to dry since before Bible times. We still see figs being sold in this way in grocery stores, especially in Italian and Greek markets. These cakes mentioned in the Bible were not the kind of cakes we think of as a dessert. Just like you can have a cake of soap, which is a pressed form of soap, you can also have a cake of figs or raisins.

Other Fruits in Health News

So much research is being done on fruits and their health-giving properties that it is difficult to keep up with it. Blueberries, strawberries, raspberries, pomegranates, grapeseeds, and grapefruit have shown some of the most fascinating health benefits.

A Few Fruits and Their Health Benefits

Fruit	Benefit
Grapefruit	Weight loss
Grapefruit	Insulin resistance[20]
Grape seeds (proanthocyanidin)	Encourage **apoptosis** in acute myeloid leukemia[21]
Grape	Improve cognitive function, anti-aging[22]
Blueberry	Reverse age-related decline in brain function, especially in amyotrophic lateral sclerosis (ALS), Alzheimer's disease (AD), and Parkinson's disease (PD); reverse cognitive decline; anti-aging, increase longevity[23]
Blueberry	Protect against radiation
Blueberry	Inhibit colon cancer cell proliferation and induce cell death[24]
Blueberry	Reduce androgen-dependent growth in prostate cancer cells
Blueberry	Reduce oxidative stress in chronic cigarette smokers and reduced cardiovascular disease in smokers [25]
Black raspberry, strawberry, blackberry	Inhibit esophageal tumors (papillomas), initiation, promotion, and progression[26]

A Few Fruits and Their Health Benefits (cont'd)

Fruit	Benefit
Black raspberry	Inhibit cell proliferation and induced apoptosis in oral squamous cell carcinoma[27]
Raspberry and strawberry	Inhibit *Candida albicans* and *Campylobacter jejuni*[28]
Cloudberry, raspberry, strawberry	Antimicrobial activity, especially on *H. pylori* and *Bacillus cereus*[29]
Apple and linseed oil	Decrease oxidative stress and DNA damage[30]
Strawberry	Anti-thrombotic, inhibit platelet function[31]
Pomegranate	Inhibit prostate tumor growth; antioxidant; inhibit cancer proliferation and cell death in colon cancer[32]
Pomegranate	Anti-inflammatory agent[33]

incontinence
involuntary loss of urine

kegel
exercises that work the muscles used in urination

prostate
a male gland at the base of the bladder

Cranberries are useful for reversing bladder infections. Many nursing homes recognize this about cranberries and on a regular basis give the juice to people prone to bladder infections.

Black cherry juice is known to reverse **incontinence** in women, especially when **kegel** exercises are done as well.

Tomatoes Are Fruits Too

Tomatoes are really fruits, even though we consider them to be vegetables. Eating tomatoes weekly can help reverse **prostate** problems for men. They are high in lycopene, an antioxidant, as well as the provitamin A compounds beta-carotene and gamma-carotene.

A Nutritional Sweetness

Snacks of fruit are very healthful and taste good too. When you or your children want a sweet snack, consider eating a piece of fresh fruit instead of candy, cakes, or cookies. It will increase your level of health and reverse the downward spiral of poor health that eating junk foods causes.

Would you rather spend sixty cents on a candy bar that robs your body of calcium and damages your teeth, or an apple or pear that can bring a sparkle to your eyes and energy and health to your body?

Olives: The Green and Black Fruits

Yes, olives are really fruits; even in Bible times they were considered fruits. Olives and olive oil are so important in the Bible diet that they have their own section in the food pyramid (see Illustration #15). Olives and/or olive oil should be eaten daily for the best of health.

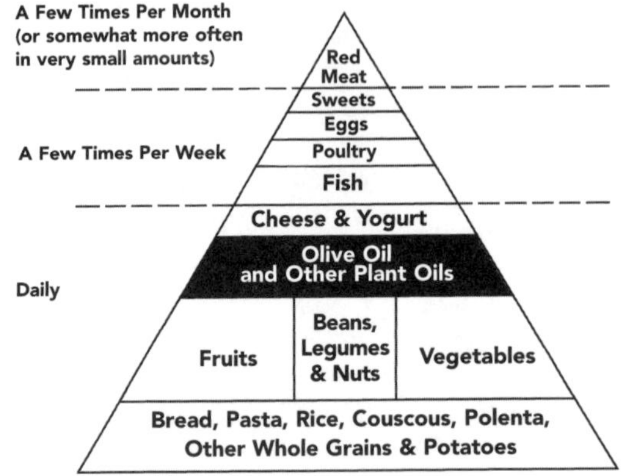

Illustration #15
The Olive Oil Section—The darkened section of this pyramid represents how much of your diet should be devoted to olive oil.

What a Curse!

DEUTERONOMY 28:40 ***You shall have olive trees throughout all your territory, but you shall not anoint yourself with the oil; for your olives shall drop off.*** *(NKJV)*

To have olive trees whose fruit drops off before being harvested and pressed into oil was among the curses given in Deuteronomy. This would really be a curse—to see your crop fail before your eyes (see Illustration #16).

The Green and Black of It

Green olives are really the unripe fruit and the black ones are ripe; that is the difference between the two kinds. Many olives are cured in salt **brine**, oil, or both as a way to preserve them. Some olives are cured with spices, lemon peel, or hot peppers. Olives are aged for different lengths of time so that the fresher ones have a milder taste and the aged ones are saltier and more concentrated in taste.

brine
salt water that is used to preserve many fruits and vegetables

Olives contain a high amount of salt. Always wash olives off with water before eating them.

The Good Fats

Olives contain monounsaturated fatty acids, which have been shown to protect the LDL from being broken down into harmful components. This has been correlated with lowered rates of coronary heart disease (CHD), **atherogenetic** disease, and the prevention of cardiovascular diseases.[34]

Illustration #16
Olive Tree—Olive trees live for several hundred years. They can survive in very rocky terrain and live in poor soil where other trees cannot flourish.

> **what others say**
>
> **Rex Russell, M.D.**
>
> Olive oil is very healthful. It contains anticancer properties, leads to more efficient **cardiac** contractions and does not lead to **vascular disease**. Olive oil apparently promotes healing of atherosclerotic plaques.[35]

It's the Phenolics That Do It

There are eight different **phenolic** compounds in olives and olive oil that are antibacterial, antifungal, **antimicrobial**, and antiviral. The phenolic compound that proved to be the most effective is oleuropein. This bitter property in olives has been shown to inhibit the growth of many bacteria, including *Escherichia coli*, *Klebsiella pneumoniae*, *Aspergillus flavus*, *Aspergillus parasiticus*, and *Bacillus cereus*.[36] It also delayed the growth of *Staphyloccus aureus*, *Clostridium botulinum*, and *Salmonella enteritidis*.[37] These bacteria and viruses are among the most troublesome and destructive factors known to mankind. They can cause illnesses from simple digestive disturbances to death.

atherogenetic
having to do with the arteries

cardiac
relating to the heart

vascular disease
having to do with the circulatory system

phenolic
aromatic

antimicrobial
against small life-forms that cause diseases including parasites

What Phenolics Can Do for You

The phenolic oleuropein is also a potent anticancer compound, and the highest amount is found in olive leaf extract and virgin olive oil. Research published in 2005 showed that oleuropein could regress tumors in the test animals in as little as nine to twelve days, rendering the tumors completely degraded.[38] The phenolic compounds in virgin olive oil reduced tumors as well and induced apoptosis and differentiation in leukemia cells.[39] The phenolic compounds tyrosol and hydroxytyrosol found in virgin olive oil also reduced the oxidative stress of LDL and therefore helped reduce cardiovascular problems.[40] Each of these studies ended with praise for the Bible diet of the Mediterranean region using virgin or extra-virgin olive oil. When you are shopping for olive oil, please make sure it is virgin or extra-virgin to ensure that it contains all the health-giving properties of pure and natural olive oil. Another study using women of postmenopausal age showed that daily intake of extra-virgin olive oil, which has the highest concentration of phenols, was partly responsible for lowered mortality, fewer incidences of cancer, and reduced risk of cardiovascular disease than the control subjects who didn't get this kind of olive oil.[41]

Olives Destroy the Dangers of Eating Out

Over the last ten years, many people have had *E. coli* and *Salmonella* poisoning from eating in restaurants or from catered picnics or parties. In most cases, either of these problems might have been avoided if people had consumed olives and olive oil as a regular part of their diets. Because olive oil and garlic are in the Mediterranean diet, most people in the Mediterranean do not get ill from these kinds of agents. If more people would add olive products into their North American diet, there might be less problems here as well.

Eating Olives and Olive Products

There are many ways to incorporate olive products into your lifestyle. Adding olives to cheese sandwiches is a great and tasty way. Cooking with virgin or extra-virgin olive oil is also a great way to introduce more olive oil into your diet. And if you substitute olive oil for the "bad-for-you fats," such as solid vegetable shortening and margarine, you will be helping your heart. I often use the French system of equal parts of clarified butter and olive oil for cooking. Some Mexican and New Mexican recipes combine olives, almonds, and raisins into many stews and stir-fries. Get creative in adding olives and olive oil into your lifestyle.

Eat the Salad Last

Following the European/Mediterranean system of eating a salad at the end of the meal consisting of romaine or leaf lettuce dressed with fresh lemon and virgin olive oil, and perhaps freshly pressed garlic, will provide two important aspects to any meal. First, it provides olive oil daily. But second, when you eat the salad last you will improve your digestion, cleanse your palate, and feel refreshed. Eating the salad first can reduce the ability to digest a heavier meal since the first few minutes that food enters your stomach determine how much digestive material your body produces. Since protein and fat take more than vegetables, you will find eating the salad last can even help improve heartburn, acid reflux, and bloating that is caused by too little digestive enzymes. Taking a digestive enzyme supplement can also help, but eating the salad last is best.

Do What God Says

DEUTERONOMY 8:8–9 . . . ***a land of wheat and barley, of vines and fig trees and pomegranates, a land of olive oil and honey; a land in which you will eat bread without scarcity, in which you will lack nothing; a land whose stones are iron and out of whose hills you can dig copper.*** *(NKJV)*

The Israelites went through testing by God in the desert where he took care of them, even though they didn't always like what he brought. God reminded them to praise him and keep his commandments and they would one day see the promised land, a land where everything would be wonderful, where they would never lack anything. There would be the things that Israelites loved most, including olive oil. That's how important olive oil is.

what others say

Pamela Smith, R.D.

Olive oil is the star monounsaturated fat. It works to protect the brain and prevent memory loss and decline in cognitive function.[42]

oleuropein
bitter aromatic substance in olives known for its health-giving properties

King Olive Tree

JUDGES 9:8–9 ***The trees once went forth to anoint a king over them. And they said to the olive tree, "Reign over us!" But the olive tree said to them, "Should I cease giving my oil, with which they honor God and men, and go to sway over trees?"*** (NKJV)

This fable compared the murder of Jotham's family by King Abimelech to the olive trees. In this way Jotham revealed that Abimelech ceased giving his oil, or killed his family, so that he could hold sway over all the people of Shechem.

Even though, in this fable, the olive tree refused to be anointed king over the trees, many people think the olive is king of the trees anyway. Olives contain a bitter property that is considered to be the king of all healing materials. This bitter substance is called **oleuropein**. It is in the olive fruit, the olive branches and bark, and in the olive leaves. Olive leaf extract is used currently for healing, especially for getting rid of viruses and parasites.

Olive, the Tree of Life?

REVELATION 22:2–3 ***In the middle of its street, and on either side of the river, was the tree of life, which bore twelve fruits, each tree yielding its fruit every month. The leaves of the tree were for the healing of the nations. And there shall be no more curse, but the throne of God and of the Lamb shall be in it, and His servants shall serve Him.*** (NKJV)

Could olive trees be the tree of life mentioned in Revelation? It certainly seems to have all the properties spoken of. The leaves really could be used to heal the nations because they work against bacteria, viruses, microbes, and parasites. The main health curses we have today are the viral diseases of herpes 1 and 2, shingles, and HIV/AIDS. Olive leaf extract is known to help eradicate these viral problems.[43]

Olive Leaf Extract and HIV/AIDS

The antiviral activity of olive-leaf extract is due to the action of oleuropein on the protein coat of the virus. It is thought to inactivate bacteria by dissolving the outer lining of the microbe.

In his book *Olive Leaf Extract*, Dr. Morton Walker documents cases of people with HIV and AIDS who used olive leaf extract therapeutically. The subjects changed their HIV antibody status from positive to negative as tested on both the ELISA and the Western Blot standard AIDS tests. The results were confirmed by retesting. He reports a case in which an HIV patient reduced his viral load from an exceedingly elevated 160,000 organisms per milliliter of blood down to 30,000 in two weeks. It continued to drop to 692 in eleven weeks. Dr. Walker comments that a fall in viral load this dramatic has never been achieved from the use of AZT.

Olive Leaves Keep Salt Away

If you are worried about consuming the salt in preserved olives, it might be a good idea to take an olive leaf extract supplement to be sure you are getting the benefits of the olive tree. Olive leaf extract is touted as giving you more energy as well as getting rid of bacteria, molds, viruses, and parasites.

Chapter Wrap-Up

- Solomon grew nuts and fruits in his garden; both are part of a healthy diet. (Song of Songs 6:11)
- Walnuts, almonds, flaxseeds, and other nuts and seeds are rich sources of EFAs (essential fatty acids), which are essential for healthy skin, hair, and arteries.
- Fruits are an important part of your daily diet. They are high in antioxidants and fiber.
- Grapes, figs, dates, strawberries, mulberries, cherries, apricots, melons, and other fruits are filled with minerals and multiple nutrients. They can help to prevent many kinds of cancers. (Genesis 1:11–12)
- Olives and olive oil contain compounds that are known to be antiviral, antimicrobial, and antibacterial. The Bible mentions them in many places as trade items. People in Bible times used the oil for lamps and for eating and cooking. They also ate the olive itself.

Study Questions

1. What did Solomon grow in his garden? And why is this food important for you?
2. Most people have read that eating fat is bad for them, but nuts contain a different fat that is actually good for you. How does this conflict make you feel about eating fat? Name three nuts mentioned in the Bible and what there is about them that makes them healthy enough to include in your diet.
3. Why is it important to eat fruit daily?
4. Which diseases are helped or prevented by fruits? What do you have to do to get the health benefits of these fruits?
5. Which three foods that we think of as vegetables are really fruits? How can you incorporate them into your diet?
6. Name the disease-fighting properties of olives. How is this related to North America and the Mediterranean region?

Chapter 6: Milk and Curds

Chapter Highlights:
- **Milk, It Does a Body Good**
- **Fermenting Helps**
- **Balance the Bacteria**
- **Cheese: Can You Stomach This?**

Let's Get Started

Dairy cattle were first domesticated for milk production in 3000 BC in Macedonia. In the first century AD Virgil wrote *Georgics*, in which he is quoted as saying, "Camel's, goat's, and ewe's milk is for humans, cow's milk is for calves."[1] This will give you some idea of how long the battle against cow's milk has been going on! For nearly two thousand years, people have said that cow's milk is bad for you, but it is still being served all over the world. There is even research that indicates cow's milk may be good for you. Very seldom do people in the West drink camel's or ewe's milk, but we do drink goat's milk. Let's just examine the facts of milk and dairy products, and you can make your own decision.

meat and milk
Exodus 23:19; 34:26; Deuteronomy 14:21

Mooooo!

GENESIS 18:8 ***So he took butter and milk and the calf which he had prepared, and set it before them; and he stood by them under the tree as they ate.*** *(NKJV)*

Abraham had a feast prepared for three guests who appeared. This is very traditional in the Middle East, even today. He served them meat and milk together because this was also traditional; God had not yet outlawed having milk and meat together. It is supposed that at least two of the three men were really angels, so Abraham would have served the best food he had.

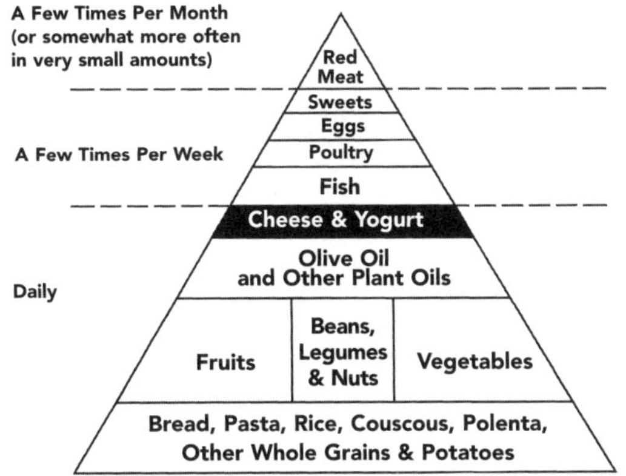

Illustration #17
Cheese and Yogurt Section—The darkened section of this pyramid represents how much of your diet should be devoted to cheese and yogurt. This is the last section of the daily foods.

summons
a calling

tyrosine
acts as a mood elevator

Low to moderate intake of dairy products contributes to the healthfulness of the Bible diet (see Illustration #17). Milk is consumed in moderation and almost always in the form of soft or aged cheeses and yogurt. The increase in plant foods like vegetables, fruits, and whole grains, as the major foods in this diet, allows for the moderate consumption of dairy products. In populations where the Mediterranean diet is followed, chronic-disease rates are low and life expectancies are long.[2]

Dairy products—mostly cheese and yogurt—have their own section in the Mediterranean diet pyramid. It is a smallish section compared to the ones for vegetables, fruits, and grains, but it is still sizable. When you look at the pyramid you can see the amount of dairy products you should have in relation to the other foods—not very much!

what others say

Don Colbert, M.D.

Mediterranean Diet yogurt is not high in sugar, but is low fat or nonfat, served plain with fresh fruit added. A common use of yogurt is as a salad dressing—generally with dill, garlic, onion, or cucumbers added to it.[3]

Why Milk?

ISAIAH 55:1 ***Ho! Everyone who thirsts, come to the waters; and you who have no money, come, buy and eat. Yes, come, buy wine and milk without money and without price.*** *(NKJV)*

The Israelites were in exile, and all of Isaiah 55 is a **summons** for them to return to Jerusalem. Wine and milk were used as symbols of abundance, and it was free! What a great place!

Milk is one of the few concentrated sources of a wide variety of nutrients. After all, it is the food for babies. Milk contains protein, calcium, phosphorus, sodium, and twice as much potassium as sodium, magnesium, zinc, copper, vitamin A, small amounts of vitamins B_1, B_2, B_3, B_6, B_{12}, and C, as well as B_9 or folate, amino acids, and monounsaturated fatty acids along with saturated fats. (For definitions of these nutritional terms, see the Glossary of Nutritional and Medical Terms at the back of the book.) The amino acid **tyrosine** is found only in meat and milk. It is essential for the normal functioning of the **thyroid gland**.[4] This makes dairy products almost essential for vegetarians, unless they are taking an amino acid supplement that contains tyrosine. Tyrosine is also noted for helping to reverse depression.

Dairy products are a great source of nutrients, especially calcium and protein. There are many different kinds of animals that give milk. Cow's and goat's milk are used for drinking and making cheeses and yogurts more than any other kind of milk (see Illustration #17).

A Land Flowing with Milk and Honey

Deuteronomy 27:3 ***You shall write on them all the words of this law, when you have crossed over, that you may enter the land which the Lord your God is giving you, "a land flowing with milk and honey," just as the Lord God of your fathers promised you.*** *(NKJV)*

There are at least eighteen references to a land flowing with milk and honey in the Bible, and each time it connotes richness. Why do you think God used milk to give the idea of richness? Perhaps because it is a rich food. It is what we have done to milk that makes it less nutritious than God originally intended. We have overbred cattle, forced them to give more milk than is natural, filled them with antibiotics and other drugs, and even given them hormones to produce more milk. Is it any wonder that so many people are allergic to milk or that so many people think it is not healthful?

God designed milk to be the perfect food for mammals. Humans are mammals and give milk for their young.

Baaaaah!

Proverbs 27:27 ***You shall have enough goats' milk for your food, for the food of your household, and the nourishment of your maidservants.*** *(NKJV)*

milk and honey
Deuteronomy 26:9, 15; 31:20

Goat's milk was one of the most common milks used in the Bible diet and is still popular. It was even given to the servants to drink. Many cheeses, like feta, for example, are still made with goat's milk. People who have trouble digesting the protein in cow's milk can

thyroid gland
regulates metabolism

milk
Judges 5:25

often digest the protein in goat's milk without a problem. This is because the protein molecules in cow's milk are larger than the protein molecules in goat's milk. Goats are smaller animals than cows, and their milk has the genetic message of growth for a smaller animal, so many people find that it is less stressful on them to use goat's milk products.

Not only is goat's milk easier to digest, but it is also a healing agent. For example, goat's milk has long been held out as a cure for arthritis. In fact, many people with arthritis keep their inflammation down by drinking a quart of goat's milk every day. Hildegard of Bingen—an abbess of a convent—used goat's milk for many different cures in the Middle Ages.

what others say

Hildegard of Bingen

Whoever has an unhealthy lung shall drink enough goat's milk and be cured.[5]

Another Baaaaah!

In Bible times, as today, people in the Mediterranean area ate cheese that is made from sheep's milk. Many of the cheeses found in Italian, health food, gourmet, and Greek stores, such as feta, brie, cheddar, and asiago, are made of goat's and/or sheep's milk. Just read the labels on some of the cheeses at your favorite store or gourmet market, and see if you can find sheep and goat cheeses.

Milk: To Drink or Not to Drink!

JUDGES 4:19 ***Then he said to her, "Please give me a little water to drink, for I am thirsty." So she opened a jug of milk, gave him a drink, and covered him.*** *(NKJV)*

In Judges 4:19 when Sisera, a commander of a Canaanite army, was hiding in the tent of Jael, a woman who was not his wife, he asked for water to drink. Jael gave him milk instead. Although the milk may have helped him fall asleep, it was not essential to the story.

Whether or not you should drink milk is still a question after thousands of years. Why is that, you ask? Perhaps it is something that was carried over from the Romans! Or could it be because many people have trouble digesting milk for many different reasons?

Milk Allergy

Some people are actually allergic to the protein in milk, which can cause acute **gastrointestinal** disturbances like cramping, diarrhea, constipation, and even vomiting in some cases. Others get allergic symptoms to milk the same as they would to any other substance that causes allergies. (Some other allergy-causing foods are peanuts, soybeans, chicken, oranges, shrimp, and other seafoods.) In a true, classic case of food allergy, the immune system overreacts, and mistakenly identifies innocent compounds in foods as enemies, like bacteria and viruses. This mistake throws the immune system into a chain reaction of alertness. It produces antibodies called immunoglobulin E (or IgE) to launch an attack on the false threats (antigens), releasing **histamines** and other chemicals that provoke symptoms of allergies. Traditionally, only reactions that involve IgE are considered truly allergic reactions.[6]

gastrointestinal having to do with stomach, small and large intestines, colon, rectum, liver, pancreas, gallbladder

histamines chemicals secreted by the immune system that act on many different body tissues

Lactose Intolerance

Some people don't have the ability to digest the milk sugar called lactose because they are low in lactase, the enzyme needed for milk digestion. This is called being "lactose intolerant." Often, as people age, they lose their ability to produce lactase in their small intestine, and become unable to digest milk. Many more Caucasians are more able to digest milk than people of Asian and African ancestry.

Milk Naysayers

1 Corinthians 9:7 ***Who tends a flock and does not drink of the milk of the flock? (NKJV)***

There are those who would have you believe that milk is not good for you, but people have been drinking milk and eating dairy products ever since Bible times. Does this sound like a dangerous food? There is a very strange situation in our schools all over the United States; soft drinks are being consumed instead of milk. Many soft drink companies are even supporting the schools with equipment and money along with soft drink dispensing machines. Elementary, middle, junior high, and high school students are consuming three to five cans of soft drinks per day. The phosphorus and sugar in soft

collard greens and kale
green leafy vegetables

drinks can rob your body of calcium. In fact, a study published in 1997 indicated that adolescent females were taking in less and less calcium from 1980 to 1992. Since 1992, it has gone down even more.[7] Calcium and magnesium are necessary for the relaxation of muscles. Therefore, is there any doubt that the decrease in calcium foods and increase in carbonated, sugary foods is responsible for some of the violence in our schools?

Milk, It Does a Body Good

There is nothing wrong with drinking milk as long as it is free of hormonal material, and that means always using organic milk, or at least milk free of growth hormones. Just read the label; it should specify if it is free of contaminants. Whole Foods, Wild Oats, and Trader Joe's all have these kinds of milk products. So will your regular natural-food store or grocery store; just ask them to carry organic milk products. It is better for children to drink milk and eat cheese and yogurt than not to consume any calcium foods at all. If your children do not eat dark green leafy vegetables or any foods listed that are high in calcium, please make sure they consume dairy products.

what others say

Pamela Smith, R.D.

Women over the age of thirty-five should get about 1,500 mg a day of calcium, yet few women get the calcium we need, and the deficiencies started when we were teenagers. Dietary sources of calcium include fat-free milk, yogurt, and cheese.[8]

Other Sources of Calcium

There are other dietary sources of calcium. Salmon, sardines, or mackerel with the bones, dried figs, tofu and other soybeans, turnip greens, **collard greens, kale**, and broccoli are all great sources of calcium. Just the foods kids and teenagers eat a lot of, right? Wrong! Now you can begin to see why God created milk to make into yogurt and cheese. It was so adults and children would get enough calcium and protein in their diets, even if they aren't eating right but use dairy products. It would be much better for growing children (including teenagers), to consume dairy products daily rather than soft drinks. I don't drink milk, but I do eat cheese and yogurt.

bioavailable
able to be utilized by your body

boron
a mineral found in dark-green, leafy vegetables

Greens and Milk

When I first studied nutrition in the 1970s with Adelle Davis, the mother of modern nutrition, she used to advise people to eat dark-green, leafy vegetables cooked in milk, or sprinkled with lemon juice. She felt that the nutrients were more **bioavailable** this way. She was right! Calcium can be absorbed and utilized in your bones more efficiently if you also eat **boron** with the calcium. This is why so many supplements that say they will prevent or reverse osteoporosis contain boron.

SOURCE: USDA Nutrient Data Laboratory, www.nal.usda.gov/fnic/foodcomp/

Calcium in Some Common Foods

Food	Amount
Milk, low-fat, 1 cup	297 mg
Cheddar cheese, 1/2 cup	476 mg
Cottage cheese, low-fat, 1/2 cup	69 mg
Tofu, 1/2 cup	130 mg
Chickpeas, 1/2 cup	38 mg
Fig, dried, one	27 mg
Oatmeal, cooked, 1/2 cup	107 mg
Almonds, 1/2 cup	195 mg
Sesame butter, tahini, 1 tablespoon	64 mg
Sardine, with bone, 1 ounce	54 mg
Broccoli, raw, 1/2 cup	20 mg
Spinach, cooked, 1 cup	245 mg
Lettuce, iceberg, 1/2 cup	6 mg
Lettuce, leaf, 1/2 cup	19 mg
Kale, cooked, 1/2 cup	47 mg

Adults need from 1,000 to 1,500 mg of calcium daily. Two glasses of milk, a handful of almonds, a serving of cooked oatmeal, and a serving of spinach would do.

what others say

Jim Shriner

The latest research has shown that the mineral boron, found in leafy vegetables and most fruits, will help improve your mental agility.[9]

What About Milk and Kidney Stones?

Many people with kidney stones, which are made of calcium, have been advised to stay away from drinking milk. Research done at the Department of Food Science and Human Nutrition at Washington State University with adult subjects who had a tendency to form kidney stones showed that drinking milk did not increase their risk of forming kidney stones.[10] This is excellent news for those with kidney stones or the tendency to get them.

If you have kidney stones and were told to avoid milk, please check with your doctor or specialist before you consume it. Write down the reference for the above study (from the endnotes) and show it to your doctor.

Should Children Be Breast-fed?

MATTHEW 21:16 ***[The chief priests and scribes] said to Him, "Do You hear what these are saying?" And Jesus said to them, "Yes. Have you never read, 'Out of the mouth of babes and nursing infants You have perfected praise'?" (NKJV)***

In many areas of the Mediterranean region, children are breast-fed until they are old enough to feed themselves, often until five or six years of age. (Many people do this in North America, too!) All mammals can breast-feed their young. If a mother is healthy, breast-feeding is the best way to nourish her children.

what others say

Joe S. McIlhaney, M.D.

Breast-feeding is superior to bottle feeding a newborn baby. Studies show that babies who are breast-fed tend to be healthier, have a lower mortality rate, seem to develop better physically and mentally, and have fewer problems with allergies later in life. In addition, other studies show that babies who nurse have greater **immunity** to **respiratory** and digestive tract disease than babies who do not. Also, babies who nurse seem to have straighter teeth and better mother/child bonding.[11]

immunity
ability to withstand attacks of germs, viruses, and bacteria

respiratory
all the breathing parts

What's So Good About Breast Milk?

Breast milk was designed by God to feed children. It contains the exact amounts and kinds of protein and other nutrients that a growing child needs. It also has the proper amount of bacteria-producing elements that aid in digestion and contribute to the balance of **microflora** in the infant's intestine. Even formula that was supplemented to have the same composition as breast milk did not function as effectively.[12] Four strains of Lactobacillus were isolated in breast milk in a recent study. The most potent strain, *L. salivarius,* even protected against salmonella.[13]

microflora
small bacteria that live in the intestines and aid digestion

immune system
the complex system of your body that seeks out and destroys invaders

thymus gland
the major gland of the immune system

spleen
organ of the immune system that deals with blood

macrophages
large cells that engulf and destroy foreign particles in your body including bacteria, cancer cells, and cellular debris

immunoreactive
a properly functioning immune system

Breast Milk Builds Immunity

Breast milk contains nutrients that build up your **immune system** by supporting the growth and health of your **thymus gland** and **spleen**. A healthy thymus gland can prevent infections and many immune and autoimmune diseases such as AIDS or cancer. A healthy spleen can help to prevent infections by secreting a substance called tuftsin, which stimulates **macrophages** in the liver, spleen, and lymph nodes. Macrophages are essential in protecting against invasion by microorganisms as well as cancer.[14] Mother's milk also contains essential fatty acids that contribute to prostaglandin production, which helps to build a healthy cardiovascular system in the newborn baby.[15]

Bedwetting and Mind Development

Children who were breast-fed longer than three months were less likely to exhibit bedwetting in childhood, reported a study published in the journal *Pediatrics.*[16] Calcium and magnesium are useful in preventing bedwetting, and they are both in breast milk. It has long been understood that omega-3 and omega-6 polyunsaturated fatty acids (PUFA) can improve brain function and cognitive development, and breast milk contains both PUFAs.[17]

what others say

Rex Russell, M.D.

Breast-fed children have a special resistance to many childhood diseases. This is because the early milk or colostrum sets up the infant's **immunoreactive** system.[18]

Langerhans cells immune cells in the skin, named after the discoverer

beta-1,3-D-glucan extracted from the cell wall of baker's yeast, immunity enhancer

allergens substances that provoke allergic responses

Number One Under the Sun

The most important thing you can do for your immune system is to avoid contact with the sun on your skin for more than five or ten minutes at a time. In other words, wear protection against the sun even when driving to the store. Use a natural moisturizer that has a sun protective factor (SPF). Whatever you do, don't sunbathe! If you are very fair or have an autoimmune disease, you might want to consider buying clothes that are sun-protective.

What's the Skinny?

Your skin is the largest immune system organ in your body. It contains **Langerhans cells**, which are part of your immune system. Your skin has macrophages the same as your thymus and spleen do. These macrophages in your skin can be damaged by harsh cosmetics, fragrances, chemicals, and sun exposure and other sources of radiation. In order for the macrophages to work, they need to be functioning fully. Use cosmetics that contain **beta-1,3-D-glucan** on your face and hands. This will fill your macrophage cells with the very nutrient that they need to function effectively and efficiently: beta-1,3-D-glucan. Each macrophage cell, whether in your skin or in the rest of your immune system, has a receptor site for beta-1,3-D-glucan.[19] Without this substance your immune system will not be able to work. Beta-1,3-D-glucan comes from the cell walls of baker's yeast, and in milder amounts from various mushrooms like maitake, shitake, and reishi.

Colostrum, the Miracle in Mother's Milk

Colostrum is also called the "first milk" because it is in the first milk secreted after the birth of any mammal. This substance has been highly researched and is shown to contain all the elements necessary for combating viruses, bacteria, yeasts, toxins, **allergens**, and other foreign substances. Colostrum stimulates your body's own immune response so that it is better able to fight off invaders on its own.[20]

Healthy Intestines Need HGF

Colostrum contains **hepatocyte** growth factor (HGF), which is an important factor in the growth of the intestinal cells in newborn babies. HGF helps to prevent intestinal problems during all stages of life, from infancy into old age.[21]

A really good diet while pregnant and breast-feeding can help keep your baby's immune system healthy. If a breast-feeding mother consistently eats a good diet that contains all of the required nutrients for health, her breast milk will provide the best food to keep her baby healthy, strong, and disease-resistant.

What If You Were Bottle-Fed?

If you were bottle-fed, as I was, what can you do? The best thing you can do for yourself is to follow a really good diet. Eat a lot of veggies every day, especially dark-green, leafy ones. Stay away from alcohol, tobacco, **MSG**, and other food enhancers or additives; don't eat processed foods of any kind; don't eat any rancid fats, **beef tallow**, **suet**, or **lard**; eat a lot of fresh foods (especially fruits and veggies) daily; keep away from animal products with antibiotics or hormones in them; eat only whole grains, and eat them in moderation; make veggies the largest portion of your daily food intake, and you will do a lot for your immune system. You might also want to take proven immune-enhancing supplements like Kyolic (the odorless garlic extract), beta-1-3-D-glucan, or **sterols** from sprouts like Super Sprouts Immune Enhancer.

Exercise daily if you want to keep your immune system working well; just don't overdo it because that will suppress your immune system.

Fermenting Helps

ISAIAH 7:15 ***Curds** and honey He shall eat, that He may know to refuse the evil and choose the good.* (NKJV)

In order to make curds, milk has to be soured or curdled with acid. You probably have done this by adding lemon or orange juice to milk to watch it form curds. In Bible times and today, many people

hepatocyte
having to do with the liver

MSG
monosodium glutamate; often causes reactions

beef tallow
commercially prepared beef fat, outlawed in the Bible

suet
fat covering the kidneys in beef cattle

lard
fat covering the kidneys in pigs

sterols
immunity-enhancing ingredients found in all plants; known to also lower cholesterol levels with no side effects

curds
solid pieces formed when milk protein is **curdled** with acid and then heated.

curdle
to "curd" or to form curds

curdle the milk to keep it longer without having to refrigerate it. The curds were eaten by adults, children drank milk. Adults know right from wrong, or at least they are supposed to. When the Christ child was to come, as the reference in Isaiah 7:15 points out, he would have baby food—milk—until he became an adult. Then he would be given curds.

In order to store milk and keep it fresh during Bible times, it was fermented so that the fermentation would keep it from going bad so quickly. Many people in the Middle East, even today, do not have refrigeration and rely on using fermented or curded dairy products. When milk is left outside refrigeration, it picks up various yeasts and bacteria in the air. They can sour the milk in an undesirable way and cause health problems. Therefore, specific agents are used to make the milk sour or ferment so that it will not go bad and cause health problems. Many dairy products are made of fermented cow's or goat's milk. Yogurt, kefir, buttermilk, cottage cheese, and other cheeses, as well as most butter, are all made from fermented milk.

what others say

Maureen Salaman

The butter referred to in Genesis 18:8 appears to have been a thick sour milk called *Laban*, a semifluid similar to yogurt or kefir.[22]

Prosperity!

Isaiah 7:21–22 ***It shall be in that day that a man will keep alive a young cow and two sheep; so it shall be, from the abundance of milk they give, that he will eat curds; for curds and honey everyone will eat who is left in the land.*** *(NKJV)*

Milk and honey were both symbols of prosperity in the Bible. However, Isaiah mentions milk and curds in this prophecy, to point out that they will have to return to the simple diet of those who live off the land.

What's So Good About Yogurt?

Yogurt with live culture and fresh fruit added can reduce serum LDL cholesterol levels in three weeks.[23] Live culture–containing yogurt reduces the occurrences of many women's problems, when eaten daily. Pasteurized yogurt, without live culture, does not help.[24] Yogurt contains both the curd and the **whey**, so it is high in many B vitamins as well as protein.

whey
clear, yellowish liquid released when curds are made; generally thrown away

probiotic
Greek for "for life," a form of "good" bacteria

what others say

Pamela Smith

Milk, cheeses, and yogurts are loaded with calcium and magnesium that keep your blood pressure more stable and [when you are pregnant] build your baby's skeletal system while keeping yours strong and intact.[25]

Yogurt Can Be Good or Bad for You

Real, true, natural, plain yogurt is good for you. It must contain a live fermenting agent or culture called *Lactobacillus acidophilus* or *Bifidobacterium bifidum*, or both. If the package does not clearly say that there is "live culture," "live bacteria," or live *L. acidophilus* in the yogurt or yogurt tablets, it does not contain the health-giving properties of natural yogurt.

Bad-for-you yogurt contains white sugar, jam, or fruit preserves made with white sugar, artificial colors and flavors, and no live culture.

Yogurt for Life

There are two kinds of bacteria—good and bad. Your intestines are supposed to have good bacteria—intestinal flora—in them to help with digestion. Antibiotics kill all the bacteria—both the good and the bad. This can cause diarrhea, unless you take some good bacteria—a **probiotic**, generally yogurt. Yogurt can restore the good bacteria that was destroyed by the antibiotics, while the antibiotics destroy the bad bacteria that made you sick.

Don't Leave Home Without Them

Many things can upset the delicate balance in your gastrointestinal (GI) tract. Some of them are bad water or poor hygiene, too many sweets or starchy foods, too many alcoholic drinks, food allergies,

tourista
popular name for illnesses caused by higher bacteria counts

dysbiosis
disturbance in the bacterial flora of the alimentary canal with resulting gut dysfunction, which may result in diarrhea, malabsorption, or the absorbing of toxins from the gut with a wide range of symptoms

prebiotic
substance that supports or nurtures the growth of probiotics

inulin
dietary fiber that encourages the growth of good bacteria in the gut

excessive stress, environmental toxins, parasites, viral illnesses, and overgrowth of undesirable bacteria or yeast. When you travel to third-world countries where "it isn't safe to drink the water," you will want to begin taking yogurt capsules before you go and continue to take them while you are there and even after you return. Doing so does not give you license to be foolish, but it will help to keep you from getting **tourista** while you are there. Kyo-dophilus is a brand of probiotic capsules that do not need to be refrigerated, so they are excellent to take with you on trips to Mexico, India, China, or anywhere that bacteria in the water and food might be different from in your hometown. Actually, it is great to take them camping too, because the water might have different bacteria than you are used to.

Balance the Bacteria

Fruits and fiber-rich vegetables provide the food for the good bacteria to create a balance of bacteria. The good bacteria should be about 85 percent of the total bacteria, and the bad bacteria around 15 percent of the total bacteria. This is considered an acceptable balance. When the so-called bad bacteria are allowed to increase to more than this amount, problems can occur and the medical term for this is **dysbiosis**. Many things can cause the good bacteria to decrease or not be produced such as stress, poor dietary habits, drugs, smoking or drinking alcohol to excess, and especially overconsumption of sugar and nutrientless foods or fast foods. When the supply is allowed to replenish by eating the nutrient-dense **prebiotic** foods of whole grains, root vegetables, onions and garlic, asparagus, and Jerusalem artichokes, and the probiotic bacteria of *Bifidobacterium bifidum, Lactobacillus acidophilus,* and *L. bulgaricus,* the body will create its own proper balance of bacteria in the intestines and help create a healthy intestinal environment. Super Probiotic/Prebiotic Bacteria Formula from Health Alive! is a great formula that contains these three ingredients in a balance with **inulin**.

Results of an imbalance of intestinal bacteria include:

- Gas, bloating, indigestion
- Frequent colds or bouts of flu
- Irritable bowel syndrome (IBS)

- Chronic fatigue and/or fibromyalgia
- Diarrhea and/or constipation
- High cholesterol levels
- Ulcerative colitis
- Skin problems like psoriasis, acne, eczema, or atopic dermatitis
- Candida-type yeast infections
- Bad breath and body odor
- Burning or itching anus
- Allergies
- Crohn's disease

Probiotics

Probiotics are also called beneficial bacteria or flora, and they are the "good" bacteria that are required by your body to have proper digestion and intestinal health. They are actually live microbial food ingredients that, when ingested in sufficient quantities, exert a health benefit on people and their digestion. Probiotics are live flora that allow for bacterial colonization of the colon, and their function is to activate the mucosal immune system and prevent pathogen colonization and translocation by strengthening the mucosal barrier interfering with pathogen colonization, and in some instances, producing secretory antibacterial substances. We all need to have these beneficial bacteria in our bodies if we want to be healthy. Super Probiotic/Prebiotic Bacteria formula contains probiotics.

Prebiotics

Prebiotics are nondigestible carbohydrates that are fermented by the colon, stimulating the proliferation of the good bacteria and producing short-chain fatty acids. Inulin is the most common prebiotic and belongs to a class of compounds known as fructans. Most inulin comes from chicory, and the best is organically grown. Inulin is resistant to digestion in the upper gastrointestinal tract and therefore reaches the large intestine (colon) essentially intact where it is fermented into indigenous bacteria.

Synbiotics

Synbiotics are a new class of digestive aid, containing both probiotics and prebiotics, which result in immunoprotective and immunosupportive factors in the body that are greatly enhanced over those resulting from probiotics and prebiotics individually.

Probiotics and prebiotics (synbiotics) can be effective for:

- Improving digestion
- Reducing bloating
- Improving mineral absorption
- Restoring intestinal function
- Increasing intestinal motility
- Improving immune function
- Balancing pH
- Reducing foul-smelling stools
- Modulating transit time
- Reducing digestive problems
- Improving constipation and/or diarrhea

Cheese: Can You Stomach This?

The story of how cheese was discovered is an old one. A soldier was taking some milk to a friend a few miles away. He had a goat-stomach bag in which he carried water, so he decided to put the milk into it instead. He strapped it onto his horse and rode to the friend's house. When he got there, the milk had soured and formed curds. He got so mad he stepped on it and pressed the curds into a fresh cheese. Why did cheese curds form in this stomach bag? The stomach acid still in the bag, from when it belonged to a goat, caused the milk to curdle. Acid—stomach acid, specifically—is used to curdle milk and make it into cheese. The stomach acid from cows is called "rennet" and is used to make most cheeses. At markets during the Middle Ages and as recently as the 1940s, cooks could buy strips of stomach lining from which to make cheese. Today, we just buy rennet in a package or tablet. There is also vegetarian rennet available for those who do not wish to mix meat with milk or who want to stay strictly vegetarian.

Little Miss Muffett Was Here

In the nursery rhyme, Little Miss Muffett sat on a tuffet eating her curds and whey. She could have been eating yogurt or what we call cottage cheese. The curds are the solid part and the whey is the liquid that is drained off when acid forms the curds. In creamed cottage cheese, cream or milk is added to the curds to make it creamy. Whey is generally yellow and transparent in color. You can see how this works if you add some lemon juice or vinegar to milk and watch the acid make curds in the milk. Rennet is a much stronger curdling agent than lemon juice or vinegar, so it makes firmer curds. If we added the curds from cottage cheese to yogurt we would really have curds and whey, just like Miss Muffett!

Illustration #18
Milk and Dairy Products—It is important to ingest a moderate amount of milk and dairy products daily.

Cheese Is Generally Well Pressed

> **Job 10:10–11** ***Did You not pour me out like milk, and curdle me like cheese, clothe me with skin and flesh, and knit me together with bones and sinews? (NKJV)***

When rennet is added to milk, whether it be whole, skimmed, or low-fat, it causes the milk to curdle. The whey is drained off and used for other purposes. The curds, which are just protein and fat along with the minerals in milk, are cooked and stirred and then pressed into a form or mold. Some cheeses are left in a cool place to age like cheddar and blue cheese. Some are called semi-soft and are not aged, but are generally cooked longer to make them sort of rubbery. Job used the example of making cheese when he was talking to God to describe a lengthy and complicated process.

what others say

Jim Shriner

A healthy, well-balanced breakfast could be as simple as a small cup of fresh fruit, a glass of nonfat milk, or a low-fat yogurt and fruit, and a slice of wheat toast.[26]

Whey More Protein

Whey is not to be thrown away; it contains a complete protein (containing all the essential amino acids)[27] that has been shown to reduce blood pressure, contribute to weight loss, and help to protect against breast cancer.[28] Whey protein is easy to digest and is often used in infant formulas, sports nutrition products, and weight-management and mood-control products. Many clinics are prescribing whey protein products as specialized enteral and clinical protein supplements. In Europe, cheese made of whey is brown and sweet and has the taste of maple sugar.

for your health

Some of the best-tasting whey proteins I have used are Jay Robb's Whey Protein and Super Protein with Digestive Enzymes from Health Alive! These proteins have a pleasant flavor and mix well into liquids. There is no strong dairy taste, and they go well with vegetable juice as well as fruit or fruit juices.

what others say

Dr. Mary Ruth Swope

Cheeses were made from the milk of several animals [in Bible times]. Soured milk which formed hard lumps was dried in the sun, and curds produced were used in cooking.[29]

A Little Goes a Long Way

When you use whole milk to make cheese, you remove some of the liquid. This makes the same volume of what is now cheese have a higher concentration of fat and other nutrients than it did when it was milk. Therefore, cheese generally has more calories than milk, so you don't need to eat a lot at one time. Cheese and yogurt are a daily part of the Bible diet. This does not mean you should drink a glass of milk at every meal, but cheese or yogurt in small amounts can be eaten daily, especially if you have some of it in the form of low-fat or nonfat cheese or yogurt.

milk
Hebrews 5:11–14

Milk in the New Testament

> **1 CORINTHIANS 3:1–2** ***And I, brethren, could not speak to you as to spiritual people but as to carnal, as to babes in Christ. I fed you with milk and not with solid food; for until now you were not able to receive it, and even now you are still not able.*** *(NKJV)*

In Bible times drinking milk was mostly for infants while different forms of milk—yogurt, cheeses, or butter—were for adults. Maybe that's why this passage is so popular; it reminds you that at least when it comes to drinking milk, you can be an infant forever. But it also tells you that milk was baby food and solid foods (like yogurt and cheese) were for adults.

Because milk was for infants, the use of the term "milk" in referring to one's spiritual life meant that he or she had not become a mature Christian. Today we often call a new Christian a "baby" Christian. They have only learned a small amount about following Christ. They have only consumed milk, not solid food.

"Solid food" was reserved for adults, or for those who had progressed in their spiritual life to become Christians of sound judgment and discernment—those who could distinguish good from evil. Solid spiritual food for a Christian comes after years of reading the Scriptures, attending Bible study, and living the life Jesus described for mature Christians in the New Testament.

Chapter Wrap-Up

- Milk is mentioned throughout the Bible, especially the milk of goats, sheep, and cows.
- Milk and milk products are high in protein, calcium, magnesium, and have small amounts of the B vitamins.
- Mother's milk is considered the best food for babies to be the healthiest. Many herbs and supplements can be used to restore the immunity of those who were not breast-fed.
- Cheese and yogurt are recommended as daily foods in the Bible diet.
- Milk in the form of yogurt can be healthful for all sorts of intestinal problems and may also help to lower cholesterol levels.
- If cheese is to be a regular part of your diet, it is best to eat small amounts at a time and to try to have more of the lower fat or part-skimmed varieties.
- In Bible times drinking milk was considered an activity for infants, not adults. (1 Corinthians 3:1–2)

Study Questions

1. Why is it a good idea to ingest dairy products daily?
2. There has been a controversy over what kind of milk and for how long?
3. Why is mother's milk so important for health?
4. What current "health food" was eaten in Bible times as part of the Bible Cure?
5. What are some reasons for eating fermented milk products?
6. In what situation did New Testament people consider it acceptable to drink milk?

Chapter 7: Fish for Five Thousand

Chapter Highlights:
- Dry Eye Syndrome
- Bone Loss
- Dementia, Aging, ADHD, and DCD
- Heart Disease and Fish Oil

Let's Get Started

Because the Mediterranean area surrounds the Mediterranean Sea, fish play a major role in the Old Testament and in the New. Fishing was an important occupation for some of Jesus's disciples, so much so that he even talked with them about being "fishers of men." Because of this, the fish is a symbol that refers to Jesus. Fish and fish oils have been shown to be very healthful for your body and mind. Perhaps the people of the Mediterranean knew how healthful fish is, and that is why they ate it almost daily in some form or another.

fishing
Mark 1:16–18; Luke 5:1–3

Catch Any?

MATTHEW 4:18–20 ***And Jesus, walking by the Sea of Galilee, saw two brothers, Simon called Peter, and Andrew his brother, casting a net into the sea; for they were fishermen. Then He said to them, "Follow Me, and I will make you fishers of men." They immediately left their nets and followed Him.*** *(NKJV)*

Fishing was a good job because people ate so many kinds of fish, so often, that a fisherman could earn a living if he could catch fish. It was hard work, but it was steady. Jesus picked his disciples from fishermen. Peter, who was a fisherman when Jesus asked him to be a disciple, later became one of Jesus's leading disciples. He even wrote 1 and 2 Peter in the New Testament.

There are fifty different types of fish mentioned in texts dating from before 2300 BC. There are forty species found in the inland waters of the Middle East, twenty-two of which are peculiar to Palestine and Syria (see Appendix B), and of these fourteen are known only to the Jordan River system (see map on page 246). That was a good variety of fish.[1]

Before eating any fish that you catch in your local waterways, check with the Wildlife Department to see if the fish are safe to eat.

EZEKIEL 47:9–10 ***And it shall be that every living thing that moves, wherever the rivers go, will live. There will be a very great multitude of fish, because these waters go there; for they will be healed, and everything will live wherever the river goes. It shall be that fishermen will stand by it from En Gedi to En Eglaim; they will be places for spreading their nets. Their fish will be of the same kinds as the fish of the Great Sea, exceedingly many.*** *(NKJV)*

If you dislike fish, you may not have cooked it properly, or it may be that you have not found a variety you like. By eating different varieties of fish, you can find a kind that you like. You are likely to find at least ten different varieties at your local market in any season.

Miracle Fish

MATTHEW 14:16–21 ***But Jesus said to them, "They do not need to go away. You give them something to eat." And they said to Him, "We have here only five loaves and two fish." He said, "Bring them here to Me." Then He commanded the multitudes to sit down on the grass. And He took the five loaves and the two fish, and looking up to heaven, He blessed and broke and gave the loaves to the disciples; and the disciples gave to the multitudes. So they all ate and were filled, and they took up twelve baskets full of the fragments that remained. Now those who had eaten were about five thousand men, besides women and children.*** *(NKJV)*

five loaves and two fish
Mark 6:30–44; Luke 9:10–17; John 6:1–13

loaves
2 Kings 4:42–44

bread of life
John 6:32–58

Synoptic gospels
Matthew, Mark, and Luke

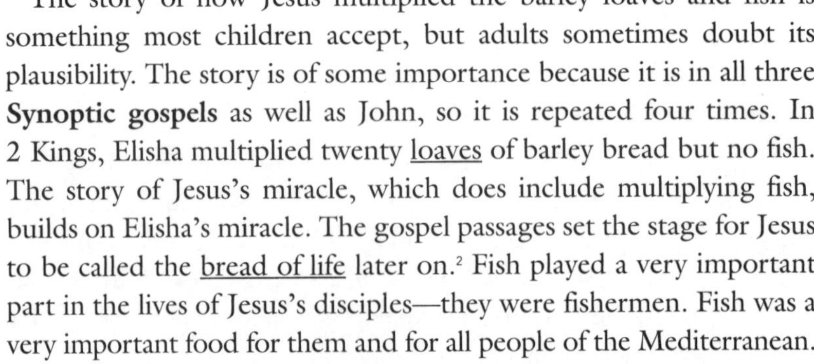

The story of how Jesus multiplied the barley loaves and fish is something most children accept, but adults sometimes doubt its plausibility. The story is of some importance because it is in all three **Synoptic gospels** as well as John, so it is repeated four times. In 2 Kings, Elisha multiplied twenty loaves of barley bread but no fish. The story of Jesus's miracle, which does include multiplying fish, builds on Elisha's miracle. The gospel passages set the stage for Jesus to be called the bread of life later on.[2] Fish played a very important part in the lives of Jesus's disciples—they were fishermen. Fish was a very important food for them and for all people of the Mediterranean. Fish can and should play a very important part in your life too.

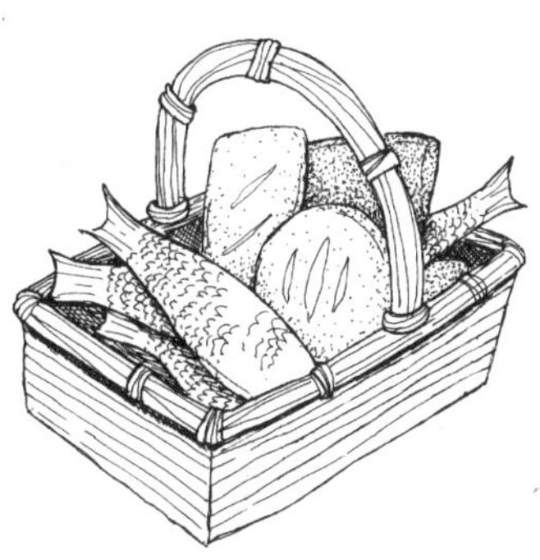

Illustration #19
Basket of Bread and Fish—"So they all ate and were filled, and they took up twelve baskets full of the fragments that remained" (Matthew 14:20 NKJV).

Fish in the Mediterranean Diet

Fish should be eaten several times a week when you are following the Mediterranean or Bible diet. Its section on the food pyramid is a bit bigger than dairy products but not much (see Illustration #20). Eating fish can provide essential fatty acids. This means that you might want to eat some form of fish or fish oil a few times a week. Sound impossible? Try cooking with fish flakes or using fish broth in cooking. If you are fond of dried (though not salted) fish, it makes a good snack; so does canned fish like the old standbys of tuna, salmon, and mackerel. Tuna can even be purchased in snack packs that can be easily opened for a school lunch.

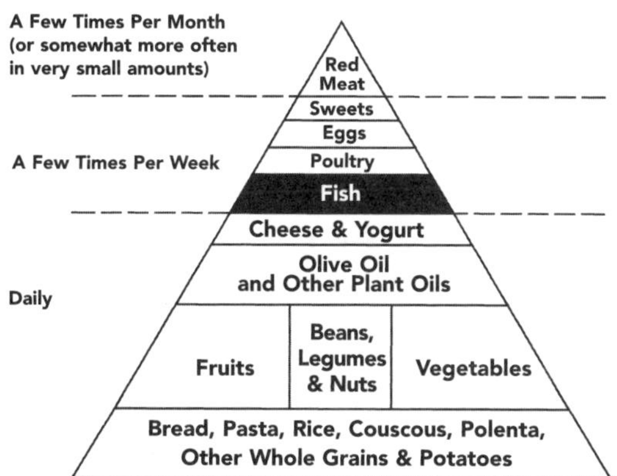

Illustration #20
The Fish Section—The darkened section of this pyramid represents how much of your diet should be devoted to fish.

The Thick and Thin of Fish

Fish come from either salt or fresh water. Farm-raised fish are generally freshwater fish. Look for the "naturally raised" label on farm-raised fish to be sure that they are not loaded with antibiotics or

omega-3 essential fatty acids
fatty acids, found mostly in fish, that can't be made in your body

growth hormones. Most fish are categorized as either round fish or flatfish. A good example of a flatfish is the flounder, which is so flat that it has both eyes on one side of its head. It swims along like a great oval platter. An example of a round fish is the salmon, which has two eyes, one on each side of its head.

Take a field trip to a fish market or look up various types of fish in a book as a family project to become more familiar with different kinds of fish. You might even want to go to a Greek, Egyptian, or other Middle Eastern restaurant, and order a traditional fish dish to taste different types of fish in their original recipes from the Mediterranean. Many Italian restaurants have fish flown in from the Mediterranean region that might even be the same as those eaten in Bible times.

The Fat and Thin of Fish

There are three classifications of fish. The classifications are: lower fat, fatty, and high fat. Fat in fish is not always bad. The lower-fat fish have less than 5 grams of fat in a 3½-ounce, cooked serving. The fatty fish have more than 5 grams of fat in a 3½-ounce, cooked serving. The high-fat fish, like Pacific herring, Atlantic mackerel, pompano, salmon, sardines, and shad, have more than 10 grams of fat for a 3½-ounce, cooked serving. The fatty and high-fat fish have the largest amounts of **omega-3 essential fatty acids**. Some lower-fat fish, such as trout, whitefish, sablefish, and tuna, also have omega-3 fatty acids. Even when canned, these fish still contain omega-3 fatty acids.

Fatty fish are naturally that way. The term "fatty fish" does not refer to breaded and deep-fried, greasy fish.

Fishy Fat

Fish Type	Examples
Lower fat	Atlantic cod, flounder, haddock, halibut, lingcod, monkfish, perch, pike, pollack, red snapper, rockfish, sea bass, smelt, rainbow trout, yellowfin tuna
Fatty	Freshwater bass, bluefish, carp, catfish, mullet, orange roughy, shark, swordfish, tilefish, bluefin tuna
High fat	Herring, Atlantic mackerel, pompano, sockeye salmon (red), sardines, shad

SOURCE: USDA Nutrient Data Laboratory, www.nal.usda.gov/fnic/foodcomp/

8-8-09

We may not like answer to prayer

IN MY OPINION
BILLY GRAHAM

Q. *I've just about given up praying because it doesn't seem to do any good. Is God testing me or something?*

We don't always know why God doesn't answer our prayers the way we wish he would. But that doesn't mean he hasn't heard them, or that he hasn't answered them. It simply means he hasn't answered them the way we wanted him to.

We see only part of the picture, but God sees the whole. We are limited in our understanding, but he is unlimited. We often think we know what is best, but only God knows what is actually best. That's why we always need to seek God's will when we pray.

But perhaps God has been testing you by not granting your prayers. If so his test may have revealed that your faith isn't as strong as it should be. If so, ask God to increase your faith – and then take steps to strengthen it by filling your soul with God's word.

Make sure above all of your commitment to Christ. Thank him for making you part of his family, and ask him to teach you to pray as you should.

Billy Graham: Billy Graham Evangelistic Association, P.O. Box 1270, Charlotte, NC 28201.

what others say

source of protein, potassium, vita-
hose who simply don't get enough
rative that you take a form of high-
day.[3]

ad done this [put their nets into deep
], they caught a great number of fish,
g. (NKJV)

ant parts of a healthy diet. Fish provides
asily prepared. Tuna fish, oysters, and
elenium; oysters and crabmeat contain
l zinc; and sardines, herring, salmon,
itamin D. All these nutrients are essen-
nore information about eating shrimp,
1 deals with clean and unclean foods.)
acids, especially **alpha-linolenic acid**,
, and docosahexaenoic acid (**DHA**).

what others say

eep-water fish, such as salmon, tuna
, and trout. These fish contain signif-
ega-3 fatty acids, which include the
r eicosapentaenoic acid. An abun-
t has been linked to lower levels of
glycerides.[4]

ed in Denver reported that consuming
3 PUFAs (polyunsaturated fatty acids)
ave glucose intolerance reduce the risk
n type 2 diabetes.[5]

Women in the Women's Health Study who had a high dietary intake of omega-3 fatty acids in relation to omega-6 fatty acids had

selenium
a mineral that inhibits the oxidation of fats

alpha-linolenic acid
an essential fatty acid found in fish, canola oil, flaxseeds, and walnuts

EPA
eicosapentaenoic acid, essential fatty acid in fish

DHA
docosahexaenoic acid, essential fatty acid in fish

cerebral palsy (CP)
a disease characterized by impaired muscular power and coordination

anti-inflammatory agents
substances that counteract inflammation

rheumatoid arthritis
inflammatory arthritis, an autoimmune disease

a reduced incidence of dry eye syndrome.[6] And it was found that eating tuna fish was of great benefit in reducing dry eye syndrome. Omega-6 fatty acids are found mostly in meats. So a Mediterranean diet of less meat and more fish and PUFA-rich vegetables, whole grains, and oils is recommended.

Bone Loss

Consumption of a balanced omega-6/omega-3 diet including long-chain PUFAs from safflower oil high in the omega-3 fatty acid DHA (docosahexaenoic acid) reduced bone loss. This is good news for women of menopause age not taking estrogen because consuming fish oil or fatty fish with safflower or high-oleate safflower oil can help reduce the bone loss often associated with menopause.[7]

A recent study showed that infant formula supplemented with DHA-rich EPA from low fish oil (oil with 10 percent EPA) could have the same health benefits as breast milk.[8] This is great news for women who are not able to breast-feed for whatever reason. Pregnant women with a family history of **cerebral palsy (CP)** should be certain to include fish in their diets to help prevent the occurrence of cerebral palsy in their children. In a study done in Greece, the mothers of children with CP were found to consume less fish and grains and more meat than control groups. The control groups comprised mothers and children who did not have CP. It was found that during pregnancy, those mothers ate more fish and cereal products as well as less meat than the mothers whose children had CP.[9]

what others say

Julian Whitaker, M.D.

The omega-3 oils are especially important in pain prevention and control, as they have anti-inflammatory, pain-relieving properties.[10]

Fish Oil Has Anti-Inflammatory Properties

Fish and fish oil are shown to be effective **anti-inflammatory agents** in cases of asthma and **rheumatoid arthritis**.[11] Feeding fish oils to laboratory animals during an experiment reduced acute and chronic inflammatory responses, improved their survival to external poisons or toxins, and improved their immune response. Fish oil has been used clinically in **acute** and **chronic** inflammatory conditions and even has had good response in inflammation following transplants.[12]

acute
comes on quickly, has limited duration

chronic
persists or recurs over an extended period

retina
lining inside the eyeball

spermatozoa
part of the male reproductive fluid (sperm)

Fish oil high in omega-3 fatty acids can reduce the pain and joint pain caused by inflammation in inflammatory bowel disease.[13] Another study showed that fish oil could even replace the use of NSAIDS (non-steroidal anti-inflammatory drugs) for the pain associated with pain in the back and neck. The subjects took 1,200–2,400 mg daily for several months and most stopped taking their NSAIDS altogether, thereby reducing the possibility of the side effects from NSAIDS such as gastric ulcers, bleeding, myocardial infarction, and in some rare cases death.[14] Fish oil also helped reduce the chronic inflammation of COPD (chronic obstructive pulmonary disease) patients so that they could walk and breathe better when taking the fish oil.[15]

Fish Feeds Your Brain

You've probably heard at some time in your life that "fish feeds your brain," and now we have the scientific evidence to back up all the old wives' tales about this. A study in Switzerland indicated that two to three portions of fatty fish per week, which comes to 1.25g EPA + DHA, is good for your heart and brain. When these fatty fish were consumed with a high-saturated-fat diet (mostly from animal products), then the fish nutrients were not as efficient as they were when other sources of omega-3 fatty acids (mostly from flaxseed and canola oil) were eaten instead of the animal fats. Low amounts of DHA in the diet have been associated with reduced functioning of the brain, **retina**, **spermatozoa**, and visual impairment in newborns.[16]

Dementia, Aging, ADHD, and DCD

It has long been known that essential fatty acids were necessary for the development of a baby's brain, but now research is showing that adults continue to need omega-3 fatty acids to help prevent several side effects of aging, Alzheimer's disease, and dementia.[17] In the

United Kingdom research was done that showed daily consumption of fish oil supplements helped improve cognitive function scores in the elderly who took part in the study. Children in a study who had ADHD had most of their symptoms alleviated by consumption of fish oil daily. The results were even more dramatic for the children with DCD (developmental coordination disorder), who experienced an increase in reading skills as well. The results of a comparison with omega-3 fish oils and Ritalin showed that the fish oil affected the ADHD index significantly more than the Ritalin did.[18] There is some indication that consuming high omega-3 fish oils daily will also benefit those with dyslexia and autism. So it is obvious that consuming fish high in DHA, EFA, and PUFA can improve mental function from the cradle to the grave. Who wouldn't want to be mentally sharp throughout their entire life?

Depression in Adults and Children

Adults who took part in a study reduced dementia and depression by adding fish and fish oils to their daily diets.[19] A diet rich in fish, walnuts, olive oil, and fish oils can also reduce the depression scores of children between the ages of six and twelve years 50 percent or more. Some of the children in the study taking the fish oil capsules experienced a complete remission of their depression.[20]

what others say

Kenneth Cooper, M.D.

It's long been known that consumption of the omega-3 oils found in deep-water fish such as salmon and tuna is associated with a lower risk of heart disease. Now a study reported in 1995 in the **JAMA** suggests that these fatty fish oils may provide protection from deadly cardiac arrhythmia, or irregular heartbeats.[21]

JAMA
Journal of the American Medical Association

sudden cardiac death
dying without warning from a heart problem

hypertensives
people with hypertension or high blood pressure

Fish Is Good for Your Heart

Arrhythmia and **sudden cardiac death** have been studied around the world, and as few as one to two meals a week of one of these fish can lower the risk from these two causes.[22] A Japanese study even suggested that overweight **hypertensives** would do better to follow a weight-loss program that included one meal a day of omega-3-rich fatty fish to reduce their blood pressure and reduce their risk of a cardiovascular accident.[23]

If you suspect that you have high blood pressure, please see your doctor before you do any home remedies. You can always eat fish, but don't start taking fish oil capsules without checking with your doctor first.

fish
John 21:12–14

Heart Disease and Fish Oil

It has long been known that the vagus nerve played a role in sudden cardiac death. New research showed that taking omega-3 oils lowered resting heart rate from an average of seventy-three beats/minute to sixty-eight beats/minute and significantly improved one-minute post-exercise heart rate recovery, which was consistent with an increase in the activity on the vagus nerve and was responsible for a decreased risk for sudden cardiac death.[24]

Pollution and Heart Rate

The elderly are most susceptible to heart rate changes due to particulate matter in the air, often called air pollution. A study conducted in Mexico City in a nursing home showed that consuming two grams of fish oil daily prevented a decline in heart variability that occurred after exposure to air pollution.[25]

Fish for Breakfast?

> **LUKE 24:41–43** ***[Jesus] said to them, "Have you any food here?" So they gave Him a piece of a broiled fish and some honeycomb. And He took it and ate in their presence.*** *(NKJV)*

Both times Jesus ate or gave fish to his disciples, it was for breakfast. Many peoples around the world eat fish for breakfast. In England, eating kippered herring, pilchards, or sardines for breakfast is considered common. Eating fish for breakfast would be better than some of the highly sugared, highly refined stuff (I can't really call it "food") that many people eat for breakfast. Try giving yourself or your family a tuna- or salmon-salad sandwich for breakfast and see how much better they think during the day. Have some sardines

broiled
cooked about six inches above or below a fire

baked
cooked in an oven or sealed up in foil or parchment paper

poached
cooked in simmering liquid

gills
the breathing vents of a fish

or herring in low-fat sauce on whole grain toast for breakfast; you might be surprised at your newfound energy. Eat some broiled fish and a salad for breakfast. Eating these kinds of meals will really feed your brain. The junk food won't! Eating fish at any meal is a good idea. Fatty fish can be an important part of a low-fat diet.

Eating Fish—Eating Out

When you are eating out, always look for simply prepared fish on the menu. Fish is healthiest for you when it is **broiled**, **baked**, or **poached**. Deep-frying and frying are not healthy ways to cook fish. A clear fish soup such as bouillabaisse would be a good substitute. Fish chowder is generally loaded with cream and/or bacon, which puts it in the category of being high in animal fats that are not omega-3 fatty acids. Many restaurants have fish that comes to them already breaded and frozen, ready to be deep-fried. This is not a good choice. However, breaded, deep-fried fish with the breading removed might be a good way to get some fish into your diet to start. You can be sure that when the children of Israel were wandering in the desert and longed for leeks, garlic, cucumbers, and fish, they were not talking about fast-food fish dinners!

What About the Fishy Smell?

When you cook fish, it should be over medium heat or at least six inches from the broiler or heat source. If it smells fishy—really, really fishy—in your house, you are not cooking it right or you have purchased fish that is not very fresh. Cooking fish on high heat will cause the fibers to shrink and allow all the vital juices to fall into the fire or the pan, which will smell fishy. It will also make the fish dry out and become fishy-smelling.

It's All in the Eyes

When you purchase a whole, fresh fish, the eyes should be clear and firm. The flesh should be firm and not smell of fish at all. The **gills** should be pink and firm. The skin should not be covered with anything. When you purchase fish that is already filleted or cut into steaks, ask to see the box or wrapper and look for any preservative chemicals that the pieces might have been dipped into. If you are at all worried about preservatives, it is better to have the fish cut in front of you than to purchase already-cut-up portions.

Chapter Wrap-Up

- The Old and New Testaments both have miracle stories wherein loaves of bread were multiplied, but only Jesus multiplied bread and fish. (Matthew 14:16–21)
- Fish is an important part of a healthy diet and plays an important role in the Mediterranean or Bible diet.
- Many health problems previously connected with aging can be helped by eating fish and fish oils.
- Components in fish oils are now being used to reduce pain when there is also inflammation.
- Fish can be eaten any time of the day. Many people around the world eat fish for breakfast, just as Jesus and his disciples did. (Luke 24:41–43; John 21:12–14)

Study Questions

1. Why do you think fish play an important role in the New Testament stories about Jesus?
2. Fish is healthy for you to eat. What makes it so?
3. What are the best kinds of fish to eat for health? Do you eat them?
4. There are at least four medical/health conditions that can be helped by fatty fish. What are the diseases, and why are they mostly modern diseases?
5. What are the best ways to cook and eat fish? Share some recipe/cooking ideas that come to mind after reading this chapter. Look at some historical books, like *The Life and Times of Jesus*, *Food in History*, or *Apicius: Cookery and Dining in Ancient Rome*, to get some ideas about the foods that were eaten in Bible times and how they differ or compare with the recipes we use today.

Chapter 8: The Passover Feast—Bitter Herbs and Unleavened Bread

Chapter Highlights:
- Parsley, the King of Herbs
- Dandelion, the Not-So-Lowly Weed
- Greens and Eye Problems

Let's Get Started

Of all the foods mentioned in the Bible, there are a few that are very important to health, both physical and mental. Garlic, fish, olive oil, and **bitter herbs** are among the most important. With just these foods you can live for a long time and live well. (Olive leaves are bitter herbs, but they were covered in the fruit chapter because olives are fruits.) The Passover Feast consists of roasted lamb, bitter herbs, and unleavened bread. The bitter herbs play an important role in the spiritual significance of the Passover. They are also an essential part of the healing and healthfulness of the Passover.

unleavened bread
Exodus 13:3–10; 23:15; 34:18; Deuteronomy 16:1–8

bitter herbs
dark green leafy vegetables; parsley, watercress, romaine lettuce, dandelion greens

Seder
meal eaten on the first night of the Passover Feast

maror
the green, bitter vegetable that stands for bitterness in the Passover Feast

haroset
reminder of the mortar used in Egypt

Passover Haggadah
order of service for the Seder

Passover Feast and Bitter Herbs

EXODUS 12:8 ***Then they shall eat the flesh on that night; roasted in fire, with unleavened bread and with bitter herbs they shall eat it.*** *(NKJV)*

God gave the children of Israel a feast to commemorate the time when they were slaves to Egypt and made to work bitterly. During the Passover Feast, which is called the **Seder**, they remember their slavery with blessings and with the eating of bitter herbs. The bitter herbs include parsley, chicory, endive, and dandelion greens (generally, parsley is used in North America). The bitter herbs are called **maror**. They are dipped in salt water to remember the tears that were shed during this hard labor. Next, the maror are dipped in **haroset**—a plate of chopped or grated apples, nuts, wine, and spices to remind them of the brick-and-mortar work they did for the Egyptians. Each time they dip the bitter herbs, they then eat them to "swallow the past bitterness."

Many Jews, non-Jews, Christians, and non-Christians still commemorate the Passover in the spring. This is a good time to cleanse your body or let it rest after a winter of inactivity and heavy food. You can find the **Passover Haggadah** for Christians in many Christian bookstores and the many different Jewish versions, from ancient texts

enzymes
protein modifiers that initiate or increase the rate of chemical reactions in the body without being used up in the process

to very modern texts, in Jewish bookstores and gift shops. Moreover, there are many sites on the Internet; just search for the words "Pesach," "Passover," or "Haggadah."

what others say

Jordan Rubin

The average American consumes less than the recommended three-to-five servings a day of "greens," and the most beneficial are the deep green, leafy vegetables.[1]

God Knows About Bitter Herbs

NUMBERS 9:11 ***On the fourteenth day of the second month, at twilight, they may keep it. They shall eat it with unleavened bread and bitter herbs.*** (NKJV)

The children of Israel ate bitter herbs at the Passover to commemorate the bitterness of having been slaves in the past, before they were able to flee. God's instructions were to eat the herbs along with roasted lamb and unleavened bread. This seems rather peculiar at first because, generally, the Hebrews ate very little meat; it was not an everyday food. But God's instructions make more sense in light of the fact that nutritionists and scientists now know bitter herbs stimulate the liver and other organs to produce **enzymes** that digest meat fat. How thoughtful of God to give a recipe that would prevent high cholesterol and gallbladder problems.

If you want to start adding bitter herbs to your diet, start cooking with herbs such as parsley, basil, oregano, marjoram, thyme, and savory (see Illustration #21). Once you are used to the wonderful flavors they offer, start adding them fresh, as garnish to food that has been cooked. Chopped, fresh parsley and watercress make a wonderful "power" garnish on soups, stews, salads, even oatmeal. Be adventurous and add fresh thyme or basil to your food.

Illustration #21
Dried Herbs—Dried herbs are used for cooking in almost all cuisines. Fresh herbs are also eaten as flavoring and for health benefits.

Why Are They So Green?

Why are the bitter herbs green? They contain **chlorophyll**, which makes them green. Chlorophyll protects you from cancer by retarding growths, and it keeps many toxins from causing health problems, especially **salmonella and drosphila**.[2] Chlorophyll can also protect you from environmental cancer-causing substances.[3]

chlorophyll
Pigment responsible for the green color in leaves; it is high in magnesium and trace minerals.

salmonella and drosphila
health-endangering bacteria

The Best Times for Bitter Herbs

Bitter herbs should be eaten daily. There are many times when it is imperative to eat dark green bitter herbs. That is whenever you eat fatty sources of protein such as a cheese sandwich, steak dinner, pork roast, etc. Never eat a burger without really green lettuce. Never eat a meat, egg, or cheese anything without bitter herbs. If you are eating eggs Benedict, please make sure that you eat green things. If you are in a restaurant, do as I do, and ask for some fresh parsley to go with it. Your liver will thank you. Dark green lettuce goes great with peanut butter, sesame butter, cheese, and even sardines. Have a salad of mixed greens daily. Never let a day go by without eating something dark green and leafy.

Try some of those mixed baby greens in the grocery store. Use them as the base of a salad. Add some tomatoes, cucumbers, celery, red and green peppers, parsley, watercress, romaine lettuce, black olives, and perhaps some tuna, salmon, or chicken. Use a fresh lemon, garlic, and virgin olive oil dressing or no dressing. Have some whole grain bread, rolls, or bread sticks. A salad like this and whole grain toast or rolls is a really great supper meal. It's best to have your lightest meal of the day at the end of the day when you aren't going to need as many calories; that's why salad is great for supper. This will make it easier to get to sleep because you will be finished digesting before bedtime.

Illustration #22
The Bitter Herbs Parsley and Watercress—Bitter herbs have been used for health food for thousands of years. Of course they didn't call it "health food" then; it was their regular food!

spring tonic
special food or drink that helps clear your body of winter heaviness and sludge

Parsley, the King of Herbs

Parsley is the bitter herb that I consider the king of herbs because of all the great things it can do for your health (see Illustration #22). For years tea made from dried parsley has been used to reduce kidney stones. Parsley also contains substances that prevent multiplication of tumor cells. It is also known to relieve gas and stimulate normal digestion.[4] Because it contains chlorophyll, parsley can sweeten your breath. It can even dispel breath problems from strong-smelling foods like garlic and onions. This is why you find it on your plate in a restaurant. It is not just a decoration. It is meant to cleanse your mouth to make you ready for the new taste of the next course.

Parsley, a Powerhouse of Nutrients

Parsley is high in iron, potassium, and vitamins A and C. It is a powerhouse of health and healing. If you could choose only one herb to take on a desert island, parsley would be the most useful. Garlic would be the most useful vegetable.

what others say

Don Colbert, M.D.

Parsley is a rich source of vitamins A and C. Two of the chemicals in parsley, apiol and myristicin, act as a mild laxative and a strong diuretic. Its diuretic action may help control high blood pressure.[5]

Dandelion, the Not-So-Lowly Weed

Psalm 104:14 ***He causes the grass to grow for the cattle, and vegetation for the service of man, that he may bring forth food from the earth.*** *(NKJV)*

Dandelion leaves have been used for many years as a **spring tonic**. They are reputed to flush the sludge of winter from your liver. This was a lot more popular in times when it was not possible for most people to get fresh vegetables in the winter, especially dark green leafy ones. Many people in the northern areas of the country ate a lot of preserved foods, meats, dried fish, potatoes, beans, breads, and biscuits with gravy, with almost no green vegetables or salads during the long winters. Some people were able to store and use dark orange squashes, carrots, and **rutabagas**, which helped provide much-needed vitamin A. In those days, large quantities of butter and heavy creams were included in the daily foods, so cleaning out the liver from all this fat was a really great idea to keep them healthy.

I still eat dandelion greens, though I buy the commercially grown ones, because most places let dogs and other animals in their yards. If you have a fenced-in yard and no animals, go for it! Eat the first-sprouted leaves of your dandelions. Your neighbors will think you are really great, digging up the dandelions and ridding the area of what they think are pests. Once the plants begin to flower, they become even more bitter than in the spring and you might want to stop eating them. If you want to gather your own dandelion greens, pick them in the early spring before they flower and in areas away from animals and exhaust. Wash the leaves well. Eat them raw in a salad or steamed lightly. According to most reference books, *Taraxacum officiale* was probably the bitter herb mentioned in the book of Numbers, and this *Taraxacum officiale* is the very one that grows so freely in our lawns!

rutabagas
a type of yellow-fleshed turnip that is generally larger than white turnips

bile
a yellow substance secreted by the liver to help digest fats

serum cholesterol
cholesterol found in your blood

uric acid
leftover substance from faulty metabolism of proteins, often causes gout

Dandelion Power

Psalm 23:2 ***He makes me to lie down in green pastures; He leads me beside the still waters. (NKJV)***

Dandelions are often thought of as the bitter herb that was mentioned in the Bible to be eaten with the Passover Feast because they are found in pastures and fields all over the Middle East. They clean your bloodstream and liver and encourage the production of **bile**. They are also known to reduce **serum cholesterol** and **uric acid**.[6]

Chinese Parsley, Cilantro, or Coriander: What's in a Name?

This dark green vegetable has a lot of names. In Chinese medicine and cooking it is called "Chinese parsley." In Spanish or Mexican medicine and cooking it is called "cilantro." North Americans know it as the green leaves of the "coriander" plant.

dental amalgams composition dental fillings containing mercury

endocrine glands ductless glands like the thyroid, adrenal, ovary, testis, and Isles of Langerhans in the pancreas

intractable stubborn, difficult to cure

Recent research in Japan has shown Chinese parsley to be of great benefit in removing mercury from the tissues and organs of people who have had their **dental amalgams** removed from their mouths and their cavities filled with synthetic materials. The strong bluish light that is used to cure the synthetic fillings was found to cause the free-floating mercury (liberated during drilling) to be deposited in the lungs, kidneys, **endocrine glands**, liver, and heart. This happened even when a dental dam was used and precautions were taken to keep the patient from mercury exposure. This mercury then contributed to **intractable** infections. The mercury deposits were removed from these people in the study by the oral intake of a 100 mg tablet of Chinese parsley four times a day.[7]

This is really great news for people who have had their mercury fillings removed, thinking that their health would improve, and yet found it to be worse. The study showed that when bacteria in the body was surrounded by mercury, it could not be successfully treated with any kind of antibiotic. The Chinese parsley removed the mercury and relief came right away.

what others say

Francisco Contreras, M.D.

Among the vegetables that best provide minerals are broccoli, spinach, watercress, coriander, lettuce, parsley, sweet peppers, tomatoes, chili peppers, prickly pears, and mushrooms.[8]

In with the Chinese Parsley, Out with the Lead

Chinese parsley can help your body excrete lead as well. High levels of lead in your body can cause mental retardation, loss of feeling in your fingers and toes, impotence, and even loss of balance. Gasoline no longer has lead in it, but you might still be affected by it or by lead paint from your childhood toys or from stripping paint from a surface that contained lead-based paint.

Lead has a half-life of fifty-two years, which means that it takes fifty-two years for lead to break down and be excreted. Many children from inner cities (where there is lead in the air from industrial pollution) are considered retarded or simple-minded when, in reality, they are suffering from an overload of lead. Before computers, when all printing was done with lead type, printers, typesetters, and proofreaders used to suffer from lead poisoning because of the lead type they used and touched frequently. In the 1960s many hyperactive children in England were found to have very high lead levels from the industrial pollution and from the smoke of cigarettes that were being smoked by their parents. Once the lead was removed from their bodies, with sodium alginate from seaweed, they were no longer hyperactive.

sea vegetables contain the heavy metal–removing agent sodium alginate

cruciferous vegetables with four-petaled flowers, suggesting a cross pattern

Many ethnic foods contain coriander or Chinese parsley, especially Mexican, Southwestern, East Indian, Chinese, and other oriental foods. Look for recipes that contain Chinese parsley or cilantro, and include them in your regular, weekly diet.

Get Your Lead Levels Checked

If you even suspect that you have had contact with high levels of lead from paint or other sources, please see your doctor. A nutritional hair analysis will show if lead is in your system and a blood test will show if it is in your blood. Eating dark green leafy vegetables, like hijiki, arame, kombu, wakame, kelp, or even dulse, especially cilantro, will help remove the lead. So will **sea vegetables** (which are also green, leafy vegetables), garlic, egg yolks, beans, and **cruciferous** vegetables like broccoli, cabbage, kale, and collard greens.

what others say

Jordan Rubin

Extraordinary foods are those that God created for us to eat and are in a form healthy for the body. If you are struggling with poor health, it is best to consume foods from the extraordinary category more than 75 percent of the time. These extraordinary foods impart health benefits and can bring about regeneration of body, mind, and spirit: leafy greens (kale, collard, broccoli rabe, mustard greens) and salad greens (radicchio, escarole, endive).[9]

Grass and Herbs: Not Just for Cows

Grass grows almost anywhere. When you "flourish like grass" you will be really healthy, and growing under all circumstances. This is

blue-green algaes
fresh water chlorella or spirulina; compact nutritional powerhouses

kelp
deep-water sea vegetable

multiple sclerosis
also called MS; a disease that causes neural and muscular impairments

because grass and all greens are high in chlorophyll and minerals. This is why so many people drink green juice, or juice made from green plants, especially grasses. It is a very powerful kind of "health food" that you can make yourself if you have a juicer. There are many companies that provide powdered green drinks that you just mix with juice or water to get the benefits of the high mineral content of greens. Many of these green-drink powders are made with alfalfa, barley grass juice, wheat grass juice, sea algaes, **blue-green algaes**, parsley, and often contain garlic, carrot, or **kelp** powder. If you have trouble eating greens every day, you might want to start out by having a green drink. Once you start to feel more energy, you will be convinced to eat more greens too.

Algae Is Good for You (Never Mind How It Looks)

Green algae and blue-green algae have been the subject of much research showing that they, too, are green plants with curative powers. Chlorella, a green algae, has been shown to prevent stress-induced ulcers.[10] Chlorella was also shown to contain an antitumor factor.[11] Another popular algae is spirulina; it has exhibited antioxidant protection and has also been shown to reduce allergic reactions.[12] Those people with **multiple sclerosis** have been shown to have a longer remission of symptoms when they are eating spirulina.[13]

Algae Is Great for Vegetarians

A strict vegetarian who eats no animal products is called a "vegan." Vegans are often deficient in vitamin B_{12} because it generally comes from animal sources. There are two vegetarian sources of this vitamin. One is the fermented soybean product from Indonesia called "tempeh" and the other is green algae.[14] Vegans would do well to include these two foods in their diet.

Popeye's Choice

Spinach is a really dark green leafy vegetable. It is high in iron, folic acid, vitamins A and C, and minerals. It is often classified as a bitter herb; just eat some raw to find out why. Spinach is added to a lot of foods in classical French cooking that are traditionally high in fat such as **quiche**, omelettes, fish, or veal. Anything with spinach in French cooking is called Florentine. Spinach will help your body digest the fat in these high-fat foods and prevent health problems. Many of these recipes go back to Bible times. The two most popular types of quiche, asparagus and spinach, were in the first cookbook ever written, which was published around the time of the life of Jesus.[15]

quiche
a pie made of eggs, cheese, and cream; eaten as a meal

oxalic acid
found in rhubarb and spinach, not suitable for people with kidney problems

Spinach is very high in **oxalic acid**. If you have kidney problems, please see your doctor before you start to eat spinach or take powdered spinach in large amounts.

what others say

Don Colbert, M.D.

Foods high in chlorophyll include spinach, kale, collard greens, beet tops, and parsley. If you eat charcoal-grilled or fried foods, I strongly suggest you consume one of these high-chlorophyll foods to block any cancer-causing chemicals that are produced as a result of frying or charcoal grilling.[16]

Green Grasses

HEBREWS 6:7 ***For the earth which drinks in the rain that often comes upon it, and bears herbs useful for those by whom it is cultivated, receives blessing from God.*** *(NKJV)*

Barley grass, wheat grass, and other cattle foods were considered useful herbs or crops in Bible times and today. Whereas in the early part of the century grasses were considered to be only cattle food, they are now considered health food because of their high nutritional content. The wheat and barley grasses that are used in green-drink powders are the leaves of the same plants that produce the seeds, which are harvested to be used as whole grains.

PH Balance and Grasses

The pH measure indicates the acidity or alkalinity of a solution and is short for potential of hydrogen. The pH scale commonly in use ranges from 0 to 14. Optimal pH of the blood is between 7.36 and

age-related macular degeneration the most common cause of blindness in the elderly

7.42. Our human bodies need to have a pH balance to stay disease-free, and that is generally measured at home by testing the urine with a pH paper or stick of some kind. The pH of urine can show a rough estimate of the pH of the body. Urine pH is generally acceptable if it is in the range of 7.0 to 7.5. Below 7.0 is considered acidic and above 7.5 is considered alkaline. Some fruits, most vegetables, and grasses are able to balance the pH and bring it to a more neutral number. Many experts have written books saying that an acidic pH is responsible for many kinds of illnesses including cancer, headaches, candida problems, and more. The general consensus is that germs, bacteria, yeast, molds, and fungus live in our bodies when they are too acidic. Meat and grains are often considered acid-forming. Fruits and vegetables are considered alkaline-forming. Taking a green drink of freshly juiced greens or using a powdered green drink can help restore and maintain the pH balance in a healthy body. Drinking water with minerals and a squirt of fresh lemon juice can help as well, since lemon juice can create an alkaline environment in the body. Eating or drinking greens every day is essential for good health.

Drinking lemon juice in water and using grasses in green drinks can help keep you healthy.

There are many wonderful green powdered drinks and some supplements containing green grasses in the market. Emerald Balance is a good-tasting one that is pH-balancing. I also like Kyo-Green, Kyo-Green's Harvest Blend, Garden of Life Perfect Food, RevivAll, and Living Multi. All of these quality products contain greens, grasses, and some even contain sprouts as well.

Greens and Eye Problems

In the last few years, much research has been done on the dietary habits of the elderly. A landmark study of almost nine hundred people, ages fifty-five to eighty, was done in Boston. They were broken into two groups: the control group had not been diagnosed with eye problems, the other groups had. The study was to assess their dietary habits over an undisclosed period of time, to assess the similarities in the diets of the people with and without eye problems. Of the group with eye problems, 356 of them had been diagnosed within one year of the study with an advanced stage of **age-related macular degen-**

eration (AMD). The results were startling, but to be expected. Those who were not diagnosed with age-related macular degeneration had the highest intake of the **carotenoids**, **lutein**, and **zeaxanthin** due to a high-frequency intake of dark green leafy vegetables, specifically spinach and collard greens. The study showed that taking vitamin E and/or vitamin C in the form of supplements did not have any effect on AMD.[17] If you want to be able to see better when you are older, eat spinach and collard greens! Another study done in the same clinic showed that women who smoked twenty-five or more cigarettes a day were also at risk for age-related macular degeneration.[18]

carotenoids
a class of compounds related to vitamin A

lutein
a carotenoid

zeaxanthin
a carotenoid

bilberry
an eye-building herb

A green drink or green-drink powder with spinach and broccoli is still considered food, not a supplement. Therefore, drinking a green drink will be of some help in fighting AMD. There are many supplements that contain **bilberry** and the ingredients of spinach and broccoli that are the most helpful: xanthophylls, lutein, and zeaxanthin. These will be very useful in fighting AMD.

what others say

Don Colbert, M.D.

Foods high in lutein include spinach, collard greens, kale, romaine lettuce, and leeks. Eating foods high in lutein seems to help prevent cataracts and loss of vision.[19]

Green and Mean (Against Cancer)

Folic acid–rich foods have been shown to prevent cancers. The foods that are high in folic acid are green vegetables, legumes, and whole grains. According to a recent study, when a person is deficient in folic acid, there is damage to the DNA that resembles damage in cancer cells.[20]

How Bitter Herbs Can Help

The Bitter Herb	The Help
Parsley	stimulates digestion dissolves kidney stones deodorizes breath and body dispels gas breaks up fat
Endive	rids body of infection

neural
of or pertaining to nerves or the nervous system

vascular disease
disease of the circulatory system

How Bitter Herbs Can Help (cont'd)

The Bitter Herb	The Help
Dandelion	spring tonic breaks up fat cleans bloodstream encourages bile production
Chinese parsley (cilantro)	removes heavy metals breaks up fat
Kelp	stimulates energy production removes heavy metals breaks up fat
Spinach	breaks up fat prevents blindness in the elderly cleans lymphatic system prevents neural-tube birth defects
Chlorella	prevents stress ulcers prevents tumors removes mercury
Spirulina	reduces allergic reactions aids MS remissions

Green Foods Fight Birth Defects and Vascular Disease

The folic acid–rich foods, which include leafy greens, were also found to prevent several kinds of birth defects, including **neural**-tube defects, or to reverse the incidents of vascular disease in women.[21] If you are planning to become pregnant or if you suspect you have **vascular disease**, please have your folic-acid levels checked. Your doctor may want to prescribe a folic-acid supplement. You would also be wise to keep track of your intake of folic acid and make sure that it is at least 400 mcg daily.

How Does This Relate to the Mediterranean Diet?

Eating dark green leafy vegetables is an important part of the Mediterranean diet. This is partly why the vegetable section on the pyramid is the largest section, to show the importance of eating a lot of vegetables, including dark green leafy ones. Try adding garnishes of parsley or watercress to every meal. Make sure that the entire family eats green things; it is very important. At my home we even put chopped fresh parsley on popcorn or scrambled eggs. Be creative in the ways you can get something green in every meal. Make your own alfalfa or other sprouts for some additional green foods.

For instructions on sprouting, see my book *Sprouts: The Savory Source for Health and Vitality,* Alive Books Natural Health Guides, Vancouver, BC, Canada.

Chapter Wrap-Up

- The Passover Feast or Feast of Unleavened Bread is significant for more than spiritual reasons. God uses it to point out that everybody should eat bitter herbs with rich proteins. (Exodus 12:8 and Numbers 9:11)
- There are many references to plants, grasses, and green leaves in the Bible. (Psalms 104:14; 23:2; and Isaiah 66:14)
- Green leafy vegetables and herbs play an important role in daily life.
- Science and medicine have taken a great interest in green plants (including algae).
- The Bible diet includes eating dark green leafy vegetables, often called bitter herbs, on a daily basis.

Study Questions

1. What Jewish feast includes bitter herbs and why? Why are they important for you to eat today?
2. Which important bitter herb grows nearly everywhere? Name some local places where it grows so you know where to harvest them in the spring.
3. Name four health benefits of eating dark green leafy vegetables. How are you going to add them to your diet?
4. Which two bitter herbs are easy to add to everything? Can you think of any benefits to doing this? Why do you suppose people ate more greens during Bible times?

Chapter 9: All the Fat Is the Lord's

Chapter Highlights:
- Forbidden Vegetable Fats
- How Much Protein Do You Need?
- You Are the Temple of God

Let's Get Started

Many people talk about the low-fat or nonfat craze, but in Scripture God gave strict orders about the kind of fat that can be eaten by his people. This mostly pertains to the hard fat around the organs of beef, lamb, sheep, goat, and pigs. There are fats that are good for you and fats that are not so good. As it turns out, the fat that God told his people to stay away from is the same fat that today's scientists say you shouldn't eat. That never changes. The Bible diet is not really a low-fat diet as much as it is a high-vegetable, low-animal-fat diet, which is different. The Mediterranean food pyramid shows that to be really healthy, you should eat olive oil, cheese, and yogurt every day (see Illustration #2).

fat
Exodus 29:13; Leviticus 7:22–25

No Fat Allowed!

> LEVITICUS 3:14–17 ***Then he shall offer from it his offering, as an offering made by fire to the LORD. The fat that covers the entrails and all the fat that is on the entrails, the two kidneys and the fat that is on them by the flanks, and the fatty lobe attached to the liver above the kidneys, he shall remove; and the priest shall burn them on the altar as food, an offering made by fire for a sweet aroma; all the fat is the LORD's. This shall be a perpetual statute throughout your generations in all your dwellings: you shall eat neither fat nor blood.*** *(NKJV)*

God instructed the Israelites to burn the fat that surrounded the organs like a cushion and the fat that was inside the body cavity of the animals, as a food offering to him. This fat, referred to in the passage from Leviticus, is the same fat that is used to make lard. It is very hard fat and is the major animal fat that is known to cause a lot of health problems. Some whole grain crackers and baked goods contain hydrogenated fat and/or palm kernel oil, a saturated fat. Hard fat is very difficult to digest. Shortening is made of vegetable oil that has hydrogen added to mimic this hard fat, or lard.

hydrogenated fat
oil that has been made hard by adding hydrogen to it

rendered
melted down

suet
hard fat from beef cattle used in cooking much like lard is

Shortening or **hydrogenated fat** is also hard to digest and can turn to fat in or on your body, which is true for any hydrogenated fat products like margarine and many processed foods. The most common place to get lard is from pigs. The hard fat is **rendered** to remove the fibrous material, and the remainder is chilled to form lard. Sometimes acid, like lemon juice or citric acid, and salt are added, but it is still the forbidden fat. The same forbidden fat is called **suet** when it comes from beef cattle. This is also very hard to digest. North Americans generally don't use the hard fat from goats, sheep, lambs, or deer.

what others say

Jordan Rubin

Our diets have increased the intake of polyunsaturated and hydrogenated fats, mainly because of the increased consumption of processed oils. Yet the verdict is in: the rate of heart disease has steadily increased, and we have a growing obesity problem in this country.[1]

These are the fats that are not good for your health. We need fat in our diet to keep our skin, hair, and nails healthy. Fat is useful because it is needed to make many hormones in your body. Fats slow the release of sugars from your foods, helping to reduce blood-sugar variations from meals. Fats make you feel fuller, so you tend to eat less food when the meal contains some fat. You do not have to give up fat altogether; just avoid lard, bacon fat, suet, and burned fat on meats.

Burn the Fat

The instructions were to burn the hard fat as an offering to God. This meant that it would belong to the Lord and not to the people. Why do you think God would declare he should get the very worst fat for humans to eat? Why was the aroma pleasing to God? Could it be because the smell reminded him that nobody was eating it? Always remove the visible fat from animal proteins before cooking them; only God gets to have burned fat. Remove all the lard, bacon fat, and shortening from your recipes; replace them with butter, olive oil, or coconut oil.

Forbidden Vegetable Fats

Vegetable oils that have been heated or have hydrogen added are called trans fats and are known to cause CVD (cardiovascular disease) and other health problems. Trans fats must be listed on packaged foods, so read the labels to make sure you aren't consuming trans fats in any prepared foods.

Today's animals live in a polluted environment, and some of the toxins produced from living in a polluted world are stored in their fat. Burning, not eating animal fat, also protects us from consuming toxins found in animal fat.

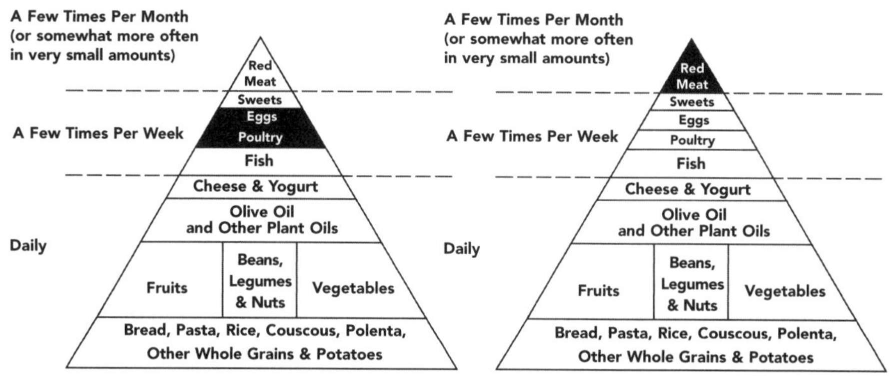

Illustration #23
Eggs and Poultry Section, Red Meat Section—The darkened section of the pyramid on the left represents how much of your diet should be devoted to eggs and poultry, while the darkened section of the one on the right represents how much of your diet should be devoted to red meat.

Choose Your Meats Wisely

The Mediterranean diet encourages low consumption of red meat, animal products, saturated fats, hydrogenated fats, and refined carbohydrates. It encourages high consumption of fruit, vegetables, and whole grains. Research has shown that high consumption of red meat is associated with increased risks of coronary heart disease (CHD) as well as colon and other cancers. A high animal-protein diet of mostly red meat is also responsible for calcium losses in the urine, which can lead to osteoporosis.[2] The Mediterranean diet suggests that red meat be eaten a few times per month, while eggs and poultry can be eaten as often as a few times per week. The most important information in the Mediterranean diet and Bible diet is to eat a lot of vegetables every day, especially dark green leafy ones, and add in some fruits, nuts, seeds, olives, and olive oil and eat the other foods sparingly. When vegetables comprise 40 to 60 percent of your daily food intake, you will have the correct balance of vegetables and protein (see Illustration #23).

what others say

Julian Whitaker, M.D.

The low-fat craze has missed the mark. The truth is that fat, consumed in moderate amounts, is important to the body. Fat slows the release of sugar into your bloodstream, helping to sustain energy. Fat is necessary for the absorption of vitamins A, E, D, and K, and beta-carotene, and for the formation of all cell membranes.[3]

Fat Gets a Bad Rap

Fat has gotten a lot of bad publicity in the last eight to ten years. It was always considered important for weight loss until North Americans developed a fat phobia—yes, a fear of fat! Fat is essential for the breakdown and absorption of the fat-soluble vitamins A, D, E, and K. If you follow a very low-fat diet, you will quickly become deficient in these vitamins. Your hair, skin, and nails will become dry, flaky, and lusterless. Many diet programs that recommended no fat have changed to low fat because people on no-fat diets were beginning to look like dried-out prunes. What's the sense of losing weight if you wind up looking like a prune in the process?

Unsaturated fatty acids are essential for proper functioning of the glands and organs in your body. Your thyroid gland will actually overfunction without vitamin F, or unsaturated fatty acids, in your diet. Eat some form of the good fat daily.

Fat keeps you from getting hungry too soon by slowing down the digestion process. If you eat a really low-fat or no-fat diet, you will be hungry all the time.

what others say

Maureen Salaman

So far as calorie content is concerned, all classes of foods are not created equal. One gram of fat contains nine calories whereas one gram of carbohydrates or protein contains four.[4]

Fat Has a Purpose

EZEKIEL 39:19 ***You shall eat fat till you are full, and drink blood till you are drunk, at My sacrificial meal which I am sacrificing for you.*** *(NKJV)*

Ezekiel is trying to tell the Israelites that they might have to endure a punishment that includes eating fat (and he means the forbidden fat) and drinking blood, also forbidden, if they don't change their ways. If they ate fat until they were glutted, that would be a lot of fat! In a normal diet, fat tells you when you have eaten enough. (I'm referring to fat in general, not the forbidden fats lard and suet.) When you feel satisfied after eating two cookies made with butter and eggs, it is because of the fat. If you eat cookies with no fat, you might find yourself eating a lot more before you feel full or satisfied. This means that you will consume a lot more calories, in the form of starch and sugar, when there is no fat. These calories from sugar and flour are really **empty calories** if you are eating refined flour and sugar, which will put fat on your body very fast. This is why a low-fat or nonfat diet could be unhealthy, even though fat has nine calories to every one calorie of starch or carbohydrate. Because fat keeps you from eating too many empty calories, you will also have less calories in your diet from either fat or starch by following the Bible diet.

empty calories
energy from food with no nutritional value, only calories

what others say

Jim Shriner

Fat has more than twice the calories per gram that protein or carbohydrates have.[5]

Fat Can Make You Fat

Animal fats have been shown to be responsible for many health problems, including atherosclerosis and prostate, colon, rectal, pancreatic, breast, and skin cancers.[6] Eating too much fat can indeed cause a person to "get fat." The proportions of fat to other foods and to the amount of exercise are the important comparisons. If most of your calories come from fat, then you will become fat. If most of your calories come from other sources, you have less chance of getting fat. You will also stand a chance of getting fat if you do not exercise, no matter how many calories you have from any source. Just because you have a lean body or low body fat does not mean that fat is not being deposited in your arteries. Many slender people have high accumulations of fat in their arteries. Fat is displaced from your body, including your arteries, by fiber from grains and vegetables along with using up the energy from the fat during your daily

purine
an organic, colorless compound

lactating
producing milk for breast-feeding

life or through an exercise program. This is why eating vegetables, especially bitter herbs, which are known to break up fat, is so important.

To lose weight, you must eat lots of vegetables and fruits and reduce your intake of animal fats. This, along with exercise, will help burn up the fat stored in your body. Do not try to lose weight by cutting out all fat and protein; this is not healthy. A diet of frequent snacks of vegetables, small amounts of protein, and nuts and seeds will be the best way to lose weight. Eating olive oil and other monounsaturated fats like flaxseed oil and hemp oil can improve your diet by reducing inflammation, joint pain, and the empty feeling of near nausea many people experience on weight-loss programs without fat. Eating whole foods is a fabulous way to start on a healthy lifestyle. Reduce the amount of white bread, fried foods, burgers, and breaded and fried chicken and fish.

There are many kinds of weight-loss diets. There are diets with only fat and protein and no carbohydrates; diets with small amounts of carbohydrates at only one meal; diets where you eat only certain kinds of protein based on the chemical **purine**; diets based on your blood type; and low-calorie or low-fat diets. Whether you're looking for a sensible diet for health, or a diet for weight loss, follow the Bible diet. Do not follow a diet that only contains vegetables and no protein sources or a diet of meat and cheese with no vegetables; all the nutrients are necessary for health.

How Much Protein Do You Need?

Protein is generally calculated by kilograms of body weight. Adults should have around 0.8 grams of protein per day for each kilogram (2.2 pounds) of body weight. Infants and growing children need more protein than adults, and older adults need less than younger adults. Infants can often require up to 2 grams per kilogram of body weight or between 13 and 14 grams a day. A 120-pound teenager would require around 64 grams and a 160-pound adult would require around 70 grams. This includes protein from all sources, not just animal sources.

If you are under a lot of stress (such as from sickness, an accident, or death of a loved one), you might need more protein to repair your body. If you are pregnant or **lactating,** you will want to make sure that you are getting adequate amounts and even add a little extra plant-based protein. A 3-ounce serving of fish contains about 20 grams of protein, 2 eggs contain about 15 grams of protein, 1 cup of tofu (a soybean product) contains about 20 grams of protein, 3 ounces of white-meat chicken contain about 18 grams of protein. By eating several 3-ounce servings of protein or 2 eggs, it is possible to maintain the required amount of protein each day. Servings of 3 or 4 ounces of protein food are a lot smaller than what most people eat at one time. Consider that a can of tuna fish is 6 or 6½ ounces; this will give you some idea of the size of a 3-ounce serving—about half a can of tuna fish.

Protein in Food

Serving of Food	Grams of Protein
Cheddar cheese, ½ cup	16.0
Cottage cheese, ½ cup	13.0
Black beans, ½ cup cooked	8.0
Tofu, ½ cup	10.0
Lentils, ½ cup cooked	9.0
Avocado, ½	2.5
Lean ground beef, 3 ounces	21.0
Chicken, light meat, ½ cup	20.0
Chicken, dark meat, ½ cup	18.0
Almonds, ½ cup	12.0
Halibut, 3 ounces	22.0
Salmon, 3 ounces	21.0

What to Do?

1 TIMOTHY 4:1–5 ***Now the Spirit expressly says that in latter times some will depart from the faith, giving heed to deceiving spirits and doctrines of demons, speaking lies in hypocrisy, having their own conscience seared with a hot iron, forbidding to marry, and commanding to abstain from foods which God created to be received with thanksgiving by those who believe and know the truth. For every creature of God is good, and nothing is to be refused if it is received with thanksgiving; for it is sanctified by the word of God and prayer.*** *(NKJV)*

Look again at the Mediterranean food pyramid in the first chapter (Illustration #2). You will see that no foods are left out of this Bible

dementia
a permanent acquired impairment of intellectual function

diet. You are not being told not to eat something. The Mediterranean diet shows that red meat should be eaten no more than a few times a month. Sweets, eggs, poultry, and fish can be eaten a few times per week. Cheese and yogurt can be eaten daily. The Mediterranean diet is the same diet that was followed for thousands of years. This is the Bible diet of the Bible lands. It is sensible and fits in with both the Old and the New Testament regulations about clean and unclean foods.

You have the option of eating foods that were considered unclean if you want to, but they are not required to be eaten. Even though beef—"oxen," as they called them—is considered clean, that doesn't mean you need to have it daily. Just a few times a month is the maximum—the same frequency at which the Israelites of old would have eaten beef or lamb—at a special holiday, banquet, party, or wedding. The Bible diet says eating red meat is acceptable, but you don't have to eat it if you don't want to. You do, however, have to eat vegetables and whole grains if you want to be healthy.

To Beef or Not to Beef? That Is the Question

Beef and other animal products contain vitamin B_{12}. There are a few nonanimal sources of B_{12} like tempeh, a fermented soybean product. However, the easiest and most foolproof way to ensure your adequate intake of B_{12} is to eat animal products. Vitamin B_{12} is needed to prevent some types of anemia, and it is also required for proper digestion and absorption of foods. It is especially essential for the metabolism of fats and carbohydrates. Vitamin B_{12} is also associated with preventing nerve damage and otherwise protecting the nerves. Lack of adequate B_{12} is associated with faulty memory and learning. This is why it is often given to older people who suffer from some form of memory impairment or even **dementia**.

Often people with a vitamin B_{12} deficiency have a shuffling gait when they walk. Other characteristics of being low in B_{12} are tiredness, general weakness, poor appetite, speaking difficulties, pernicious anemia, nervousness, neuritis, brain damage, and growth failure in children. This makes vitamin B_{12} a really important part of your diet.

Meat for Breakfast

When I was in high school I did not like eating cold cereal or sweet things for breakfast, like pancakes or French toast, at least not during the week. My mother was at a loss about what to have available for me for breakfast. One day I just said that leftovers from dinner the night before would be fine. She thought I should have some meat so she got me a pound of ground beef. She then divided it into six servings and individually wrapped them and put them in the freezer. Each day for breakfast I would have all the leftover vegetables, any gravy leftover, and a very small patty of ground beef, which I cooked up. I felt great and never had mid-morning slumps. Even then I ate vegetables for breakfast!

If you have a steak or some other serving of meat that is over four ounces, do not have any more fat or animal proteins for the rest of the day. Stick to veggie proteins.

Eggs in the Jewish Diet

There is evidence that eggs were eaten in Bible times because, as seen above, there are references to eggs in the Bible. The eggs they had were from both domesticated birds and wild birds, as this passage points out.

Young Jewish boys used to discuss, as part of their schooling, whether it was lawful for a chicken to lay an egg on the Sabbath, because no work was to be done on the Sabbath. So you can be sure that eggs were part of the Jewish diet.

> **what others say**
>
> **Maureen Salaman**
>
> Eggs are mentioned in various parts of the Scriptures, and it is common knowledge that they were eaten in Old and New Testament times, when available.[7]

How Much Can I Have?

The Mediterranean diet suggests that you eat poultry and eggs a few times a week. When you are eating a diet high in vegetables (especially soybeans), whole grains, nuts, and seeds, a few times a week, you can supplement these vegetable proteins and fats with animal protein from poultry, fish, and eggs.

choline
a nutrient beneficial for your nerves, brain, gallbladder, and liver, found in eggs and soybeans

inositol
a nutrient beneficial for nerves, hair growth, and fat metabolism, found in eggs, soybeans, molasses, and whole grains

lecithin
a component of all cells, made of choline and inositol

You don't want to eat eggs every day, but a few a week are generally recommended. Eggs are part of a good diet. White and brown eggs have the same nutritional values. Whether or not eggs are healthy is determined not by their color but by what the hens were fed. Hens fed naturally grown grains and vegetables produce eggs that are healthy. Eggs contain **choline** and **inositol**, which feed your brain in such a way as to allow you to think better. Eggs do contain cholesterol, but they also contain **lecithin**, which helps the cholesterol to be used up. Cooking eggs on medium or low heat is advised to prevent the protein from becoming too tough or from releasing sulfurous compounds, which could cause gas and are difficult to digest.

All protein foods should be cooked on medium or low heat. If you are broiling meat, fish, or cheese, always keep it six inches from the heat source. Meat and eggs should be cooked through but never blackened.

Eggs—The Perfect Food?

For many years eggs were considered the perfect food. Consequently, eggs were the standard on which to base all proteins. This meant that any proteins for human consumption had to "measure up" to the complement of protein in eggs, or they were judged inadequate. In other words, each protein food was assigned a "protein efficiency ratio" (PER), and because eggs contained 100 percent of the amino acids for complete protein, they were given the number 100. Fish, milk, meat, and soybeans also have a PER of 100. All other protein foods have a PER of less than 100.

what others say

Maureen Salaman

If any food can be called perfect, the egg can, inasmuch as it contains all the amino acids essential to our health. Over and above its protein richness, the egg boasts many vitamins and minerals. Few foods are as digestible, contain as few calories, and cost as little per unit weight.[8]

Eggs make a great snack or main meal. Consider having eggs for dinner when you are in a hurry or want a light meal. Really fresh eggs have not formed an air pocket inside and, when hard-boiled, the shell will be more difficult to remove.

What About the Chickens?

MATTHEW 23:37 ***O Jerusalem, Jerusalem, the one who kills the prophets and stones those who are sent to her! How often I wanted to gather your children together, as a hen gathers her chicks under her wings, but you were not willing!*** **(NKJV)**

muscle
the part of the animal that is eaten

In Bible times many people were in touch with the elements and their surroundings. Examples of animals were used for clarification in many stories. This passage from Matthew 23:37 uses the example of a hen gathering her chicks under her wings to give the all-encompassing feeling of how God wants to shelter the people spoken to here.

Grain-fed, chemical-free, antibiotic-free chickens and eggs are the best kinds to eat. There is much controversy about whether the skin on chickens and the yolks of eggs are okay to eat. Research has shown that chicken with and without the skin has about the same health benefits. There is a lot more fat in and around the skin, so if you are watching your fat intake, you will have to count this extra fat. For example, 100 grams of roasted white-meat chicken without the skin has 173 kilocalories and 4.5 grams of fat, while 100 grams of roasted white-meat chicken with the skin has 222 kilocalories and 10.85 grams of fat. Just remember that the measurement in grams is a weight measurement and muscle weighs more than fat, so you are getting more fat per weight than you would **muscle** for the same weight.

One Picture's Worth a Thousand Words

Look at the pyramids at the beginning of this chapter (Illustration #23). You will see that poultry and eggs have a small section. Red meats have an even smaller section. Poultry, which includes chicken, duck, geese, and other birds, can be eaten a few times a week. Eggs, which include scrambled, boiled, or poached, as well as eggs used in cooking (in baked goods, as a thickening agent in sauces, and in custards—both sweet and savory), can be eaten a few times a week. Many foods, like ice cream and muffins, have eggs hidden in them.

unclean
Leviticus 11:1–8; Deuteronomy 14:7–8. 12–19

rock hyrax
a rabbit-sized mammal, resembling a guinea pig, whose closest relative is the elephant

Keep It Clean

DEUTERONOMY 14:4–8 *These are the animals which you may eat: the ox, the sheep, the goat, the deer, the gazelle, the roe deer, the wild goat, the mountain goat, the antelope, and the mountain sheep. And you may eat every animal with cloven hooves, having the hoof split into two parts, and that chews the cud, among the animals. Nevertheless, of those that chew the cud or have cloven hooves, you shall not eat, such as these: the camel, the hare, and the* ***rock hyrax****; for they chew the cud but do not have cloven hooves; they are unclean for you. Also the swine is unclean for you, because it has cloven hooves, yet does not chew the cud; you shall not eat their flesh or touch their dead carcasses. (NKJV)*

The Israelites were told not to eat hard fat, blood, or certain meats. These meats were considered to be unclean for a variety of reasons. They were also not to eat anything found dead—no roadkill.

Are These Rules for You?

ACTS 10:10–15 *Then he became very hungry and wanted to eat; but while they made ready, he fell into a trance and saw heaven opened and an object like a great sheet bound at the four corners, descending to him and let down to the earth. In it were all kinds of four-footed animals of the earth, wild beasts, creeping things, and birds of the air. And a voice came to him, "Rise, Peter; kill and eat." But Peter said, "Not so, Lord! For I have never eaten anything common or unclean." And a voice spoke to him again the second time, "What God has cleansed you must not call common." (NKJV)*

There are those who say that everyone should be a vegetarian, there are those who say we should follow the clean and unclean food instructions of Deuteronomy and Leviticus, and there are those who say everyone should do neither of these choices. All base their ideas on something they have read in the Bible. It is up to you to follow these rules in the way that you feel comfortable.

Let me say, however, that there are often several reasons for not eating animals the Old Testament calls unclean. They might be carriers of diseases or fleas that bring the plague, they might eat rotting foods that could carry bacteria or viruses with them, or they may simply be high in fat. I have known many people who do not eat fish without scales and fins such as shrimp and lobster, nor would they eat pork. They were healthy without them. You may have known any number of people who eat pork and lobster, and they also are healthy.

You Are the Temple of God

> **1 Corinthians 3:16–17** ***Do you not know that you are the temple of God and that the Spirit of God dwells in you? If anyone defiles the temple of God, God will destroy him. For the temple of God is holy, which temple you are.*** *(NKJV)*

A good way to honor God is to keep your body healthy. Putting foods or items into your body that are not healthy for you is definitely defilement. We have discussed many so-called foods that can harm a human body. Those are the items that are unclean and unhealthy. Soft drinks, sugarcoated and sugar-filled products, white flour, white rice, and foods containing chemicals such as MSG and preservatives such as BHT and BHA are not good for your body. Smoked foods, preserved food, processed foods—all these terms should be a red flag to let you know to stay away from them. Look at the foods you eat. Are they defiling your body, creating high cholesterol, giving you diabetes or heart disease? We know that smoking tobacco can cause lung cancers and emphysema, so that is surely defilement to your body. Do not drink, smoke, or eat anything that is going to cause your body to experience poor health. This passage is given to let us know that we can have good and vital health if we don't defile our bodies with junk and garbage that can cause damage.

Refined and processed foods are never good for your health, so don't eat them.

Chapter Wrap-Up

- God prohibited the Israelites from eating the hard fat found around the organs. (Leviticus 3:14–17)
- The hard fat and all visible fat on meat was to be burnt as an offering that would please God. (Leviticus 3:14–17)
- Chicken and eggs do have a place in a healthy diet and can even be part of a reduced-fat diet for weight loss.
- Nutritionists recommend that 15 to 20 percent of your calories come from fat and that 15 to 20 percent come from proteins.
- The rest of your calories should come from the carbohydrates in whole grains, vegetables, and fruits. This is about the same percentage as in the Bible diet.
- The New Testament says that it isn't necessary anymore to be concerned with the clean and unclean foods. (Acts 10:10–15)

Study Questions

1. Why does the Bible say all the fat belongs to the Lord?
2. Which fats were prohibited to the Israelites, and where do you find these fats in our foods today?
3. Why don't we just quit eating fat altogether?
4. What does the Bible diet say about eating eggs and poultry, and when should we eat them?
5. Which foods are to be eaten a few times a week? Are you eating more of them than you need to? Are you willing to cut back to be healthier? When do you pledge to do this?
6. Which foods in your diet are considered clean, and which foods in your diet are considered unclean? Does it matter?

Chapter 10: Sweets, Salt, Water, and Wine

Chapter Highlights:
- **Land of Milk and Honey**
- **Salt in the Bible Diet**
- **Water: Liquid of Life**
- **Wine in the Mediterranean Diet**

Let's Get Started

Sweets and alcohol are the last two food sections of the Mediterranean diet pyramid (see Illustration #24). The Mediterranean diet allows sweets to be eaten a few times per week, but this does not necessarily mean what you think it means, as you will see. Salt and water are essentials of life, so they must also be covered. Last, alcohol is a tricky subject, but after reading this chapter, you will have a better understanding of how it fit into the diet of people in Bible times, and how it should fit into yours.

carob pods
high-fiber, beanlike pods grown on trees of the locust family in the Middle East; also called "St. John's bread" after John the Baptist

reduced
when water added during pressing is boiled off, reducing the volume

Land of Milk and Honey

EXODUS 3:8 ***So I have come down to deliver them out of the hand of the Egyptians, and to bring them up from that land to a good and large land, to a land flowing with milk and honey, to the place of the Canaanites and the Hittites and the Amorites and the Perizzites and the Hivites and the Jebusites.*** *(NKJV)*

There are two kinds of honey mentioned in the Bible. One is the kind you know of that comes from honeybees and the honeycomb. The second is "honey" that comes from a syrup of fruits or **carob pods**. Date honey is made from **reduced**, pressed dates, just like maple syrup is the boiled or reduced sap of maple trees. It is boiled or just set out in the sun to allow some of the liquid to evaporate. Date honey and carob honey (or carob syrup) are still popular in the Middle East.

The most interesting thing about the way Mediterranean people have been eating this sweet "honey" since Bible times is that they always have it with some form of protein such as milk. This kind of honey, as well as honey from bees, is little more than carbohydrates. Honey contains so little protein, it can't be measured. It also contains no fat. Eating straight carbohydrates was not done in Bible times, and it shouldn't be done today either. To redress the situation, Middle Easterners always have milk, or some other form of

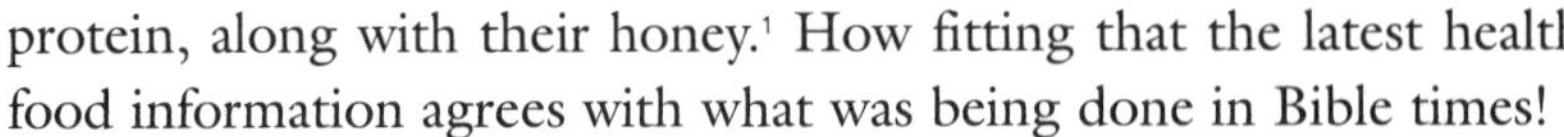

protein, along with their honey.[1] How fitting that the latest health food information agrees with what was being done in Bible times!

Milk and Honey: A Marvelous Match

milk and honey
Leviticus 20:24;
Numbers 13:27;
Deuteronomy 6:3;
Joshua 5:6;
Jeremiah 11:5;
Ezekiel 20:6

PSALM 19:10 ***More to be desired are they than gold, yea, than much fine gold; sweeter also than honey and the honeycomb.*** *(NKJV)*

Psalm 19:10 compares the sweetness of honey, which is very sweet, with the sweetness of the Lord's revealed laws, which are even sweeter than honey. God's laws were really sweet to them and should be to you as well.

Honey can be eaten directly from the honeycomb. This unrefined honey is from honeybees and is very sweet, a little bit sweeter than honey made from dates might be. Protein and sweets together are the newest health food necessity. Because North Americans have been eating so many refined sugars and carbohydrates over the years, there is an epidemic of people who react very quickly to sugar. These people find that they should always eat some form of protein with fruit or other sweets. Generally, nutritionists suggest that protein (from low-fat cheese or nuts) be eaten with fruits and other sugars to avoid the sudden rush of blood sugar. People in Bible times tried to avoid the very same sort of reaction by having milk and honey together.

This is why the many Bible references to a "land of milk and honey" meant the place mentioned would be paradise—nobody would get sugar rushes or other health problems from eating honey by itself because there would also be milk products like cheese and yogurt to balance the honey, since honey (and honey from the comb) was very sweet. A place with both would be a really excellent place to live; it would have all the essential foods provided by God.

Illustration #24
A Well-Balanced Meal with Dessert—Note how large the portion of vegetables is and how small the portions of meat and dessert are.

what others say

Don Colbert, M.D.

Perhaps because it is so sweet, honey is a major symbol for the abundance of God's blessings in the Bible. Instead of processed sugar, people in Bible times used natural honey as a sweetener or ate the honeyed pulps of fresh fruit.[2]

Sweets in the Mediterranean Diet

Sweets, other than fruit, are allowed when you are following the Mediterranean diet or Bible diet (unless you react to sweets, that is). It is best to train your taste buds to want fruits of some kind when you want something sweet, rather than refined sugar. The more complex the sugar is, the slower it enters your bloodstream; and the slower it enters your bloodstream, the less likely you are to have a "sugar rush." If you want to have a muffin, for example, bake your own out of whole grain flours. This way you will be able to monitor the amount of sugar you are getting.

They Don't Make 'Em Like They Used To

Until about the 1970s, muffins were considered a healthy food. A dozen muffins made with two and a half cups of flour had two tablespoons of sugar, and so they were considered healthy snacks. Then came the muffin popularity, and stores that sold muffins popped up everywhere. In order to sell enough to make it a viable business, they added more sugar. Recipes for homemade muffins are being influenced too. Nowadays, a recipe for a dozen homemade muffins calls for one cup of sugar. This is indicative of how the taste for sweets has really grown in North America. Don't believe any of the estimates about how much sugar the average person consumes in a year; most estimates are far behind the actual consumption. Sugar consumption has changed all over North America. In the 1940s and 1950s, for example, schools gave children snacks of graham crackers and milk, or fruit. Now they serve soft drinks in the schools. Soft drink companies are even paying for school equipment (like basketball hoops and team scoreboards) and putting soft drink machines in the schools. Many schoolchildren consume five soft drinks a day on the average.

Trend Reversed

Many schools have heard the news of the health problems of sugar and soft drinks, and they are changing. Some school boards are even banning soft drinks and replacing them with fruit drinks and fresh fruit. This is because many parents and nutritionists spoke out against so much sugar in schools. If your neighborhood schools still allow sugar-laden soft drinks, coffee, or burgers and fries, take a stand and help change this for your children.

If You Know What's Good for You . . .

> ISAIAH 55:2 ***Why do you spend money for what is not bread, and your wages for what does not satisfy? Listen carefully to Me, and eat what is good, and let your soul delight itself in abundance.*** *(NKJV)*

God designed your body to function from the fuel in whole grains, fruits, vegetables, and proteins. Man designed the refined foods that so many people eat today, like sugary snacks, white-flour breads, and soft drinks. Do you spend your money on white bread, which is not really nutritious because it isn't made from whole grains? Do you eat mostly the foods that are good? Too many people take the foods that God designed for human bodies and change them in such a way that they are causing countless health problems. There are many foods that fit into this category: refined grains, refined sugars, margarine and other hydrogenated fats, and processed foods filled with unhealthy fats and chemicals.

Sugar by Any Other Name

Sugar has a lot of different names. Look for these on products that you buy: sucrose, dextrose, fructose, maltose, corn syrup, brown sugar, honey, and high-fructose corn syrup. You will be getting sugar in products with those ingredients. The more natural sugars are fruit juice, honey, brown rice syrup, dehydrated cane juice, evaporated cane juice, barley malt syrup, and fruit purées. The more natural sugars are not refined, so they contain the B vitamins and minerals in the original food. The sugar source in its natural state has fiber in it as well. B vitamins, minerals, and fiber are all used to help your body assimilate the sweet part efficiently. When sugar is refined and the vitamins, minerals, and fiber are removed, it is more difficult for your body to handle.

There are many brands of natural foods that contain **organic** cane sugar or **dehydrated cane juice**, which contains less sugar, and therefore less sweetness, and no chemicals or additives. Even my local supermarket carries several brands of sorbet, ice cream, and sherbet made with whole sugar.

There are two kinds of carbohydrates: simple and complex. Simple carbohydrates are often called simple sugars. They are fructose (fruit sugar), sucrose (table sugar), and lactose (milk sugar). Complex carbohydrates are found in vegetables, whole grains, dried peas, and dried beans. Both sugars are converted into **glucose** in your body. The simple sugars go directly into your bloodstream, causing a rise in blood sugar. The complex carbohydrates are called "slow release" because they release sugar more slowly than simple sugars do.

organic
grown without pesticides or artificial fertilizers

dehydrated cane juice
dried juice of the sugar cane plant

glucose
the sugar that fuels your body and brain

insulin resistance
Body cells are unresponsive to insulin.

Is Sugar Bad for You?

Natural sugar in moderate or low doses, as prescribed by the Mediterranean diet, along with a low animal-fat, natural diet, is not bad for you. What is bad for you is a diet with very little nutrients, very little whole foods, lots of stimulants like caffeine and nicotine, lots of sugar, and no vegetables, especially no green vegetables. Sugar is acid-forming and can throw off the pH balance in your body, creating an acidic condition that can lead to many disease states.

what others say

Joyce Meyer

For years I was caught in the trap of not eating until mid-afternoon. I'd spend those days drinking coffee, smoking cigarettes, and in the evening eating ravenously. And I wondered why I never lost weight and felt bad all the time.[3]

Carbohydrates and Syndrome X

Syndrome X, one of the latest diseases to come along in medicine, was first written about in 1988. Syndrome X is also called **insulin resistance** syndrome. Many people who have syndrome X develop

NIDDM
non-insulin-dependent diabetes mellitus, diabetes that doesn't require the person to take insulin either orally or by injection

hyperlipidaemia
high blood fats

hypertension
high blood pressure

obesity
condition of being overweight

cardiovascular disease
disease of the heart and/or circulatory system

NIDDM later. Syndrome X is characterized by **hyperlipidaemia**, **hypertension**, **obesity**, **cardiovascular disease**, and insulin resistance.[4] Much research has been done on syndrome X and diet over the last six years, and most of the results point to a high-fat, refined-sugar diet as being partly responsible for the syndrome.[5] Insulin resistance has become a predictor for cardiovascular disease[6] and coronary artery disease.[7] Syndrome X is present even in children as young as nine years old. In one study, a program that used a special diet and exercise program proved to be the best treatment, but most of the children were not eager to comply with this program even though it could prevent major disease symptoms.[8] A low-fat, complex-carbohydrate diet, much like the Bible diet, was found to be the most effective treatment for syndrome X.

what others say

Reginald Cherry, M.D.

Fiber is turning out to be a major factor used to lower blood sugar.[9]

It's Simple: Food = Energy

ISAIAH 44:12 *He is hungry, and his strength fails; he drinks no water and is faint.* (NKJV)

Food supplies the energy to run your body. If you eat no food, you will have no energy. If you get hungry and don't eat, you'll lose your strength. It's as simple as that! If you follow the Mediterranean diet, you will have strength, energy, and be on the path to a healthy life. The more you eat denatured or refined foods, the more you will have low energy, loss of strength, and diseases that might have been prevented with a more appropriate lifestyle.

How Can I Tell What's Bad for Me?

By keeping a log you can easily tell what you are doing right or wrong in your diet. Write down what you eat and when you eat it. Write down how you feel. After a week or so you should begin to see some patterns.

Once you can assess your lifestyle and your energy levels, you can pretty much see what you are doing right or wrong.

Questions to Ask Yourself

- Did I eat breakfast?
- Did I eat lunch?
- Did I get tired?
- Did I have a mid-morning or mid-afternoon slump?
- Was I too tired to fix dinner at the end of the day?
- Did I lose my temper?
- Did I crave anything with sugar, carbohydrates, alcohol, caffeine, or nicotine?
- Did I want or have a candy bar or coffee to "perk me up"?
- Did cheese give me a headache?
- Did I have raw vegetables?

If you answered no to all but the last one, you really need to change your lifestyle to follow the recommendations in this book. If you answered yes to the last question, you are doing a good job in your lifestyle.

Salt in the Bible Diet

MATTHEW 5:13 ***You are the salt of the earth; but if the salt loses its flavor, how shall it be seasoned? It is then good for nothing but to be thrown out and trampled underfoot by men.*** *(NKJV)*

Although salt is used in the Bible many times to mean something essential or stable, it does not have a section on the Mediterranean diet pyramid. Salt is to be used in small amounts, and should never be used during cooking. This means you can add small amounts of salt to your food at the table but not on a regular basis. You will want to keep away from processed foods that are typically high in salt, sugar, and hydrogenated fats. These refined and processed foods are not part of a healthy diet anyway. Stick to fresh vegetables, raw or lightly steamed; small amounts of cheese or yogurt; broiled, baked, or poached fish; olive oil as a dressing; beans; peas; tofu; nuts; and fresh or dried fruits for your daily diet. This will automatically give you a low-salt diet. Only the cheese, and perhaps the yogurt, is likely to contain salt.

brine
liquid with preservatives and pickling agents

natural practicing doctors
doctors who use natural methods first and drugs as a last resort

edema
water retention

How Salty?

Job 6:6 ***Can flavorless food be eaten without salt? Or is there any taste in the white of an egg?*** *(NKJV)*

In Bible times salt was the main preservative of fish and meat. For hundreds of years salt has often been an ingredient of the **brine** used in meat-smoking processes. Recently, in the last fifty years or so, salt has become an addiction for many people. You've probably seen people put salt on their food even before tasting it. They know there will never be enough salt for them. Perhaps you are one of these people. Many women are addicted to salt and prefer salt over sugar any day. Most **natural practicing doctors** will tell you that when you have either exhausted or overactive adrenal glands, you will have low blood pressure, and you will crave salt. You might also crave salt if you are low in iodine, because most salt has iodine added to it. For many people, salt is their only source of iodine.

what others say

Jordan Rubin

Extraordinary foods are those that God created for us to eat: Celtic sea salt, RealSalt, sea salt.[10]

How Much Can You Have?

You need some salt in your diet, because it is a valuable mineral that will help keep the fluid balanced in your body. It is only when you start to take in too much that it becomes a problem. Sodium chloride, regular table salt, is also useful to maintain normal stomach, nerve, and muscle functions. Excessive sodium intake can lead to **edema**, high blood pressure, potassium deficiency, and liver and kidney disease.

Not All Salt Is the Same

Not all salt is the same. The ordinary table salt that most of us eat is too refined; it lacks the minerals we need. Also, additives and preservatives are added to prevent caking; dextrose is even added to improve flavor. About half of all table salt is supplemented with potassium iodide, which wards off goiter. Whole, natural salt like

RealSalt contains fifty naturally occurring trace minerals like calcium, potassium, sulfur, magnesium, iron, phosphorus, manganese, copper, iodine, and zinc. Celtic Sea Salt is another form of whole, real salt that contains the minerals that are supposed to be there.

The sodium found in salt is an essential nutrient. Sodium, together with calcium, magnesium, and potassium, helps regulate the body's metabolism. In combination with potassium, it regulates the acid-alkaline balance in our blood and is also necessary for proper muscle functioning. When we don't get enough sodium chloride, we experience muscle cramps, dizziness, exhaustion, and, in extreme cases, convulsions and death. Salt is essential to our well-being. Salt helps maintain the normal volume of blood in the body and also helps keep the correct balance of water in and around the cells and tissues. It is also necessary for the formation and proper function of nerve fibers, which carry impulses to and from the brain, and plays an important part in the digestion of food and is essential in making the heart beat correctly. Sodium holds water in and postassium releases it; this goes on all day and night long in a body that has the correct balance of sodium and potassium. If you have more sodium than potassium, you will have water retention. If your salt source is balanced between sodium and potassium, there should be no water retention.

In the 1950s, most hot places in the United States like Texas had salt machines for newcomers to get salt tablets to keep from losing so much water due to perspiration that they became dehydrated. In hot climents like in the desert in India, people eat salty nuts and salty soup to keep from becoming dehydrated. Now we drink plenty of water to keep from becoming dehydrated instead of taking salt tablets.

Should You Cut Back?

In a study done with elderly people, many people who did not have a history of hypertension, but had a high-sodium intake, had strokes.[11] Because this was the case, it was suggested that all elderly people evaluate the amount of salt in their diets and reduce any excess intake. This would mean not using salt in cooking and adding very little to food at the table. It would also mean eliminating those foods high in salt such as bacon, ham, potato chips or pretzels, and using sodium-reduced crackers, juices, and salad dressings when possible. Always consult with your doctor if you are planning to make

mouth breathing regularly breathing through your mouth instead of your nose

some dietary changes. If you suspect that you are eating too much salt or sugar, have your doctor prescribe a visit with a nutritionist or dietitian who can evaluate your diet.

> **what others say**
>
> **Pamela Smith, R.D.**
>
> Once your fluid stores drop below a certain level, your thirst mechanism cuts off altogether. What turns on is a desire for salt—or salty foods. Because extra sodium holds more fluids in the body, the salt craving is a survival mechanism to slow life-threatening dehydration.[12]

What's It Taste Like?

Many habits that you may have can dull your taste buds. Drinking very hot or very cold liquids, eating very hot or very cold foods, eating spicy-hot foods, smoking cigarettes, **mouth breathing**, low zinc in your diet, and B vitamin deficiencies all can contribute to some part of your mouth or tongue becoming unable to taste well. There are five basic tastes: salty, sweet, bitter, pungent, and sour. Each taste is experienced in a different place on your tongue. If you have desensitized your tongue and/or your taste buds, you may want to add enough salt so that you can taste it, when really you are adding too much.

Test yourself out. Ask a child to taste some of your food, before you add salt, and get his or her reaction. Then you taste it. Next add salt until it is the taste you like and ask the child to taste it again. Note the child's reaction. Did he or she think it was too salty the way you like it? Children are often sensitive to strong tastes because they have not yet engaged in habits that would destroy their sense of taste.

> **what others say**
>
> **Kenneth H. Cooper, M.D.**
>
> People who have high blood pressure should severely restrict their salt intake. One reason for this restriction is that a number of problems have been linked to high salt intake, including loss of calcium and bone deterioration, stroke, heart enlargement, kidney stones, and asthma.[13]

Salt sensitivity and insulin resistance are often related in both hypertensives and nonhypertensives. In fact, one study even suggested that salt sensitivity actually contributed to insulin resistance, and that this could lead to cardiovascular disease.[14] This finding would suggest that everybody should restrict their salt intake to the lowest required amount. Give up the salty snacks! Give up adding salt to store-bought foods, because they are already high in salt. Use reduced-salt items when appropriate and eat more potassium-rich vegetables and fruits, such as bananas, potatoes, red and green peppers, and tomatoes.

Water: Liquid of Life

> **1 Samuel 30:11–12** ***Then they found an Egyptian in the field, and brought him to David; and they gave him bread and he ate, and they let him drink water. And they gave him a piece of a cake of figs and two clusters of raisins. So when he had eaten, his strength came back to him; for he had eaten no bread nor drunk water for three days and three nights.*** *(NKJV)*

Water makes up a large percentage of your body weight and volume. There are many figures about how much of a human body is water, somewhere between 70 and 90 percent. Different people have different percentages of their bodies made up of water. Babies have the most, as a newborn's weight is about 78 percent water. By one year of age, however, that amount drops to about 65 percent. In adult men, about 60 percent of their bodies are water. In adult women, about 55 percent of their bodies are water. Fat men also have a lower percentage of water than thin men. Without water you will dry up, you will be dehydrated. That is what happened to the Egyptian in the passage from 1 Samuel; he was dehydrated. You can tell you are dehydrated if you have apathy, confusion, nausea, and fatigue.

These same symptoms can also occur if you have had too much water. The official name for this condition is *hyponatremia*. Although some individuals show no symptoms at all, if untreated, hyponatremia can lead to coma and even death. So don't overdrink liquids; check with your doctor to get confirmation of how much water you need for your activity and weather needs.

what others say

Jordan Rubin

Only God could come up with a calorie-free and sugar-free substance that regulates body temperature, carries nutrients and oxygen to the cells, cushions joints, protects organs and tissues, removes toxins, and maintains strength and endurance. Water makes up 92 percent of your blood plasma and 50 percent of everything else in the body. [15]

How Much Should You Drink?

Eight 8-ounce glasses is the least amount of water you should drink every day. There are weight-loss plans that suggest drinking a gallon of water every day, but that is very difficult to do. As soon as you get up in the morning, drink a large glass of fresh water. Always let the water run for a while, so that you aren't drinking water that was in the pipes overnight. Many of the pipes used in modern kitchens can allow water to leach out chemicals that you don't want to be drinking if water is left standing in the pipes. Before you go to bed, drink a large glass of water. That makes two of the required eight glasses of water. Drink an additional glass between each meal; that's three more. Then drink at other times during the day. I always carry a bottle of water with me in my purse or car. You can always stop at a convenience store and purchase a bottle of fresh water, so there is no excuse for not having water. The more you drink, the better you will feel!

And If You Don't Drink It?

GENESIS 21:19 ***Then God opened her eyes, and she saw a well of water. And she went and filled the skin with water, and gave the lad a drink.*** *(NKJV)*

Your body will respond to low water levels in a lot of ways—lower energy and reduced performance, inability to concentrate, and irritability, just to name a few. Please don't wait until you feel thirsty to drink. By then you really need the water; you might even be dehydrated already.

Drink regularly! Mountain bikers and hikers know that it is essential to drink whether they are thirsty or not, especially when exercising. Because of this they always carry water so that they can drink on a schedule. When doing any exercise that might make you sweat and, therefore, lose water, it is essential to drink frequently before, during, and after. If you work out in a gym or do anything aerobic, you need more water. If you take walks, you need more water. Every day you require at least eight 8-ounce glasses of water; when you exercise, you need even more.

Getting Up at Night

If you find yourself getting up at night to urinate, you will want to have a thorough checkup at your family doctor. Generally, having to urinate is not the real reason people get up at night. There are many health problems that might be diagnosed early, if you mention getting up at night to urinate to your doctor.

Wine Is a Mocker!

PROVERBS 20:1 ***Wine is a mocker, strong drink is a brawler, and whoever is led astray by it is not wise.*** *(NKJV)*

Yes, wine and beer have been leading people astray for a long time. Even in Bible times people were picking fights because they drank too much wine or beer. All through the Bible there are warnings against being drunk. Much research has been published lately showing the health benefits of drinking wine. However, the same benefits can come from other fruits and vegetable juices just as well. You can also drink nonalcoholic wine. If you do, select a nonalcoholic red wine, which contains beneficial substances.

what others say

Don Colbert, M.D.

There are several health alternatives you should consider in place of alcohol. One alternative is to take an extract of the beneficial properties of red wine in supplement form, which does not contain alcohol.[16]

Alcohol and B Vitamins

Wine and other alcohol misuse can produce deficiencies of the B vitamins, especially B_1 and B_3. Low amounts of vitamin B_2 have been associated with a desire to drink wine or other alcoholic beverages. During the early days of vitamin therapy, and again today, many natural practicing doctors treat alcoholics with injections of B vitamins, especially B_2, because it makes people lose their taste for alcohol.[17]

Is It the Same Wine?

In Bible times there were three different kinds of wine used. One was very high in alcohol and was called strong drink, similar to the brandy we have today. The second type was very weak and was generally diluted, quickly fermented, and called new wine. The most common wine mentioned in the Bible is a third type, which was made from boiling grape juice down into a heavy syrup. This allowed the grape juice to be preserved in a day when refrigeration was unknown. The New Testament word for this kind of wine is *oinos*, and the word simply means "juice of grapes." This syrup would be reconstituted with water to make a beverage, and that made it nearly nonalcoholic.

Even the strong alcoholic wine made in biblical times was diluted with water as much as twenty-to-one before drinking. Generally, naturally fermented wine has an alcohol content of 11 percent. The strongest wine normally consumed in Bible times was mixed in a three-to-one water/wine ratio and meant that the wine would have an alcohol content of around 2.75 percent. In many areas of the ancient world, water supplies were contaminated with bacteria. Mixing wine with water actually helped purify the water and made it fit to drink.

All the Benefits, None of the Hassle

EPHESIANS 5:18 ***And do not be drunk with wine, in which is dissipation; but be filled with the Spirit.*** *(NKJV)*

Although there are many passages in the Bible where people drink wine, there are many passages warning against getting drunk. Many companies produce wine without alcohol. The benefits of wine come from the skins and seeds, not from the alcohol. This is why so many health food stores sell capsules of grape seed and grape skin extract—they are powerful antioxidants! If you want to experience how wine can be of benefit to your health, you can easily purchase one of these products, which contain all the benefits of wine without the alcohol. Or, better yet, eat grapes—skins, seeds, and fruit.

Wine in the Mediterranean Diet

Although there aren't the same problems with sanitation in North America that existed in the Mediterranean in Bible times, there are many health reasons for not drinking wine. Of course there is the problem with getting drunk, which is very bad for your body and mind. If you have *Candida albicans* or other problems with yeast and mold, you must never touch wine or beer. If you have a blood-sugar problem, you must never touch wine or beer. You do not have to drink wine in order to follow the Mediterranean diet; grape juice contains the same healthful properties as wine without being fermented. There are many varieties of superb grape juice that can be festive, and often they are organic so there are no additives. We have refrigeration so we don't need to ferment the grape juice.

Chapter Wrap-Up

- The Bible has many references to the land of milk and honey. It was a phrase that meant the land was rich and balanced. (Exodus 3:8)
- Sweets are not forbidden on the Mediterranean diet/Bible diet. It is suggested they be eaten a maximum of a few times per week. Eating fruit is okay anytime.
- Salt was essential in Bible times, but it is not as essential today because we consume it in so many different vegetables. For some people salt causes health problems. (Matthew 5:13)
- Water is the most essential liquid in any diet; six to eight glasses should be drunk each day. (Isaiah 44:12)
- Wine is not an essential food for modern people. Although wine is part of the Mediterranean diet, experts concede it is not the alcohol that is the healthy part of wine; it is the bioflavins, which are also found in the skins and seeds of grapes and other fruits.

Study Questions

1. What were the different kinds of honey used in the Middle East and where did they come from? Why did they always mention milk and honey together?
2. How many sweets should we eat? Which are the best forms of sweets to eat? How will this information allow you to change your diet?
3. What health problems are attributed to eating salt and how can you reverse them? Why do you think that people could eat more salt in Bible times than we can now?
4. What is the most important liquid for health? When should you drink it? Why do you think there has been more emphasis on drinking water in the last five years?
5. When are the most important times to drink wine? What does your church say about drinking wine? How do you feel about that now?
6. What are the benefits of wine, and which foods have the equivalent nutrients?

Part Two
GOD'S WORD ON GOOD HEALTH

Chapter 11: All Food Is Clean

Chapter Highlights:
- Is It Kosher?
- Meat and Milk Together
- Safe Food Handling
- Regulations About Mildew or Plague

Let's Get Started

Chapter 9 touched on clean and unclean foods. Jews were not supposed to eat the meat or flesh of many animals, fowl, and birds.

clean and unclean
Leviticus 11:1–47

Clean land animals, the Law read, chewed their cud and had a split hoof. Unclean land animals either chewed cud but did not have a split hoof, or had a split hoof but did not chew cud. Examples of unclean animals are pigs, camels, and rabbits. Animals living in the waters that did not have fins and scales—trout, lobster, shrimp, scampi, octopus, clams, oysters, mussels—were also considered unclean. Many Jews, even today, do not eat these foods.

In the New Testament, Peter had a vision of a new way of looking at these prohibitions, as God showed him that all foods were clean. Although the clean and unclean foods were prescribed by God for spiritual reasons, scientists recently have found the unclean foods to actually be unhealthy.

Is It Kosher?

The word *kosher* is the Anglicized form of the Hebrew *kasher*, which literally means "good" or "proper," but came to indicate an item fit for ritual use. *Kashrut* is the term that means fitness for ritual use. The Hebrew word for nonkosher is *trayf*, from the word *terayfa*, or *torn*, which is taken from the commandment in Leviticus 22:24 not to eat meat that has been torn by other animals.

For those who keep kosher, observance of the dietary laws is both an opportunity for obedience to God and for preserving Jewish unity and identity.

How Do They Do It?

In order to be considered kosher, animals must be ritually slaughtered. The primary goal of ritual slaughter is to rid the animal of as

trayf
not kosher

much blood as possible, which is done by cutting the animal's throat with an extremely sharp knife with no nicks. The meat must then be kashered, or made kosher, by hanging the carcass to drain as much blood as possible. The meat must then be washed, salted, and cooked.

Are You Eating Unclean Foods?

DEUTERONOMY 14:6–10 *And you may eat every animal with cloven hooves, having the hoof split into two parts, and that chews the cud, among the animals. Nevertheless, of those that chew the cud or have cloven hooves, you shall not eat, such as these: the camel, the hare, and the rock hyrax; for they chew the cud but do not have cloven hooves; they are unclean for you. Also the swine is unclean for you, because it has cloven hooves, yet does not chew the cud; you shall not eat their flesh or touch their dead carcasses.*

These you may eat of all that are in the waters: you may eat all that have fins and scales. And whatever does not have fins and scales you shall not eat; it is unclean for you. (NKJV)

Meat and Milk Together

Meat and dairy products are not to be combined or eaten at the same meal. Although the Bible merely prohibits boiling a goat in its mother's milk, for centuries learned scholars and rabbis have interpreted this as forbidding meat and dairy to be eaten together. However, fish with dairy or eggs with dairy are permitted. *Fleishig* is the word that means "meat," and *milshig* means "made from milk or milk products." Even the smallest amounts of meat or dairy matter. Many kinds of margarine, which can contain whey, would be considered dairy products. *Pareve* is a term that means the food contains neither meat nor dairy and can therefore be eaten with either one. So foods that contain a kosher mark, and there are several, were prepared following the Jewish dietary laws. So both meat and dairy products can be kosher, but they are still not to be eaten together.

People who keep kosher at home have separate dishes, separate sinks, separate ovens, separate dishcloths and towels, and separate serving and eating utensils for meat and milk products. No food that is **trayf** is allowed into the house. That means no leftovers from a restaurant can be brought into the house unless they come from a restaurant that serves kosher food.

scavengers
animals that feed on dead or decaying matter

antibiotic-resistant
when bacteria have mutated in such a way that there is no antibiotic that will eradicate them

The unclean animals of the Old Testament are the same animals that could carry disease, harbor bacteria, or have rotted flesh inside them that would taint the meat. These animals are generally **scavengers**. In this day and age, when so many foods are becoming contaminated because of handling problems, it would be wise to avoid meats that are likely to be contaminated before or while being slaughtered. If you know where your meat is coming from and it is raised under the strictest standards, the need for concern may be less.

what others say

Dr. Mary Ruth Swope

Jesus would not have eaten pork in any form—not even barbecued or grilled on an open pit. Our favorites of baked ham, broiled pork chops, fresh pork with sauerkraut, or even the famous BLT (bacon/lettuce/tomato) sandwich would all have been "unclean" to Jesus.[1]

Blech!

Much animal meat is tainted with new contaminants that did not exist in Bible times. Generally, animal producers use these contaminants to make animals grow faster, protect them from some real or imagined infection, and to make them fatter and therefore weigh more. Many of these chemicals and additives can cause allergic reactions in people who eat the meat. They often cause other health problems, and many of them are dangerous to the environment if they are not properly taken care of.

In the last ten years or so antibiotics have been forbidden in slaughtered animals, so meat producers have stopped feeding them to animals a few days before they are sent to the killing plant. Many people feel that the overuse of antibiotics in meat and dairy products was responsible for so many people being allergic to antibiotics, especially penicillin, and that this also contributes to **antibiotic-resistant** strains of bacteria. Perhaps if meat producers and meatpackers followed God's instructions for raising, killing, and processing animals found in the Bible, we would not have this problem. One can only speculate that if modern man had not raised, killed, and processed

organically grown
grown or raised without petrochemicals

feedlot
place where cattle are sent to get fattened up before slaughter; often considered a breeding ground for diseases and ill health

petrochemicals
made from coal tar

"unclean" animals, they would not have needed to use as many antibiotics and other chemicals. Most states have laws prohibiting the use of antibiotics three days before the slaughter of animals used for eating.

what others say

Anne and David Frähm

Current practices in livestock and poultry management are producing meat products that are laden with production chemicals and drugs that undermine human health. These substances, unlike bacteria, which can be killed by cooking, remain in the animal products when consumed by humans.[2]

Where's the Beef?

Meats that are raised without the use of chemicals, antibiotics, hormones, steroids, or other growth hormones are generally called **organically grown**. Some farmers also feed their livestock organically grown food, which results in meat that is cleaner and has less contamination.

Grass-fed beef is popular because it also means that the animals have not been sent to a **feedlot**.

what others say

Jordan Rubin

Regarding the consumption of meat in your diet, I strongly urge you to eat meats that are organically raised, or designated as grass-fed or at least free-range. When these animals are fed grasses supplemented with organically grown grains, they lead healthy, happy lives and eat the foods they were meant to eat.[3]

If you are allergic to antibiotics or **petrochemicals**, consider eating only organically grown meats and dairy products.

Peter's Vision

Acts 10:9–16 ***The next day, as they went on their journey and drew near the city, Peter went up on the housetop to pray, about the sixth hour. Then he became very hungry and wanted to eat; but while they made ready, he fell into a trance and saw heaven***

opened and an object like a great sheet bound at the four corners, descending to him and let down to the earth. In it were all kinds of four-footed animals of the earth, wild beasts, creeping things, and birds of the air. And a voice came to him, "Rise, Peter; kill and eat." But Peter said, "Not so, Lord! For I have never eaten anything common or unclean." And a voice spoke to him again the second time, "What God has cleansed you must not call common." This was done three times. And the object was taken up into heaven again. *(NKJV)*

unclean
Acts 11:4–10; Matthew 15:10–11, 18

deceit
misleading people

lewdness
obscene, being preoccupied with sex and sexual desires

Peter followed the Jewish dietary laws of the time and did not eat any unclean or impure animal products. Jesus had already been teaching his followers that it was not what they ate but what they said that made them clean or unclean. This vision appeared to Peter to reinforce Jesus's teachings.

Jesus was a practicing Jew, so he followed the clean and unclean food rules, but he was more concerned with spiritual health. Jesus said that following the "rules" set out in the commandments was more important than mindlessly following rituals. He taught that all people should be more concerned with what they said and did to themselves and others than with observing conventional customs.

Jesus's Response

Mark 7:18–23 ***So He said to them, "Are you thus without understanding also? Do you not perceive that whatever enters a man from outside cannot defile him, because it does not enter his heart but his stomach, and is eliminated, thus purifying all foods?" And He said, "What comes out of a man, that defiles a man. For from within, out of the heart of men, proceed evil thoughts, adulteries, fornications, murders, thefts, covetousness, wickedness, deceit, lewdness, an evil eye, blasphemy, pride, foolishness. All these evil things come from within and defile a man."*** *(NKJV)*

You do not have to follow the rules set up for the Israelites in Old Testament times for the sake of following the rules. Jesus declared that you should be more concerned with what comes out of your mouth than with what goes into it. However, if you want to be really, really healthy, you will want to pay attention to why these foods were unclean. Scavengers eat rotting and infected foods. Scavengers were designed by God to be the garbage collectors of the world.

Many of the seafoods that were forbidden are now found to contain contaminants such as mercury, lead, dioxins, PCBs, and pesticides. The Food and Drug Administration in the United States publishes information on contaminants in fish and seafood at cfsan.fda.gov/seafood1.html. If you have any questions about the safety of any foods check this Web site: foodsafety.gov. Food safety in the United States, Canada, Australia, New Zealand, and many parts of Europe is now under the direction of the Food Codex (codexalimentarius.net).

what others say

Jordan Rubin

I strongly believe there are meats that you shouldn't eat, the meats that God called "unclean" in Leviticus and Exodus. I'm talking about pork, shrimp, and lobster, to name three of the most popular foods in America.[4]

Help, This Scares Me!

If you find this frightening, you should! There are so many sources of parasites today that it has become big business to sell potions and supplements to rid your body of them. What can you do? Stay away from any unclean foods, including spoiled foods. Eat only wholesome foods that have been raised chemical-free, and wash off your vegetables with soap and water. Include those foods and herbs in your diet that have been shown to clean out your body or kill various parasites. These foods include garlic, onions, bitter herbs, papaya seeds, pumpkin seeds, olives, olive oil, and olive leaves. Stay away from refined sugar and white flour products (they are considered garbage anyway), as they can reduce the effectiveness of your immune system. When your immune system is not functioning fully, you can be even more susceptible to parasites and illnesses. If you even suspect that you have a health problem related to your consumption of these unclean foods, please see your doctor for testing and treatment. Abdominal cramps and pain, constipation, diarrhea, fatigue, fever, flatulence, food allergies, headaches, hives, indigestion, and lower back pain are symptoms associated with parasitic infection.

This Is Confusing!

1 Timothy 4:1, 3–5 ***Now the Spirit expressly says that in latter times some will depart from the faith, . . . forbidding to marry, and commanding to abstain from foods which God created to be received with thanksgiving by those who believe and know the truth. For every creature of God is good, and nothing is to be refused if it is received with thanksgiving; for it is sanctified by the word of God and prayer.*** *(NKJV)*

Even in New Testament times there were people saying that you shouldn't eat this or that because it wasn't clean by Old Testament standards. Often people interpret this passage to mean that they shouldn't be vegetarians, since that is forbidding them from eating any meat. The Old Testament says to keep away from "unclean" animals, not meat in general, and Jesus says it doesn't matter as much as how you act toward others.

Pray a Lot

Colossians 2:16 ***So let no one judge you in food or in drink.*** *(NKJV)*

If you decide to eat these foods that are unclean or impure to Jews, just be sure to receive them with thanksgiving and pray over them. I would also suggest you eat raw or odorless garlic, pumpkin seeds, olive oil, and take olive leaf extract. If you have chosen to eat any foods that others find objectionable, remember that only God can judge you. It is your right to choose to eat these foods or to eat meat at all.

Just Try It

If these "unclean" foods are in your diet on a regular basis and you feel really great, don't be too concerned. However, if you eat these foods and you have headaches, unexplained muscle pain, fever, or swelling on a regular basis, or you just don't feel really great, go off them for two weeks. If you begin to notice that you feel better, stay off them. It really takes much longer to get rid of parasites, and you must see your doctor for treatment. However if the antibiotics they use to kill the bacteria in the "unclean" animals is causing you health

washing
Exodus 29:4; 40:12; Leviticus 8:6

problems, then you will notice a lifting of your energy right away. Wouldn't you rather feel great than eat something that made you feel bad?

All Food Is Clean

> ROMANS 14:20 *Do not destroy the work of God for the sake of food. All things indeed are pure, but it is evil for the man who eats with offense.* (NKJV)

It seems obvious that by the time this verse was written in Romans, the New Testament Christians were going around and around about this matter of clean and unclean foods, so I don't expect it to be solved here either.

Wash Those Hands and Feet

> EXODUS 30:18–20 *You shall also make a laver of bronze, with its base also of bronze, for washing. You shall put it between the tabernacle of meeting and the altar. And you shall put water in it, for Aaron and his sons shall wash their hands and their feet in water from it. When they go into the tabernacle of meeting, or when they come near the altar to minister, to burn an offering made by fire to the LORD, they shall wash with water, lest they die.* (NKJV)

Hand washing was both a common practice and ceremonial ritual for thirty-five hundred years after God gave these instructions to Moses. God gave Moses instructions for washing hands and feet, and for washing clothes of wool, linen, anything woven or knitted, and leather. The clothes-washing instructions were for removing contaminants and for general purification. Hand washing was for sanitation and ritual purification.

A Reason for Sadness

For many years autopsies were performed on dead bodies by doctors who left the autopsy room and went in to examine pregnant women in another hospital ward. One out of every six of these women died. The physicians thought it was due to unrelenting constipation, bad air, or some other thing wrong with the women. In the 1840s, after Ignaz Semmelweis instituted a process of hand washing between the autopsies and the pelvic examinations, the death rate was one in every forty-two. After a month of the practice, the death rate was one in every eighty-four. This is most astonishing! And yet Dr. Semmelweis was ridiculed for his idea. He was shunned and eventually left the hospital in disgrace.

> **what others say**
>
> **S. I. McMillen, M.D.**
>
> Many centuries before Semmelweis, however, God gave to Moses detailed instructions on the safest method for cleansing the hands after handling the dead or the infected living. Semmelweis's method went a long way in preventing many deaths, but it would not be accepted in any hospital today.[5]

You Wash Your Hands Before?

I am really strict about hand washing. I always wash my hands after touching a dog, cat, horse, or other animal. I also wash my hands in the ladies' room before I go into the cubicle and after I come out. I often get a lot of strange looks when women see me washing and then going into the toilet. I realize that when I am out in public shopping and touching objects that an infected person could have touched, I could actually contaminate myself if I didn't wash my hands before using the toilet. Moses told Aaron to wash before and after entering the Tent of Meeting. There must be some message for everybody in this. Even though a healthy body is less susceptible to bacteria, viruses, and germs than a poorly nourished body, it is wise to follow the hand-washing rituals no matter how healthy you are!

Safe Food Handling

DEUTERONOMY 23:12–13 ***Also you shall have a place outside the camp, where you may go out; and you shall have an implement among your equipment, and when you sit down outside, you shall dig with it and turn and cover your refuse.*** *(NKJV)*

Almost weekly you see some TV special talking about the importance of hand washing in the bathroom and the kitchen. They always show the bacteria on the kitchen sponge and cutting board. In a kitchen that looks spotless, there is always the most bacteria on the cleaning rag because someone forgot to wash it out with soap and water after doing the dishes and wiping the counter. Several times a year you hear about an epidemic in a nursing home, day care, or hospital, because someone made a sandwich on a cutting board that had held raw chicken without washing it in between (see Illustration #25). We still don't have complete sanitation and safety in our houses!

Illustration #25
Cutting Board with Bleach—After cutting meat, be sure to sanitize the cutting board with a chlorine solution.

This Is Not the Same Clean

Although this chapter starts with "all food is clean," it does not mean that all food is bacteria-free. That is up to the person raising the animal, killing the animal, cleaning the animal, preparing the animal, cooking the animal, and serving the animal. It is essential to take charge of your health by frequent hand washing and by following the cleanliness rules in the Food Safety list (see page 187). As far as whether you should eat the foods declared "clean" and "unclean," that is really up to you.

Food Safety

The Food Safety and Inspection Service of the U.S. Department of Agriculture recommends:

- Hands should be washed, gloved or not, for twenty seconds before beginning preparation; after handling raw meat, poultry, seafood, or eggs; after touching animals; after using the bathroom; after changing diapers; or after blowing the nose.
- Always wash your hands, counters, equipment, utensils, and cutting boards with soap and water immediately after use.
- Counters, equipment, utensils, and cutting boards can be sanitized with a chlorine solution of one teaspoon liquid household bleach per quart of water.
- Thaw food in the refrigerator, never on the counter.

If you are interested in all of their recommendations, you may contact the USDA Meat and Poultry Hotline at 1-800-MPHOTLINE. Or go to their Web site: fsis.usda.gov.[6]

Dig a Hole

God told his people to bury their excrement. This, too, is something relatively new. You probably remember from history classes reading about people throwing human waste out of windows into the streets of Europe. A lot of the basic rules of cleanliness and sanitation that we follow today come from the Old Testament. Many people are alive today because some ancestor followed God's instructions and washed his hands and buried his excrement. Many places in the world use human excrement for fertilizer on crops. Eating fruits and vegetables fertilized this way can cause major intestinal upsets. This is one of the reasons we get "tourista" or traveler's disease in other countries. When traveling in other countries, always drink and wash with water that has been boiled or is safe bottled water.

If you are traveling to a place that has unsafe water or high levels of bacteria, it is wise to take a probiotic and prebiotic product such as Kyo-Dophilis, Primal Defense, or Super Probiotic/Prebiotic Bacteria, or drink Stonyfield Farm's Smoothie or use another yogurt product containing *l. acidophilis* and *bifidus* to provide the good bacteria to balance out the bad bacteria. There are many good dairy and soy products available with these bacteria in them, but when traveling you will need a product that doesn't require refrigeration.

> **what others say**
>
> **S. I. McMillen, M.D.**
>
> Up to the close of the eighteenth century, hygienic provisions, even in the great capitals, were quite primitive. It was the rule for excrement to be dumped into the streets, which were unpaved and filthy. Powerful stenches gripped villages and cities. It was a heyday for flies as they bred in the filth and spread intestinal diseases that killed millions. Such waste of human lives could have been prevented if Europe had only taken seriously God's provisions for freeing man of diseases. With a single sentence the Bible pointed the way to deliverance from the deadly epidemics of typhoid, cholera, and dysentery.[7]

Regulations About Mildew or Plague

LEVITICUS 14:35 ***And he who owns the house comes and tells the priest, saying, "It seems to me that there is some plague [mildew] in the house." (NKJV)***

Mildew is something that we don't think too much about, and yet various kinds of mildews and molds in houses are causing serious problems for a lot of people. God gave Moses and Aaron information about how to deal with mildew in the house and on clothes that still is useful today.

Sorry, We're Out

LEVITICUS 14:37–38 ***And he shall examine the plague; and indeed if the plague is on the walls of the house with ingrained streaks, greenish or reddish, which appear to be deep in the wall, then the priest shall go out of the house, to the door of the house, and shut up the house seven days. (NKJV)***

When mildew was found, people were to tell the priest and leave the house so he could come in and examine it. If someone was in the house, he may be declared unclean. When the priest did find mildew, he closed up the house for seven days. If the mildew had spread by the time the priest returned, the house had to be cleaned by either scraping off the mildew and even the plaster, or replacing the contaminated stones with clean ones. If the mildew returned, the entire house had to be torn down and replaced. All the contaminated matter was to be removed and placed in a designated place outside of town.

sick building syndrome
illnesses that develop because impure air is allowed to circulate from room to room

alternaria
a common mold

sick building syndrome symptoms
headaches, coughing, sinus problems, stomachaches, and rashes

what others say

S. I. McMillen, M.D.

Could submitting to a code of "restrictive" rules lead to freedom from sicknesses? Could this promise remain pertinent even in the twentieth century? Yes! Medical science is still discovering how obedience to the ancient prescriptions saved the primitive Hebrews from the scourges of epidemic plagues; and medical research is constantly proving the timeless potency of the divine prescription for modern diseases.[8]

Is Your Home Dangerous?

Should the priest be coming to your home, daycare center, or office to look for mildew? The most common illnesses associated with mildew or mold in the home or workplace are asthma, wheezing, headaches, and **sick building syndrome**. Children with mold allergies often develop persistent coldlike symptoms in a moldy environment.[9] In a recent study, children with asthma were very susceptible to **alternaria** even in the desert.[10] The indoor pollution and **sick building syndrome symptoms** were often found to be caused by one or more of three common molds—aspergillus, cladosporium, and penicillium. These microfungi were most prevalent in damp buildings and buildings with basements, especially basements that had standing water.[11] In the places that had air-conditioning, the symptoms were not as great as they were in non-air-conditioned places.

If more schools followed God's instructions about mold and mildew, perhaps there would be less absenteeism and better grades. If children are being subjected to mold and mildew at day care or school, they could be developing reactions that would make it difficult to concentrate, stay awake, or be alert. It might also influence their health by compromising their immune systems, allowing them to be more susceptible to colds, the flu, asthma, or bronchitis.

scourge pestilence

Pulmonary Hemosiderosis bleeding in the lungs

mycotoxins poisonous substances produced by a fungus or mold

what others say

Francisco Contreras, M.D.

Our homes often lack adequate ventilation so that pure air is limited and harmful elements can reach very high levels. The danger represented by indoor contaminants is aggravated by the lack of information about the problem.[12]

Stachybotrys: The New Scourge?

A new **scourge** has been causing severe health problems and even death in many areas of the country, especially to young infants. It is a mold called *Stachybotrys*, which grows on wood or paper that has gotten wet. It is generally black (though not all black mold is *Stachybotrys*) and slimy and often has white edges. This mold is causing **Pulmonary Hemosiderosis**. Infants and children as well as adults around the country are becoming very ill and even dying from the toxins this mold produces. *Stachybotrys* can also produce inflammation in the intestines, stomach, lungs, and throat, and can suppress the immune system.[13] If you suspect that you have this mold, ask the health department to check it and call in some professional help to clean it up.

Most walls are made of plaster that is covered with paper; this is called wallboard or plasterboard. Ceiling tiles made of cellulose, newspapers, cardboard boxes, wall paneling, and cotton items are possible places for this mold to grow if they remain wet for at least a week.

What Can You Do?

Always keep your house, office, and school areas clean and free from mildew, mold, and other fungi. Use approved air cleaners, air conditioners, and dehumidifiers. If there is water damage, clean it up immediately; seek professional help to do this if the damaged area is large. Some studies have shown that raw garlic, onions, and green onions can inhibit the growth of aspergillus, so you might want to be sure you are eating these foods if you come into contact with mildew or mold.[14] The best thing to do is call the board of health to inspect the mold. Then do whatever they suggest. **Mycotoxins** are found in many places where there has been water damage, and most insurance companies will give you the names of fire and water cleanup professionals who can remove any contaminants from a house or business. Please have this done professionally if you have had water damage.

Follow the instructions God gave Moses and Aaron, and have the walls scraped or removed. If the water damage is very bad from a leak, flood, or other problem, you might have to tear the house down and rebuild, as God prescribed in Leviticus.

Let's Wrap It Up!

The information in this chapter might be somewhat scary. Just remember that when you live in the West, you live in one of the cleanest countries possible. There is no longer excrement in the streets. Doctors and nurses always wash their hands between seeing patients and before any surgical procedure. Your food is not allowed to be fertilized with human excrement. And even though many people are trying to separate church and state, be happy that this is one of the areas where they have not succeeded.

Chapter Wrap-Up

- God gave the Old Testament Jews special rules regarding which foods to eat, calling some foods "clean" and others "unclean." (Deuteronomy 14:6–10)
- Many of the foods that were considered "unclean" in Bible times are still not considered clean today because of parasites.
- God gave Peter a vision. All foods were to be considered "clean" because they were made clean by God. (Acts 10:9–16)
- Jesus instructed his disciples to pay more attention to what they said and how they treated people than to whether they were following rituals. (Mark 7:18–23)
- God instructed Moses and Aaron to wash their hands on many different occasions. This was a cleanliness ritual, but it was also very practical and hygienic. (Exodus 30:18–20)
- Raw meat can contaminate objects in the kitchen, and everything that touches it should be washed carefully with soap and water, preferably hot water, and chlorine bleach.

- The rules regarding mildew are just as important and necessary today as they were in Moses's time. You don't usually "call in the priest" to look at the mildew, but you should call the health department.

Study Questions

1. Name some "clean" and "unclean" animals. Name one unclean animal that many people eat. Why do you think some animals are still considered unclean today?
2. What was Peter's vision and why was he so shocked about it?
3. What two cleanliness rules did God institute that are still in use today?
4. List some things that you should do when selecting and preparing food.
5. What is the name given to foods grown without pesticides and chemicals? Do you think this is necessary?
6. What did God say to do about mold in your house?

Chapter 12: Elijah and Ahab

Chapter Highlights:
- Ahab: Eat, Eat, Eat!
- The Most Incredible Diet!
- Music Lifts and Depresses the Soul
- Gifts of Healing

Let's Get Started

Depression is not a modern disease, and using diet and nutrition is not a new way of dealing with depression. Elijah had depression and Ahab had **sullenness**. God chose nutrition and diet therapy to help these two overcome their problems. You will be able to do the same thing once you read this chapter.

sullenness
a type of depression

Elijah's Story: Does This Sound Familiar?

1 KINGS 19:3–5 ***And when he saw that, he arose and ran for his life, and went to Beersheba, which belongs to Judah, and left his servant there. But he himself went a day's journey into the wilderness, and came and sat down under a broom tree. And he prayed that he might die, and said, "It is enough! Now, LORD, take my life, for I am no better than my fathers!" Then as he lay and slept under a broom tree, suddenly an angel touched him, and said to him, "Arise and eat."*** *(NKJV)*

Have you ever felt stressed out? Have you felt that people were chasing you, after you, or bugging you to do something, be somewhere, go somewhere, when all you really wanted to do was lie down and escape in a nap? Are there times when you just wish the world would stop or go away and leave you alone? Or perhaps you wish you weren't even here to be caught up in all this running around, schedules, and frantic lifestyle. This used to be called "a case of the blues." Now experts are discovering that brain chemicals are involved. You could be suffering from depression. Look at the list of depression symptoms and see if you have any of them; you need at least three to even be considered depressed. From what we can tell, Elijah had numbers 3, 6, and 8 on this list. There are many levels of depression, and Elijah had one of them. He was so far down that he wanted God to take his life.

insomnia
chronic inability to sleep

hypersomnia
excessive sleep habits

Clinical Depression Symptoms

According to the American Psychiatric Association, in its Diagnostic and Statistical Manual of Mental Disorders (DSM-IV), there are eight primary criteria for diagnosing depression. If you have five of these eight, you are a candidate for clinical depression. If you have even three, please go directly to your family doctor and discuss this with him or her. Many disorders have some of these symptoms, so only your doctor can really diagnose if you have depression and need medication.

Depression Symptoms

- Poor appetite accompanied by weight loss, or increased appetite
- **Insomnia** or **hypersomnia**
- Physical hyperactivity or inactivity
- Loss of interest or pleasure in usual activities, or decrease in sexual drive
- Loss of energy, feelings of fatigue
- Feelings of worthlessness, self-reproach, or inappropriate guilt
- Diminished ability to think or concentrate
- Recurrent thoughts of death or suicide

You must have at least five of these eight symptoms for at least one month to be clinically depressed. If you have at least four symptoms, you are probably depressed.

Woe Is Me

1 Kings 18:46 ***He . . . ran ahead of Ahab to the entrance of Jezreel.*** *(NKJV)*

Elijah ran in front of Ahab's chariot. This appears to be symptom number three: physical hyperactivity. He also had feelings of worthlessness and self-reproach, loss of energy, hypersomnia, and thoughts of death. There also could have been a diminished ability to think and a loss of pleasure in usual activities, though it is not really clear.

Of these eight symptoms you need the presence of five to have the diagnosis of clinical depression, which means if Elijah were alive today, he would most likely be on antidepressants.

dysthymia
mild depression, used to be called "depressive personality" or "depressive neurosis"

> **what others say**
>
> **Dr. Suzan Johnson Cook**
>
> Depressed people tend to think pessimistically and are highly critical of others and themselves. Additionally, they may feel lethargic, cry frequently, over- or undereat, oversleep or suffer from insomnia, and mask symptoms with irritability and excessive worry. With all those negatives, depression could easily be called the major emotional energy drain.[1]

A Sliding Scale

Depression can range from mild feelings of depression to serious considerations of suicide. Elijah had serious considerations of suicide and even asked God to take his life. With mild depression, often called **dysthymia**, the symptoms are less serious clinically but are still very serious to the person with the symptoms.

Dysthymia Symptoms

1. Low self-esteem or lack of self-confidence
2. Pessimism, hopelessness, or despair
3. Lack of interest in ordinary pleasures and activities
4. Withdrawing from social activities
5. Fatigue or lethargy
6. Guilt or ruminating about the past
7. Irritability or excessive anger
8. Lessened productivity
9. Difficulty concentrating or making decisions

You must be depressed most of the time for at least two years and have at least three of these symptoms to have mild depression.

what others say

Dr. Suzan Johnson Cook

If you're struggling with depression, I urge you to seek help, particularly if you have entertained any suicidal thoughts. If you do see a therapist, ask God to bless your actions.[2]

Do not attempt to diagnose or treat yourself. See your doctor for an assessment, and then work with him or her on a recovery program that includes a good diet, medicinal herbs, or medications.

No Better Than His Ancestors

Even Elijah in his despair and depression was judging himself against his ancestors. He was beaten, scared, and depressed, and all he could think of to tell God was that he wasn't as good as the rest of his family, as if they were judging him. Studies of college students with depression have indicated that a lifetime exposure to interparental violence is associated with depression, anxiety, interpersonal problems, and violence. Indeed, it seems that if you have parents who are constantly making cutting remarks to each other, displaying physical and verbal aggression to each other, and even acting out physical and sexual abuse on you, you will end up no better than your ancestors. You will become just like them unless you get some help.[3] Another study showed that children with a depressed parent had a 40 percent chance of experiencing an episode of major depression before turning twenty.[4] If you have a parent with depression, no matter how minor, please see your doctor for an assessment. It is up to you to become better than your ancestors.

Depression is a real illness; it is not caused by a lack of discipline, failure, laziness, or punishment from God. Do not be ashamed if you have any of the symptoms listed here. You will have more cause for shame if you do not seek treatment than if you do. Once you are treated you will be a healthy person on medication. If you are not treated, you could be hiding at home or causing trouble in public. What a waste!

Illustration #26
God Sends an Angel to Elijah—"Suddenly an angel touched [Elijah], and said to him, 'Arise and eat'" (1 Kings 19:5 NKJV).

Angelic Help

1 Kings 19:5–8 ***Then as he lay and slept under a broom tree, suddenly an angel touched him, and said to him, "Arise and eat." Then he looked, and there by his head was a cake baked on coals, and a jar of water. So he ate and drank, and lay down again. And the angel of the Lord came back the second time, and touched him, and said, "Arise and eat, because the journey is too great for you." So he arose, and ate and drank; and he went in the strength of that food forty days and forty nights as far as Horeb, the mountain of God. (NKJV)***

When Elijah was depressed and wanted to die, God sent an angel to feed him (see Illustration #26). That's right! He sent whole grain bread baked on coals and water. Whole grain bread of wheat and/or barley contains carbohydrates, which can improve your blood-sugar levels and lift your spirits. Whole grains also contain folate or folic acid, selenium, chromium, vitamin B_3, vitamin B_6, and vitamin B_5; all of these nutrients are known to help prevent or reverse several different kinds of depression. Research conducted in Japan has shown what health food advocates have known for forty years: B vitamins can reduce postpartum depression. B vitamin–rich foods should always be eaten, but it is imperative that women eat these foods during pregnancy to avoid postpartum depression.[5] (Please do not begin to eat vast quantities of bread if you have depression, as this would be very foolish. Instead, see your doctor.)

Food: The Basic Unit of Energy

God designed your body to run off food, and a constant supply of food is needed. If you do not eat, you will not have enough fuel to operate your body or your mind. When the basic unit of fuel in your body, blood sugar, gets low, you can have depression, just like Elijah. A diet with whole grains is helpful for preventing depression. It is essential to eat frequently to avoid drops in your blood sugar. Research with both type 1 and type 2 diabetics showed that good glycemic (blood sugar) control can contribute to improvements in mood and perceptions of well-being. This holds true for anybody with fluctuating blood-sugar levels due to lifestyle and dietary choices.[6] Studies have indicated that a carbohydrate-rich and protein-poor diet is one of the best for people who have depression or a tendency toward depression.[7] The carbohydrates should be in the form of fruits, vegetables, soybeans, and whole grains to supply the nutrients essential to help overcome depression. Omega-3 polyunsaturated fatty acids can also help reverse some forms of depression.[8] Omega-3 fatty acids are found in fish and flaxseeds. (See chapters 5 and 7 for more information.)

what others say

Jim Shriner

Carbohydrates are converted to glucose [blood sugar] for energy, but if a body doesn't take in enough carbohydrates each day, it will convert protein to glucose. The brain can't function without glucose. It needs more than sixty percent of the body's blood glucose for fuel every day.[9]

The angel that appeared to Elijah was pretty smart, smart enough to bring the food God wanted Elijah to have. Are you that smart? Do you feed your body the food that God meant for you to have to be healthy? Do you eat several meals a day? Do you have a balance of lots of vegetables, fruits, whole grains, beans, nuts and seeds, olives and olive oil, dairy products, and fish? Do you eat to sustain your body? Or do you eat to satisfy a craving for sweets, fat, and salt? Does your lifestyle put you in danger of having Elijah's type of depression?

Ahab: Eat, Eat, Eat!

1 Kings 21:4–5, 7 *So Ahab went into his house sullen and displeased because of the word which Naboth the Jezreelite had spoken to him; for he had said, "I will not give you the inheritance of my fathers." And he lay down on his bed, and turned away his face, and would eat no food. But Jezebel his wife came to him, and said to him, "Why is your spirit so sullen that you eat no food?" . . . Then Jezebel his wife said to him, "You now exercise authority over Israel! Arise, eat food, and let your heart be cheerful; I will give you the vineyard of Naboth the Jezreelite." (NKJV)*

Judging from the above Scripture, the remedy for depression and ill humor seems to be eating. How interesting that two men, Elijah and Ahab, who were fighting with each other, both had health or mental problems that could have been remedied by eating. Of course, Ahab's wife wasn't exactly implying that eating would cheer him up. Rather, she was saying that he should not be sullen but take action, and since he couldn't or wouldn't, she would get him the vineyard he wanted. She knew this would cheer him up.

The Most Incredible Diet!

You probably have guessed by now that the diet Elijah and Ahab ate was the Mediterranean or Bible diet. It is a diet with small, frequent meals—generally six meals, or three small meals and three snacks. The food is in its natural state, not refined or processed, so there are only whole grains, lots of fresh vegetables and fruits, dairy products, olives and olive oil, fish, chicken and eggs, and small amounts of red meat and sweets. Eating foods in the two bottom sections of the Mediterranean diet pyramid (see Illustration #2) every day can help you get the fuel you need to stay healthy.

Eating the foods in the lower sections of the Mediterranean diet pyramid (see chapter 1) frequently during the day can help you have the fuel you need to avoid mood swings, energy slumps, and mild depression. This is a lifestyle high in vegetables, beans, and other legumes, fruits, nuts and seeds, and whole grains and up to four ounces of protein at meals.

If you eat when your body runs out of energy or just before that happens, you will have plenty of energy, and you will eat just the right amount of food. If you eat only enough to take care of your energy needs at that time, you will not eat too much and what you do eat, you will use, and it will not turn to fat. Your brain will have a constant supply of the correct fuel for functioning efficiently.

Once you keep your blood sugar from going too high or dropping too low, you will be surprised at how some forms of depression will just lift. If you have any kind of depression or even suspect that you do, please talk to your doctor for an assessment. Let your doctor monitor your diet change. Also, let your doctor know before you go off any medication.

> **what others say**
>
> **W. David Hager, M.D., and Linda Carruth Hager**
>
> The neurotransmitter serotonin plays a critical role in an individual's mood. Increasing serotonin by dietary means or by using antidepressants can improve mood and depressive symptoms. The best sources of serotonin are bananas and meat, especially turkey. Carbohydrates are necessary to enhance the absorption of serotonin by the body.[10]

How Often Should I Eat?

Most people will need to eat every three or four hours in the beginning. This will keep your blood-sugar levels stable, and your energy levels up. Eating this regularly will constantly feed your brain with the brain foods it needs. The whole grain carbohydrates will provide the pathways for all the brain chemicals you will need to be healthy. You must make sure that you eat dark green leafy vegetables and dairy products to provide the folate and tryptophan that your body needs.

People often tell me that they don't have time to eat. What so many people don't realize is that the time they spend eating will greatly reduce or eliminate the time they waste in depression. Hopefully, with this in mind, you can see how eating is worth whatever time it takes. Eating healthily will oftentimes put you in a good mood, while not eating healthy can set you up for depression.

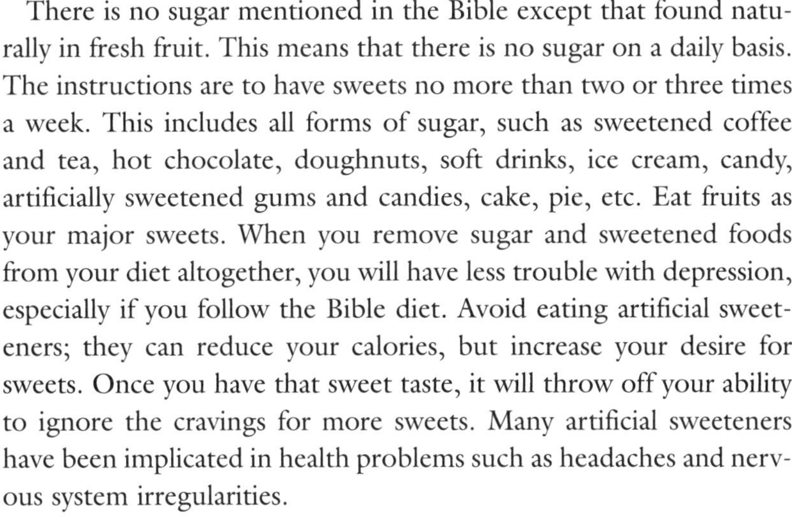

Put Down That Chocolate Bar

despondent
feeling dejected or disheartened

There is no sugar mentioned in the Bible except that found naturally in fresh fruit. This means that there is no sugar on a daily basis. The instructions are to have sweets no more than two or three times a week. This includes all forms of sugar, such as sweetened coffee and tea, hot chocolate, doughnuts, soft drinks, ice cream, candy, artificially sweetened gums and candies, cake, pie, etc. Eat fruits as your major sweets. When you remove sugar and sweetened foods from your diet altogether, you will have less trouble with depression, especially if you follow the Bible diet. Avoid eating artificial sweeteners; they can reduce your calories, but increase your desire for sweets. Once you have that sweet taste, it will throw off your ability to ignore the cravings for more sweets. Many artificial sweeteners have been implicated in health problems such as headaches and nervous system irregularities.

Keep away from low-fat diets if you have depression because research has shown there is a direct relationship between decreases in dietary fats and decreases in energy and/or in moods. The best fats are the olive oil and the omega-3 fatty acids, which have been explained in previous chapters.[11]

Music Lifts and Depresses the Soul

> 1 Samuel 16:14, 23 ***But the Spirit of the Lord departed from Saul, and a distressing spirit from the Lord troubled him . . . And so it was, whenever the spirit from God was upon Saul, that David would take a harp and play it with his hand. Then Saul would become refreshed and well, and the distressing spirit would depart from him.*** *(NKJV)*

In Bible times it was well known that the right kind of music, played in the right manner, could lift the spirits of a person who was **despondent**, sullen, fearful, or depressed. It still works today. Generally, classical music does this, but many other kinds of music will too. Rock music in all its forms can suppress the immune system and bring on many forms of sullenness and depression. And if the words are also depressing, it could mean big trouble.

It is almost certain that a teenager who constantly listens to music with a rock beat that has negative messages in the words, especially words that say "kill yourself" or "women are stupid" or any of the many other negative phrases that are in rock music today, will eventually find himself in a sullen or depressed state. Many precious children are selling their souls into the slavery of negative thinking and depression, because they are bringing themselves into a deep negative state with their music and not getting out of it. This negative state might even be an evil spirit brought on by the words of the music itself.

According to Dr. John Diamond in his 1989 book *Your Body Doesn't Lie,* there is a specific beat in most rock music that is detrimental to your health and can suppress your thymus gland, reduce your immunity, and weaken you. Generally it is the beat of punk rock, death rock, and gangster rap that has the worst effect.[12] There are already enough things that are weakening us like pollution, junk food, and stress, without listening to music that also weakens us. But by the same token, uplifting music can have a curative effect by positively stimulating the thymus gland and improving well-being and immunity.

There are many musicians who record songs even they don't believe in, as long as they sell. Such songs could be the very ones that might destroy your mind or your hearing.

The Mozart Effect

The music of Mozart is now being touted as promoting learning and creativity as well as increasing positive moods and promoting relaxation. If you are depressed, start with some Mozart!

Music Soothes the Soul

Many classical music pieces were composed as church music and are extremely uplifting. There are even modern Christian pieces that will do the same, as long as they don't have the rock beat that can bring you down. Let yourself go into the spirit of the music when listening to religious music; it is intended to praise God, and praising God is always helpful for dispelling depression.

what others say

Jordan Rubin

Music therapy is the use of specific music to promote relaxation and healing. Research in music therapy supports its effectiveness in a wide variety of health-care and educational settings.[13]

Just Get Over It

PROVERBS 17:22 ***A merry heart does good, like medicine, but a broken spirit dries the bones.*** *(NKJV)*

According to Proverbs, a merry or cheerful heart is good medicine. This is wise counsel for everyone, and especially for people who are suffering from depression and who need to work at being positive and cheerful. People used to tell a person with depression to "just get over it" or "cheer up," thinking he or she might just snap out of it. There are times you might be feeling low when a change of heart, taking some positive action, laughing at a joke or story, or listening to music will change your attitude. But there may be other times when your depression is more serious, and it's important to remember that before true depression can be helped, a chemical change must take place in your brain.

Don't let well-meaning friends make you feel worse than you already do because you can't force yourself to cheer up. If you would like to start the healing process by changing your diet, see your doctor or a nutritionist. If you want to start by taking antidepressants, see your doctor and perhaps when you start feeling better, you can begin changing your diet. When you have been on antidepressants for a length of time and then change your diet, you will begin to feel well enough for your doctor to reduce your prescription.

Prayer

PROVERBS 4:20–22 ***My son, give attention to my words; incline your ear to my sayings. Do not let them depart from your eyes; keep them in the midst of your heart; for they are life to those who find them, and health to all their flesh.*** *(NKJV)*

The words of Solomon can be health to your whole body if you keep them in your heart. This theme is followed throughout the entire Bible. Prayer is good for you. God answers prayers in his time; you must just keep praying.

I have met many people who have been healed by prayer. The most startling one is the use of prayer for healing of Down syndrome. This is a condition where a child is born with an extra chromosome. Although slow development is associated with Down syndrome, there are also features of a flat facial profile: an upward slant to the eyes, small ears, and an enlarged tongue. I have met several children who have recovered from this just through prayer. They were bright and had none of the facial features or developmental delays that they were born with. The progression of the healings was remarkable, and the children seemed completely normal, even though the photographs of their early days showed they had been Down syndrome children.

Many prayer groups around the world have documented healings attributed solely to prayer. I have been involved in several prayer groups in both Canada and the United States where people have experienced healings through prayer. Much research is being done on healing with prayer, but scientists try to dispel the idea and the media try to reduce the miraculousness of this intervention into our lives by God.

Psychoneuroimmunology

Since 1976 when the term was coined for the science of psychoneuroimmunology, we have known that negative influences can reduce the health of people by suppressing their immune system. Books have been written and articles published. This is the basis of the renewed interest in mind/body healing. This is not much different from the message in Proverbs 17:22: "A broken spirit dries the bones" (NKJV). If negative thinking and influences can reduce one's health, then positive thinking and influences, especially prayer, can positively influence one's health. There are many forms of healing, and not everyone who receives a healing is freed of a disease, but their spirit is uplifted and in tune with God. This is the kind of spiritual healing that was spoken about in Proverbs 4:20–22.

Group Prayer and Prayer Groups

> JAMES 5:13–16 *Is anyone among you suffering? Let him pray. Is anyone cheerful? Let him sing psalms. Is anyone among you sick? Let him call for the elders of the church, and let them pray over him, anointing him with oil in the name of the Lord. And the prayer of faith will save the sick, and the Lord will raise him up. And if he has committed sins, he will be forgiven.* ***Confess*** *your trespasses to one another, and pray for one another, that you may be healed. The effective, fervent prayer of a* ***righteous man*** *avails much.* (NKJV)

confess
admit the truth, acknowledge

righteous man
a morally right person

prayer warriors
people who pray fervently for others every day

Praying alone may not be suitable for you; you will need to have others pray for and with you. This is why there are prayer groups, prayer circles, and **prayer warriors**! Both the Old and New Testament churches were founded on and filled with prayer. These verses in James explain the basis of healing: Recognize that you have missed the mark, confess it, ask for God's forgiveness, and then let go of it.

what others say

Rita Bennett

If the depression is too deep, and he is too debilitated to pray himself, the prayer partners may need to allow him to simply rest while they do the praying. If the person is suicidal, check with your pastor for guidance or referral.[14]

Magnets: They're Not Just for the Refrigerator Door

For thousands of years, magnets have been used for healing. You will probably remember hearing about the "lodestone," which was a magnetic stone on which sick people were placed to become well. The idea is that a magnet replaces the magnetic pull of the earth that is lost by being out of balance. Modern scientists realize that magnets contribute to increases in blood circulation, thereby reducing healing time and accelerating feelings of well-being. In Israel magnets are being used with great success for people with mania as well as depression.[15]

what others say

Julian Whitaker, M.D.

The research is equally clear that electromagnetic fields speed up the healing of bone fractures and soft-tissue injuries to a remarkable degree, and can be effective in treating stress-related disorders, including anxiety, insomnia, and depression, even in patients resistant to drugs.[16]

Gifts of Healing

1 CORINTHIANS 12:27–28 ***Now you are the body of Christ, and members individually. And God has appointed these in the church: first apostles, second prophets, third teachers, after that miracles, then gifts of healings, helps, administrations, varieties of tongues.*** *(NKJV)*

The body of Christ will always have people who have received the gifts of healing and are obligated to perform healing, in his name, for those in need of healing. It can be with medicine, prayer, or nutrition; all are considered healing.

Chapter Wrap-Up

- Elijah became fearful and ran for his life when he was threatened. (1 Kings 19:3–5)
- Elijah didn't notice how stressed out and depressed he was becoming; he went off by himself and asked God to take his life.
- Twice God sent an angel to Elijah to give him food and water to regain his strength.
- Ahab's wife, Jezebel, realized that Ahab was sullen and needed to eat. (1 Kings 21:4–5, 7)
- God provided you with all the nutrients you need to be healthy, including those that cure many different diseases. These nutrients are in the vegetables, fruits, dairy products, fish, olives, meats, and grains that he created for your body to eat.

Study Questions

1. What happened to Elijah, and why is he important in this chapter?
2. What did the angel tell Elijah, and why is it important to you?
3. Name some symptoms of depression.
4. What are the two most important things you can do for yourself if you think you have depression?
5. How did David help Saul with his depression? Which music do you find helps you feel more positive?

Chapter 13: Food Cravings, Weight Loss, and Eating Disorders

Chapter Highlights:
- **How Your Body Works**
- **Do You Take Sugar?**
- **Eating Disorders in the Bible**

Let's Get Started

Of all the problems that plague modern man, weight loss, weight gain, and out-of-control eating are near the top of the list. There was a time when being plump was a sign of wealth and prosperity; now most people think of plump people as lacking in self-control.

Why have the size, shape, and flexibility of your body become a subject for discussions, diets, loathing, and concern? Something is out of balance in a society where people are more concerned with how thin they look than with helping neighbors or spending time with God every day. Some people feel that it is the influence of the "me generation" of past decades. There are many other reasons for society's obsession with thinness, some spiritual and some biochemical. Could the food you eat (or don't eat) be causing the real problem? The Bible is filled with people who have weight problems, eating problems, and even eating disorders.

cubit
length of a forearm

hilt
handle of a dagger or sword

Overweight in Bible Times

JUDGES **3:17** ***So he brought the tribute to Eglon king of Moab. (Now Eglon was a very fat man.)*** *(NKJV)*

Eglon may have been the king of Moab, but the most they could say about him was he was a fat man. And not just fat but very fat. He was so fat that when Ehud stabbed him in the belly with a dagger that was a **cubit** long and double-sided, the fat closed over the entire dagger, including the **hilt**. So he was really fat! He was a king, and consequently he didn't have to do any physical activity so he didn't take the opportunity to do any exercise or even move around. People just came to him.

Fatness was often associated with wealth, and there are still places in the world today that equate being overweight with being wealthy or rich. Even in food, we refer to something with a lot of fat as "rich." In the Old Testament, being fat is often unpleasing to God and is not something to be desired.

raining down
Exodus 16:4–5

craved
Numbers 11:4–6

meat
Numbers 11:18–22

Adam and Eve
Genesis 3:1–24

Israelites
Numbers 11:4–6

Jesus
Matthew 4:1–4

angels
Matthew 4:11

manna
Miracle food that God supplied daily, it was oily and had the taste of coriander seeds.

Is This All We Get?

PSALM 78:23–25, 27, 29 *Yet He had commanded the clouds above, and opened the doors of heaven, had rained down* ***manna*** *on them to eat, and given them of the bread of heaven. Men ate angels' food; He sent them food to the full . . . He also rained meat on them like the dust, feathered fowl like the sand of the seas . . . So they ate and were well filled, for He gave them their own desire.* (NKJV)

When Moses led the Israelites into the desert, God provided for them by raining down manna from heaven every night except on the Sabbath. On the sixth day he sent double the amount because Jews were not supposed to do any work on the seventh day, the Sabbath, and gathering the manna would have been considered work. They grumbled and mumbled about having to eat the stuff and craved meat, garlic, leeks, cucumbers, fish—all the foods they had eaten in Egypt and now didn't have. So God made them eat quail until the meat "[came] out of [their] nostrils" (Numbers 11:20 NKJV), just so that they would learn to like the manna and be obedient.

Don't Fall for It

MATTHEW 4:3 *Now when the tempter came to Him, he said, "If You are the Son of God, command that these stones become bread."* (NKJV)

Adam and Eve were tempted by forbidden food, and eating it got them in big trouble. The Israelites were tempted by the fancy food they had eaten before they went into the desert. The devil tempted Jesus to turn stones into bread, which was the first of three temptations he had to endure when he was in the desert.

Being tempted by food is nothing new, and look at some of the consequences for failing to resist this kind of temptation. Adam and Eve caused the fall of man, and the Israelites were forced to eat meat until it oozed from their noses. Jesus, however, did not fall for the temptation, so the devil left, and angels came to Jesus's aid.

what others say

T. D. Jakes

Remember, you are not the enemy. You're a victim of a tempter who has been around for a long time. Food was the first thing the devil used to tempt Eve. Adam didn't hold up against the temptation when Eve said, "Look at what we can have if we eat this food." And eating something they shouldn't had fatal consequences. Eating the food God had made for them would have kept Adam and Eve where they wanted to be.[1]

crave
to have an intense desire for, to need urgently

Are you also tempted by foods? Most of the foods that tempt people consist of fat, carbohydrates, caffeine, or sugar (which also includes alcohol). The Israelites had perfect food, and yet they wanted meat, fish, and vegetables. At least they craved decent food, while most North Americans crave salt, fat, sugar, starch, or all of the above. How long has it been since you heard someone say, "I really **crave** a piece of lettuce?" Probably never! People crave only those foods that will give them a quick fix, a lift, perk them up. Keeping your blood-sugar levels stable can really help prevent cravings. Once your blood-sugar levels begin to fluctuate due to eating habits, you can begin to crave those foods that will bring up your blood-sugar levels, foods like caffeine, sugar, empty carbohydrates, and even nicotine.

How Your Body Works

God created your body, and God created food for your body. In chapter 12 you learned that an angel told Elijah to eat several times a day. This gave him strength and self-confidence. Your body is the same. It is essential to eat only the food you need just before you are going to need the energy the food produces. You also need to eat only the foods that contain the nutrients and energy you need. Many health problems are related to changes in blood sugar. Eat foods that don't trigger blood-sugar changes. This sounds simple, doesn't it? It is.

hyperglycemia high blood sugar or glucose

hypoglycemia low blood sugar or glucose

It's Very Simple

FOOD = ENERGY

NO FOOD = NO ENERGY

All the parts of your body—skin, hair, organs, muscles, even your brain—need energy to function. All food changes into the basic unit of energy once it is in your body. This basic unit of energy is called blood sugar. Blood sugar feeds every part of your body so it can function; without this energy, nothing will work. When your blood sugar goes up it is called **hyperglycemia**; when it drops down it is called **hypoglycemia**.

what others say

Joseph Mercola, M.D.

The fact is that any meal or snack high in carbohydrates from grains or sweets generates a rapid rise in blood glucose.[2]

What Does It Feel Like?

When your blood sugar drops it is very uncomfortable. The symptoms could be allergies; anger; anxiety; depression; crying spells; confusion; compulsive eating; lack of coordination; cravings for sugar, starches, or alcohol; exhaustion; drowsiness; headaches; fears; forgetfulness; incoordination; indecisiveness; irritability; nervousness; nightmares; poor concentration; sighing and yawning; staggering; twitching and jerking of the muscles; weak spells; lack of sex interest; insomnia; and even tremors. You might get very sleepy or glassy-eyed when you eat too much, which makes your body produce too much blood sugar, or when you eat too seldom, which causes your blood sugar to drop and produce no energy for your body. Either way, eating too much or eating too seldom is bad for your body.

Do You Take Sugar?

Eating sugar can be the main way to cause these fluctuations in energy/blood sugar. All food turns into blood sugar, but sugar can, in some people, cause a greater rise in blood sugar. Insulin is released from the pancreas to use up the blood sugar. If the meal is large, has a high-starch content, contains a high amount of sugar, or contains alcohol, the blood-sugar levels can go very high, which causes a high amount of insulin to be released. This insulin uses up the blood sugar more quickly and the levels will fall quickly, causing hypoglycemia. Hypoglycemia can also occur when an insulin-dependent diabetic takes too much insulin.

If you have any of these symptoms or have blood-sugar problems in your family, see your doctor for a six-hour, oral glucose tolerance test (GTT) to determine the cause of the problem.

what others say

Dr. Mary Ruth Swope

Sugar causes a rapid rise in blood sugar levels—sometimes causing a person to swing from hypoglycemia to diabetes within a one-hour period (or less). Headaches, fatigue, forgetfulness, irritability, and blurred vision can result.[3]

Wrong Foods at the Wrong Times

Isaiah 44:12 ***He is hungry, and his strength fails; he drinks no water and is faint.*** *(NKJV)*

When you get hungry and begin to feel a loss of strength, this is generally when your blood-sugar levels have dropped because you have eaten no food. You have actually gone too long without eating at this point. This is when many people crave sweets, caffeine, alcohol, or nicotine. When you feel hungry and know that you need to eat something, eat food that does not contain sugar or caffeine. In the long run this will give you more energy and help to stabilize your energy levels. If you choose sweets or caffeine to perk you up, you could drive your blood-sugar levels higher, only to have them fall again very soon. Pay attention to when you eat and what you choose to eat when you have gone without eating long enough to "lose your strength."

Illustration #27
Two Choices—When you have not eaten in a while and have lost your strength, make the right food choice! In the long term, eating healthily will give you more energy than eating foods with a lot of sugar or caffeine.

Some soft drinks contain sugar and caffeine. This is a double whammy that can stimulate your blood-sugar levels to go out of control.

> **what others say**
>
> **Joseph Mercola, M.D.**
>
> It is primarily your body's response to the over indulgence of grains and sugars, not your intake of fat, that makes you fat.[4]

The mother of modern nutrition, Adelle Davis, used to say: Eat breakfast like a king, lunch like a prince, and dinner like a pauper. This was her idea of how to be healthy. It is good advice to follow because it will give you the most food when you need the most energy. Even though she said this in the 1960s and 1970s, it is still a basic rule to follow today. Almost every nutritionist will agree that breakfast is the most important meal of the day.

Yeah, Yeah, but I Want to Know About Weight Loss

Many people who are trying to lose weight think they can cut down on calories by cutting out breakfast and lunch. This is a grave error! Doing so can set up a really big stress in your body that makes you crave sweets, starches, and perhaps alcohol. God designed your body to run on the fuel of foods like fish; whole grains; vegetables; dark green leafy vegetables; squash; meat; milk; cheese; and olives and other fruit. These foods contain the nutrients necessary for health and energy. If you do not eat the right foods at the right time, your body will make you crave the foods that will turn into fat in your body. Foods like lettuce, celery, parsley, cabbage, and broccoli do not trigger severe blood-sugar swings.

metabolism
the physical and chemical processes involved in the maintenance of life

what others say

Jim Shriner

Let's take a closer look at how important breakfast really is. Think about it: you've just come off a seven-to-eight-hour period of sleep where there was no food available in your stomach to be converted to energy. Within only minutes of waking up, your body will be in search of vital nutrients. As soon as you get up in the morning and get moving, your metabolism begins to rise, and just by eating a well-balanced breakfast, you can boost your daily **metabolism** by as much as fifteen percent. That could mean burning as many as two hundred to three hundred more calories per day! Still thinking about missing breakfast?[5]

Do Yourself a Favor: Eat Breakfast!

Breakfast is the most important meal of the day. Eating breakfast is how God meant for you to get the fuel to run your body every day. If you do not eat breakfast, your brain may get so little fuel that you are unable to think correctly, and you may choose to eat the wrong foods or not to eat at all, which in turn will set you up for craving sweets, starches, and high-calorie foods. Or, you may lose control altogether and just keep eating and eating and eating.

You may have heard the famous quote from limerick writer Ogden Nash: "Candy's dandy, but liquor's quicker." He was not talking about blood sugar or craving, but it is true for both. If you go without eating breakfast and your blood sugar drops, you learn to take whatever you can to bring up your blood sugar so you can function. This is often how people become addicted to candy, caffeine, or nicotine; they are using it to bring up their blood-sugar levels so they can function. A sensible breakfast (and that's one with no sugar or caffeine) can prevent these energy slumps or blood-sugar drops midmorning and keep you from a day of cravings and poor choices.

what others say

Pamela Smith, R.D.

Make breakfast a must. Getting the day off to a good start is the single greatest factor in stabilizing hormone and appetite levels throughout the day. Breakfast takes your body out of its morning resting metabolic state and serotonin deficit, balancing your blood sugars and boosting both energy and hormone-producing capability.[6]

Mood swings or energy slumps at mid-morning and mid-afternoon are often a reaction to dropping blood-sugar levels. If you have either of these problems, try eating a breakfast that does not contain any sugar or caffeine. After a few days you will feel really strong and energetic all day long with no drops in energy or concentration. Read the labels on your morning food, whether it is cereal or a protein shake, to determine if there is any sugar in it.

Fish for Breakfast? Why Not?!

JOHN 21:12–13 ***Jesus said to them, "Come and eat breakfast." Yet none of the disciples dared ask Him, "Who are You?"—knowing that it was the Lord. Jesus then came and took the bread and gave it to them, and likewise the fish.*** **(NKJV)**

When the disciples came back from a fishing expedition, onshore Jesus had a fire ready to cook the fish. He asked them to bring some of their catch and have breakfast with him. Jesus gave fish to his disciples for breakfast. Fish and barley bread would be a great breakfast. It is worth noting that Jesus did not eat sugarcoated cereal, or anything similar, but rather real whole foods—foods that would stimulate his metabolism and give him energy without the energy fluctuations that sweets cause. A small steak and a salad would be a great weight-loss breakfast, because it would contain protein, vegetables (including dark green leafy ones), and no sugar, especially if you have no dressing on the salad.

Broiled fish or even tuna fish salad is great for breakfast. Either will give you the correct kind of protein and nutrients that you need for thinking and concentrating. Don't fall into the cold cereal or sugar-laden, quick-breakfast habit if you want to have lots of energy. Who said you had to eat pastries, pancakes, or cold cereal for breakfast? Surely not the Bible.

Eat a Little Food a Lot of Times

acute psychotic state
state in which a person hears voices and sees things that are not really there

Small, frequent meals of low-calorie whole foods are the best way to lose weight. Eat a baked potato for breakfast with some low-fat yogurt and chopped, fresh parsley. Then for lunch or dinner eat a four-ounce piece of meat and some vegetables with lemon juice or fresh herbs. For supper eat a salad with some avocado, a boiled egg, or a small amount of low-fat cheese. Generally, this would have been one meal, right? Baked potato, steak, veggies, and salad would all have been eaten at one sitting before you realized that this was going to cause you to gain weight. Now that you know you can eat these foods throughout the day, you will soon begin to lose weight. Between meals, eat low-calorie snacks to keep your energy up—things like whole grain crackers, of which you only need three or four with some low-fat cheese or peanut butter. A snack of a hard-cooked egg and lettuce is also great. Any veggies can be eaten as snacks as long as they are *au naturel*, not coated with anything. Even dill pickles and a few almonds would be a good snack.

what others say

T. D. Jakes

Always carry a couple of snacks with you so you won't get hungry. It isn't good to go too long without food.[7]

Herbert Wagemaker, M.D.

Hypoglycemia is the opposite of diabetes, and though it usually occurs in diabetics, it also appears in nondiabetics. Some patients with this condition may be suffering from bipolar illness, experiencing the delusions, the hallucinations, and the excitement associated with an **acute psychotic state**. They may complain of feeling faint, of feeling shaky or weak, or of having headaches. Patients respond to diet regulation, eating high-protein snacks and meals five times a day rather than three, and cutting back on sugary foods.[8]

These Foods Can Make You Thin

The foods mentioned in the Bible diet are the foods that make you thin, when eaten in moderation and frequently during the day. There is no secret to weight loss. A sensible diet of nutritious foods at the right time in the right amounts will allow your body to obtain its optimum weight. Follow the basic rule: If God made it, eat it; if

nitrates
compounds used in curing meats; can lead to nitrosamines, which are known to cause cancer

nitrites
compounds used in curing meats, similar to nitrates

MSG
monosodium glutamate, a flavor enhancer in many foods; often causes allergic reactions or water retention

man made it, leave it. This means do not eat processed foods; artificial sugars or sweeteners; processed cheeses or meats; foods filled with preservatives like **nitrates**, **nitrites**, or **MSG**; partial foods like white-flour products or instant mashed potatoes; anything with sugar added; anything with salt added; anything with fat as the first or second ingredient; or anything that promises it has had the calories removed. Look at the Do Eat/Don't Eat chart for more ideas.

But I Need a Special Diet

If you eat these whole, natural foods that God made for your body and eliminate anything that has man-made chemicals or preservatives, or has been processed, you will not need a restrictive diet. When you begin to add daily stretching, walking, and gentle exercises to this regimen of whole food—when you follow the Bible diet—you will not need a special diet.[9]

Dos and Don'ts of the Bible Diet

Do Eat	Don't Eat
100 percent whole grain bread, bagels, crackers, pretzels, pasta	White-flour bread, bagels, crackers, pretzels, pasta
Romaine, leaf, mesclun, escarole	Iceberg lettuce
Yogurt, cream cheese, low-fat cheese	Processed cheeses, cheese food
Unsweetened whole grain cereal	Sugarcoated, refined cereals
Fresh or frozen veggies	Canned veggies
Veggies with a drizzle of olive oil	Canned veggies with margarine
Broiled, baked, roasted meats; fish	Breaded, deep-fried meats; fish
Steamed, baked potatoes	Breaded, deep-fried potatoes
Fresh potatoes with skin on	Peeled, packaged potatoes
Homemade macaroni and cheese	Packaged white macaroni and cheese
Sweet red, green, and yellow peppers	Candy snacks
Frequent snacks, regular meals	No snacks, poor meals
Fresh fruit snacks	Fruit roll-ups
Protein snacks	Carbohydrate-only snacks
Beans, soybeans, tofu, tempeh	Canned, sweetened baked beans
Whole grain cookies	Low-fat, refined-flour cookies

Eating Disorders in the Bible

1 Samuel 1:2, 5–8, 17–20 ***And he had two wives: the name of one was Hannah, and the name of the other Peninnah. Peninnah had children, but Hannah had no children . . . But to Hannah he would give a double portion, for he loved Hannah, although the Lord had closed her womb. And her rival also provoked her severely, to make her miserable, because the Lord had closed her womb. So it was, year by year, when she went up to the house of the Lord, that she provoked her; therefore she wept and did not eat.***

Then Elkanah her husband said to her, "Hannah, why do you weep? Why do you not eat? And why is your heart grieved? Am I not better to you than ten sons?" . . .

Then Eli [the priest] answered [Hannah's prayer] and said, "Go in peace, and the God of Israel grant your petition which you have asked of Him." And she said, "Let your maidservant find favor in your sight." So the woman went her way and ate, and her face was no longer sad.

Then they rose early in the morning and worshiped before the Lord, and returned and came to their house at Ramah. And Elkanah knew Hannah his wife, and the Lord remembered her. So it came to pass in the process of time that Hannah conceived and bore a son. *(NKJV)*

According to Isaac Schiff, M.D., and Morty Schiff in the medical journal *Fertility and Sterility*, Hannah had the eating disorder anorexia nervosa. Partly it was brought on by the torment she received from Elkanah's other wife, Peninnah, and partly it was brought on by refusing to eat. First, she was not able to conceive, and this caused her to stop eating. Because she was not eating she was unable to conceive. The Schiffs speculate that God closed Hannah's womb, because she was listening to her tormentors instead of him. When Hannah became able to praise God and turn her situation over to God, she was able to eat again. Once she ate and gained her strength, she conceived and gave birth to a son.[10]

This is one of the first references to an eating disorder that is brought on by being tormented or teased. Modern psychiatrists and psychologists have developed many ways to treat eating disorders. Hannah's prescription—eat something and turn your infertility over to God—was simple and very much in line with the recommendations of the Bible diet.

anorexia nervosa
disorder wherein the person refuses to eat, suffers from underweight, poor body image, and other symptoms including lack of circulation

Eating a really good diet, small frequent meals, and avoiding caffeine and sugar are the first steps of working on overcoming eating disorders and infertility. In order for your body to function, it needs a wide variety of nutrients—all of which come from food. Avoiding food can cause many health problems due to depriving your body of nourishment.

what others say

Joe S. McIlhaney, M.D.

Menstruation can be erratic or absent [with eating disorders] even though weight is normal. This does not permanently damage one's body, but pregnancy is often impossible.[11]

What Are Eating Disorders?

There are several kinds of eating disorders. **Anorexia nervosa** is an eating disorder wherein the person with it cannot or will not eat. Bulimia nervosa is a disorder wherein the person often eats to excess and then purges the excess food with laxatives of many different kinds or by forced vomiting. In rare cases the person exercises excessively to purge the body of extra food. There are many theories about why these disorders exist. Doctors and nutritionists who practice natural medicine have found that low levels of certain minerals like zinc, chromium, or copper can cause a distorted mental image of what someone sees in the mirror. Unstable blood sugar has also been known to contribute to the lack of self-confidence that often triggers one of these disorders. Critical adults or self-criticism can often lead a child into an eating disorder as a way of exhibiting power over either themselves, adults, or their parents.

Tough Stuff

There are no solutions that will work for every person with an eating disorder. Some people may just have an imbalance of serotonin, which causes depression and may lead to an eating disorder. In one study, a serotonin-active antidepressant was suggested to correct eating disorders.[12] This type of antidepressant could be a prescription drug or a natural remedy.

Many anorexics have found solutions by following a program like the diet recommended in this book:

- Breakfast in the first half hour of getting up
- Small meals
- Eat every three hours
- Eat a lot of fresh veggies
- Chew each mouthful until liquid
- Drink eight glasses of pure water
- Eat some protein with all carbohydrates
- Protein for breakfast
- Digestive enzymes
- Fish almost daily
- Multivitamin and mineral three times a day
- Slow, deep breathing
- Smiling for no reason
- Avoid caffeine, nicotine, sugar, refined foods
- Avoid MSG

A trained professional who can do nutritional and psychological counseling can also help.

Anorexia nervosa can significantly affect the gastrointestinal tract and brain mass. Self-induced starvation can lead to delayed gastric emptying, decreased gut motility, and severe constipation. This can lead to the feeling of the abdomen or tummy being too large and create the distortion of seeing oneself as too fat. Digestive enzymes are always in order for this kind of problem to ensure the functioning of the gastrointestinal tract. There is also evidence of structural brain abnormalities, often tissue loss, with prolonged starvation, which appears early in the disease process and may be of a very serious nature. While it is clear that some reversibility of brain changes occurs with weight recovery, it is uncertain whether complete reversibility is possible. To minimize the potential long-term physical complications of anorexia nervosa, early recognition and aggressive treatment are essential for young people who develop this illness.

A hair analysis from a reputable nutritionist or doctor who is skilled in the correct interpretation of the lab work can assess any mineral imbalances or toxic metal levels, many of which can contribute to eating disorders. A psychologist can often help with family dynamic problems. A family study of Dr. Kevin Leman's *Birth Order Book* or any number of different books on temperaments or personality types can help a family accept a member who has an eating disorder and find ways to relate to him or her. This kind of family involvement can go a long way in raising self-esteem and releasing rage.

There is a Christian Center in Edmonds, Washington, that specializes in eating disorder problems using biblical principles, nutrition, counseling by trained medical personnel, and is run by Dr. Gregory L. Jantz, Ph.D., CEDS. He has twenty-two years of experience in helping people recover. His Web site is aplaceofhope.com /index.html, and he can be reached at 1-425-771-5166 or 1-888-771-5166. Eating disorders of any kind are complicated, and medical support is always indicated. For a list of other clinics, go to caringonline.com/eatdis/treatment.htm.

what others say

Florence Littauer

As you look through your family's background, be alert to signs of negative patterns that need to be changed so that the REAL YOU can stand up.[13]

Is It in Your Family?

Many families have patterns, habits, or lifestyles that get passed on from generation to generation. If someone in your family has an eating disorder, here are some questions to answer that can begin the healing process:

- What does he or she do that is typical of a person with an eating disorder?
- Is he or she the first child?
- Does he or she have a personality type different from those of the other family members?
- Does he or she have an addiction to sugar and junk foods, or perhaps even alcohol?

- Are the parents too busy to pay attention to the children?
- Did or do the parents allow the oldest child to be the responsible one, robbing him or her of a childhood?
- Do the parents pay so little attention to food that many family members end up going without eating when they are young?
- Do the parents provide regular meals for the family and a stable home life?
- Does the family eat mostly nutritionless foods?
- Is there a really strong spiritual family life?
- Does the family pray together and read the Bible together?

Chapter Wrap-Up

- God provided manna for the Israelites while they were in the desert and they wanted to have other foods. They were sent there because of disobedience to God, and they didn't trust God to give them food. They became more disobedient when they began to grumble and complain about the manna. (Psalm 78:23–25, 27, 29)
- Adam and Eve were tempted by food and caused the fall of man. (Genesis 3:1–24)
- Jesus was tempted by the devil, who used food as a way to get Jesus to turn stones into bread. Jesus was able to resist this temptation. (Matthew 4:1–4)
- Every part of your body needs blood sugar to function. Healthy food is the source of the most stable blood sugar.
- Eating several times a day, either three meals and three snacks or six small meals, is the best way to have lots of energy.
- Hannah was an example of a woman who suffered from an eating disorder and also infertility; she was restored to good health and fertility by prayer and eating regularly. (1 Samuel 1:1–20)

Study Questions

1. What are some examples of being tempted by food in the Bible? Why is it important to know about them?
2. What are two opposite blood-sugar conditions and how can you avoid them?
3. What did Jesus give to the disciples for breakfast? Why do you think he did so?
4. Name some foods you usually eat that are not healthy for you and healthy foods you can eat instead. Why do you think God created food that was not good for health?
5. What medical problems did Hannah have, and what do these problems mean to people now? Why was Hannah considered to have an eating disorder?
6. What are two common eating disorders and who gets them? Why do eating disorders exist?

Chapter 14: Wasting Disease

Chapter Highlights:
- Whew!
- Not Enough Love
- The Cure!
- Things to Avoid
- Pray for One Another

Let's Get Started

There are many places in the Bible where people are cursed with plagues and diseases because of disobedience. Many times God prescribed a special diet, like he did for Ezekiel (see chapter 3). The curses in Deuteronomy 28 are for disobedience. The Israelites seemed very headstrong and often disobedient to God. The really good news is that the diet God prescribed in the Bible for the Israelites' disobedience is the exact same diet that is prescribed by physicians today. Could it be that North Americans are just as disobedient as the Israelites were? Or perhaps even more disobedient?

When I say disobedient, I mean collectively, not individually. Look around at the unbridled pollution that is harming people; this is very disobedient! This is harming people and the earth. Look at all the families broken apart because of sin, alcoholism, drugs, and stress. This is disobedient. Look at how our diets have changed—from the natural foods that God gave us to eat and pure water to drink, to food filled with chemicals and devoid of nutrition and water filled with diseases and chemicals (which may or may not be harmful to us) used to purify it; we don't even know really. How many people truly take one day a week as a day of rest? Not very many; this is disobedient.

All of these kinds of things can suppress our immune systems and make us susceptible to many illnesses, including those described as inflammation and scorching, and the effects of mildew. We have already discussed how inflammation is responsible for so many different diseases, from irritable bowel to heart disease, from high cholesterol to diabetes. Inflammation is one of the curses that God promised to a society that does not obey his commandments. But inflammation can also come from yeast, molds, and mildews as well, just as the Bible says. Pollution can suppress your immune system, and a suppressed immune system is more susceptible to pollution.

mildew
Leviticus 13:47–59; 14:33–57; Haggai 2:17

commandments
orders

statutes
authoritative orders having the force of law

curses
appeals or prayers for evil or injury to befall someone

rebuke
to reprove sharply or reprimand

forsaken
given up, abandoned

consumption
illness that gradually deteriorates the body, sapping strength or energy

mildew
fungi or yeast-type mold

fungi
plural for more than one fungus

Whew!

DEUTERONOMY 28:15, 20–22 *But it shall come to pass, if you do not obey the voice of the LORD your God, to observe carefully all His* ***commandments*** *and His* ***statutes*** *which I command you today, that all these* ***curses*** *will come upon you and overtake you . . . The LORD will send on you cursing, confusion, and* ***rebuke*** *in all that you set your hand to do, until you are destroyed and until you perish quickly, because of the wickedness of your doings in which you have* ***forsaken*** *Me. The LORD will make the plague cling to you until He has consumed you from the land which you are going to possess. The LORD will strike you with* ***consumption****, with fever, with inflammation, with severe burning fever, with the sword, with scorching, and with* ***mildew****; they shall pursue you until you perish. (NKJV)*

The New King James Version of the Bible calls this section "Curses for Disobedience." Whew! That is really a heavy curse, and yet I have met thousands of people who are suffering from this today, just as people did in Bible times. This curse is called "the yeast syndrome," or *Candida albicans* infection. Mildew is considered so gross a thing that there are entire sections of the Bible under the ritual laws that deal specifically with mildew and specifically with mildew and cleansing yourself and your house from mildew.

Is There a Fungus Among Us?

Mildew and plague are both **fungi** that can damage your crops, your house, and your body. It has been so since Bible times! In the late 1970s, C. Orian Truss began talking about how a specific fungus or mold called *Candida albicans* can affect your body and mind. People used to joke about there being a "fungus among us" without realizing the seriousness of this particular fungus and the many different kinds of health problems that are possible once this fungus is allowed to overrun one's body.

what others say

William Crook, M.D.

In the late fall of 1979, I learned from C. Orian Truss, M.D. of the relationship of *Candida albicans*, a common yeast, to many chronic illnesses. Then, following his recommendations, I began treating some of my difficult patients with a special diet and a safe antifungal medication. Nearly all were adults with complex health problems, including headache, fatigue, depression, irritability, digestive disorders, respiratory disorders, joint pains, skin rashes, menstrual disorders, loss of sex interest, recurrent bladder and vaginal infections and sensitivity to chemical odors and additives. Almost without exception, they improved, and some improved dramatically.[1]

thrush
the candida problem that is in the mouth, throat, and lungs

rhinorrhea
drainage from the nose

postnasal drip
persistent dripping of fluid from the nasal passages into the back of the mouth

biofilm
thin, usually resistant layer of microorganisms (of bacteria) that form on and coat various surfaces like catheters or water pipes

What Can Mold and Mildew Do?

If you have yeast syndrome, it is important to avoid exposure to mold and mildew, as they can make a bad situation worse. Many people with AIDS have suppressed immune systems; they also have raging candida problems like thrush. Small children often get **thrush** due to *Candida albicans* overrun, especially if they are allergic to dairy products and are being given cow's milk nonetheless. Studies of children with persistent coldlike symptoms found that they were very sensitive to molds in the environment.[2] They often had the additional symptoms of bloodshot eyes, mouth breathing, **rhinorrhea**, nasal voice, **postnasal drip**, and headache.

Candida infections are the most frequent cause of fungal infections in patients hospitalized in an intensive-care unit. Although Candida albicans accounted for 52 percent of the infections, there are other strains of candida becoming more frequent and more dangerous to patients in intensive-care units.[3] Nearly 93 percent of diabetic foot ulcers in a recent study were caused from some form of candida that allowed the infection to progress despite antibiotic therapy. This was true for insulin-dependent diabetics (IDDM) with an ulcer infection persisting more than thirteen weeks and non-insulin-dependent diabetics (NIDDM) with a picture of deep ulcer and abscess in the plantar region, no matter how long they have had the infection.[4] The opportunistic fungal pathogen Candida albicans contributes to implanted medical device–associated infections because the Candida forms a **biofilm** that has dramatically reduced susceptibility to antifungal therapy.[5]

what others say

William Crook, M.D.

I began to see and help many patients with candida-related health problems. The great majority were women and over

fibromyalgia
disease with painful muscles

PMS
premenstrual syndrome, discomfort experienced just before a woman's period

impotence
being incapable of sexual intercourse

MS
multiple sclerosis; degenerative disorder of the central nervous system

psoriasis
scaly skin disease

autism
brain disorder

yeast connection
popular name for yeast problems coined by Dr. William Crook

> three-quarters were in their thirties. Their complaints included fatigue, irritability, PMS, headache, and depression. Most gave a history of recurrent vaginal infections, loss of libido, painful intercourse, and recurrent urinary tract infections.[6] . . .
>
> Many different factors play a part in making you sick. Yet I am convinced that repeated courses of broad spectrum antibiotics are the main "villain." These antibiotics cause yeast overgrowth in your intestinal tract and vaginal yeast infections. And these infections, like a stream cascading down a mountain set off disturbances which can make you feel "sick all over."[7]

Sick All Over

Many people who are bothered by the candida problem report feeling "sick all over" most of the time. Many diagnosed diseases or disorders also can be influenced by candida. A course of treatment for candida problems can often be helpful in treating a score of other health problems like hyperactivity, memory loss, learning difficulties, muscle pain (even **fibromyalgia**), **PMS**, **impotence**, fatigue, **MS**, **psoriasis**, **autism**; the list goes on and on.

If you want more information on this health problem, please see your doctor. If your doctor is not familiar with these kinds of problems, and you think you might be suffering from a yeast-related illness, look for a doctor who can treat you.

for your health

If going into a house with a basement or an old barn or garage makes you feel queasy, swimmy-headed, or gives you a headache or runny nose, have yourself checked out for yeast problems.

How Do I Get This?

According to Dr. Don Colbert, there are many things that can contribute to your becoming susceptible to yeast problems. Taking broad-spectrum antibiotics and/or birth control pills is a really major way to start the vicious cycle that becomes the **yeast connection**. The antibiotics kill all the good "germs" along with the bad. This allows the yeast that is in the air and on everything to multiply in your body until it is out of control.

If you also have a diet rich in yeasts, fermented foods, sugar, refined carbohydrates, or have exposure to chemicals or molds, you can expect that your immune system will not be able to handle all of this, and the yeasts will multiply (see Illustration #29). In the act of multiplying, the yeasts make some **gross toxins**, the most common of which is alcohol, which further suppress your immune system, and you will likely begin to get any number of symptoms that come when your immune system is not functioning 100 percent. Doctors have various names for all these symptoms, but most of them are related to poor immune functioning. Nutritional deficiencies, food and **inhalant** allergies, not enough exercise, and emotional stress or deprivation also contribute to this downward cycle.

gross toxins
crude poisons

inhalant
something you breathe in

acidophilus culture
the good bacteria that makes yogurt

Antibiotics can be lifesaving. Taken on a regular basis, however, they can suppress your immune system and allow a yeast problem to develop. Always take **acidophilus culture** or live yogurt when you are taking antibiotics; this will prevent the antibiotics from causing diarrhea and will help to prevent yeast overgrowth.

Not Enough Love

MARK 12:28–31 ***Then one of the scribes came, and having heard them reasoning together, perceiving that He had answered them well, asked Him, "Which is the first commandment of all?" Jesus answered him, "The first of all the commandments is: 'Hear, O Israel, the LORD our God, the LORD is one. And you shall love the LORD your God with all your heart, with all your soul, with all your mind, and with all your strength.' This is the first commandment. And the second, like it, is this: 'You shall love your neighbor as yourself.' There is no other commandment greater than these."*** ***(NKJV)***

Of all the causes for candida that Dr. Crook mentions in *The Yeast Connection*, the one I have found to be the most common is not enough love. We would do well to take Jesus's words to heart—loving God, your neighbor, and yourself are the most important commandments—because he may have had our health in mind when he said so.

I have counseled many women with candida problems who felt they were not loved as children. In some cases the mother had another baby while the first was still an infant; in others the parents had wanted their child to be a different sex; sometimes the parents were not ready to have children and said so while the child was in the womb, making him or her feel unloved before being born; and in still others the mother had tried to abort the child. There are many ways to make a child feel unloved. They are children, after all, and do not think as adults do.

Illustration #29
Fermented Foods—Fermented foods are not good for people with candida overgrowth. Soy sauce, cheese, bread, crackers with yeast, wine and beer, vinegar, and any food with mold in or on it can contribute to a yeast problem.

The Cure!

> DEUTERONOMY 29:5–6 ***And I have led you forty years in the wilderness. Your clothes have not worn out on you, and your sandals have not worn out on your feet. You have not eaten bread, nor have you drunk wine or similar drink, that you may know that I am the LORD your God.*** *(NKJV)*

When the Israelites were disobedient, they were cursed with mildew; when they decided to obey and renewed their covenant with God, he gave them the cure for the curses—eat no fermented foods, drink no fermented drinks, and go to a place where there is no mold. This is exactly the same cure for the yeast problem! You must also eat foods that improve your immune system and foods (not necessarily the same foods) that destroy the fungus. Among these foods are garlic, yogurt, and olive oil.

Things to Avoid

If you think that you might be suffering from too much yeast, mold, or fungus in your body, see your doctor for a test. You can also start a special diet that is designed to prevent the yeast from multiplying. This is a diet with no yeast; no fermented foods such as wine, beer, or vinegar; nothing made with vinegar such as pickles, mayonnaise, and other salad dressings; no cheeses (except for cottage cheese, which is not fermented); and no bread or crackers made with yeast and no soft drinks. Many people find they can't have sugar, not even fruit, for a period of time because yeast and other fungi love to grow on fruit and fruit juices. Many people do not eat any grains or carbohydrate vegetables like corn, peas, lima beans, and potatoes. Some people cannot eat dairy products because of the **lactose** in them that causes the yeast to grow. Stay away from peanuts and cashews since they may have mold and other **mycotoxins** on them.

lactose
milk sugar

mycotoxins
toxins produced by fungus

what others say

Don Colbert, M.D.

Milk and milk products contain lactose, which also encourages candida growth. Small amounts of butter are acceptable for most individuals with less-severe cases of candida.[8]

Experience this yourself by going off all these foods for at least a month and then gradually adding in one new food a week. If your symptoms start to subside while you are off the offending foods and return when they are added back in, you have the answer to your problem!

Too Much Yeast in Your System?

Foods to Avoid	Foods to Eat Instead
Bread made with yeast	Unleavened bread
Cheese—aged or ripe	Soy and almond cheeses or cottage cheese
Leftovers	Freshly made foods
Vinegar	Lemon juice
Pickles	Fresh cucumbers
Dried and fresh fruits	Vegetable sticks
Canned vegetables	Fresh vegetables
Rollmop herrings	Fresh fish
Bagels, sweet rolls, pastries, etc.	No-yeast whole grain crackers
Beer, wine	Water
Soft drinks	Unsweetened herbal teas
Coffee, tea	Water
Fruit juice	Water
Fast-food hamburgers	Broiled meat and no bun
Corn chips and salsa	Veggies and salsa

biotin
a member of the B vitamin family[9]

melaleuca
tea tree oil

beta-1,3-D-glucan
immune builder from the cell walls of baker's yeast, contains no yeast protein

Well, What Can I Eat?

Just eat whole natural foods. Avoid sugar and sugar-laden foods, refined foods, and processed foods. Have small amounts of fish, meat, yogurt, cottage cheese, or nuts and seeds every day. Add to this a lot of raw and steamed vegetables. You may have butter, olive oil, or flaxseed oil on them. Put raw garlic on everything! So a great breakfast would be fish and a salad, or eggs and veggies. Even tofu and veggies is great for you. Generally, almond- or soy-milk cheeses are not fermented, so experiment with eating these. After a few days or weeks you will start to feel better.

Nutritional Supplements That Help

- Odorless garlic extract
- Low-dose B complex vitamins, three times a day
- **Biotin**
- Olive leaf extract
- Acidophilus liquid or tablets/capsules
- Probiotics/prebiotics
- **Melaleuca**
- **Beta-1,3-d-glucan**
- Beta-sitosterol from sprouts
- Oregano oil
- Grapefruit extract

Pray for One Another

JAMES 5:13–16 ***Is anyone among you suffering? Let him pray. Is anyone cheerful? Let him sing psalms. Is anyone among you sick? Let him call for the elders of the church, and let them pray over him, anointing him with oil in the name of the Lord. And the prayer of faith will save the sick, and the Lord will raise him up. And if he has committed sins, he will be forgiven. Confess your trespasses to one another, and pray for one another, that you may be healed. The effective, fervent prayer of a righteous man avails much.*** *(NKJV)*

It is very important to pray for those who are sick. If they have sinned, they must confess it and then be forgiven through prayer. This is the work of prayer groups, elders, and healing ministries in many churches. Even if you are not a member of their church, they are obligated to pray for you, believing that you will be healed. Confess your sins—the times that you missed the mark. Confess when you cheated on your taxes, took too much change at the grocery, yelled at your children for no reason, belittled your husband, wife, children, or mother-in-law. Any time you were not 100 percent loving to God, your neighbor, or yourself is a sin to be confessed.

Prayer can lift your spirit and improve immune function. Praising God can improve immune function and improve well-being almost immediately. This is what it means to "love the LORD your God with all your heart . . . [and] love your neighbor as yourself" (Mark 12:30–31 NKJV). According to Jesus, these are the two great commandants. According to modern holistic medicine, they are essential for total health. Love can build up your immunity and improve your health immensely.

what others say

Don Colbert, M.D.

Leaky gut occurs when the lining of our intestines lies down on the job. This can happen when candida damages our GI tract. Leaky gut opens a door for bacteria, yeast, viruses, parasites and undigested food molecules, as well as yeast and their toxic waste, to enter the blood stream. They then begin circulating. The partially digested food molecules activate the immune system, creating food allergies and food sensitivities. This further damages the lining of the GI tract, creating symptoms of fatigue, rashes, diarrhea, abdominal pain, memory loss, arthritis, autoimmune diseases, psoriasis and acne.[10]

Body, Mind, and Spirit

MATTHEW 22:37–39 ***Jesus said to him, "'You shall love the LORD your God with all your heart, with all your soul, and with all your mind.' This is the first and great commandment. And the second is like it: 'You shall love your neighbor as yourself.'" (NKJV)***

Healing encompasses the body, mind, and spirit of a person. If you have anger or hatred in your heart, you might have a suppressed immune system. This can make you more susceptible to all kinds of illnesses. Do not hold on to anger or hold something against a person; confess it and let it go. God will forgive you, and you should forgive yourself. Eat sensibly, pray without ceasing, and remember to forgive all people (including yourself). This will put you on the road to a healthy body, mind, and spirit.

Chapter Wrap-Up

- God found the Israelites to be disobedient because they turned away from him. (Deuteronomy 28:15)
- God put a curse on the Israelites because of their disobedience. He sent mold and mildew along with other curses. (Deuteronomy 28:20–22)
- The curse of mildew is very similar to a modern illness that has many symptoms. The mildew or fungus that is the scourge of modern civilizations is *Candida albicans*, often called the "yeast syndrome."
- God forbade the Israelites from eating bread, wine, and other fermented foods and drinks. Staying away from these foods and drinks will help you to overcome the health problems related to mold and mildew. (Deuteronomy 29:5–6)
- Many outside substances—fermented food, junk food, preservatives, mold on leftovers, and various yeasts and molds—can affect your immune system and allow your body to have too much candida in it. Lack of love can also have a great effect on your immune system, causing suppression that can also lead to a wide range of symptoms and diseases.
- Prayer can do a lot toward healing all afflictions. (James 5:15–16)

Study Questions

1. Why did God curse the Israelites? And with what?

2. If the Israelites were disobedient and God cursed them with mildew and plague, what do you think is happening in the world today that has brought back the curse of mold and mildew even more widespread than in Bible times? Relate this to a modern plague.

3. What foods did God keep from the Israelites in the desert that are good to stay away from in light of the modern yeast and fungi plague? What do you imagine modern people have in common with the Israelites, that they would both receive the same curses on their health and bodies?

4. What else can you do to improve your immune system and your health? Why do you think so many people are reluctant to look at their own level of health and try to assess what God wants for them in their lives? (I assume that they are reluctant because there are so many sick people who are suffering from faulty-lifestyle-related illnesses.)

Chapter 15: God's Sacred Temple

Chapter Highlights:
- Your Body Is God's Temple
- How Can I Know What to Do?
- The Rainbow of Hope

Let's Get Started

Many external substances such as mildew, mold, air pollution, noise pollution, overcast skies, and unkind words can affect your body. You are also affected by the thoughts you put in your mind and the words that come out of your mouth. God has given many herbs and foods that can help you find health in your body and mind. God has also given complete instructions on how to know him. He created your body to be turned over to him as a temple for him to dwell in.

temple
1 Corinthians 6:19

Your Body Is God's Temple

1 CORINTHIANS 3:16–17 ***Do you not know that you are the temple of God and that the Spirit of God dwells in you? If anyone defiles the temple of God, God will destroy him. For the temple of God is holy, which temple you are.*** *(NKJV)*

God created you in his image; you bear his image in your body, in your cells, in every part of you. This alone should be enough to make you want to respect your body and take care of it. Most people take better care of their car or truck than they do their body, and yet their car or truck was not made in the image of God. When you feed your sacred temple of God less-than-nutritious food, you are defiling it; you might actually be destroying it. What you do to your body, whether it be smoking, drinking alcohol, eating junk food, being angry, or telling lies, directly affects the temple that God has given you. Is this any way to treat the temple you have been entrusted with?

what others say

Don Colbert, M.D.

Lack of sleep also impairs immune function. Medications such as corticosteroids and antibiotics may deplete the body of B vitamins and zinc, thus impairing immune function. Alcohol and cigarette smoke also impair the immune system.[1]

present
Romans 6:13

aorta
the main trunk of the body's arteries

habits
constant and often unconscious inclination to perform acts, acquired through frequent repetition

You Can Become a Temple

ROMANS 12:1–2 ***I beseech you therefore, brethren, by the mercies of God, that you present your bodies a living sacrifice, holy, acceptable to God, which is your reasonable service. And do not be conformed to this world, but be transformed by the renewing of your mind, that you may prove what is that good and acceptable and perfect will of God.*** *(NKJV)*

By offering or presenting your body to God, you can become a sacred temple. Every day you must present your body and mind to God. A really simple way to do this is to say, "God, I offer you my body and mind today, to do with as you will." Or, "My body is your body, O God." You don't have to say much; just present your body to God first thing in the morning and in the evening before going to bed. This will bring you closer to God, and remind you of your sacred responsibility to care for his temple.

> **what others say**
>
> **Jordan Rubin**
>
> Anger, acrimony, apprehension, agitation, anxiety, and alarm are deadly emotions, and when you experience any of these feelings—whether justified or not—the efficiency of your immune system decreases noticeably for six hours.(This is the same amount of time your immune system shuts down when you eat large amounts of sugar.)[2]

Hypertension can be aggravated by drinking coffee, adding salt to food, and excessive use of alcohol. Eating fish and flax oils will help to reduce high blood pressure.[3] Eating garlic on a regular basis can reverse the aging process of your arteries by keeping the **aorta** elastic and less stiff.[4] Even keeping your bones in great shape is possible. Research shows that elderly people who eat high-calcium foods and take a vitamin D supplement or get adequate sunlight exposure can reduce osteoporosis and hip fractures. Of course, scientists suggest reducing caffeine intake as a preventative.[5]

God gave you the choice to choose the foods you eat and the habits you develop and keep. It is up to you to decide which things you do are damaging your body and which things you could add to your lifestyle or **habits** that will build up your body to become a glorious temple of God. By following all the recommendations in the first half of this book, you will be well on your way to building a clean and beautifully functioning temple for God to inhabit.

poultices, plasters
soft, moist substances put over injuries

sebaceous cyst
skin growths containing oil and proteins

> what others say
>
> **Jordan Rubin**
>
> So if you're one of those people on your way to work while motoring down I-95, minding your business while biting into a Krispy Kreme, only to become unglued by fifty-mile-per-hour senior citizens clogging up the road, your immune system could be shot for the whole day. Welcome to the Angry Doughnut Crowd![6]

A Poultice of Figs

2 KINGS 20:1–5, 7 ***In those days Hezekiah was sick and near death. And Isaiah the prophet, the son of Amoz, went to him and said to him, "Thus says the LORD: 'Set your house in order, for you shall die, and not live.'" Then he turned his face toward the wall, and prayed to the LORD, saying, "Remember now, O LORD, I pray, how I have walked before You in truth and with a loyal heart, and have done what was good in Your sight." And Hezekiah wept bitterly. And it happened, before Isaiah had gone out into the middle court, that the word of the LORD came to him, saying, "Return and tell Hezekiah the leader of My people, 'Thus says the LORD, the God of David your father: "I have heard your prayer, I have seen your tears; surely I will heal you. On the third day you shall go up to the house of the LORD."'" . . . Then Isaiah said, "Take a lump of figs." So they took and laid it on the boil, and he recovered.*** *(NKJV)*

Many fruits and vegetables are made into **poultices** or **plasters** for healing. Some draw out poisons, which could have been the case with the poultice of figs in 2 Kings 20. Figs contain ficin, an enzyme that is useful for treating a variety of parasites, including roundworm. It works in a manner similar to papain, the enzyme from papaya, by attacking proteins mainly and expelling or destroying parasitic worms. Some bring heat to the skin on the surface and increase the blood flow to the area, as a mustard plaster does. Aloe vera gel from the leaf is used to relieve the sting of burns and speed healing. Comfrey leaves are used to draw out poisons. Even ginger root can draw out a **sebaceous cyst**. Because Hezekiah cried out to the Lord for healing and his friends put a poultice on him, God healed him and gave him fifteen more years of life.

forgive
Colossians 3:13

molested
harassed sexually

Forgiveness

MATTHEW 6:14–15 *For if you forgive men their trespasses, your heavenly Father will also forgive you. But if you do not forgive men their trespasses, neither will your Father forgive your trespasses. (NKJV)*

Jesus makes it clear in Matthew 6:14 and 15 that it is essential to forgive anyone who sins against you. If you cannot do so, God won't be able to forgive you. This is a basic theme in Jesus's teachings—you must forgive others when they have sinned against you. You have all heard this before, but how hard it is to do! It doesn't matter who has sinned against you—your father, mother, aunts, uncles, the grocery store manager, your first-grade teacher—you must forgive them all.

Practice Forgiveness

Each time you have a memory of something hurtful that someone did to you, just forgive them. Turn it over to God. I remember hearing in a sermon that C. S. Lewis, the great Christian writer, spent twenty-five years trying to forgive someone. You must forgive people whether you want to or not. The very practice of doing it when you least want to is an act of forgiveness to yourself.

It is easy enough to say, "I forgive you (name the person or problem here), and I forgive myself for holding on to it, and now I turn this over to God." Forgiving is an act of love, and Jesus tells us we must love our neighbors as ourselves. Therefore it is logical to forgive others and forgive ourselves as well.

what others say

Mark Pearson

Often people block their healing—by clinging to resentment. I ministered to a man who had been sexually abused as a child. One day one of the people ministering to him asked him if he had forgiven the person who had **molested** him. "No," he responded. "I hate him!" He was reminded that our Lord tells us to forgive others and pray for those who persecute us. Indeed, Jesus said that if we do not forgive others, we ourselves will not be forgiven. Forgiving the man who molested him had not been easy, but it had brought healing.[7]

How Can I Know What to Do?

drunkenness
Luke 21:32–36

anger
Ephesians 4:31

wrath
divine retribution for sin

malice
a desire to harm others or to see others suffer

> MATTHEW 18:21–22 ***Then Peter came to Him and said, "Lord, how often shall my brother sin against me, and I forgive him? Up to seven times?" Jesus said to him, "I do not say to you, up to seven times, but up to seventy times seven."*** (NKJV)

If you have a question regarding correct actions or what to do in a certain situation, consult your Bible. When someone sins against you, you must forgive them; this is exactly what Jesus said to do. It is a simple act but not always easy. When somebody cuts in front of you on the road, don't get angry; forgive them. Say out loud, "I forgive you for doing that." When your child spills his milk, say to him, "I am not mad at you, I forgive you for having an accident. Please clean it up." Then give him a hug, and you will both be on the way to better health. If you are tempted to eat something that you know is bad for you, just ask yourself, *What does the Bible say about this, or what would Jesus have done?* He would not have eaten junk food or gotten drunk. Especially since there was no junk food, and we know that he spoke against drunkenness.

Turn to God

> COLOSSIANS 3:5–10 ***Therefore put to death your members which are on the earth: fornication, uncleanness, passion, evil desire, and covetousness, which is idolatry. Because of these things the wrath of God is coming upon the sons of disobedience, in which you yourselves once walked when you lived in them. But now you yourselves are to put off all these: anger, wrath, malice, blasphemy, filthy language out of your mouth. Do not lie to one another, since you have put off the old man with his deeds, and have put on the new man who is renewed in knowledge according to the image of Him who created him.*** (NKJV)

God makes it quite clear that you are not to take part in anger, wrath, malice, or many other actions and reactions that we now call "stress response." If you really expect to spend time with God and to be healthy, you are to get rid of any worldly ways. Most of the actions and emotions that God tells man not to take part in are those of the "fight or flight" response. This response occurs when you do not follow a sensible diet, eat too much sugar and caffeine, and allow your blood sugar to go way up and then to drop way down, creat-

type A behavior typical behavior of heart attack personality

ing a stress that triggers the "fight or flight" response. The "fight or flight" response is also a response to the failure to handle stressful situations in your life.

Perhaps you are doing more than your body can handle, perhaps you are not eating right, perhaps you are not sleeping enough, perhaps you are in over your head. Perhaps you have gone without eating and not taken care of your "temple." You can "put to death" these stresses in your life by turning them over to God.

Anger and Rage

Of all negative emotions, anger and rage can do the most damage to your body. Research is showing that **type A behavior**, thought to be responsible for heart disease and heart attacks, can now be called "type anger." Scientists have found it is anger that damages the heart muscle, not the other behaviors of a type A personality. Even infants can cause damage to their heart muscles, over time, if left to cry so long that they become angry frequently.

For more information on anger, how it can harm your body and how to overcome it, see my book *The Anger Cure,* published by Basic Health Publications.

what others say

Kenneth H. Cooper, M.D.

A failure to handle the pressures of life can increase cholesterol, blood pressure, and other risk factors linked to heart disease.[8]

Mark Pearson

Increasingly, articles are being published both in medical journals and in the popular press demonstrating the relationship between sickness and the inappropriate handling of emotions. Bitterness, resentment, anxiety, inappropriately expressed anger—all of which the Scripture calls sin—besides harming others, harm ourselves, spiritually, emotionally and physically.[9]

The Rainbow of Hope

GENESIS 9:13–16 ***I set My rainbow in the cloud, and it shall be for the sign of the covenant between Me and the earth. It shall be, when I bring a cloud over the earth, that the rainbow shall be seen in the cloud; and I will remember My covenant which is between Me and you and every living creature of all flesh; the waters shall never again become a flood to destroy all flesh. The rainbow shall be in the cloud, and I will look on it to remember the everlasting covenant between God and every living creature of all flesh that is on the earth.*** *(NKJV)*

The rainbow appears after storm and rain. It takes the sun shining on the wetness to form a rainbow. Each time you feel gray or stormy, remember the rainbow and the hope it brings to you. Let the rainbows in your life remind you that God has a covenant with you. If you keep his commandments and follow his precepts and advice, you will see the rainbow and be reminded that God loves and cares for you and has given instructions for you to feel really great.

Chapter Wrap-Up

- You were created in the image of God. The Bible tells you that you are to be a temple of God. (1 Corinthians 3:16)
- God often instructed his prophets to use common substances for healings. He instructed Isaiah to use a poultice of figs to cure a boil. (2 Kings 20:1–5, 7)
- Over and over again Jesus talked about the importance of forgiveness. He even said we should forgive our brother seventy-seven times. (Matthew 18:21–22)
- Jesus warns everybody about anger, wrath, and other negative emotions. (Colossians 3:5–10)
- God gave the Israelites a rainbow to remind them of his covenant with them. (Genesis 9:13–16)

Study Questions

1. Why is your body a temple?
2. When it comes to healing, what is the role of God, and what is the role of medicines or remedies?
3. Why was Jesus so adamant about forgiving? Why should you be too?
4. Which emotions can harm your body? How do they do this?

Chapter 16: And Jesus Went A' Walkin'

Chapter Highlights:
- Jesus the Walker
- Not Your Everyday Stroll
- Walking Is Good for Older Folks
- Make It Really Count

Let's Get Started

Deciding what kind of exercise to do can be confusing—should you walk, bicycle, lift weights, do aerobics? What you do is really up to you, but why not start with walking? Walking is easy to do, does not require any special equipment, can be done in almost any environment, and it's free! Jesus and his disciples walked everywhere they went. Everybody knows how to walk, but did you know there is a correct way to walk for health?

mountain
Matthew 5:1

traveling
Luke 24:13–29

chronic obstructive pulmonary disease
persistent difficulty in breathing because lung tissues cannot function effectively; emphysema or severe asthma

Jesus the Walker

MATTHEW 4:18–20 ***And Jesus, walking by the Sea of Galilee, saw two brothers, Simon called Peter, and Andrew his brother, casting a net into the sea; for they were fishermen. Then He said to them, "Follow Me, and I will make you fishers of men." They immediately left their nets and followed Him.*** *(NKJV)*

Jesus and his disciples walked because they didn't have automobiles, airplanes, or subways (see Illustration #30). He walked up on a mountain to deliver the Sermon on the Mount. Jesus was traveling—that is, walking—with his disciples even when he returned to the world after his resurrection. What other choice did they have? The only other modes of transportation were donkeys, donkey carts, and boats. Often he took a boat, but according to Scripture, more often he walked.

Walking Is Great!

If you don't exercise at all, and you start to do regular walking, you will soon find yourself feeling better, even if you didn't think you felt bad in the first place. A recent study of patients with **chronic obstructive pulmonary disease** (COPD) showed that when COPD sufferers added walking and cycling to their daily lifestyle, they had increased muscle strength, got out of breath less, and enjoyed an improved quality of life.[1] Men with **benign prostatic hyperplasia** who walked two to three hours a week had a 25 percent lower incidence of urinary tract symptoms.[2] Walking helped to improve the bone mineral density after hip surgery in both men and women.[3]

Illustration #30
Map of First-Century Palestine—Jesus and his disciples walked from the Dead Sea to Galilee in their ministry travels.

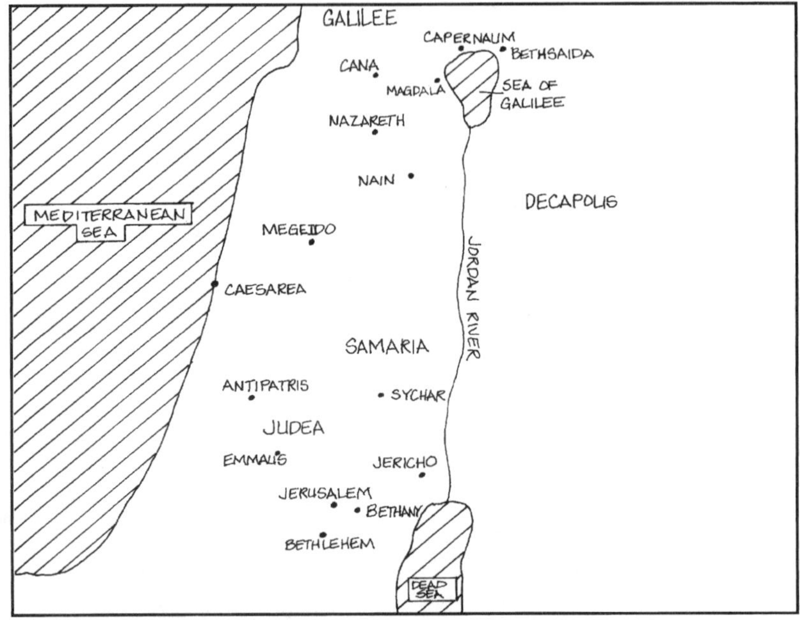

what others say

Don Colbert, M.D.

Certain exercise promotes psychological well-being. Exercise reduces stress and anxiety by enabling a person to burn off the stress chemicals that fuel anxiety. It increases the release of endorphins in the brain; endorphins are hormonelike substances that elevate mood and give a person a sense of well-being.[4]

benign prostatic hyperplasia
enlargement of the prostate gland including overproduction of prostate cells

lactic acid
by-product of muscle use that often causes temporary pain when trapped in muscles

What Else Does It Do?

Walking is an excellent exercise to help relieve the symptoms of fibromyalgia, along with physical therapy, massage, and relaxation techniques.[5] Although it is often difficult for people with fibromyalgia to do any exercise because of the chronic pain and fatigue associated with the disease, it will improve their well-being in many ways. Walking can help remove some of the pain caused by the **lactic acid** that is trapped in the muscles. When a person with fibromyalgia starts a walking program, it may be painful and difficult; but with regular walking, the pain decreases, the heart rate improves, and there will be an increase in stamina and energy. Regular walking can reduce high blood pressure and increase blood flow in the arms and legs for older **hypertensives**.[6] Daily walking was shown in another study to increase bone mineral density in postmenopausal women.[7] When bones lose their density there will be a problem with osteoporosis. Always consult with your doctor before starting any type of exercise program, even walking.

hypertensives people with high blood pressure

Weight-bearing exercise, especially walking, can help restore calcium to bones, increasing their density and helping to prevent osteoporosis and breaking bones. Steamed broccoli, sardines, and salmon with bones, tofu, and chard are all good sources of dietary calcium. Did you know many women have a greater need for exercise after menopause than before? After hearing all this, how can you not walk? Ask your doctor if you can exercise by starting a walking program.

Not Your Everyday Stroll

JOHN 4:3–5 ***He left Judea and departed again to Galilee. But He needed to go through Samaria. So He came to a city of Samaria which is called Sychar, near the plot of ground that Jacob gave to his son Joseph.*** (NKJV)

The distance between Judea and Galilee could be as much as fifty miles depending on where they went in each place. Do you ever walk that far just to see friends? Or to do your work? Yet, in Jesus's day, walking was the usual mode of transportation. In many places in the world, walking is still the main mode of transportation; perhaps you can make it your main transportation (see Illustration #31).

Walking Is Good for Older Folks

Two studies done thousands of miles apart show that walking is very important for a great life. In one study in Maryland, people between the ages of seventy and eighty-two who did walking and other types of movement exercise several times weekly had a 32 percent lower risk of mortality than people who didn't do any or did very little walking. You can actually live longer by walking.[8] The other study done in Finland with 134 women who were postmenopausal showed that women who did about 2 km of brisk walking daily in either one bout or broken up into two bouts and also did a small amount of resistance training, improved in lower-extremity muscle strength and in walking time.[9]

Illustration #31
Walking in Bible Times—In Bible times people walked everywhere!

God Walked Too!

> **Genesis 3:8** ***And they heard the sound of the Lord God walking in the garden in the cool of the day.*** *(NKJV)*

From Genesis 3:8 it appears that even God liked to go walking. When you go out walking, consider it your daily time with God. Take a CD player every now and then and listen to uplifting songs and praise God while you walk. Make your walking time your time with God.

Make It Really Count

When you walk, it is important to do so at a brisk pace. Start by walking a little more with everything you do. Take the stairs for one flight instead of the elevator or escalator, or park your car a few yards farther from the store. Walk to the post office or visit a museum or art gallery for additional walking. Many older adults start a walking program by joining the "mall walkers" in their favorite shopping mall. Because it's enclosed, bad weather is never an excuse. Once you are in the habit of walking more, pick up the pace a little each time that you walk. Walking is best for your body if you can increase your pulse a little. Obviously you need to take your pulse when you are resting so you can tell what your resting pulse is. (For instructions, see the Pulse Chart below.)

Pulse Chart

- Sit in a comfortable chair for at least ten minutes, until you are relaxed.
- Place your fingertips on your throat next to your Adam's apple or voice box.
- Swallow to find the location of the center of your throat.
- Using your fingertips, feel around in the area of your neck beside the Adam's apple until you find a beating pulse.
- Look at a clock with a second hand and count the number of beats or pulses for one full minute. That will be your resting pulse.
- You can also count the beats for fifteen seconds and multiply by four to get the one-minute pulse.
- A true resting pulse of sixty to seventy-five first thing in the morning (before you get out of bed) is the general range for an adult.
- A first-thing-in-the-morning pulse of one hundred or more calls for a visit to your doctor.

On the Pulse of It

Once you know your resting pulse, take your pulse before you walk. Check it while you are walking and then when you are finished. Ask your doctor what your normal resting and exercise pulse should be. This way you will know how high you can increase your pulse for your age or health level.

Good Exercise Choices

- Aerobics
- Bicycling
- Bowling
- Dancing

- Gardening
- Golfing
- Heavy Housecleaning
- Ping-Pong
- Stair Climbing
- Stationary Bike
- Swimming
- Tennis
- Treadmill
- Walking
- Weight Lifting

Walking the Straight and Narrow

When you decide to start walking for exercise, check out your equipment. First look at your shoes. Do not wear shoes that are run-over or uncomfortable. Wear shoes with firm but flexible soles and low or no heels. The heels of your shoes should fit snugly around your heels. If they don't, purchase some heel grips for inside your heels. They are very inexpensive and can keep you from getting blisters while you walk.

Once you have comfortable shoes and an outfit that allows you to move freely, it is time to begin. Start by stepping forward with one foot. Your heel should touch the ground first, and the rest of your foot should be rounded to allow you to rock up onto the ball of your foot. Walking coaches often describe the posture of the foot during walking as being like the rockers of a large rocking chair. Each time you place your heel down, rock up onto the ball of your foot. Keep doing this with your knees slightly bent and your body lifted high as if you were going to float off at any minute. Rock onto one foot and then the other until you are walking briskly. Your arms should be swinging, left arm forward when the right foot is forward, right arm forward when the left foot is forward. This is just the natural way to walk. If you have any doubts, look at a young child. Do not roll your feet to the side. Keep both feet pointed straight ahead, as if you were walking along either side of a narrow, drawn line.

Don't Forget to Breathe

aerobic
reaction that occurs in the presence of oxygen

When you are walking along briskly, take slow deep breaths in and out as you walk along. You should be able to feel your heart rate increasing a little, and be a little out of breath but still able to carry on a conversation. Brisk walking is an **aerobic** activity that increases your oxygen intake, and this will happen best if you concentrate on doing gentle deep breathing.

what others say

Julian Whitaker, M.D.

Current recommendations for aerobic activity are for 20 to 30 minutes at least three days a week. You should aim to work at a level where you feel that your breathing is heavier but where you can still hold a conversation.[10]

Chapter Wrap-Up

- When Jesus began his ministry he called fishermen to walk with him. (Matthew 4:18–20)
- Walking is a great form of exercise for you today.
- Jesus and his disciples often walked forty to fifty miles to get to the places they visited. (John 4:3–5)
- Walking can improve a person's general health, and it can improve some specific health problems. It is one of the best overall exercises.
- God used to walk with Adam and Eve in the Garden. (Genesis 3:8)

Study Questions

1. Why do you think Jesus and his disciples walked everywhere?
2. What is the best way to start exercising? Are there exercises you are doing now that can be increased to improve your health level? What are they?
3. Children are generally more active. How has your attitude about exercise changed since you were a child and why?
4. What are some of the health benefits that can be gained by exercise and walking in general? Does your church have an exercise group? If not, when are you going to start one?

Chapter 17: Feasting, Feasting, Feasting

Chapter Highlights:
- Seven Feasts
- They Ate on a Couch
- Why Can't I Eat That Anymore?
- It Makes Me Feel Strange

Let's Get Started

The Bible has many passages about feasts. Many people assume feasting means to eat a lot, but this is not always the case with the "feasts" mentioned in the Bible. There were seven feasts specifically for the Israelites. They were often warned against **winebibbers** and people who overindulged in food, because this is what Romans and pagans did. Feasts were used to honor religious remembrances, for weddings and funerals, and for other special occasions. In the New Testament, Jesus warns people to keep away from overindulging in alcohol, anger, vile talk, hatred, and unforgiveness. This chapter will explore not only what the Bible says about feasting but also what nutritionists say about it. Too much feasting, specifically eating too much, can actually cause food sensitivities, exhaust your body, and prevent you from being able to handle stress.

feasts
Genesis 26:30;
Psalm 81:3;
Matthew 26:5

winebibbers
Proverbs 23:20

holy convocation
Leviticus 23

winebibbers
people who drink a lot of wine

Seven Feasts

LEVITICUS 23:1–2 *And the LORD spoke to Moses, saying, "Speak to the children of Israel, and say to them: 'The feasts of the LORD, which you shall proclaim to be holy convocations, these are My feasts.'"* (NKJV)

God gave the Jews seven holy convocation days to observe forever: Passover, Unleavened Bread, First Fruits, Pentecost, Trumpets, Atonement, and Tabernacles. All of them required special eating and feasting except for the Feast of Atonement, when they were to deny themselves. They were required to do no work, and this meant no eating.

Feasts with Lots of Eating

To the Hebrews, a feast was not simply a meal with lots of food, the way it was for the Romans. The seven feasts were festivals—religious remembrances—and sometimes they made animal sacrifices to

weaned
Genesis 21:8

wedding
John 2:1–11

Passover
"Pesach," commemorates the flight of the Jews from Egypt

leavening
any substance such as yeast, sour dough starters, or cream of tartar, used in batter to produce fermentation

matzah
unleavened bread, like a large cracker

God. These feasts included special meals and often lasted for several days, but people did not eat a huge amount or drink too much. Feasts were held for special occasions, such as the one held to commemorate Isaac's being weaned, funerals, and weddings. As a matter of fact, Jesus performed his first miracle at a wedding feast when he turned water into wine.

The Feast of Unleavened Bread

EXODUS 12:14–16 ***So this day shall be to you a memorial; and you shall keep it as a feast to the LORD throughout your generations. You shall keep it as a feast by an everlasting ordinance. Seven days you shall eat unleavened bread. On the first day you shall remove leaven from your houses. For whoever eats leavened bread from the first day until the seventh day, that person shall be cut off from Israel. On the first day there shall be a holy convocation, and on the seventh day there shall be a holy convocation for you. No manner of work shall be done on them; but that which everyone must eat—that only may be prepared by you. (NKJV)***

The feast that non-Jews are the most familiar with is the Feast of Unleavened Bread, which begins with the **Passover** meal. For seven days, nothing may be eaten with **leavening** in it. Besides yeasted breads, that includes vinegar, corn syrup, brown sugar (because it may contain yeast), baking soda and powder, and more strict Jews even omit beans, peas, grains, corn, and seeds. There is a special meal at the beginning of the period called the "Seder." The Seder is a family ritual to remember the time when the Israelites had to leave in a hurry and did not have time to let the yeast work in their bread, so they ate unleavened bread. During this meal they do not eat any foods with leaven or yeast or anything that might ferment and become leaven. Wine drinking is part of the remembrance, and so are other ritual foods like bitter herbs, boiled eggs, and lamb shanks, which are eaten along with the **matzah**.

You Call This a Feast?

LEVITICUS 16:29–31 ***This shall be a statute forever for you: In the seventh month, on the tenth day of the month, you shall afflict your souls, and do no work at all, whether a native of*** *your own country or a stranger who dwells among you. For on that day the priest shall make atonement for you, to cleanse you, that you may be clean from all your sins before the* L*ORD. It is a sabbath of solemn rest for you, and you shall afflict your souls. It is a statute forever.* (NKJV)

atonement
Ezekiel 45:17

The **Day of Atonement** is one of the feasts required by God, and during it there is no eating at all! This day of at-one-ment is marked by a series of five restrictions, or afflictions: (1) no eating or drinking, (2) no bathing, (3) no anointing of the body with oil, (4) no wearing of leather shoes, and (5) no sexual relations. This is a day to remember one's sins, ask for forgiveness, and repent. It's definitely not what we normally consider a feast. It is, however, a festival, with services in the synagogue, reading from the holy books, and lighting of candles.

Day of Atonement
also known as "Yom Kippur"

Why Feast?

In Bible times the feasts were held at certain times of the year, especially before and after harsh weather. First, a feast was held to prepare for winter when people didn't go out as often. Then a feast was held after winter was over, to thank God for getting them through it. Feasts also were held on many important occasions like birthdays, marriages, and harvests. Often, during these nonreligious feasts, there would be much drinking of wine and eating of rich food.

They Ate on a Couch

Amos 5:21; 6:1, 4, 6–7 ***I hate, I despise your feast days, and I do not savor your sacred assemblies . . . Woe to you who are at ease in Zion, and trust in Mount Samaria . . . Who lie on beds of ivory, stretch out on your couches, eat lambs from the flock and calves from the midst of the stall . . . Who drink wine from bowls, and anoint yourselves with the best ointments, but are not grieved for the affliction of Joseph. Therefore they shall now go captive as the first of the captives, and those who recline at banquets shall be removed.*** (NKJV)

During Old and New Testament times, Israelites, Romans, and most of the known world ate reclining on a kind of couch. In fact,

gluttonous consuming large, immoderate amounts of food and drink

Jesus and his disciples were reclining at the Last Supper. This means that when they had a special feast or banquet, they were relaxing while they ate. They were fully engrossed in eating and fellowship. Times were different then. They weren't distracted by the evening news on TV as many people are today. When you are under stress or tension, your digestion slows down. Today people might do well to do nothing else when they eat except relax, enjoy the company of friends and family, and leave the worries of the world behind. This would really help improve digestion, stress levels, and family relations. Perhaps if everyone did nothing else while eating, there would be less need for antacids and digestive aids.

Forget God, Let's Eat

Many of the Israelites who belonged to the house of Joseph (because they were his descendants) had given up on God and were feasting without the religious aspect. They were eating and drinking to excess because they were separated from God. Many of the feasts, holidays, celebrations, and even the clean and unclean food rules were given to them in hopes of making them remember God. It didn't work. They just became more sinful and **gluttonous**. Sounds a bit like the modern-day Christmas celebration, doesn't it?

what others say

Don Colbert, M.D.

Your body will enter into a deep state of relaxation when you praise and worship God and meditate on the Word of God.[1]

When the Israelites began to drink wine, eat lots of food, and forget God during religious feasts and at other times, they were in a lot of trouble. God sent them away so that they had to stop eating and drinking so much. God knew that eating too much was bad for their bodies, and forgetting him was bad for their hearts and minds.

Why Can't I Eat That Anymore?

Proverbs 23:20–21 ***Do not mix with winebibbers, or with gluttonous eaters of meat; for the drunkard and the glutton will come to poverty, and drowsiness will clothe a man with rags. (NKJV)***

subconsciously
without awareness

How interesting it is that the writer of Proverbs places eating too much and drinking too much in the same category. So do many people concerned with health. Eating and drinking too much can overload your body and cause many health problems. Stuffing yourself at any meal, whether it be a feast, potluck, Sunday dinner, or breakfast, is not good for your health. Each time you eat a big meal you ask your body to go into the stress mode. Eventually this can overwork your body to such an extent that it starts to break down.

Such a Comfort

A person may be tempted to overeat because doing so **subconsciously** reminds him or her of what it felt like to be a bottle-fed baby. Often a mother will insist or encourage her baby to drink a certain number of ounces, whether the baby wants to or not, which leaves the baby with a full tummy and that groggy feeling that comes from eating too much. When a baby is fed in his mother's arms, the baby also begins to equate eating too much, and feeling full and groggy, with comfort and Mother's love. This can cause a lifetime of eating for comfort and overeating.

It Makes Me Feel Strange

Food sensitivities often can be the result of eating too much at one time, or generally eating too much. It has been known for thirty years that if you eat the same foods over and over, day after day, you can develop sensitivities to that food. Food sensitivities can then cause health problems such as headaches, joint pains, being overweight, skin rashes, sinus problems, indigestion, depression, achy muscles, fatigue, and fluid retention. Many people inaccurately refer to "food sensitivities" as "allergies." With a true allergy there is some form of swelling; with food sensitivities, you may not even know that you are being affected by the food.

what others say

Don Colbert, M.D.

Many individuals have food allergies and food sensitivities. You could be one of them. It's critically important to identify, eliminate or desensitize food allergies to properly restore immune function.[2]

Metabolic Syndrome

Oftentimes, overeating at feasts can lead to chronic overeating. This is probably the worst sin you can commit against your body. First of all, you will eat way more than your body can handle, which can cause digestive upsets. Second, if you eat more calories than you use or work off during exercise, you will gain weight and even cause health problems that can lead to cancer. Third, there is a danger of developing syndrome X or metabolic syndrome, a condition with the "cluster" symptoms of hypertension, glucose intolerance, high blood fats, and obesity.[3] Chronic overeating, feasting, and stuffing yourself are partly responsible for the epidemic levels of type 2 diabetes (or adult-onset diabetes) in North America (see Illustration #32).

Syndrome X or metabolic syndrome is responsible for many heart attacks. If someone you know has a heart attack and he or she tells you then that he is also a diabetic, he has syndrome X. Metabolic syndrome has reached epidemic proportions in North America because of our lifestyles of caffeine, sugar, nicotine, and going without eating. These habits can lead to the breakdown in sugar metabolism and create heart problems and other serious health problems or diseases. For more information on this and how it happens, see my book *The Anger Cure*, Basic Health Publishers.

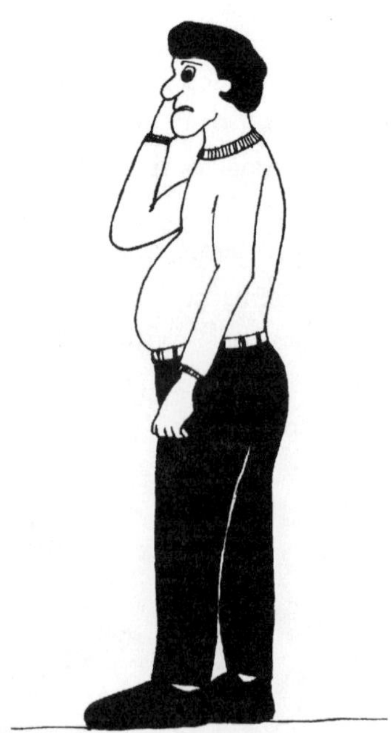

Illustration #32
Man with Food Sensitivities—Eating the same foods over and over again can cause you to become overweight and have any number of health problems. Many people think they are suffering from the flu when actually they have food sensitivities.

Okay, So What Should I Do?

Break the connection between good times and food. If you are going to go to a feast, potluck, or dinner party, eat a little something before you go so that you won't be so hungry that you eat too much of everything. Never eat a big meal when you have not eaten for more than four hours. This could be a disaster for your body, mind, and health. Eat slowly by chewing every mouthful well; this will show respect for your digestive organs. Remember Horace Fletcher, who went around the country in the early 1900s telling people to chew every mouthful until it was liquid—"fletcherizing" they called it.[4]

Remember that God made your body to live sensibly, eat sensibly, and pray sensibly. When you are involved in a feast, always make sure God is there, first, before any food. Don't be like the disobedient children of God who forgot him and got involved with eating and drinking too much. Even overeating healthy food is still overeating.

what others say

Jordan Rubin

God definitely healed me, but He did it in the natural, practical way I have shared with you—through the Maker's Diet. My mother says it best; I was healed "as I feasted on the Word of God" and applied His principles—including dietary—to my life. Believe me, these principles of divine health are completely reproducible in your life, too.[5]

T. D. Jakes

I find it depressing when I do something against my better judgment, so I take my own low-fat food to parties. It keeps me from a relapse into my old bad habits. Sometimes you have to nibble on something to keep others from feeling like you have broken fellowship. Our society is food-oriented, and some people make you feel like you haven't celebrated until you "break bread" together.[6]

Chapter Wrap-Up

- God gave instructions to the Israelites for seven appointed feasts spaced throughout the year as a way for them to remember God. (Leviticus 23:1–2)
- Each of the feasts is really a festival and includes the public reading of the holy books, services at home, in the synagogue, or both.
- The Feast of Unleavened Bread, which starts with Passover (Pesach), and the Day of Atonement (Yom Kippur) are the two of the seven feasts that Christians know most about.
- There are many verses in the Bible that indicate God was not happy about the way Israelites were doing their feasting. (Amos 5:21; 6:1, 4, 6–7)
- God did not intend for you to eat more than your body was designed to hold or use. Many diseases such as cancer, digestive disturbances, and allergies can come from overeating.

Study Questions

1. What are the holy convocations, and why did God give them to the Israelites?
2. What sort of feasting did the children of God do on Yom Kippur?
3. What was dangerous about the feasting of Old Testament times? How do you do the same things?
4. What are some of the health problems that can be associated with overindulgence in food, and what can you do to overcome them?
5. What was the real reason for most of the feasts? What part should God play in your feasts today?

Chapter 18: Fasting, Fasting, Fasting

Chapter Highlights:
- Fasting from What?
- Why Fast?
- Some Toxic Substances
- The Reward of Fasting

Let's Get Started

There are many kinds of fasts. When you go in for a physical checkup, the doctor will often ask you to fast from food after 9:00 p.m. and from liquids after midnight. Perhaps you didn't know you were fasting during these times, but you were!

together
2 Chronicles 20:1–4

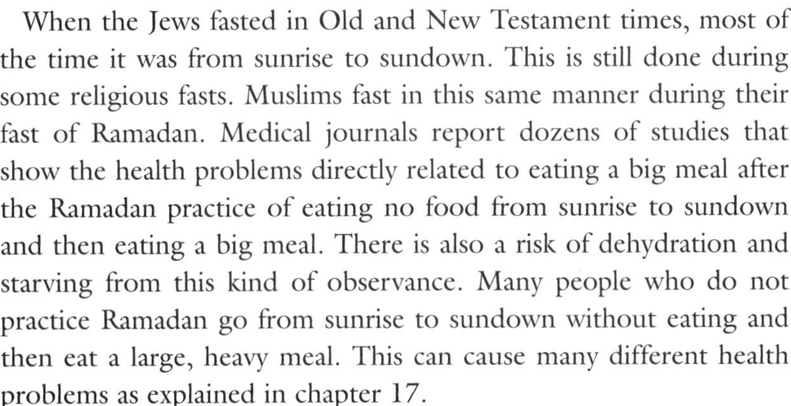

When the Jews fasted in Old and New Testament times, most of the time it was from sunrise to sundown. This is still done during some religious fasts. Muslims fast in this same manner during their fast of Ramadan. Medical journals report dozens of studies that show the health problems directly related to eating a big meal after the Ramadan practice of eating no food from sunrise to sundown and then eating a big meal. There is also a risk of dehydration and starving from this kind of observance. Many people who do not practice Ramadan go from sunrise to sundown without eating and then eat a large, heavy meal. This can cause many different health problems as explained in chapter 17.

Fasting from What?

JEREMIAH 36:9 ***Now it came to pass in the fifth year of Jehoiakim the son of Josiah, king of Judah, in the ninth month, that they proclaimed a fast before the LORD to all the people in Jerusalem, and to all the people who came from the cities of Judah to Jerusalem.*** (NKJV)

A day of fasting was proclaimed because of a national emergency, which historians suspect to have been the Babylonian attack of 605 BC. Fasting was used as a way to bring the people together, to petition the Lord to help them. Fasting was not used for health purposes but for religious purposes. Apparently, they were allowed to have water during this kind of fast, but no food (see Illustration #33).

major fasts
All eating and drinking was prohibited twenty-four hours a day.

minor fasts
All eating and drinking was prohibited from sunrise to sunset.

Four Fasts

ZECHARIAH 8:19 ***Thus says the LORD of hosts: "The fast of the fourth month, the fast of the fifth, the fast of the seventh, and the fast of the tenth, shall be joy and gladness and cheerful feasts for the house of Judah. Therefore love truth and peace."*** *(NKJV)*

Fasts were normally for commemorating historical occurrences. These four mentioned in Zechariah were to commemorate, respectively, the destruction of the first temple, the destruction of the second temple, the destruction of Jerusalem, and the destruction of the independent Jewish state in ancient times.[1] Although originally these fasts were to be **major fasts**, the latter two eventually became **minor fasts**. Holy texts, readings, and prayers of petition were regular parts of the proclaimed fasts.

what others say

T. D. Jakes

Many people are discovering the pleasure of fasting and are renewing the biblical observance of using the day of fasting to pray and seek direction from the Lord.[2]

A Whole Forty Days!

MATTHEW 4:1–4 ***Then Jesus was led up by the Spirit into the wilderness to be tempted by the devil. And when He had fasted forty days and forty nights, afterward He was hungry. Now when the tempter came to Him, he said, "If You are the Son of God, command that these stones become bread." But He answered and said, "It is written, 'Man shall not live by bread alone, but by every word that proceeds from the mouth of God.'"*** *(NKJV)*

Forty days without eating is about how long it takes to use up all the stored energy in your body. This is not recommended for most Westerners. With the introduction of junk foods, soft drinks, processed foods, air pollution, and high stress levels, most Westerners are not in good enough shape to do a forty-day fast and remain healthy afterward. The medical journals are filled with articles reporting hundreds of negative health results because of the Ramadan fasting that Muslims do. They fast for only one month, and then it is only from sunrise to sunset. This creates a great stress on human bodies, especially if, after not eating during the day, one eats a large meal after sundown.

Illustration #33
Water Pot and Ladle—Although some biblical fasting required refraining from drinking water during a fast, during non-fasting times it is best to drink six to eight 8-ounce glasses of water daily.

If you decide that you want to try fasting in order to seek the Lord, please do it sensibly! Start by outlining how you will do it, which will be covered in depth in this chapter. Write it down. Then go see your doctor for a physical, show him the outline of your fasting plan, and then ask your doctor to approve your fast. Even if you decide to go to a clinic or retreat to do your first fast, let your doctor know and get his approval.

Why Fast?

> ACTS 13:2–3 ***As they ministered to the Lord and fasted, the Holy Spirit said, "Now separate to Me Barnabas and Saul for the work to which I have called them." Then, having fasted and prayed, and laid hands on them, they sent them away.*** *(NKJV)*

Basically, people fast for either religious or health reasons. People who fast for religious reasons do so to get closer to God, to ask for forgiveness, to petition God for something, to confess sins and repent before God, to wait on God for an answer to a petition (as in Acts 13), or just to feel God's presence with them. Some call this last sort of fasting "practicing the presence of God." These are the same reasons people fasted in Bible times.

People who fast for health reasons do so to have blood tests done, to clean out the "sludge of winter," to remove toxins or heavy metals, to improve digestion, to give the body a rest from eating and digesting, to stimulate healing, to test for allergies or sensitivities, or to get over a specific sickness, which is generally coupled with prayer, repentance, and forgiveness. When you fast from food, your body doesn't have to concentrate on all the bodily functions that go with

totally healthy
having no diagnosed diseases or disorders

juice
the liquid part of fruits and vegetables

clear liquids
vegetable broth, pure water with lemon juice, flavored and unsweetened mineral water

pure water
water with no chlorine or other chemicals in it

not totally healthy
have a diagnosed or suspected disease

eating, digesting, and eliminating. Instead, your body can use its energy for other purposes such as healing and spiritual matters.

Fasting eliminates a host of concerns that normally go with eating—where to eat, what to eat, when to eat, etc. It gives you more time for meditating, reading Scripture, and petitioning God. Fasting one day a week, when properly done, can improve your health.

what others say

Cheryl Townsley

Regular fasting is one of the easiest ways to cleanse the body. When we stop eating, we transfer all of the energy used to process food into eliminating body toxins. Fasting one day a week (for twenty-four to thirty-six hours) totals fifty-two days a year of cleansing the body. Those fifty-two days become days of rest—cleansing restoration for the body, mind, and soul.[3]

I Don't Know About This . . .

You have already been doing a mini-fast almost every day! You go from sometime in the evening, say dinnertime, to the first meal of the day called breakfast ("break the fast"). So, you are already going without food for eight to twelve hours, depending on whether you snack after dinner or before bedtime. The Jews most often fasted from sunrise to sunset. That is about the same time you already fast, but at the other end of the day. Hopefully, knowing this will help to calm any fears you may have about fasting.

Start Slow!

If you are **totally healthy**, you might want to start with just taking **juice**, **clear liquids**, and **pure water** all day long for a period of twenty-four to thirty-six hours (see Illustration #34). Your first food after this period should be something light like a fruit plate or a salad plate with just veggies and some lemon juice, and perhaps a touch of olive oil. Then you can eat something more substantial after that for the next meal. If you are **not totally healthy**, say you have diabetes, hypoglycemia, cancer, arthritis, high blood pressure, asthma, kidney disease, heart disease, or any other health problem, see your doctor first! Then, when you get the okay, start slowly and keep your doctor informed of what you are doing. Likewise, if you are fasting for spiritual reasons, inform your pastor, minister, or priest in case you have a need to call them, just as you might call your doctor, but about spiritual, emotional, or mental problems.

Juice fasts are popular because even though you don't eat food, you still get some food source fuels to feed the blood sugar and prevent a blood-sugar crisis. Many companies produce powdered nutrients that can be used as meal replacements when doing partial or selected fasts. They are generally made of easily digested foods so that when in liquid form your body doesn't have to digest foods. This is not actually fasting, but is advisable for those who have trouble going without food or who have stressful lives, making it inadvisable to do a fast during the workday. Living Fuel is one of these foods. So is Ultra Meal from Metagenics and Dream Protein, both available through holistic health practitioners.

Illustration #34
Fruit and Vegetable Juice—Provided you are totally healthy, start fasting by drinking only fruit and vegetable juice for a period of twenty-four to thirty-six hours.

what others say

Rex Russell, M.D.

Hippocrates, the father of medicine, used fasting to combat disease 2,400 years ago. The ancient Ayurvedic healers of the Hindu religion prescribed fasting weekly for a healthy digestive system. Most nationalities, religions and languages have a tradition of fasting handed down from their ancestors.[4]

The First Days

Prepare by reading Scripture and praying about the wisdom of fasting. Then write out what you plan to do and accomplish. This would include the number of days for each phase as detailed earlier, the time limit you are setting for the fast, and your method of coming off the fast. On the first day of preparation, abstain from eating fat, meat, and all animal products, including milk and eggs. On the second day, eliminate all foods made of grains, including gravy, bread, crackers, and pretzels. On the third day, begin to drink several more glasses of water than you usually would and eat only raw fruits and vegetables. On the fourth day, switch to fruit and vegetable juices. Use juice that is as fresh and unprepared as possible and dilute it half and half with pure water. Stay away from juice with salt, EDTA, or preservatives. Eliminate all caffeine as well. Drink some diluted juice every hour or two throughout the day and night as long as you are awake. If you feel hungry, drink a little juice or water and breathe deeply several times to relax your digestive organs. On the fifth day, you can go to only water if you wish. This can be maintained as long as you feel healthy. If you begin to feel really, really hungry, go off the fast.

Many people feel really terrible the first day or two of a juice or water fast. This is to be expected if you have a blood-sugar problem, eat poorly, or have been around toxic substances (see the following list). It is also to be expected if you have been addicted to any foods or substances like caffeine, nicotine, sugar, salt, wheat, or dairy products. This period of feeling terrible is called "withdrawal." It generally takes at least three days for withdrawal effects to go away. Exercise, do deep breathing, relax, and drink a lot of pure water.

Some Toxic Substances

- Tobacco smoke
- Acrylic and gel fingernails
- Alcohol
- Gasoline fumes
- Aluminum cooking pans
- Mold
- Cleaning fluids
- Deodorant with zinc or aluminum
- Exhaust fumes
- Preservatives

- Heavy metals like lead and mercury
- Hair dyes and perms

Get Me Off This, Fast!

To go off a fast, just reverse the process. Drink juices for a day. Then eat fresh fruit and veggies. The following day add in grains, and on the last day add in meat, eggs, fish, and milk.

If you are on water and feel great and then upon eating fruits and veggie juices you begin to experience strange symptoms, like headaches, a runny nose, coughing, or pain anywhere, you might have a food allergy or sensitivity. Go back on the water until the symptoms clear up. Then take the diluted juice of only one fruit. If adding the juice causes no change in how you feel, you may add in another type of juice the next time you take juice. Continue to add one new juice each time. When you begin to eat solid foods, eat one type of food at a time. Add a new food, if you wish, each time you take some sustenance. If you come across a juice, vegetable, grain, or other substance that makes a really noticeable change in how you feel, you will be well on your way to discovering what is making you sick. (This is called "food challenging" and is a very popular way to test for food allergies or sensitivities.) See an allergist with this information for confirmation or a remedy. Be suspicious of any of the following: dairy products, corn and corn syrup, wheat, sugar, eggs, chicken, oranges, pork products, preservatives, peanuts, and potatoes. But that's not to say other foods or substances won't cause an allergic reaction; they might.

what others say

Rex Russell, M.D.

Don't expect mental miracles on your first fast. Addiction and withdrawal symptoms (irritability, anger, headaches, and so on) could override any first-time benefits. Examples of fasting's positive effect on the mind, however, are even more striking.[5]

Fasting Cures

Leviticus 16:29–31 *This shall be a statute forever for you: In the seventh month, on the tenth day of the month, you shall*

nocebo effect
illness created by the power of suggestion

schizophrenia
disease that includes disordered thinking and perception, emotional changes, behavioral disturbances, and loss of contact with reality

rheumatoid arthritis
inflammatory arthritis

afflict your souls, and do no work at all, whether a native of your own country or a stranger who dwells among you. For on that day the priest shall make atonement for you, to cleanse you, that you may be clean from all your sins before the LORD. It is a sabbath of solemn rest for you, and you shall afflict your souls. It is a statute forever. *(NKJV)*

Many Christians believe that diseases and unclean states are caused by sins; this is why so many churches require a confession of sins before a healing service or prayer for healing. Atonement and repentance are very important parts of a cleansing fast for spiritual or physical healing.

The definition of sin is missing the mark. Many people feel guilty for things they do that are considered sin and hold on to this and create a kind of immune suppression in their body because of it. When the immune system is suppressed, many diseases can occur as a result. Releasing the guilt by confessing it and asking for forgiveness can stop the immune suppression and allow healing to take place. This is part of what is now called the body-mind connection. Confessing sins can also be a kind of placebo effect and reduce illness as well. Or the disease could be caused by a **nocebo effect** and the problem will be lifted as well. This is especially true of anxiety and depressive disorders.[6] In James 5:15–16 we read: "The prayer of faith will save the sick, and the Lord will raise him up. And if he has committed sins, he will be forgiven. Confess your trespasses to one another, and pray for one another, that you may be healed. The effective, fervent prayer of a righteous man avails much" (NKJV). And that clearly points out that confession of sins can help with healing.

In the last thirty years I have heard of many people who have been cured of many different diseases by fasting. **Schizophrenia** and **rheumatoid arthritis** are the most popular diseases for using fasting, because often they can be caused by food allergies.

Abraham Hoffer, M.D., used to discuss many different cases of schizophrenics who were suffering from food allergies, even people in catatonic states, who recovered when they fasted and found out what foods were causing the condition. We had many discussions about schizophrenia and allergies and fasting when he gave talks at the Nutritional and Preventative Medical Clinic in Toronto where I was a nutritionist. Dr. Hoffer is one of the founders of the system of healing called Orthomolecular Medicine, which uses varying doses of vitamins and other nutrients for healing as well as fasting and other kinds of medical testing.

fools
Proverbs 26:3–8

Migraines, stomach problems, allergies, sinus conditions, and mild depression all have been reported to have been cured by fasting or fasting and prayer together. All of these fasting cures were done in clinical settings with supervision and should not be attempted without medical supervision.

The Reward of Fasting

> MATTHEW 6:16–18 ***Moreover, when you fast, do not be like the hypocrites, with a sad countenance. For they disfigure their faces that they may appear to men to be fasting. Assuredly, I say to you, they have their reward. But you, when you fast, anoint your head and wash your face, so that you do not appear to men to be fasting, but to your Father who is in the secret place; and your Father who sees in secret will reward you openly.*** *(NKJV)*

When Jesus speaks of fasting to know God, he speaks of the rewards that God will bring you. They are peace, joy, love, forgiveness, and the wonder of knowing God in a new and refreshing way. Just be sure that when you fast, you do it sensibly. God is not impressed with fools.

Chapter Wrap-Up

- God assigned four fasts to the Israelites that were to be joyful experiences. (Zechariah 8:19)
- The Jews observed two kinds of fasts. Major fasts required no food or drink for twenty-four hours. Minor fasts required no food or drink from sunrise to sunset.
- Fasting was done for spiritual reasons in Bible times, especially to receive information from God. (Acts 13:2–3)
- Fasting is also done for health reasons. Through the ages many nationalities have fasted as a group for spiritual and health reasons.
- Jesus warned people to fast in silence if they were doing a spiritual fast, because it is between the one who is fasting and God. (Matthew 6:16–18)

Study Questions

1. What does the Bible say about fasting?
2. What were the different fasts that were followed in Bible times? Why are they of importance today?
3. Which fasts are done today by Christians and for what reasons? Do you think it is effective to do these kinds of fasts?
4. What is the right way and what is the wrong way to fast?
5. Why do you think Jesus said people should keep their fasting secret from all but God?

Chapter 19: Recipes for Healthy Living

Chapter Highlights:

- **Breakfast**
- **Soups**
- **Lunch or Dinner**
- **Snacks or Appetizers**
- **Breads**
- **Salads**

Life is fun! Well, at least it should be. Eating healthy should never be seen as an option, but as a daily endeavor. Our bodies were meant to be fueled by food, whole food in as natural a state as you can eat it. Have you noticed that as our food, water, and air supplies become more adulterated we become susceptible to more and more diseases? The diseases that were considered "old people's diseases" just fifty years ago are now commonplace among teenagers and children. As fast food and toxic chemicals in the food and water supplies have increased, so have diseases like diabetes, autism, heart disease, high cholesterol, and flu plagues. Antibiotic-resistant organisms are running rampant in schools, hospitals, and nursing homes. Many elderly are living out their lives in nursing homes and hospitals, whereas fifty years ago most elderly died of old age.

Changing your diet can help! Following the Mediterranean diet style of eating can help you feel better and live a more vibrant life, and I have a few tips that can help:

If God made it, eat it. If man made it, leave it. This is my most famous saying of all time. That should be all you need to know when shopping or eating out. Just look at the food and ask, "Is this the way God intended this food to be?" If the answer is no, then don't bother with it.

We were not designed to live on caffeine, sugar, and preservatives. They can destroy your body little by little. If you ate junk food and woke up with a headache or a hangover, it might be obvious, but it generally isn't that fast. Eating nutrientless food is a slow, insidious, and downward descent to ill health. It starts when you are a child.

Believe me when I say there are those who actually think that the devil made junk food. I don't believe it. I think man, greedy man, unthinking man, corporate man, made the junk food. And that brings me to another of my favorite sayings. Ask yourself, *Is this food made for eating or for selling?* Will someone make a huge profit from this with no concern for your health? Or is a farmer or farm cooperative going to make a living from this food? Hopefully for most of the food we eat the answer will be "The farmer will make his living from this food."

Eat green at every meal. If you eat something green or take a green powdered drink at every meal, you will start on the path to better health. Never serve a sandwich without green lettuce. Never eat cheese without lettuce.

Eat colored foods daily. Every day, eat a variety of different-colored foods, especially dark blue, red, orange, yellow. These foods have the highest amount of nutrients. How smart of God to make it so easy for us to be healthy. I have met people who say they don't eat anything white, and that just won't work. How can you live without cauliflower? Actually it is supposed to be green. It is bleached by farmers who tie up the leaves over the growing head of cauliflower so the sun can't turn it green. Look for brocco-flower for a greener variety. White sugar and white bread are two white foods to stay away from.

Garnish with sprouts and chopped herbs. Add chopped parsley or dill and sprouts to every meal. This will give you enzymes, chlorophyll, and vitality.

Drink water regularly. Fill a large container of fresh, filtered, or well water every morning and drink it throughout the day. Forget the ice; it will just slow down your digestion. Add lemon to your water to make it more alkaline. It might take a few weeks to get used to drinking un-iced water as your main beverage, but soon you will enjoy it as you train yourself to want the wholesome drink that God gave us for health.

Eat whole grains. If you are going to eat grains, eat only whole grains and whole grain products. There're everywhere; it's easier now than ever before. Sure, it takes a little more time to cook brown rice than white rice, so plan ahead.

Use whole grain flours. Every recipe I have ever tried with flour can be turned into a whole grain recipe without much problem. Just remember, if you are using whole wheat flour, use pastry flour for things that are not going to be treated roughly like pancakes, waffles, biscuits, cakes, cookies, piecrust, muffins, and quick breads. If it takes kneading, use bread flour; it's that simple. If you sift the dry ingredients first, you can sift out any bran that is in overabundance and replace it with a little more flour. Save the bran and use it for cooking or put it in a shake.

Use only whole salts. Research is starting to show that the health problems associated with salt are associated only with refined salt, sodium chloride. When you use a whole salt like Real Salt or Celtic Sea Salt, you also get all the minerals that should be in the salt so the health issues will be less.

How to Cook with Success

1. Read over the recipe before you start.
2. Allow enough time to get ready, make the recipe, cook it, and clean up.
3. Check your supplies to see if you have all the necessary ingredients.
4. Make a list and purchase what you need.
5. Clean off the surface you are going to use with a damp cloth and dry it.
6. Get out all the utensils you will be using.
7. Get out all the ingredients you will be using (all ingredients should be room temperature unless otherwise specified).
8. Make the recipe as it is written the first time to see how it comes out. Then make substitutions if you want to.
9. Set a timer that will ring when the time is up so that you won't forget it.
10. Clean up as soon as you have finished cooking, baking, or making food.

Whole Grains, God's Most Perfect Food

Whole grains are all the rage these days, and it's no wonder. They are the total food, the complete food, that God intended us to eat.

Whole grains contain fiber, protein, and carbohydrates and many nutrients like vitamin E, B vitamins, and vitamin F, depending on the type of grain. The current thinking is that we all need to eat at least 25 grams of fiber a day and that eating fresh vegetables and fruits along with whole grains will provide this. This is why it is good to substitute whole grains for refined grains like white flour or wheat flour; brown rice for white or refined rice. Try adding whole grains into soups and stews, substitute whole wheat pastry flour equally for all your delicate baking needs like cakes, pies, cookies, and muffins. Use whole grain flours in bread baking and for making sauces and thickenings.

Simple Grain Breakfast

Cook desired quantity of oatmeal, millet, buckwheat, or commercial hot cereal. While cooking, add one or more of the following:

- lima beans
- corn
- carrots, chopped or grated
- peas
- green beans
- precooked beans (like kidney or pinto)

Ladle cooked mixture into bowls and top with butter or olive oil or a mixture of both, flaxseeds, chopped fresh parsley, and soy sauce or Real Salt brand sea salt.

Simple Vegetable Breakfast

Using a steamer or steamer basket inside a large pot, bring water to full steam. Cut up and steam vegetables, starting with those that take the longest to cook—potatoes, brussels sprouts, broccoli stems, onions, beet and other roots, and sweet potato. Veggies that are cut into about one-half-inch cubes should take 10 to 12 minutes to fully cook.

Add other veggies to the pot as the first ones continue to cook.

Peas, green or yellow beans, mushrooms, zucchini, summer squash, broccoli florets, peppers, or precooked veggies will take less time to cook. These can be added after the first vegetables have cooked for 6 or 7 minutes. Chopped spinach and other greens only take a minute or two.

Serve with butter or olive oil, chopped fresh parsley, cumin seeds, sunflower seeds, or even natural or homemade catsup. Salt and pepper, if desired.

You may add an egg or two for each person. Bring the egg to room temperature by covering it with hot water for 3 or 4 minutes. When the chopped greens have been added to the steaming veggies, carefully lower the eggs into the steamer and leave them for the last 4 minutes of cooking time. When the meal is finished cooking, remove the eggs to cold water to stop the cooking. Break the egg shell by hitting it with a table knife so it opens into two halves. Scoop out the egg from each half into the veggies and serve with a little olive oil, chopped parsley and freshly squeezed raw garlic. Small cubes of cheese may be added instead of the eggs, or add cream cheese, or even tuna fish or leftover meats. Fresh herbs can be added to the meal at serving time.

This recipe provides variety for breakfast because it can be made from any seasonally available vegetables.

BREAKFAST

Tofu Shake

For each serving:

½ block tofu, drained

1 cup fresh fruit or vegetable juice

1 teaspoon green powder or ½ cup fresh sprouts

1 tablespoon sunflower seeds or flaxseeds or both

½ teaspoon cinnamon

Pinch of cayenne pepper, optional

Blend all ingredients until smooth. Serves one.

Eggs Florentine

For each serving:

1 teaspoon butter or olive oil

1 small clove fresh garlic, chopped

1 green onion, sliced

7–10 spinach leaves, washed and sliced

1–2 eggs

Water as needed

Salt and pepper to taste

Heat a small fry pan over medium heat; add the butter or olive oil. Sauté the garlic and onion until just starting to go soft. Add the spinach, and when it has cooked down a little make a slight depression in the spinach and put the egg into it. Make sure there is some spinach on the bottom of the pan to hold the egg. You may need to add a little bit of water, up to a half cup, depending on how wet the spinach was. Cover and simmer until the egg is cooked just the way you like it. Serves one.

Scrambled Tofu and Veggies

For each serving:

½ piece tofu in water

1 teaspoon olive oil

¼ cooking onion, chopped

½ stalk broccoli, chopped and separated

2 mushrooms, chopped

⅛ red pepper, chopped

Soy sauce to taste

Drain tofu in several layers of towels. Heat oil over medium heat. Sauté onion, broccoli stalk, and mushrooms until soft. Mash the tofu. Add broccoli florets to onion, broccoli, and mushrooms, and stir; then add red pepper and stir. Add the mashed tofu and soy sauce to taste; heat through. Soak up the water that is released during the cooking of tofu with a paper towel before serving.

Any combination of veggies can be used in this. Cumin, basil, oregano, tomatoes, curry powder, or salsa can be added to change the flavor. Tofu has no taste, so you will want to add seasoning. Keep away from salt, though. Soak up any excess water with a paper towel before serving.

High-Fiber Breakfast Muffins

Mix together:

1 cup grated carrots

1 cup grated zucchini

1 egg, beaten

1 cup milk, low-fat or whole

¼ cup evaporated sugar cane juice or Sucanat

2 tablespoons coconut oil

1 15-ounce can or jar of beans* (pinto, great northern, white, etc.), slightly mashed

½ cup quick-cooking oats

Sift together:

1½ cup whole wheat pastry flour

¼ teaspoon baking soda

1 tablespoon baking powder

Preheat oven to 400°F. Grease or paper 16–18 muffin tins. Sift dry ingredients into wet and stir until it is just barely mixed together. Spoon into muffin tins. Fill to within ¼ inch of the tops. Bake for 25 to 30 minutes.

**Look for organic beans with no chemicals, spices, or preservatives. I like to use Haines or Eden Foods brands.*

Cheese Muffins: Add a teaspoon of grated cheddar cheese to the top of each muffin before baking.

Muffins Like Ezekiel Might Have Eaten

¼ cup cooked millet*

½ cup cooked beans, drained well and mashed

2 tablespoons melted butter

¼ cup organic evaporated sugar cane juice

1 large egg

¾ cup natural yogurt + water to make 1 cup

½ cup raisins, finely chopped

1 cup whole wheat pastry flour

½ cup barley flour

½ cup spelt flour

2 teaspoons baking powder

1 teaspoon ground coriander or cinnamon

Mix the first seven ingredients together. Sift the remaining dry ingredients together into the wet and mix until just mixed together. Spoon into oiled or papered medium muffin cups. Bake in a preheated 350°F oven for 30 minutes. Makes 12 medium muffins.

I often do this in the food processor as it saves time and mashes the beans while mixing the wet ingredients.

These are not the light, sweet, fluffy white-flour muffins most people have gotten used to. These are dense and filling and require chewing.

***Use leftover cooked millet or cook some up for this recipe using 1 tablespoon of hulled millet to 1¼ cups water. Heat to boiling and then turn to low and cook covered until soft. Add a small pinch of salt if desired.**

Breakfast Sandwich

For each sandwich use:

2 slices whole grain bread

Cheese sliced thin to cover each slice of bread (cheddar, Muenster, Monterey Jack, etc.)

4–6 green olives, sliced

2 slices tomato

3 slices red or green pepper

Garlic, peeled and sliced in half (optional)

Rub bread with garlic, place half the cheese on one slice of bread. Cover with olives and veggies, then remaining cheese, cover with bread. Grill or heat through until cheese is melted. You could use mozzarella cheese and pizza sauce to make pizza sandwiches.

You can use whole grain pita bread, tortillas, or wraps.

Breakfast Smoothie

1 cup fresh sprouts (alfalfa, mung bean, radish, mixed, etc.)

¾ cup milk or juice

¼ cup plain yogurt*

½ piece of fruit (banana, peach, pear, or mango)

Blend all ingredients together and serve. Serves one.

*Make sure the yogurt has live bacteria cultures in it.

SOUPS

Basic Winter Stock

1½ tablespoons butter

3 medium carrots, not peeled, coarsely chopped

2 medium onions, not peeled, coarsely chopped

1 medium turnip, coarsely chopped

1 medium parsnip, coarsely chopped

2 stalks celery, chopped

3 quarts water

2 cloves garlic, pressed or chopped

½ cup fresh parsley, chopped

½ teaspoon each dried thyme, ground cumin, and black pepper

In a large soup pot, heat butter and sauté vegetables for 15 minutes or until lightly golden. Add water, herbs, and pepper. Turn to medium-high until soup begins to give off steam. Turn to simmer and cook for 1–2 hours. Strain. Discard vegetables.

This stock is very flavorful and can be used as a broth by itself. It can be made into a different soup by adding precooked beans or precooked grains after simmering.

Black Bean Soup

3 tablespoons extra-virgin olive oil

1 large onion, chopped

2 ribs celery, chopped

2 cloves garlic, pressed or chopped

1 tablespoon whole wheat bread flour

6 cups cold water or stock

3 cups cooked black beans (two 15-ounce cans, washed and drained)

¼ cup parsley, chopped

2 teaspoons natural liquid smoke

2 bay leaves

1 teaspoon ground cumin

½ cup dry sherry (look for a nonalcoholic one)

2 tablespoons white wine vinegar (optional)

Salt and freshly ground pepper to taste

1 cup sour cream, low-fat is best, for garnish

Jalapeño peppers for garnish

Heat soup pot over medium heat and add oil. Sauté onion, celery, and garlic until onion is translucent. Sprinkle flour over mixture and stir to coat. Cook 1 minute or more, until it gives off a nutty fragrance. Add water and stir. Add beans, parsley, smoke, bay leaves, cumin, sherry, vinegar, and salt and pepper, stir. Allow to come to just barely simmering, reduce heat to keep it simmering and cook, covered, for 1 hour or more. Serve with a dollop of sour cream and chopped jalapeños on top. Serves 6–10.

To make this vegan, use nondairy sour cream.

Mushroom and Barley Soup

¾ pound mushrooms

1 tablespoon olive oil

2 tablespoons butter

⅓ cup pearl barley

6 cups boiling water or stock

1 stalk celery

1 teaspoon salt

2 sprigs parsley

2 tablespoons chopped parsley

Clean mushrooms, remove stems from caps and separate. Slice mushroom caps. Heat oil and butter in soup pot over medium heat. Sauté caps for 2 minutes or until they change color; remove from pan and set aside.

Add barley to oil and sauté until it just starts to turn golden. Chop mushroom stems and add. Stir. Cook until barley is very golden and mushrooms are cooked. Add water, celery, and salt and turn heat to high. Boil for 3 minutes. Turn heat to low, add parsley sprigs, cover and cook for 20 to 45 minutes more or until barley is soft. Remove celery and parsley and discard. Add mushroom caps and simmer for 4 minutes to heat caps. Garnish with chopped parsley. Serves 4.

This soup is even better reheated the next day, keeps well in the freezer, and makes a great after-school snack.

To make this vegan, use all olive oil and eliminate the butter.

French-Style Onion Soup

2 tablespoons virgin or extra-virgin olive oil

1 tablespoon butter

3 cooking onions, peeled, quartered, and sliced thin

2 Spanish onions, peeled, halved, and sliced thin

1 clove garlic, chopped or pressed

2 quarts cold water or stock

½ cup nonalcoholic sherry

1 teaspoon thyme

1 tablespoon miso paste* diluted in 2 tablespoons water

Heat oil and butter over medium heat in soup pan until mixture foams up. Add cooking onions, stirring until very golden brown. Add Spanish onions and garlic, stir and cook until they are transparent. Add water and turn heat to medium-high. Bring just to the boiling point. Turn to simmer and add sherry while soup is cooling down. When it is simmering, add thyme and miso paste. Simmer 5 minutes. Serves 6.

**Miso paste is made of fermented soybeans and can be purchased in natural food stores or the health food department of your supermarket. You can also use Marmite to give the soup body and a dark color.*

Traditionally, French onion soup is made by browning beef shoulder bones in the oven and then using them to make the stock. This takes hours of preparation. Sautéing the onions until brown gives almost the same stock in way less time.

To make this vegan, use all olive oil and eliminate the butter.

Quick Vegetable Soup

1 tablespoon olive oil

2 tablespoons butter

1 cooking onion, peeled, quartered, and sliced thin

1–3 cloves garlic, chopped

2 cups mixed vegetables, chopped (no leaves or flowers*)

2 ripe tomatoes, peeled and seeded; or 2 slices lemon with peel

4 cups cold water

1 teaspoon salt, optional

2 teaspoons dried savory

Heat oil and butter in soup pot over medium heat until butter melts. Add onion and garlic and stir. Sauté until golden, but not burned. Add vegetables, starting with the ones that take the longest to cook, like potatoes, broccoli stems, parsnips, and carrots. Continue to add another type when each changes color. Add tomatoes last. Add lemon here if using instead of the tomatoes. Add water, turn heat to medium-high and bring just to the boil. Turn heat to low and simmer for 6–15 minutes, depending on the vegetables used. Add salt and/or savory and simmer for an additional 5 minutes. This soup can be made with any combination of veggies. Carrots, potatoes, celery, peas, green and yellow beans, and tomatoes are the most common. Okra, broccoli, mushrooms, corn, pea pods, zucchini, turnips, etc., can all be used in combinations. Serves 4.

**Add broccoli florets and chopped leaves of veggies or spinach at the very end.*

To make this vegan, use all olive oil and eliminate the butter.

LUNCH OR DINNER

Magic Meal

The magic part is that this is just a technique that can be adapted to many different kinds of recipes. By changing the seasonings, thickenings, or the basic starch, you can create dozens of different-tasting recipes without much effort. One of my male cooking school students in Toronto found that this made him a fabulous dinner party host. He actually served the same veggies every week to his friends using different seasonings, and he was a huge hit. They all thought he had become a gourmet cook. One week he did French-style, the next Chinese, the next East Indian, and the last Italian. He went from a man who had never cooked anything to a gourmet chef in one lesson. Now that's magic.

Festive Risotto

1 tablespoon extra-virgin olive oil

1 onion, medium-sized, peeled and finely chopped

1 cup arborio rice*

1 cup fresh mushrooms, chopped

2 tablespoons fresh red pepper, minced

¼ cup dry white nonalcoholic wine

¼ cup chopped Just Tomatoes (dried tomatoes) soaked in ½ cup water

2 cups chicken or vegetable broth

1 teaspoon whole dried rosemary

¼ cup grated Parmesan cheese

¼ cup Italian parsley, finely chopped

In a 2-quart Duromatic Pressure Frypan or larger pressure cooker, heat olive oil over medium-high heat. Add onion and sauté until translucent. Add the rice and sauté until golden, stirring often. Add mushrooms and peppers and stir to coat with oil. Add the wine and stir to mix. Drain tomatoes and add, stirring into mix. Add the broth and increase heat to high until mixture comes to a boil. Stir. Add rosemary.

Close the lid and bring pressure to the first red ring over high heat. Reduce heat to stabilize the pressure at the first red ring. If using another brand of pressure cooker, bring it to the stage where the rocker is lightly rocking and keep it at that pressure. Cook 7 minutes.

Remove the pressure cooker from the heat and release the pressure by running cool water over the rim of the pan, avoiding the steam valves. Remove the lid and stir. Stir in the Parmesan and parsley. Serves 4–6.

**Never wash or rinse arborio rice before cooking. This may keep it from getting creamy during cooking.*

Clarified Butter

Melt 1 pound unsalted butter over low heat or in microwave. Separate milk solids from clear oil, either by chilling or by using a skimmer or separator. In India, clarified butter is called ghee and is made by heating butter over medium heat until the solids have separated out. The solid matter becomes firm and can then be strained away from the golden liquid. Be very careful not to burn the solids or the ghee will taste burned.

Roux

Start with equal parts of oil or clarified butter and flour. There is no precise measurement for the flour and fat. It depends on the type of flour used and the amount of bran and gluten. Use whole wheat, spelt, or other bread flour. Traditionally, clarified butter is used for this, but you could also use olive or coconut oil.

In a heavy pan over medium heat, begin to mash the flour and fat together. All the flour should be coated with fat and all the fat should be saturated with flour. No visible oil or flour should be remaining in the pan. Adjust the mixture by adding more fat or flour.

Cook and mash with a fork until it begins to bubble up and give off a smell of toasted nuts. Reduce heat. If you want to use it for light sauces, remove it from the heat. You can continue to heat and brown it until it is darker if you want a deep-colored sauce. This is very traditional in French cooking. Keep the finished roux in a glass container with a tight lid in the refrigerator. This will prevent rancidity.

To use roux, add 1 heaping tablespoonful to 1 cup near-boiling liquid. Stir until thickened. For a thicker sauce, add more roux.

Roux can be used to thicken soup and stews or to give sauces body. The darker roux will add a richer taste to "flat" soups.

French-Style Tempeh* and Veggies

2 tablespoons clarified butter or oil, or a mixture (more as needed)

1 medium onion, chopped

1 package tempeh or tempeh burgers*

2 garlic cloves

1 bunch broccoli (or 1 small head cauliflower)

½ pound mushrooms

½ red or yellow pepper

1–3 tablespoons flour (whole wheat is best)

¾ cup cold water

1–3 cups hot water as needed

1 teaspoon salt

1 teaspoon ground cumin

2 teaspoons basil or 1 teaspoon tarragon

Chopped fresh parsley as garnish

Heat oil in large heavy pan over medium or medium-high heat. Add chopped onion. Chop tempeh and garlic and stir in, coating with oil. Cut stems from broccoli into small pieces. Add and stir. Slice mushrooms if small or chop if larger, and stir in. Chop pepper. Cut florets into bite-sized pieces. When broccoli stems are nearly cooked, add enough flour to coat all the veggies and tempeh. Sprinkle the flour on and stir. Cook and stir until the flour is toasted. Then add cold water while stirring. It should foam up. Keep stirring and add hot water as needed to make the desired consistency of sauce. Add salt, cumin, florets, and peppers, and stir. Turn the heat down to simmer. When the mixture is simmering, add basil or tarranon. Let simmer for 3–5 minutes and serve over brown rice or whole grain pasta. Serves 4–6.

**Tempeh is an Indonesian fermented soybean product and can be found in the refrigerated Asian section or freezer section of the supermarket or natural food store. It is one of the vegetarian sources of vitamin B_{12}. You could use beef, veal, or chicken in place of the tempeh if desired.*

East Indian Magic Meal

Ingredients from the French-Style Tempeh and Veggies, except for the cumin and basil or tarragon.

¼ teaspoon ground cloves

1 teaspoon each of ground cinnamon, cardamom, turmeric, coriander, ginger, and fenugreek

Chopped fresh cilantro as garnish

Sauté veggies as above. Pull veggies away from the center after stirring in the mushrooms. Add 1 teaspoon additional oil or ghee. When ghee has melted, add the spices to the ghee. Let them cook until the fragrance is strong, about 30 seconds or so. Stir in the veggies and cook 1 minute. Add the flour and continue on as above. Serve over brown rice or whole grain pasta. Garnish with chopped cilantro. Serves 4–6.

Chopped cilantro could be added with the dried spices if desired.

Chinese Magic Meal

Ingredients for French-Style Tempeh and Veggies except for the flour, basil or tarragon, and cumin

1- to 2-inch piece fresh ginger, grated

2 garlic cloves

1 tablespoon tamari

1 heaping tablespoon cornstarch

Cold water to dilute

Hot water, as needed

Follow directions for French Veggies. After mushrooms have started to soften, pull veggies away from the side of the pan. Blend seasonings and cornstarch with enough cold water to make a runny paste. Pour into the center of the wok or pan and let it cook until it begins to get clear around the edges; stir into veggies. Add hot water as needed to dilute to desired consistency. Add florets and cook to the crisp stage. Serve over brown rice or mix with rice noodles. Serves 4–6.

Open-Faced Bean Sandwich

1 15-ounce can of precooked beans (pinto, lima, butter, etc.)

⅛ red bell pepper

2 sprigs fresh parsley, dill, or other herb

4 slices multigrain or whole grain bread

Mayonnaise to moisten

Salt and pepper to taste, optional

2 lettuce leaves for garnish

Rinse and drain beans thoroughly, pat dry with a paper towel. Finely chop the pepper and herbs and mix together with the beans and mayonnaise. Assemble two sandwiches by placing two slices of bread on each plate. Spoon beans onto each slice and spread on the slices. Garnish with lettuce leaves. Serves 2.

This is a high-fiber kind of meal that is tasty and eye-pleasing. Even children love this sandwich. It is also elegant enough for a fancy luncheon.

Tea-Poached Salmon

4 cups boiling water

6 tea bags of green tea

4 large sprigs fresh dill weed or 2 tablespoons dried

1 2-pound fillet of wild caught salmon

1 tablespoon cornstarch

2 tablespoons cool water

Pour boiling water over the tea bags and let steep for up to 10 minutes. Don't leave it too long or it might get bitter. If using dried dill, add it to the tea and steep. If using fresh dill, layer it in the bottom of a pan large enough to just hold the fish. Pour tea in and heat to simmering over medium heat. Cut the fish into 4 even-sized portions and gently place in the pan skin side down. If using dried dill, place a rack in the bottom of the pan to suspend the fish so the tea can surround the fish while poaching. Cover and slow-simmer for 6–8 minutes or until cooked through. Tea should cover the fish while cooking.

Remove fish to a heated plate and keep warm while you make the sauce. Remove fresh dill, turn heat to medium-high, dissolve cornstarch in water. Once tea is just starting to break a boil, stir in cornstarch mixture and stir to thicken. Add more hot liquid as needed to desired consistency. Spoon over the fillets and serve with a green salad on the side dressed with lemon juice and extra-virgin olive oil. Serves 4.

Savory Scones would be a great addition to this meal.

Sloppy Joe

- 2 teaspoons olive oil
- 1 small onion, chopped
- ½ green pepper, chopped
- 1 clove garlic, chopped
- 1 pound low-fat ground beef or turkey
- 6 ounces tomato sauce or catsup
- 1 teaspoon soy sauce
- 1 teaspoon veggie or regular Worcestershire sauce
- ½ teaspoon chile powder

Heat oil in heavy pan, add onion, green pepper, and garlic, and sauté until transparent. Add crumbled ground meat. Continue to cook until all are lightly browned. Add remaining ingredients and simmer 5 minutes or to desired consistency. Serve over whole wheat buns. Serves 4.

Tofu and Winter Veggie Pot Pie

Filling:

1 potato (Yukon gold or White Rose are best)

1 small turnip

1 small carrot

1 package firm tofu, drained or smoked

1 small onion

2 garlic cloves

2 tablespoons oil or butter

2–3 tablespoons whole wheat bread flour

½ teaspoon salt

1 tablespoon red or brown miso paste or marmite or 1 tablespoon veggie bouillon, chicken or beef*

½ teaspoon ground cumin

2 teaspoons dried thyme

Dice potato, turnip, and carrot into half-inch cubes and steam for 3–4 minutes to precook. Slice tofu into half-inch slabs and wrap in towels to drain, if using the regular tofu.* Chop onion and garlic. Heat oil or butter and sauté the onion and garlic until slightly brown. Stir in flour and salt. All the fat should be absorbed in the flour. There should be no flour that is not coated with oil in the pan. Stir and cook over medium-high heat until flour is toasted. Add about ½ cup of cold water and stir. As mixture begins to thicken, add more water or bouillon to make a gravy (the veggies will give off liquid while cooking). Add the miso paste, diluted with a small amount of water. Stir in the veggies and herbs. Dice tofu into the same-size pieces as the veggies and add.

**Not essential if using smoked tofu.*

Crust:

2 cups whole wheat pastry flour

⅔ cup butter or soy margarine

1 teaspoon salt

5–6 tablespoons cold water or other liquid (milk, soy milk, or broth)

Preheat oven to 425°F. Sift flour and salt into food processor. Add butter, cut into small pieces. Process until a coarse meal forms. Add 5 tablespoons liquid and pulse until ball forms. Add remaining tablespoon as needed. Roll out into 2 round crusts.

Place larger crust in 9 or 10″ pie pan, being careful not to stretch the bottom or sides. Put in filling. Dampen edges of crust and place top crust over it. Seal edges and flute. Prick the top with fork to allow steam to escape. Bake for 12 minutes and reduce heat to 375°F and bake 40–50 minutes more or until crust browns. Serve warm with a green salad. Serves 4–6.

Chicken and Winter Veggie Pot Pie

Follow the recipe for Tofu and Winter Veggie Pot Pie and substitute 1 cup diced chicken for the tofu. Add it to the browning onions and garlic and follow the recipe as written.

Tofu Dinner Loaf

2 onions

2 carrots

2 stalks celery

2 cloves garlic

2 tablespoons cooking oil (optional, see note)

1 pound tofu

1½ cups cooked whole grains such as rice, buckwheat, millet (the grains are optional)

¾ cup dry breadcrumbs

1–2 tablespoons miso paste

5 sprigs fresh dill or 2–3 tablespoons dried herbs such as thyme, marjoram, tarragon, or basil

Grate or finely chop first 4 ingredients. Heat oil over medium heat and sauté the vegetables, stirring constantly, until deep brown, but not burned.

Drain tofu in colander. Using a potato masher, mash tofu and all ingredients together. Or blend half the tofu until smooth and mash in remaining ingredients. Or using the plastic blade in a food processor, process tofu and add remaining ingredients until mixed. Spoon into oiled loaf pan and bake at 350°F for one hour or until lightly browned. Serves 4–6 as a main protein serving. Serve with a baked potato and green salad.

Note: You can eliminate the oil by braising the chopped veggies in water with 2 tablespoons low-sodium soy sauce added. Eliminate the miso paste.

The Sautéing of the vegetables gives body to the loaf. The vegetables can be varied depending on how much body you want. This is one of those recipes that can be changed according to your mood or stock of food in the house.

Variations: Substitute rolled oats for the grains and dried breadcrumbs. Use a small can of tomato paste, and substitute 2 teaspoons basil and 1 teaspoon oregano for the dill. This is just like the meat loaf that Mother used to make except that it isn't meat. You could also add chopped green peppers.

A favorite is made from tofu, tarragon, onions, garlic, carrots, celery, cashew or hazelnut pieces lightly dry-toasted, and miso paste. Serve it topped with fresh mushroom gravy and a baked potato with tofu sour cream and a green salad.

Not Meat Loaf

Make the tofu dinner loaf and use 2 packages of Gimme Lean or other ground veggie protein in place of the tofu. You may use breadcrumbs, tomato paste, basil, oregano, and green peppers as described above.

Macaroni, Veggies, and Cheese

- 1½ cups boiling water
- 1 teaspoon salt
- 1 cup whole grain elbow macaroni
- 2 cups chopped mixed veggies (onion, garlic, mushrooms, carrot, celery, broccoli, green beans, red peppers, etc.)
- ¼ cup milk (cow or soy)
- ¼ cup milk powder (optional)
- 1½ cups shredded or cubed cheese

Bring water to a boil in 2-quart pan, add salt (optional). Add macaroni slowly so that the water continues to boil. Stir. Cook for 10 minutes. Stir in veggies, starting with the ones that take the longest to cook first. Preheat oven to 325°F. Cook for another 10 minutes. Remove from heat and stir in milk, milk powder, and 1 cup of the cheese. Put in buttered baking dish and top with remaining cheese. Bake for 20 minutes. Serves 2–4. Serve with a green salad.

Dried herbs, chopped tomatoes, or fresh parsley may also be added.

Tempeh* and Sweet Potato Stew

4 tablespoons oil, butter, or a mixture of the two

2 small onions

1 package tempeh

2 cloves garlic

1 package tempeh burgers (or all regular tempeh)

3–4 tablespoons whole wheat bread flour

3 teaspoons ground coriander

About 2 cups cold water, more or less as needed

3 sweet potatoes, cleaned

1 bunch fresh cilantro

In a large soup pot, melt butter over medium heat. Chop onions and tempeh into 1-inch pieces. Sauté until golden. Press the garlic into the pot, add the tempeh burgers in smaller pieces than the regular tempeh, stir. Add the flour, stir. When it begins to toast, add the ground coriander. Turn heat to medium-high and stir in 1 cup of cold water. Add enough water to make a good consistency. Add sweet potatoes diced into half-inch pieces. Stir. Add more water as needed. Reduce heat to medium. Cook until potatoes are done. Chop the cilantro and add half to the stew after it has cooked for 6 minutes. Use the rest as a garnish on the top of each serving. Stir frequently while the sweet potatoes are cooking. Serves 4–6.

**Substitute diced chicken or veal if desired.*

Millet Casserole

1 cup hulled millet

5 cups water

1 tablespoon virgin olive oil

½ teaspoon sea salt

1 2-cup package shredded low-fat mozzarella and fresh Parmesan combined

¼ teaspoon olive oil to oil the casserole pan

1½ tablespoons extra-virgin olive oil

½ pound crimini mushrooms, cleaned and stems removed

1 small cooking onion, chopped

2 large cloves garlic, chopped

1 pound low-fat ground beef or turkey

2 teaspoons dried thyme

1 teaspoon rubbed or crumbled sage

1 teaspoon organic Worcestershire sauce

¼ teaspoon red hot pepper sauce or more to taste, optional

Soak millet 6–10 hours to speed cooking if desired. Cook millet, water, olive oil, and sea salt in a saucepan with lid by bringing the water to a boil with the ingredients in it. When it boils for 2 minutes, turn the heat to medium, cover the pan, and simmer for 20–30 minutes until fully cooked and like porridge. Stir in ½ cup of the cheese. Spread into a layer in a casserole pan that has been oiled.

While millet is cooking, prepare the topping by heating the 1½ tablespoons olive oil in a heavy pan over medium heat. Finely chop the mushroom stems and add to the oil and sauté for 4 minutes, then add the chopped onion and garlic and sliced mushroom caps. Stir and sauté, adding the crumbled ground beef until all has been added. Cook until onions are transparent and beef loses its redness. Remove from the heat and add the thyme, sage, Worcestershire sauce, and pepper sauce if desired. Spread over the millet in the casserole dish and top with the remaining cheese. Cover and bake at 350°F for 30 minutes. Uncover and bake another 5 minutes to brown the cheese. Serves 4–6.

SNACKS OR APPETIZERS

Lettuce Roll-Ups

Kids love these, and it's a great way to get them to eat greens.

10–15 firm lettuce leaves (romaine, leaf, butter, Bibb, etc.)

Maranatha, Eden Foods, Arrowhead Mills, or other all-natural nut butter*

Toothpicks

Wash and dry the lettuce very well. Carefully spread each lettuce leaf with a tablespoon of nut butter. Roll up and use a toothpick to keep it from unrolling. Make sure you can see the toothpick so it doesn't get eaten. Or you can slice each roll into pinwheels. Serves 5.

**All-natural nut butters do not contain sugar, dextrose, fillers, or anything other than nuts or seeds and salt.*

Veggie Sticks

Prepare several kinds of vegetables and keep them covered in the refrigerator ready to grab and eat. Carrots, celery, green peppers, cucumbers, zucchini, jicama, any veggies will do.

Pizza Pinwheels

This is made of staple ingredients that you can keep around the cupboard so you can make this any time guests or kids drop in.

Filling:

¾ pound low-fat ground beef

2 tablespoons olive oil

1 small onion, chopped

1–2 cloves garlic, chopped fine

1 stalk celery, chopped

¼ cup sliced black or green olives

½ teaspoon ground black pepper

½–1 teaspoon hot pepper sauce, optional

1 teaspoon Real salt or other natural sea salt

½ teaspoon natural soy sauce

½ cup or 1 small can organic tomato paste

1 teaspoon basil

2 teaspoons oregano

1 cup grated or shredded mozzarella

Heat a heavy pan over medium heat and lightly brown ground beef, drain off excess oil. Add olive oil, onion, garlic, and celery and sauté until transparent. Stir in other ingredients and let cool while you make the pastry crust.

Crust:

1½ cups whole wheat pastry flour

½ cup yellow cornmeal

1 teaspoon Real salt or other sea salt

1 teaspoon no-aluminum baking powder

½ cup butter

¾ cup milk

Put dry ingredients into food processor and mix. Add butter in chunks and pulse off and on until the mixture looks like a coarse meal. Add milk and pulse until it is mixed and holds together. Turn out onto a lightly floured surface and knead for a few minutes. Transfer to a lightly floured pastry cloth. Roll out into a rectangle about 12 inches by 15 inches.

Putting it together:

Preheat the oven to 425°F.

Spread the pastry evenly with the cooled pizza mix, leaving a strip along one side about 1 inch. Sprinkle the cheese in a strip in the middle of the filling going the long way. Starting with the side that has the filling all the way to the edge, the 15-inch side, use the cloth to roll the pastry gently into a roll (like a jelly roll), ending with the strip of pastry with no filling. Press lightly to seal. Transfer to a baking sheet with the seam side down. Using a fork, seal the ends by pressing the fork into the pastry. Bake for 15–25 minutes or until it is lightly golden brown. Serves 4 as a main dish with a salad. Or serves 8–10 as an appetizer.

You can also make this into two narrower rolls and have pinwheels for a party appetizer. This should yield about 20 pinwheels.

Many will like this cold as a snack. I generally serve it warm as an appetizer.

Mushroom Paté

This makes a great appetizer for a party.

1 tablespoon each olive oil and butter or 2 tablespoons olive oil

2 cooking onions (8-ounce), chopped

3 garlic cloves, chopped

2 celery stalks, finely chopped, no leaves

1 pound white or crimini mushrooms, divided

½ cup white grape juice or wine

1 cup hazelnuts or almonds, chopped and toasted

⅓ cup fresh parsley, chopped

1½ cups dry whole wheat bread crumbs

1 package tofu (14-ounce)

¼ teaspoon ground sage

1 teaspoon marjoram

1 teaspoon thyme

¼ teaspoon dry mustard powder

¾ teaspoon sea salt, optional

Cooking spray, parchment paper

Preheat oven to 375°F. Heat olive oil and sauté onions, garlic, celery, and half of the mushrooms, very finely chopped. Cook and stir until it makes a paste. Add grape juice and remaining mushrooms, coarsely chopped. Stir and cook until soft, using metal blade in a food processor, or process parsley, breadcrumbs, tofu, herbs, and salt with metal blade until smooth. Replace blade with plastic blade and blend in veggies and nuts. Spray pans with cooking spray and spoon in paté. Bake 45 minutes to an hour or until it is firm and starts to brown around edges. Run knife around edges to loosen. Release from mold onto plate and garnish with parsley. Serve with whole grain crackers.

Tofu Bean Paté

2 cups firm tofu (500 mL)

1 cup cooked black beans

1 tablespoon olive oil

1 large cooking onion, finely chopped

1–2 cloves garlic, finely chopped

1 tablespoon miso paste or tamari

1½ tablespoons dried thyme

Ground black pepper to taste

Wrap tofu in several layers of paper towel to drain. If using canned beans, drain and rinse them. Heat oil over medium heat and sauté onions and garlic until brown. Mash or process beans and tofu together, add remaining ingredients. Spray pan with cooking spray and spoon in mixture. Bake in 375°F oven for 45 minutes to an hour or until firm and browned.

These can be made in small foil pans. It makes 3 baby loaves. Or a larger bread pan can be used.

This appetizer tastes so much like fancy-grade liver paté that your guests won't be able to tell the difference.

Easy Whole Grain Crackers

3½ cups whole wheat pastry flour

½ cup sesame seeds, optional

1¼ teaspoons salt (or less)

½ cup natural oil, include 1 tablespoon toasted sesame oil

1 cup + 2 tablespoons cool water

Using plastic blade in food processor, mix flour, seeds, and salt. Blend oil and water together and add to flour, process until blended. Roll out very thin on lightly floured surface or cloth. Prick all over with a fork and cut into shapes. Bake on ungreased baking sheet in 350°F oven for 15–20 minutes or until lightly brown.

You may save the salt to sprinkle on the tops before pricking and cutting instead of putting in the crackers. Dill, curry, caraway seeds, cumin seeds, poppy seeds, etc., can be used on top.

Chickpea and Roasted Red Pepper Spread

2 cups cooked chickpeas

1 red pepper, seeded, roasted, and peeled

3–4 tablespoons lemon juice

2 teaspoons ground cumin seeds

⅛ teaspoon cayenne pepper

1 teaspoon vegetarian or regular Worcestershire sauce

1 tablespoon roasted sesame tahini

5 garlic cloves, roasted

Wash off chickpeas and drain. Put everything in food processor and process until almost smooth. Add more of anything to taste. Some like a lot more cayenne than this, but it is an acquired taste. Use as an appetizer with crackers or spread on warmed whole grain tortillas or wraps and roll up. Slice into pinwheels and serve.

Green Olive Tapenade

1¼ cups pitted Manzanilla olives, rinsed and drained

1 teaspoon vegetarian or regular Worcestershire sauce

1 large garlic clove, pressed

1 teaspoon lemon juice

¼ cup extra-virgin olive oil

1 tablespoon cilantro or parsley, finely chopped

Chop olives in food processor. With motor running, add remaining ingredients except greens. Process to blend. Stir in parsley or cilantro. Serve with crackers or on slices of crusty whole grain French baguette.

Lettuce Snacks

10–15 very green lettuce leaves, washed and dried

10–15 tablespoons natural peanut, almond, cashew or other nut butter

Toothpicks

Spread each leaf with a tablespoon of nut butter and roll up like a jelly roll. Secure with a toothpick.

This is a fabulous snack that children of all ages love, and it is also a great way to get them to eat lettuce.

Laban Snacks

Laban is a yogurt cheese easily made in your own kitchen and traditionally eaten in the Middle East.

1 32-ounce tub of natural, unsweetened yogurt

1 tablespoon dried or fresh chives, minced

¼ teaspoon garlic powder

1 sprig fresh parsley, finely chopped

½ cup sprouts, chopped

Drain* the yogurt overnight in the refrigerator and reserve the whey. Mix all ingredients into the curd that is left. Roll into balls a little smaller than a golf ball or Ping-Pong ball. Arrange on a plate so they are not touching one another and refrigerate uncovered overnight to firm them up. Serve with fresh bread or crackers. Put one ball on the bread and spread it around. Add a few drops of extra-virgin olive oil or natural sesame oil for variety.

You can keep them submerged in sesame oil in or out of the refrigerator for hours or even days. That's how they transported them around in the desert in Bible times.

**There are several ways to drain the laban or cream cheese. You can use a large coffeepot with a paper filter or cone in it. Just make sure there is no coffee smell or taste left in the pot. Or you can use several layers of cheesecloth in a nylon strainer over a bowl or over the tub the original yogurt came in.*

The whey is excellent for watering houseplants, as it is rich in nutrients and will make them very green. Or you can add some lemon juice to it and drink it for a refreshing and cooling drink. In Europe a fermented whey drink is used as part of a natural weight-loss program.

BREADS AND QUICK BREADS

Use Your Recipes for Bread

Most bread recipes can be made of all whole wheat bread flour, even if the recipe calls for all white flour or just part whole wheat. Always use bread flour for bread. If the flour has a lot of bran, you will want to sift it out to prevent the end product from drying out. Once you find a brand of flour that you can use, adjust your recipes to deal with using this brand of flour. If there is more bran, you will need to add less water, or more flour to make up for the space the bran takes up in the measuring cup.

How to Recover Dry Bread

Preheat oven to 250°F. Crumple up a paper bag. Wet it under the tap. If the bread is very hard, wet the bag fully, being careful not to let it rip. If the bread is just stale, wet the bag lightly. Put the bread into the bag and put it in the oven for 20 minutes.

Olive/Egg Bread

2 packages dry, noninstant yeast

2¾ cups warm water

5 tablespoons Sucanat, or other dehydrated cane juice or natural sugar

2 teaspoons sea salt

¼ teaspoon ground cardamom

4 eggs

⅓ cup olive oil

3 cups whole wheat bread flour, high-protein if available

1 cup kalamata olives, pitted and chopped

2 cups whole durham flour

2¾ cups unbleached white or all-purpose flour (or use all whole wheat)

olive oil as needed

1 egg yolk, blended with 1 teaspoon cold water

4 teaspoons sesame or poppy seeds

Warm a large mixing bowl with hot water. Dissolve dry yeast in the warm water with half of the Sucanat by stirring it in. Leave it to foam up for 10 minutes. (If yeast does not foam up, it may be inactive. Start over with fresh yeast.) Put the remaining Sucanat, salt, cardamom, eggs, oil, and foamed yeast mixture into the warmed bowl. Beat for 2 minutes with a whisk or electric mixer.

Add the whole wheat flour and beat until all is mixed in. Add olives and stir with a wooden spoon. Add the durham flour and mix. Add the remaining flour in small amounts and stir in. When the mixture begins to leave the sides of the bowl, stop adding flour. Sprinkle a generous amount of the remaining flour onto a clean, dry surface—a bread board or cloth is easier to clean up than a countertop, but not necessary. Dump bread onto floured surface.

Knead the bread using the heels of your hands, turning it to ensure even kneading of each section. Add flour as needed. Knead until dough is smooth and elastic; it should have the same texture and feel as your earlobe.

Rinse the bowl with hot water and dry it, then oil it with the olive oil. Oil the dough with a small amount of olive oil and place in bowl, smooth side up. Cover bowl with a clean, dry cloth and put it in a draft-free warm place. Allow to rise for 1½ hours or until it is triple in bulk.

Punch dough in the center with your fist and make a dent to the bottom, to release the dough. Then turn it onto a clean, dry surface. Gently knead dough again for about 1 minute. Divide it into 12 equal portions.

Roll each of the 12 into equal-sized 8-inch rolls and set aside. Cover with a dry cloth. Remove three and braid together, turning the ends under to seal. Do this with the remaining rolls. Place in well-oiled bread pans, or on a baking sheet for a free-form loaf.

Cover with a dry cloth and let rise in a warm place 45 minutes, or until about triple in bulk.

Mix egg yolk and water and carefully brush the tops of the risen loaves. Sprinkle each with some of the seeds. Bake in a preheated 375°F oven for 25 to 30 minutes or until golden.

Makes 4 loaves. You can also make smaller loaves in small tins, free-formed rolls on baking sheets, or dinner rolls by placing little braids in muffin tins.

Whole Wheat Bagels in the Food Processor

½ cup lukewarm water

1 package dry yeast

1½ tablespoons natural sugar, evaporated cane juice, or Sucanat

½ tablespoon salt

3¼ cups whole wheat bread flour

1 tablespoon olive oil

¾ cup lukewarm water

Put the lukewarm water and half of the sugar into a warm cup and sprinkle the yeast over it. Stir the yeast. Let it stand for 8 to 10 minutes until it foams up. Sift the dry ingredients into the bowl of the food processor, add the oil. Process for 6 to 8 seconds. Add the dissolved yeast mixture and process for 10 seconds. Add water through the feeder tube while the machine is still running. Process until the dough forms a ball on the blades. Let the machine knead the dough for about 30–40 seconds from the time the ball stage is reached.

Turn out onto a lightly floured board and knead for 1–2 minutes until the dough is smooth and elastic. Lightly oil or butter a bowl and put the dough in it. Cover with a clean towel and leave it in a warm place to rise for 20 minutes. Turn the dough out onto a lightly floured board and divide it into 12 equal pieces. Roll each piece into an 8-inch rope, join the ends to form a circle. Cover with a cloth and let rise for another 20–30 minutes. (Push your finger into the dough. If it leaves a dent, it is ready. If the hole springs back, it has to rise longer.) In a large soup pan, put 4 cups water, 1 teaspoon salt, and 1 tablespoon honey. Bring to a boil. Gently put 2 or 3 bagels in the boiling water and cook 30 seconds on each side. Remove from the water, place on a baking sheet that has been greased or covered with cornmeal. Bake in a preheated 400°F oven for 25 minutes.

Note: This recipe takes about an hour and a half or more to prepare. Please allow enough time when you are making this recipe. Keep the dough away from any drafts, especially cold ones.

Use Your Recipes for Quick Breads and Pastries

When you use your regular recipes, you can substitute whole wheat pastry flour equally for the white flour. If there is a lot of bran, sift it out with a coarse sifter to remove the bulk of it so that your cookies or cakes do not dry out. Save the bran and add it to cereal. Experiment with different brands of whole wheat pastry flour. There are many different varieties available. Some brands have more bran than others and some brands are organically grown. Start with a recognized quality brand such as ArrowHead Mills, Bob's Red Mill, Purity Foods, Eden Organic, Giusto, or ask your health food store owner for a recommended brand.

Biscuits

2 cups whole wheat pastry flour

2 teaspoons baking powder

½ teaspoon salt

5 tablespoons cool butter

½ cup milk or more as needed

Sift dry ingredients together into a bowl or the bowl of a food processor. Cut in the butter* or pulse in the food processor until the butter is in small pieces like tiny peas. Add the milk and fluff with a fork or pulse with the food processor. When the dough comes together, put it on a floured surface and knead it two or three times. Using a floured rolling pin, roll it until it is about ¼ inch thick. Spread it with butter and fold it over, or just fold it over. Roll lightly to press together. Cut biscuits with a floured biscuit cutter or the top of a glass. They can be any size you want from 2 inches to 4 inches. Place them on an ungreased pan so that the edges just touch and bake in a preheated 450°F oven for 12 minutes or until evenly browned. Makes 9 to 12 biscuits depending on the size of the cutter.

**Cut in the butter. Use 2 knives held next to each other and chop the butter until it is all in very tiny pieces. A pastry blender can be used for this. Kitchenware stores or supermarkets often have this. It is a D-shaped implement with many blades on the rounded part and a handle on the straight edge. Use this to cut into the butter to break it up into small pieces.*

Herbed Biscuits

Add in 2 tablespoons chopped fresh herbs during the brief kneading stage and bake as directed.

Shortbread Biscuits

Make as above and add 2–3 tablespoons of natural sugar or evaporated cane juice. This makes a great base for strawberry shortcake. Or can be used as a topping for cobbler.

Corn Bread

1 cup yellow or blue cornmeal
1 cup whole wheat pastry flour
½ teaspoon sea salt
4 teaspoons baking powder
¼ cup natural sugar
1 egg, slightly beaten
1 cup milk
¼ cup melted butter or olive oil

Sift dry ingredients together into a large bowl. Mix remaining ingredients together and stir into dry ingredients. Stir until well mixed. Bake in a greased 8-inch pan at 400°F for 30 minutes or until lightly browned.

Sweet Corn Bread Cobbler

Slice fresh fruit, or berries, into a 9-inch cake pan. Make a layer of fruit about ½ inch deep. Spoon the corn bread over the top andbake as directed.

Savory Corn Bread Cobbler

Lightly brown sausages, meat or vegetarian, and place them in the bottom of a lightly oiled pan in a sunburst or wagon-wheel pattern. Spoon the corn bread batter over and bake as directed.

I often add chopped fresh parsley to the corn bread for this recipe. You can also make a gravy from the sausages or make tempeh gravy and put that on top of the sausages and then the corn bread. This is a Sunday morning favorite at our house. Serves 4–6.

Quick Onion Cheese Bread

1 tablespoon butter

½ cup finely chopped onion (I like to use a "sweet" variety)

1½ cups whole wheat pastry flour

3 teaspoons baking powder

½ teaspoon salt

2 tablespoons cold butter

1 cup sharp cheddar cheese, grated

1 large egg

½ cup milk

3 tablespoons fresh parsley, chopped

Preheat oven to 400°F. Grease an 8-inch round or square pan. In 1 tablespoon of butter, gently sauté onion until golden brown and set aside. In a large mixing bowl or the bowl of a food processor, sift the flour, baking powder, and salt. Add the butter and cut in* or pulse until the mixture is crumbly. Stir in ½ cup of the cheese and the parsley. (In food processor switch to the plastic blade for this.) Mix the onion, egg, and milk together and add to the cheese mixture. Press into the pan and sprinkle the remaining cheese over the top. Bake for 25 minutes or until golden.

This makes a great base for a vegetarian evening meal. Add a dark green leafy salad that includes ripe olives, red peppers, carrots, cucumbers, tomatoes, and other raw vegetables. Top with a light dressing of olive oil and lemon juice.

**See the instructions for this under Biscuits.*

Scones

2 cups whole wheat pastry flour (or half wheat and half spelt)

2 teaspoons baking powder

½ teaspoon baking soda

½ teaspoon ground nutmeg

½ teaspoon salt

4 ounces cold, unsalted butter (¼ cup)

1 cup raisins or currants

2 tablespoons natural sugar

1 egg yolk

¼ cup buttermilk

Sift first 5 ingredients together. Cut in the butter or work it in with your fingers until it is the size of peas. (I generally use the food processor.) Stir in the raisins or currants and the sugar. Beat the egg yolk with the buttermilk and stir it into the mixture. Mix until blended. Turn it out onto a floured surface and knead 10–12 times. Cut it in half and pat into two 6-inch circles. Slice each into 6 wedges and transfer them to an ungreased baking sheet. Bake in a preheated 375°F oven for 18–20 minutes.

Savory Spelt Scones

2 cups spelt flour

2 teaspoons baking powder

½ teaspoon baking soda

½ teaspoon salt

⅓ cup noninstant milk powder

⅛ teaspoon garlic powder

1 tablespoon each dill weed and chives

1 egg

⅔ cup water

⅓ cup coconut or olive oil

Mix dry ingredients together in bowl. Mix wet ingredients together until egg is beaten and oil is blended in. Pour wet mixture over dry and mix. Dust the working surface with spelt flour. (You might need to use up to ⅓ cup.) Knead it 12–15 times and pat it flat. Divide into 12 even pieces by cutting strips to form diamonds or use a large biscuit cutter. Transfer to an ungreased baking sheet and bake in a preheated 375°F oven for 18–22 minutes.

Banana Loaf

Mix together with a potato masher, electric mixer, or food processor:

2 tablespoons soft butter

2 tablespoons canola or coconut oil

2 tablespoons honey

2 ripe bananas

2 eggs

¼ cup milk

1 teaspoon pure vanilla extract

Sift together into the wet mixture:

2½ cups whole wheat pastry flour*

1 teaspoon baking powder

1 teaspoon ground cinnamon

½ teaspoon salt (if using unsalted butter)

Preheat oven to 375°F. Grease an 8-inch loaf pan. Spoon mixture into pan and bake for 50–60 minutes or until a toothpick comes out clean when inserted in the thickest part.

**Substitute 1 cup spelt flour for 1 cup of the whole wheat pastry flour.*

SALADS

"Eggless" Salad

1 package firm or extra-firm tofu

½ package soft tofu

½–¾ teaspoon celery seeds, finely ground

1 tablespoon fresh parsley, finely chopped

4 green onions, chopped

⅛ cup green olives, chopped (optional)

1 stalk green celery, finely chopped

½–¾ teaspoon turmeric powder, for color

2 teaspoons Dijon mustard

Tofu "mayo" to taste

Drain tofu and wrap in towels to absorb extra water. Mash the soft tofu and add turmeric. Chop the firm tofu. Add to bowl with remaining ingredients and stir. Let stand for 1 hour or more, for best flavor. Makes 4–6 sandwiches.

Note: If you are planning to make sandwiches for a picnic or to take to work for lunch, don't. Pack the bread and lettuce in plastic wrap. Put the tofu "eggless" salad in a jar. Put the sandwich together just before eating. The water might soak into the bread and make it soggy.

Tofu "Mayo"

8 ounces soft tofu, Chinese-style, or firm Japanese-style

¼ cup olive oil or canola oil, or a mixture

¼ teaspoon salt

¼ teaspoon dry mustard or ½ teaspoon Dijon mustard

¼ teaspoon paprika

1 tablespoon each lemon juice and vinegar

Wrap tofu in several layers of towel to drain well. Place all ingredients except tofu in blender and blend. Remove feeder tube and add tofu in 3 pieces. Blend or process until desired consistency is obtained. Store covered in the refrigerator for 2 weeks. If water separates out, drain it off or stir it back in.

This is a fabulous recipe if you are trying to watch your cholesterol or fat intake because it tastes like regular mayonnaise and has no eggs and very little fat. If you use it in a sandwich, assemble the sandwich just before eating, as the Tofu Mayo releases water into the bread and can make it soggy.

Cabbage Salad

½ head green cabbage

½ cup sliced natural almonds

½ cup green salad olives

½ cup unsulfured raisins

½ cup sunflower sprouts

2 tablespoons parsley, finely chopped

½ cup virgin olive oil

1 teaspoon toasted sesame oil

¾ cup freshly squeezed orange juice

Finely slice cabbage and chop. Chop almonds. Mix cabbage, olives, almonds, raisins, sprouts, and parsley and stir. Whisk together oils and juice and pour over salad and toss. Serves 4–6 as a side salad.

Rice Salad

2 cups cooked brown rice, chilled

½ green pepper, chopped

½ red pepper, chopped

4 sprigs parsley, finely chopped

Toss together and add Green Dressing (see page 312). Chill and serve. This is nice to take to potlucks and parties, especially at holiday time. This will serve 6–8, depending on the size of portions. Or even 10 at a buffet.

Add cooked chickpeas to this for extra protein.

Green Dressing

2 green onions

1 bunch fresh parsley, cilantro, basil, or dill

1–2 cloves garlic

½ cup olive oil

1–2 teaspoons lemon juice

Chop onions and parsley and put all ingredients into a blender or food processor and blend with remaining ingredients.

Dinner Salad

For each person, use:

1 leaf green leaf lettuce

1 leaf red leaf lettuce

1 leaf romaine lettuce

2 leaves butter lettuce

4 leaves curly endive or escarole

2 leaves spinach

⅛ red pepper

⅛ green pepper

1/16 English cucumber

6 ripe olives

1 green onion

½ carrot, grated, or 3 baby carrots

Wash and dry leaves and slice or tear into bite-sized pieces. Put into the bottom of a large soup bowl. Chop the other vegetables and add arranged in groups or spread evenly over the top. Then add some protein source.

Protein sources for each person:

1 firm cooked egg, sliced or chopped

2 slices real cheddar cheese

3 slices smoked tofu or natural tofu sandwich slices*

2 slices Monterey Jack, Colby, or other cheese

¼ can drained tuna fish

2 slices precooked chicken, salmon, or shrimp

Arrange in pleasing design or toss with greens and vegetables. Add dressing of your choice and serve. This is a meal in itself. Or you may add some fresh whole grain rolls or bread to the meal.

**You might cut julienned slices of any naturally cured meats. Just make sure that it doesn't have nitrates, nitrites, or sulfitic agents in it.*

Salad Niçoise

Use the green lettuce base in Dinner Salad and add precooked green beans and cubed potatoes, tuna fish, and niçoise olives. The traditional dressing for this is made of 3 parts olive oil to 1 part lemon juice, ½ teaspoon dried tarragon, and freshly ground black pepper and pressed garlic to taste.

Chapter 20: Sources of Nutrients

Chapter Highlights:
- Recommended Dietary Allowance
- Conversions
- Vitamins
- Minerals

Where Did This Information Come From?

Nutritional breakdowns have changed over the years, and there are many different sources for nutritional information. I have chosen to use information furnished by the USDA (United States Department of Agriculture) in handbooks and on the official Web site. The USDA does not publish the full range of known nutrients in any of their nutrient guides. For this reason there is a limited number of listings in this book. If you wish to find a complete nutritional breakdown for any specific food, please utilize their Web site, called the USDA Nutrient Database at:

nal.usda.gov/fnic/foodcomp/search and
ars.usda.gov/nutrientdata.

In this database you can search for specific foods by name. It will give you breakdowns of amino acids, fatty acids, vitamins, minerals, protein, carbohydrates, calories, and other nutrients.

Recommended Dietary Allowances

The Recommended Dietary Allowances (RDA) are a set of nutritional standards established by the Committee on Dietary Allowances in the United States. These recommendations have been published since the early 1940s and are continually adjusted to meet changing needs and information levels of consumers. The RDAs are the average daily intakes of energy and nutrients considered adequate to meet the needs of most healthy people under usual environmental stresses. If you have greater needs, you will want to seek professional help from your doctor, nutritionist, or other health-care practitioner who is knowledgeable about nutrition and health. The foods and RDAs listed are suggested for an average adult.

It's As Easy As 1, 2, 3!

To get the most out of this information, use the following three-step process:

1. Look at what your RDA is for a certain nutrient.
2. Look at how much of that nutrient the listed foods contain.
3. Consume as much as you need to reach your RDA.

Conversions

½ cup=4 ounces=8 tablespoons

1 cup=16 tablespoons

¼ cup=2 ounces=4 tablespoons

⅓ cup=5 tablespoons

g=gram=1,000 milligrams

mg=milligram=1/1,000 gram

mcg=microgram=1/1,000,000 gram

Vitamin A

RDA for women: 8,000 IU (if obtained from fruits and vegetables); 2,640 IU (if obtained from animal sources)

RDA for men: 10,000 IU (if obtained from fruits and vegetables); 3,300 IU (if obtained from animal sources)

The foods listed here have about the equivalent of approximately 500 IU of vitamin A:

½ cup tempeh
1½ tablespoons butter
½ cup diced cheddar cheese
½ cup diced Colby cheese
2½ tablespoons cream cheese
¼ cup Edam cheese
⅓ cup diced Gruyère cheese
½ cup diced Monterey Jack cheese
½ cup Muenster cheese
½ cup whole-milk ricotta
1½ large eggs
1½ cups whole-milk yogurt
1 dried apricot
½ avocado
2 cups sweet cherries
⅔ cup raw elderberries
1/16 mango
1¼ cups papaya cubes

½ raw peach
1 cup watermelon
¼ cup cooked oatmeal
⅛ teaspoon ground paprika
1½ ounces simmered beef kidney
1/7 ounce chicken liver
4 ounces bluefish
2 ounces pickled Atlantic herring
½ cup cooked chinook salmon
2 medium globe artichokes
⅔ cup green beans
½ cup raw broccoli florets
½ cup cooked brussels sprouts
½ cup cooked savoy cabbage
2 tablespoons cooked Chinese cabbage (bok choy)
3 medium baby carrots
1½ tablespoons cooked chopped Swiss chard
1½ tablespoons cooked collard greens
1½ tablespoons garden cress
½ cup raw endive
3 teaspoons cooked kale
1 cup butterhead lettuce
⅓ cup shredded romaine lettuce
½ cup shredded leaf lettuce
8 pods cooked okra
2½ tablespoons parsley
½ cup green peas
½ cup chopped green bell pepper
3 tablespoons cooked pumpkin
2 teaspoons cooked spinach
½ cup cooked zucchini
½ cup baked acorn squash
1½ teaspoons baked butternut squash
1½ teaspoons baked hubbard squash
½ medium cooked tomato
5 tablespoons watercress
3 ounces pan-fried beef liver=30,689 IU
½ cup chopped chicken liver=1,146 IU
1 medium baked sweet potato=25,752 IU
1 egg=260 IU

Vitamin B1—Thiamin

RDA for women: 1.1 mg

RDA for men: 1.5 mg

The foods listed here have approximately the equivalent of 0.25 mg of thiamin:

WOMEN: 4 SERVINGS

MEN: 6 SERVINGS

½ teaspoon brewer's yeast
½ cup cooked black beans
⅔ cup great northern (white) beans
½ cup kidney beans
1 tablespoon wheat germ
½ cup raw pistachio nuts
¼ cup brazil nuts
1½ tablespoons tahini (sesame seed butter)
1 cup cooked lentils
⅔ cup cooked navy beans

¼ cup peanuts
⅔ cup soy milk
1 cup tempeh
1 cup tofu cubes
1 whole wheat English muffin
1 piece whole wheat pita bread
¾ cup cooked couscous
1 cup cooked millet
⅓ cup cooked oat bran
1 cup cooked oatmeal
1 cup cooked brown rice
1½ cups cooked whole wheat spaghetti
½ cup kidneys
½ cup liver
¼ cup filberts
6 tablespoons Atlantic salmon
6 tablespoons bluefin tuna
½ avocado
1 cup orange juice
2 cups plain yogurt

Vitamin B2—Riboflavin

RDA for women: 1.3 mg

RDA for men: 1.7 mg

The foods listed here have approximately the equivalent of 0.25 mg of riboflavin:

WOMEN: 5+ SERVINGS

MEN: 6+ SERVINGS

1¾ teaspoons brewer's yeast
2 tablespoons wheat germ
½ cup cooked soybeans
1½ cups soy milk
½ cup cheddar cheese
1 cup uncreamed cottage cheese
⅔ cup creamed cottage cheese
2 tablespoons feta cheese
1½ tablespoons semisoft goat cheese
1 avocado
2 mangoes
2 slices rye bread
⅔ cup oatmeal
6 tablespoons beef tenderloin
6 tablespoons broiled lean ground beef
1 teaspoon kidney meat
⅔ teaspoon liver
3 ounces (6 tablespoons) lamb
⅔ cup roasted dark meat chicken
1½ tablespoons chicken liver
⅓ cup whole almonds
4 tablespoons cooked mackerel
⅓ cup orange roughy
4 tablespoons Atlantic salmon
½ cup chum salmon
1 cup raw mushrooms
1 cup green peas
1¼ cups cooked pumpkin
⅓ cup spinach
1 sweet potato
2 soft or hard-boiled eggs
2 bananas

Vitamin B3—Niacin

RDA for women: 15 mg

RDA for men: 19 mg

The foods listed here have approximately the equivalent of 5 mg of niacin:

WOMEN: 3 SERVINGS

MEN: 4 SERVINGS

1½ tablespoons brewer's yeast

6 tablespoons dry-roasted peanuts

5 tablespoons peanut butter

1½ cups tempeh

2 avocados (California) or 1 avocado (Florida)

2 cups cooked pearl barley

1 cup cooked couscous

1½ cups cooked millet

1¼ cups cooked oatmeal

2 cups brown rice

4 ounces (½ cup) beef eye of round

4 ounces lean beef tenderloin

3½ ounces broiled lean ground beef

6 tablespoons beef kidney

1½ ounces (3 tablespoons) beef liver

3 ounces roasted leg of lamb

2 ounces broiled or roasted veal

⅓ cup roasted and diced light-meat chicken,

½ cup roasted and diced dark-meat chicken

½ cup sunflower seeds

3 ounces bluefish

6 ounces Atlantic or Pacific cod

4 ounces haddock

3 ounces Atlantic and Pacific halibut

3 ounces mackerel

4 ounces orange roughy

2 ounces Atlantic or chinook salmon

4 ounces sardines

1½ ounces swordfish

3 ounces rainbow trout

1½ ounces fresh tuna

1½ cups green peas

2 baked potatoes

Vitamin B6—Pyridoxine

RDA for women: 1.6 mg

RDA for men: 2.0 mg

The foods listed here have approximately the equivalent of .25 mg of pyridoxine:

WOMEN: 6+ SERVINGS

MEN: 8 SERVINGS

¼ cup cooked chickpeas
1 cup cooked great northern beans
1 cup cooked kidney beans
¾ cup cooked lentils
¾ cup cooked lima beans
¾ cup cooked navy beans
3 tablespoons natural peanut butter
½ cup soybeans
½ cup tempeh
2 cups tofu
1 cup white beans
2 cups plain yogurt
½ avocado
⅓ cup sliced bananas or ½ large whole banana
¾ cup dates
¾ cup elderberries
1½ cups grapes
1 mango
1¼ cups melon balls
2½ cups orange juice
1 cup pineapple juice
½ cup prune juice
⅔ cup seedless raisins
1 cup watermelon balls
1½ pieces whole wheat pita bread
¼ cup brown rice flour
½ cup dark rye flour
2 cups cooked buckwheat
1 cup cooked couscous
¼ cup cooked oatmeal
1 cup cooked brown rice
¼ cup toasted wheat germ
1 cup cooked wild rice
6 tablespoons braised beef brisket
6 tablespoons roasted chuck
7 tablespoons braised beef short ribs
3 tablespoons beef eye of round
3 ounces (6 tablespoons) broiled lean ground beef
¼ cup beef kidney
1 tablespoon liver
⅓ cup chicken liver
4 ounces tongue
3 ounces roasted veal leg
⅓ cup roasted diced light-meat chicken
½ cup roasted dark-meat chicken
1½ ounces (3 tablespoons) filberts
⅔ cup pistachio nuts
¼ cup sunflower seeds
⅔ cup unroasted Brazil nuts
⅓ cup black walnuts
⅔ cup unroasted cashew nuts
3 ounces striped bass
2 ounces bluefish
3 ounces Atlantic or Pacific codfish
3 ounces flounder or sole
2½ ounces grouper
3 ounces haddock
3 ounces Atlantic or Pacific halibut
7 tablespoons canned mackerel
3 ounces monkfish
3 ounces orange roughy
5 tablespoons chinook salmon
3 ounces pink salmon
5 tablespoons sea bass
5 tablespoons snapper
3 ounces rainbow trout
1½ ounces bluefin tuna
1 ounce yellowfin tuna
3 ounces turbot
1 globe artichokes
1 cup shredded savoy cabbage
1 cup shredded Chinese cabbage (bok choy)

1¼ cups grated raw carrots

1 cup cooked cauliflower

1 cup kohlrabi

1 cup onions

⅔ cup green peas

⅔ cup chopped green bell peppers

½ baked potato

⅔ cup cooked spinach

1 cup cubed cooked butternut squash

⅔ cup cubed cooked hubbard squash

1 medium sweet potato

1 medium ripe tomato

Folate, Folic Acid, or Folacin (used to be called Vitamin B_9)

RDA for women: 400 mcg

RDA for men: 400 mcg

The foods listed here have approximately the equivalent of 30 mcg of folate:

WOMEN: 13 SERVINGS (25 IF PREGNANT OR PREPARING TO BE)

MEN: 8 SERVINGS

2 tablespoons cooked black beans

3 tablespoons cooked broad beans

3 tablespoons cooked chick peas

2 tablespoons cooked kidney beans

1½ tablespoons cooked lentils

3 tablespoons cooked lima beans

2 tablespoons cooked navy beans

4 tablespoons cooked split peas

1½ tablespoons natural peanut butter

5½ tablespoons cooked soy beans

5½ tablespoons tempeh

1 cup cubed tofu

1½ cups whole-milk cottage cheese

1 cup nonfat cottage cheese

1 cup ricotta cheese

1 extra large egg

1 cup plain yogurt

⅓ avocado

1 cup sliced banana

⅔ cup blackberries

1¼ cups unsweetened grapefruit juice

1 kiwi fruit

1 mango

1 cup cantaloupe balls

⅔ orange

⅓ cup orange juice

⅔ cup cubed papaya

⅔ cup pineapple juice

1 cup raspberries

1 cup cubed strawberries
1 heaping cup cooked pearl barley
1¼ cups cooked buckwheat
1 cup cooked bulgur
⅔ cup cooked millet
2½ tablespoons cooked oatmeal
2 teaspoons wheat germ
1 ounce cooked kidney
1 tablespoon beef liver
1½ teaspoons chicken liver
8 tablespoons almonds
1½ ounces (3 tablespoons) filberts
⅓ cup pistachio nuts
1½ tablespoons sunflower seeds
2 tablespoons sesame seed butter or tahini
4 ounces chinook salmon
½ globe artichoke
2 spears asparagus
⅔ cup green beans
¼ cup beet slices
⅔ cup raw broccoli florets
⅓ cup brussels sprouts
1 cup shredded cabbage
½ cup shredded cooked savoy cabbage
½ cup raw cauliflower
1 cup diced raw celery
⅓ cup raw endive
⅔ cup shredded butterhead lettuce
⅓ cup shredded romaine lettuce
1 cup shredded looseleaf lettuce
1 cup shiitake mushrooms
7 pods cooked okra
1 cup chopped raw onion
⅓ cup raw parsley
⅓ cup parsnips
5 tablespoons green peas
1 cup chopped green pepper
⅔ cup cooked mashed rutabaga
2 tablespoons cooked spinach
¾ cup cooked acorn squash
¾ cup cooked mashed butternut squash
1 cup cooked hubbard squash
⅔ large cooked sweet potato
2 medium ripe tomatoes
1 cup chicken liver=1,080 mcg
1 cup cooked spinach=263 mcg
1 cup green peas=100 mcg

Vitamin B_{12}—Cobalamin

RDA for women and men: 2 mcg

The foods listed here have approximately the equivalent of 1 mcg vitamin B_{12}.

¾ cup tempeh
1 cup cheddar cheese
⅔ cup cottage cheese
½ cup Gruyère cheese
½ cup Muenster cheese
1¼ cups milk
⅔ cup plain yogurt
1½ ounces beef brisket
1½ ounces beef tenderloin
1½ ounces lean ground beef
½ ounce roasted leg of lamb
3 ounces roasted veal
2 cups light-meat chicken
½ ounce sea bass

3 ounces carp
1½ ounces flounder or sole
3 ounces haddock
3 ounces halibut
1½ ounces orange roughy
1½ ounces salmon
1 ounce red snapper
1½ ounces turbot
3 ounces liver=95 mcg
¼ cup chicken livers=6.7 mcg
3 ounces rainbow trout=5.36 mcg

Vitamin C

RDA for women and men: 60 mg

The foods listed here have approximately the equivalent of 30 mg vitamin C:

⅓ cup apple juice
½ cup apricot nectar
2 cups raw apricot halves
1 cup blackberries
¾ pint blueberries
2½ tablespoons dried black currants
¾ cup elderberries
1 heaping cup fresh gooseberries
⅓ cup grapefruit sections including their juice
⅓ cup unsweetened grapefruit juice
⅓ large kiwi fruit
½ mango
⅓ cup cantaloupe balls
½ orange
¼ cup orange juice
1 large tangerine
¼ papaya
1 cup raspberries
5½ tablespoons sliced strawberries
3 tablespoons canned pimento
½ cup liver
¾ cup chicken livers
½ cup raw broccoli florets
⅓ cup brussels sprouts
1½ cups shredded raw cabbage
¾ cup shredded raw red cabbage
⅔ cup raw cauliflower
1 cup cooked Swiss chard
1¼ cups cooked collards
⅔ cup cooked kale
⅓ cup cooked kohlrabi
3½ tablespoons chopped green bell peppers
3½ strips yellow bell peppers
1½ baked potatoes
⅔ cup cooked rutabaga
½ cup cooked spinach
1 cup cubed cooked mashed butternut squash
¾ cup fresh chopped tomatoes
1 medium tomato

Vitamin D

RDA for women and men: 5 mcg (5 mcg = 200 IU)

The foods listed here have approximately the equivalent of 50 IU:

4 SERVINGS

1¼ cups Kellog's cornflakes

¾ cup Nutri-Grain wheat cereal

1¾ ounces (4 tablespoons) Swiss cheese

2 boiled chicken eggs

4 tablespoons chicken liver

1½ ounces canned salmon

2 ounces canned tuna fish

½ cup milk fortified with vitamin D*

**Most dairy products and even some baked goods are fortified with vitamin D; please read the labels of prepared foods.*

Please Note: Vitamin D is made on your skin from the sun shining on it. If you are a person who goes out in the sun even for 10 minutes a day, you are probably getting enough vitamin D that way. If you live in an area where the sun doesn't come out for days or months on end, you will want to make sure that you consume the necessary amount of vitamin D. When you do go in the sun, it takes very little exposure for this to happen, so do not eliminate the use of sunscreen. If you feel you are low in vitamin D, see your doctor for a test before you begin to consume large amounts of it in the form of supplements. Perhaps your basic daily vitamin and mineral tablets have the RDA in them. Please look before you begin to take supplements.

(References for Vitamin D from *Food Values of Portions Commonly Used*, Jean A. T. Pennington and Helen Nichols Church, Harper and Row, New York, 1985.)

Vitamin E

RDA for women: 8 mg

RDA for men: 10 mg

The foods listed here have approximately the equivalent of 1 mg:

WOMEN: 8 SERVINGS

MEN: 10 SERVINGS

7 tablespoons Edam cheese

7 tablespoons Parmesan cheese

7 tablespoons Swiss cheese

4½ tablespoons butter

1½ teaspoons corn oil

2 teaspoons olive oil

2 teaspoons peanut oil

2 teaspoons soybean oil

½ teaspoon sunflower seed oil

1½ teaspoons Atlantic salmon

½ mango

14 tablespoons (¾ cup = 2 tablespoons) whole barley

1½ teaspoons wheat bran

7 tablespoons dry whole wheat cereal

½ small avocado

3½ tablespoons raw asparagus

3½ tablespoons beet greens

3½ tablespoons raw green cabbage

3½ tablespoons raw chard

3 tablespoons raw dandelion greens

1 heaping tablespoon raw kale

3½ tablespoons raw mustard greens

4 tablespoons raw parsley

7 tablespoons parsnip

6 tablespoons raw green bell pepper

4 tablespoons raw spinach

1½ tablespoons raw sweet potato

3 tablespoons raw turnip greens

1½ teaspoons almonds

1 tablespoon Brazil nuts

1 teaspoon filbert

1 tablespoon natural peanut butter

5 teaspoons pistachio nuts

4½ tablespoons walnuts

7 tablespoons almonds=15 mg

7 tablespoons filberts=21 mg

7 tablespoons sunflower seeds=44 mg

7 tablespoons wheat germ=14 mg

7 tablespoons raw sweet potato=4.56 mg

(References for Vitamin E from *Food Values of Portions Commonly Used*, Jean A. T. Pennington and Helen Nichols Church, Harper and Row, New York, 1985)

Calcium

RDA for women: 1,500 mg (Old recommendations were 800 mg.)

RDA for men: 1,000 mg

The foods listed here have approximately the equivalent of 100 mg:

WOMEN: 15 SERVINGS

MEN: 10 SERVINGS

2 cups cooked black beans
1½ cups cooked broad beans
1¼ cups cooked chickpeas
¾ cup cooked great northern beans
2 cups cooked kidney beans
¾ cup cooked navy beans
½ cup cooked soybeans
⅔ cup tempeh
⅓ cup tofu
⅔ cup cooked white beans
2 tablespoons cheddar cheese
¾ cup creamed cottage cheese
½ ounce Edam cheese
1½ tablespoons feta cheese
½ ounce Gouda cheese
2 tablespoons Monterey Jack cheese
1 ounce whole-milk mozzarella cheese
2 tablespoons Muenster cheese
½ cup Neufchâtel cheese
2½ tablespoons part-skim ricotta
1 tablespoon Swiss cheese
3½ eggs
⅓ cup low-fat milk
⅓ cup goat milk
⅓ cup sour cream
⅓ cup plain yogurt
⅔ cup dried black currants
4 dried figs
2 oranges
4 dried pear halves
4 slices whole wheat bread
½ cup cooked oatmeal
2½ teaspoons poppy seeds
⅓ cup almonds
⅓ cup Brazil nuts
4 tablespoons hazelnuts or filberts
2 tablespoons Atlantic sardines with bone
2 cups green beans
¾ cup shredded raw Chinese cabbage (bok choy)
1 cup Swiss chard
1 cup cooked kale
1¼ cups raw parsley
¾ cup mashed cooked rutabaga
⅓ cup cooked spinach
1 heaping cup cooked cubed acorn squash
2 sweet potatoes

Magnesium

RDA for women: 280 mg

RDA for men: 350 mg

The foods listed here have approximately the equivalent of 100 mg magnesium.

WOMEN: 2¾ SERVINGS

MEN: 3½ SERVINGS

¾ cup cooked black beans
1¼ cups cooked great northern beans
1½ cups chickpeas
1¼ cups cooked kidney beans
1¼ cups cooked lentils
1¼ cups cooked lima beans
1 cup cooked navy beans
1 cups split peas
4 tablespoons dry roasted peanuts
4 tablespoons natural peanut butter
½ cup + 2 tablespoons cooked soybeans
¾ cup tempeh
¾ cup tofu
¾ cup cooked white beans
1 Florida avocado
2½ pieces whole wheat pita bread
1¼ cups cooked buckwheat
1 cup cooked millet
1¼ cups cooked oat bran
2 cups cooked oatmeal
¼ cup cooked brown rice
¼ cup wheat germ
4 tablespoons almonds
⅓ cup Brazil nuts
4 tablespoons unroasted cashews
¼ ounce filberts
¾ cup pistachio nuts
¾ cup sunflower seeds
⅓ cup walnuts
3 ounces chinook salmon
⅔ cup cooked Swiss chard
⅔ cup cooked spinach

Potassium

RDA for women and men: 2,000 mg

The foods listed here have approximately the equivalent of 250 mg of potassium:

8 SERVINGS A DAY

⅓ cup cooked black beans
½ cup cooked broad beans
½ cup cooked chickpeas
⅓ cup cooked great northern beans
⅓ cup cooked kidney beans

⅓ cup cooked lentils

¼ cup cooked lima beans

⅓ cup cooked navy beans

2 tablespoons natural peanut butter

⅔ cup soy milk

½ cup tofu

⅔ cup milk

¾ cup whole-milk yogurt

⅔ cup low-fat yogurt

1 cup apple juice

½ cup raw apricot halves

1 cup apricot nectar

¼ avocado

½ cup sliced bananas

1 cup blackberries

1 cup sweet cherries

3 tablespoons dried currants

3 tablespoons dates

2 dried figs

¾ cup grape juice

1 kiwi

¾ mango

½ cup cantaloupe balls

1 nectarine

1 large orange

½ cup orange juice

⅔ cup cubed papaya

1 medium peach

1 large pear

1½ plums

½ cup prune juice

3 tablespoons raisins

1 cup strawberry halves

Iron

RDA for women: 15 mg

RDA for men: 10 mg

The foods listed here have approximately the equivalent of 1 mg of iron:

WOMEN: 15 SERVINGS

MEN: 10 SERVINGS

¼ cup cooked black beans

¼ cup cooked broad beans

⅓ cup cooked chickpeas

⅓ cup cooked great northern beans

3 tablespoons cooked kidney beans

2 tablespoons cooked lentils

¼ cup cooked lima beans

3½ tablespoons cooked navy beans

⅓ cup cooked split peas

4 tablespoons natural peanut butter

⅛ cup cooked soybeans

⅔ cup soy milk

⅓ cup cooked tempeh

2 tablespoons tofu

1 cup part skim ricotta cheese

1¼ cups raw apricot halves

1 cup apple juice

1 cup apricot nectar

½ avocado

3 tablespoons dried currants
½ cup pitted dates
⅓ cup raw elderberries
3 dried figs
2 halves dried peach
⅓ cup prune juice
4 tablespoons raisins
1 slice whole grain bread
½ piece whole wheat pita bread
½ cup cooked barley
½ cup cooked buckwheat
⅔ cup cooked bulgur
⅔ cup cooked millet
½ cup cooked oat bran
2 tablespoons cooked oatmeal
1 cup cooked brown rice
1½ tablespoons wheat germ
1 teaspoon cumin seeds
1 teaspoon fenugreek seeds
3 ounces of most cuts of beef or lamb
⅓ cup chicken
3 tablespoons almonds
4 tablespoons Brazil nuts
⅓ cup cashews
½ cup shredded unsweetened fresh coconut
1 ounce dried unsweetened coconut
1 ounce filberts
10 pecan halves
1½ teaspoons sesame tahini
⅓ cup sunflower seeds
2 ounces bass
6 tablespoons grouper
3 ounces haddock
3 ounces halibut
4 ounces all-fresh salmon
3 ounces fresh tuna
⅓ globe artichoke
⅔ cup green beans
¾ cup sliced beets
½ cup brussels sprouts
¼ cup cooked Swiss chard
¾ cup cooked kale
1 cup raw mushrooms
¼ cup raw parsley
⅔ cup peas
½ baked potato
¾ cup cooked pumpkin
⅔ cup cooked rutabaga
2½ tablespoons cooked spinach
1 cup cooked zucchini
½ cup cooked acorn squash
¾ cup cooked butternut squash
1 large cooked sweet potato
1 large tomato
1 cup cooked oatmeal=8 mg

Sodium

RDA for women and men: 500 mg (This is actually called estimated safe and adequate daily intake.)

The foods listed here have approximately the equivalent of 100 mg of sodium:

TRY TO KEEP SODIUM UNDER 500 MG A DAY, 2–4 SERVINGS.

1 ounce canned chickpeas

½ tablespoon salted peanut butter

⅛ teaspoon soy sauce (tamari)

2 tablespoons grated cheddar cheese

2 tablespoons Colby cheese

2 tablespoons cottage cheese

½ ounce Gouda cheese

2 tablespoons mozzarella cheese

2 tablespoons Neufchâtel cheese

½ cup whole-milk ricotta

1 cup whole-milk

½ cup 2% or nonfat milk

¾ cup sour cream

1 cup whole-milk yogurt

¾ cup low-fat or nonfat yogurt

2 teaspoons margarine

2 medium ripe olives

⅛ bagel

1 whole wheat dinner roll

¼ whole wheat English muffin

½ white hamburger or hot-dog roll

4 Triscuits or woven wheats

⅛ cup cooked oats prepared with salt

1 teaspoon catsup

¾ cup most meats

1 slice cooked bacon

1½ teaspoons ham

1 cup roasted or stewed chicken

½ slice bologna

¼ hot dog

6 tablespoons baked carp

6 tablespoons cod

4 tablespoons canned sardines

1 cup cooked fresh tuna

2 cups shredded Chinese cabbage

2½ cups grated carrots

3 cups cooked cauliflower

1 cup raw diced celery

¾ cup cooked spinach

Copper

RDA for women and men: 1.5–3 mg (This is actually called estimated safe and adequate daily intake.)

The foods listed here have approximately the equivalent of 1 mg of copper:

1–3 SERVINGS

- 1 cup tempeh
- ½ cup almonds
- ½ cup Brazil nuts
- ⅓ cup cashews
- 8 tablespoons hazelnuts or filberts
- ¾ cup pistachio nuts
- 3 tablespoons unsalted sesame seeds
- 4 tablespoons lobster

Most foods contain trace amounts of copper.

Zinc

RDA for women: 12 mg

RDA for men: 15 mg

The foods listed here have approximately the equivalent of 1 mg of zinc:

WOMEN: 12 SERVINGS

MEN: 15 SERVINGS

- ½ cup cooked black beans
- ⅓ cup cooked chickpeas
- ⅔ cup cooked great northern beans
- ⅓ cup cooked lentils
- ½ cup cooked navy beans
- ½ cup cooked split peas
- 2 tablespoons peanuts or peanut butter
- ½ cup cooked soybeans
- ⅓ cup tempeh
- ½ cup tofu
- ¼ cup diced cheddar or Colby cheese
- ¾ cup cottage cheese
- 1 cup most milks
- ½ cup yogurt
- 1 piece whole wheat pita bread
- 2 slices whole grain bread
- ⅔ cup cooked barley
- 1 cup cooked buckwheat groats
- 1 cup cooked bulgur
- ½ cup cooked millet
- 1 cup cooked oats

⅔ cup cooked brown rice

1 cup cooked whole wheat cereal

1 cup cooked whole wheat macaroni

1 cup cooked whole wheat spaghetti

2 tablespoons most meats

⅔ cup cooked chicken

2 tablespoons almonds

2 tablespoons Brazil nuts

2 tablespoons cashew nuts

3 tablespoons filberts or hazelnuts

⅔ cup pistachio nuts

2 tablespoons sunflower seeds

½ cup shiitake mushrooms

½ cup green peas

⅔ cup cooked spinach

Appendix A - Glossary of Nutritional and Medical Terms

acid. A chemical compound, often sour to the taste, that has a low pH. Many fruits have a high acid count, especially lemon, which accounts for its tart or sour taste. Acid is the opposite of alkaline, which has a high pH. Lemon is known for its ability to change to an "alkaline-forming food" when eaten.

acidophilus culture. An agent used to make yogurt. It is also available in capsules, liquid, and powder. Acidophilus is used to change the bacteria in the intestines. Many illnesses occur when dangerous bacteria get out of balance in the intestines. Taking acidophilus culture can replace the "good" bacteria destroyed by antibiotics. Many B vitamins need intestinal bacteria in order to be absorbed. Candida albicans lives in gastrointestinal areas of the body that are depleted of the "good" bacteria, which can be replaced by taking acidophilus.

acute. An acute illness occurs quickly, lasts relatively short periods of time, and goes quickly.

age-related macular degeneration (AMD). In some people the macula of the eye begins to degenerate with age, causing blindness. This condition is the main cause of blindness in people over fifty-five years of age in the U.S. It may occur gradually or suddenly. Research has shown that people who regularly eat spinach, broccoli, and collard greens have less possibility of developing this than people who do not eat these foods regularly. It is good for all people who have eye problems to eat beta-carotene in their food.

AIDS. Stands for acquired immunodeficiency syndrome. A disease of the immune system that compromises the body's ability to defend itself from outside invaders.

alpha-linolenic acid. An omega-essential fatty acid found in canola oil, flaxseed oil, and walnut oil.

amaranth. A cereal grass that grows in farms and waste places. It is high in protein and being used around the world to make a high-protein food, especially in places where there is drought.

amino acids. The building blocks of all cells. These nutrients are essential for life in its simplest form.

antioxidants. Any substance that inhibits or blocks harmful reactions with oxygen.

arteriosclerosis. *See* **atherosclerosis/arteriosclerosis**

artificial sweeteners. Sweeteners that have been manufactured from other foods to taste sweet but have less calories than sugar or honey. Many artificial sweeteners have been found by people to cause adverse reactions, especially saccharine and aspartame. The most common complaints are diarrhea, headaches, stomach problems, swimmy-headedness, irritability, and faintness.

asafoetida. A yellow powder obtained from the roots of several different plants. It is used in East Indian medicine as a digestive aid. Many health food stores sell this product also known as hing or yellow powder. It can also be purchased at East Indian stores.

atherosclerosis/arteriosclerosis. These diseases are characterized by a buildup of deposits on the inside of the artery walls, which can cause a thickening or hardening of the arteries. In arteriosclerosis the deposits are made up of mostly calcium. In atherosclerosis the deposits are made up of mostly fatty substances. Both of these conditions involve high blood pressure, and can ultimately lead to angina, heart attack, stroke, and/or sudden cardiac death.

B complex vitamins. Vitamins are organic substances that are essential for life and health. B complex vitamins are essential to help maintain the health of your nerves, eyes, skin, hair, liver, mouth, brain, and gastrointestinal tract. The B complex is composed of B_1 or thiamine, B_2 or riboflavin, B_3 or niacin (niacinamide, nicotinic acid), B_5 or pantothenic acid, B_6 or pyridoxine, B_{12} or cyanocobalamin, folic acid (previously called B_9), choline, inositol, biotin, and PABA (paraminobenzoic acid). Brewer's yeast, a by-product of the brewing industry, is a source of most of the B complex vitamins. B_{12} is found mostly in animal products but can also be found in soybeans, tempeh, kelp, and alfalfa. *See also* **vitamins**.

beef tallow. The fat in cattle that is found around the organs, especially the kidneys. It is often used for deep-frying foods in fast-food restaurants. This is one of the fats that God told the Israelites not to eat.

beta-1,3-D-glucan. A component of the cell wall of baker's yeast. This is one of the most-researched natural chemicals for the immune system. Many pharmaceutical companies sell this in injectable form to use for shrinking tumors.

beta-carotene. A precursor of vitamin A known to destroy free radicals and carcinogens. Beta-carotene is found in dark orange and dark green foods.

bilberry. A fruit that is used extensively in Europe, the U.S., and Canada to improve eyesight.

bok choy. A Chinese vegetable used in stir-fry dishes and many other Chinese meals. It has many leaves growing from one stem, much like celery. It has very white stems and very dark green leaves. The stems stay crunchy when cooked, therefore giving a crispness to many dishes.

bran. The outer layer of many grains including wheat, rice, and oats. A very essential fiber for aiding digestion.

bromine. A heavy, volatile, corrosive, reddish-brown, nonmetallic liquid element, having a highly irritating vapor. It is often used in producing gasoline antiknock mixtures, fumigants, dyes, and photographic chemicals.

buckwheat. A three-cornered grain that is really the seed of a plant in the rhubarb family. It is green when dried but is often toasted to become brown before being eaten. Toasted buckwheat cooks up like most grains and cam be used with rice in many dishes such as stuffed cabbage, peppers, or squash. It gives a stronger taste, and many people find that when buckwheat is used in this way it gives the idea that meat is included.

bulgur wheat. Wheat that has been cooked, chopped, and dried. This makes an easy grain to prepare since it is already cooked. Simply pour 2 cups of boiling water over 1 cup of bulgur wheat, cover, and leave for 45 minutes to an hour and it will be ready to add to salads, cereals, or serve as a main dish with vegetables.

calcium. A mineral that is essential for the health of teeth, bones, and gums. Calcium is found in dairy products, the edible bones of salmon and sardines, almonds, and dark green leafy vegetables.

carbohydrates. Mostly of plant origin, this substance provides your body with energy. The best sources for carbohydrates are whole grains, fruits, and starchy vegetables such as corn, peas, beans, and potatoes.

carcinogenic hormones. Hormones that cause cancer.

carcinogens. Substances that are capable of causing cancerous changes in your body.

carob pods. The fruit of a tree that grows wild in most of the Bible lands. The pod is very fibrous and contains large, very hard seeds. Many people toast the powder of ground carob pods or beans to use as a chocolate substitute. It does not contain the caffeinelike substance that cocoa beans do. Carob pods are a good source of calcium and other minerals.

carotenoids. A class of compounds that are related to vitamin A. Some even act as precursors to vitamin A. Beta-carotene is the best-known carotenoid.

cellulose. Plant fiber that is essential to a healthy digestive system.

chlorogenic acid. A phytochemical found in tomatoes thought to prevent cancers.

cholesterol. A necessary component of cells manufactured by all creatures with backbones. *See also* **LDL cholesterol** and **HDL cholesterol**.

choline. A nutrient beneficial for your nerves, brain, gallbladder, and liver, found in eggs and soybeans.

chronic fatigue syndrome. There are many theories of how this debilitating disease is contracted, and they are just theories; no one really knows for sure. Most speculate that the Epstein-Barr virus is responsible; others feel it is the aftermath of a shock or some stress. The only thing that medical and scientific people agree on are the symptoms. They also agree that the main symptom, persistent fatigue that is not relieved by bed rest and that reduces your average daily activity by at least 50 percent for at least six months, must be present for the diagnosis to be chronic fatigue syndrome. The other symptoms are: aching muscles and joints, anxiety, depression, difficulty concentrating, fever, intestinal problems, headaches, irritability, mood swings, muscle spasms, upper respiratory tract infections, sensitivity to light and heat, sleep disturbances, sore throat and/or swollen glands, and extreme and debilitating fatigue.

complete protein. Containing all the essential amino acids in a nearly equal complement.

Crohn's disease. Chronic and long-lasting ulceration of a section or sections of the digestive tract. The symptoms are similar to ulcerative colitis, with the exception that in Crohn's disease all the layers of the intestinal tract are involved. The symptoms include loss of weight and appetite, abdominal pain, general malaise, diarrhea, and rectal bleeding.

cruciferous. Forming a cross. These plants have a leaf pattern that forms a cross.

dementia. Irreversible deterioration of intellectual faculties with accompanying emotional disturbances resulting from an organic brain disorder.

detoxify. To remove toxins and other waste matter from your body. There are many methods including fasting, nutritional supplements, herbs, injections, chelation, and colonics. The best method is to eat a high-fiber diet and reduce animal products. Include those vegetables that are known to help remove foreign matter from your system like cabbage, broccoli, sea vegetables, beets, watercress, dandelion, daikon radish, parsley, and beans, especially soybeans.

DHA. Docosahexaenoic acid, essential fatty acid in fish.

diabetes. There are two kinds of this disease: diabetes insipidus (which is rare) and diabetes mellitus (which is common). The mellitus type is divided into two different types: type 1, often called insulin-dependent or juvenile diabetes; and type 2, often called non-insulin-dependent or adult-onset. All types of diabetes are related to the rise and fall of blood sugar and insulin in the body and require supervision by your doctor.

diverticulitis. A condition in which the mucous membranes that line the large intestines become inflamed and form pockets or pouches in the intestinal walls, which trap food and then become further inflamed or cause infection.

EDTA. A solution used to remove toxins, especially lead and arterial fat, from your body. The letters stand for: ethylenediaminetetraacetic acid.

EPA. Eicosapentaenoic acid, essential fatty acid in fish.

endocrine glands. Those glands in your body that secrete directly into your blood stream. They are thyroid, adrenal, islands of Langerhans (in the pancreas), ovary (female only), and testis (male only).

enzymes. A protein-based substance found in every cell of every living plant and animal, including the human body. Enzymes are essential for health and are found mostly in raw and unprocessed foods.

essential amino acids. Tryptophan, leucine, isoleucine, lysine, valine, threonine, methionine, and phenylalanine.

essential fatty acids (EFAs). Fatty acids that are essential for life and cannot be manufactured in the body. They are considered the building blocks of which fats and oils are composed. Every living cell needs EFAs. There are two categories of EFAs: omega-3 and omega-6. Included in the omega-6 groups are linoleic and gamma-linolenic acids found mostly in raw nuts and seeds, legumes, and unsaturated oils such as borage, grape seed, sesame, and soybean. The omega-3 groups include alpha-linolenic and eicosapentaenoic (EPA) fatty acids found mostly in fresh deep-water fish, fish oil, flaxseed oil, and the vegetable oils canola, flaxseed, and walnut.

estrogen. One of a number of hormones made in women's bodies that regulate the female cycle.

fat. An oily solid or semisolid that is the main part of many animal tissues.

fat-soluble vitamins. Vitamins that can be absorbed in your body when there is fat present in the same meal as the vitamins are taken. They are vitamins A, D, E, and K.

fiber. The indigestible part of plants.

fibromyalgia. A disease that is characterized by chronic achy muscular pain that has no obvious cause. Often depression, anxiety, irritable bowel, and impaired coordination are also involved. There are also nine pairs of "tender points" that are abnormally tender to the touch that help your doctor make the diagnosis. They are around the lower vertebrae of the neck, at the insertion point of the second rib, around the upper part of the thigh bone, in the middle of the knee joint, in muscles connected to the base of the scull, in the muscles of the neck and upper back, in muscles of the mid-back, on the side of the elbow, and in the upper and outer muscles of the buttocks. A visit to your doctor for a diagnosis is a good idea if you have any of these symptoms.

flavonoids. Crystalline compounds found in plants.

folic acid. If begun before pregnancy, 400 mcg a day in the diet of a pregnant woman can prevent neural-tube birth defects.

food allergies. An irritation of your body tissues or an inflammation caused by a specific food. There are many different symptoms that can occur including migraine headaches, diarrhea, eczema, hyperactivity, anginalike symptoms, and even a flare-up of rheumatoid arthritis. Some symptoms can occur within twenty minutes of eating the offending food. Others may be chronic or take longer to be detected.

free radical. A highly reactive molecule that can bind to and destroy body components. Free radicals produce "oxidative" damage in your body that can contribute to aging, heart disease, and cancer. This is why you need to take antioxidants to prevent this damage from occurring. Eating processed foods, rancid fats, and being in polluted environments can contribute to free radical damage.

gamma-carotene. One of the many carotenoids. Part of the vitamin A complex. Included in this group are beta-, alpha-, and gamma-carotene, lutein, and lycopene. All are considered to be antioxidants.

genistein. One of the phytonutrients in soybeans.

glucose tolerance test (GTT). A test that is helpful in determining if a person has diabetes or hypoglycemia. The test is administered after overnight fasting. The person is given a solution to drink and blood is drawn at frequent intervals over six hours to test the rise and fall of blood sugar.

HDL cholesterol. High-density lipoprotein, the good cholesterol.

high blood pressure. A term used to indicate when the normal blood pressure of 120/80 is exceeded. The elevation is significant of many health problems including risk for strokes and cardiovascular diseases. Borderline high blood pressure is 120–160/90–94, mild is 140–160/95–104, moderate is 140–180/105–114, and severe is 160+/115+.

histamines. Compound responsible for producing allergic reactions. This is why you take antihistamines for allergic reactions.

immune system. That system of your body whose job it is to identify and eliminate foreign substances such as bacteria. The liver, spleen, thymus, bone marrow, and lymphatic system all play vital roles in the proper functioning of your immune system.

inositol. A nutrient beneficial for nerves, hair growth, and fat metabolism, found in eggs, soybeans, molasses, and whole grains.

iodine. A mineral needed in trace amounts to help your body metabolize fats. It is useful for the functioning of your thyroid gland and to prevent goiter. Good sources of iodine are saltwater fish, seafood, kelp, and iodized salt. It is also found in minute amounts in asparagus, dulse (a sea vegetable), garlic, lima beans, mushrooms, sea salt, sesame seeds, soybeans, summer squash, Swiss chard, and turnip greens. Many foods can inhibit your body's ability to utilize iodine when eaten in large amounts. These foods are brussels sprouts, cabbage, cauliflower, kale, broccoli, peaches, pears, raw spinach, and turnips.

iron. A mineral needed in your body to produce hemoglobin (blood cells) and to add oxygen to your red blood cells. Prolonged use of antacids or excessive coffee or tea consumption can often result in an iron deficiency. Iron is found in eggs, meat, fish, poultry, green leafy vegetables, whole grains, almonds, avocados, beets, brewer's yeast, dates, dulse, kelp, kidney and lima beans, lentils, millet, peaches, pears, dried prunes, pumpkins, raisins, rice and wheat bran, sesame seeds, soybeans, and watercress.

isoflavone. Plant-based hormone.

kegel. Exercises performed by women that have been shown in medical reports to reduce the problem of incontinence, or urine loss.

LDL cholesterol. Low-density lipoprotein or "bad" cholesterol.

lecithin. A component of all cells, made of choline and inositol.

lignin. A type of fiber that is good for lowering cholesterol and helping to prevent gallstones. Found in Brazil nuts, carrots, green beans, peaches, peas, potatoes, strawberries, tomatoes, and whole grains.

lutein. A carotenoid.

lycopene. One of the more than 10,000 phytochemicals found in tomatoes. It plays an important role in preventing cancers, especially of the lungs and prostate. Lycopene also is a defender against ultraviolet skin damage.

lymphatic system. The system in your body that circulates a clear fluid called lymph that nourishes tissues and returns waste matter to your bloodstream.

lysine. An amino acid that is thought to block the herpes simplex virus from causing cold sores and herpes sores.

macrophage. The cells in your immune system that do the majority of its work. The name means "big eater." The macrophage have long "arms" that pull in toxins and eat or otherwise destroy them.

magnesium. A mineral that is vital to health. It assists your body in using calcium and potassium. A deficiency of magnesium can interfere with the transmission of nerve and muscle impulses, causing irritability and nervousness. A deficiency is often implicated in certain heart conditions such as sudden cardiac arrest and hypertension. Asthma, chronic fatigue, chronic pain syndromes, depression, insomnia, irritable bowel syndrome, and pulmonary disorders are associated with a magnesium deficiency. Many forms of hyperactivity in both children and adults are thought to be magnesium deficiencies such as ADD and

ADHD. Magnesium is found in dairy products, fish, meats, seafood, apples, apricots, avocados, bananas, brewer's yeast, brown rice, cantaloupe, dulse, figs, garlic, green leafy vegetables, kelp, lentils, lima beans, millet, nuts, soybeans, tofu, watercress, and whole grains.

manganese. A mineral that helps to prevent repetitive strain injuries and tennis elbow. Manganese is needed in small amounts to allow protein and fat metabolism. It is found in avocados, nuts and seeds, sea vegetables, blueberries and blueberry leaf tea, egg yolks, legumes, dried peas, whole grains, and green leafy vegetables.

menopause. That time in a woman's life when her hormonal levels change to stop her monthly periods.

minerals. Nonliving elements that are essential to the functioning of the human body.

monounsaturated fat. Fat found in butter, olive oil, and canola oil that is thought to be helpful in lowering cholesterol levels.

natural practicing doctor. A doctor who uses natural methods as his or her first choice when dealing with any health problem or disease. Oftentimes they use natural methods in conjunction with prescription medicines. This is called complementary medicine.

omega-3 essential fatty acids (EFAs). Found in raw nuts and seeds, legumes, grape seeds, soybeans, and other vegetable oils.

organically grown. A term used to mean grown without the use of any farm chemicals that are produced from coal tar or petroleum. Plant-based and animal-based pesticides and fertilizers are often used.

p-courmaric acid. A phytochemical found in tomatoes and thought to help prevent cancers by interfering with certain chemical unions that can create carcinogens.

perimenopause. That time in a woman's life leading up to the ending of menstruation. It is characterized by many symptoms due to hormonal imbalances such as fatigue, mood swings, erratic menstrual periods, and often heavy flow during menses.

pH. A scale used to measure the relative acidity or alkalinity of substances. The scale runs from 0 to 14. A pH of 7 is considered neutral. Numbers that go down from 7 are considered increasingly acidic. Numbers going up from 7 to 14 are considered increasingly alkaline.

phosphorus. A mineral needed for tooth and bone formation, cell growth, contraction of the heart muscle, and kidney function. It is found in asparagus, bran, brewer's yeast, corn, dairy products, eggs, dried fruits, garlic, legumes, nuts, sesame seeds, sunflower seeds, pumpkin seeds, salmon, and whole grains.

phytic acid. A type of fiber found in grains, especially wheat.

phytochemical. Health-protective substance in plants.

phytoestrogens. Plant-based female hormonal substances.

phytohormones. Plant-based hormones.

phytonutrient. Plant-based nutrient.

polyunsaturated fats. Come from vegetable sources.

polyunsaturated fatty acids. Fat found in corn, soy bean, safflower, and some fish oils; may help to reduce cholesterol and inflammation.

potassium. Mineral essential for muscle function.

premenstrual syndrome (PMS). This is a condition that occurs in women younger than those who are in menopause and is characterized by symptoms ranging from tiredness, crankiness, and often short temper. It is generally relieved with a natural diet, progesterone cream, and mineral supplementation.

protein. The basic element of all plant and animal tissues.

provitamin A. A chemical that can be converted into vitamin A.

respiratory system. That part of your body involved in the process of breathing, the intake of oxygen and the expulsion of carbon dioxide.

rubidium. A basic element found in nature.

saturated fat. Fat that is solid at room temperature. It is generally found in animal sources, although coconut oil is also solid at room temperature.

schizophrenia. A disease characterized by disordered thinking and perception, emotional changes such as tension and/or depression, behavioral disturbances ranging from catatonia to violent outbursts, delusions, and loss of contact with reality. Generally a person with this disease is in a world of his or her own.

scleroderma. Literally means hardening of the skin.

selenium. A mineral that prevents the breakdown of fats.

serum cholesterol. Concentrations: amount of cholesterol in your blood.

sodium. Sodium chloride, table salt.

starch. A carbohydrate found in plants.

thymus gland. A gland located just below the thyroid, behind the breast bone, that is an important part of your immune system.

thyroid gland. A gland located at the base of your throat that is responsible for metabolism in your body. It is often called the body's internal thermostat.

titanium. An element used in paint pigment.

toxins. Foreign matter that enters your body possibly from air and water pollution, bacteria pollution, or ingesting substances that are not part of your body's required nutrients such as lead, aluminum, airborne pollens, and viruses.

triglycerides. The form in which fat is stored in your body.

unsaturated fatty acids. Vegetable fats that are liquid at room temperature.

vascular disease. A disease of the circulatory system.

vitamins. A substance required in small quantities for life and health.

xanthophylls. A class of carotenoids found in dark green leafy vegetables, especially spinach and collard greens. They are reported to be useful in preventing and perhaps reversing many eye conditions, including macular degeneration.

zeaxanthin. One of a class of xanthophylls known to prevent eye problems.

zinc. A mineral essential for overall heath. It is especially necessary for the health of the prostate gland and the growth of the reproductive organs. It promotes wound healing and a healthy immune system. A zinc deficiency is often indicated in loss of the sense of taste. It is found in brewer's yeast, dulse, egg yolks, fish, kelp, lamb, legumes, lima beans, liver, mushrooms, pecans, oysters, pumpkin seeds, sardines, seafood, soy lecithin, soybeans, sunflower seeds, and whole grains.

Appendix B - Map of the Mediterranean Region

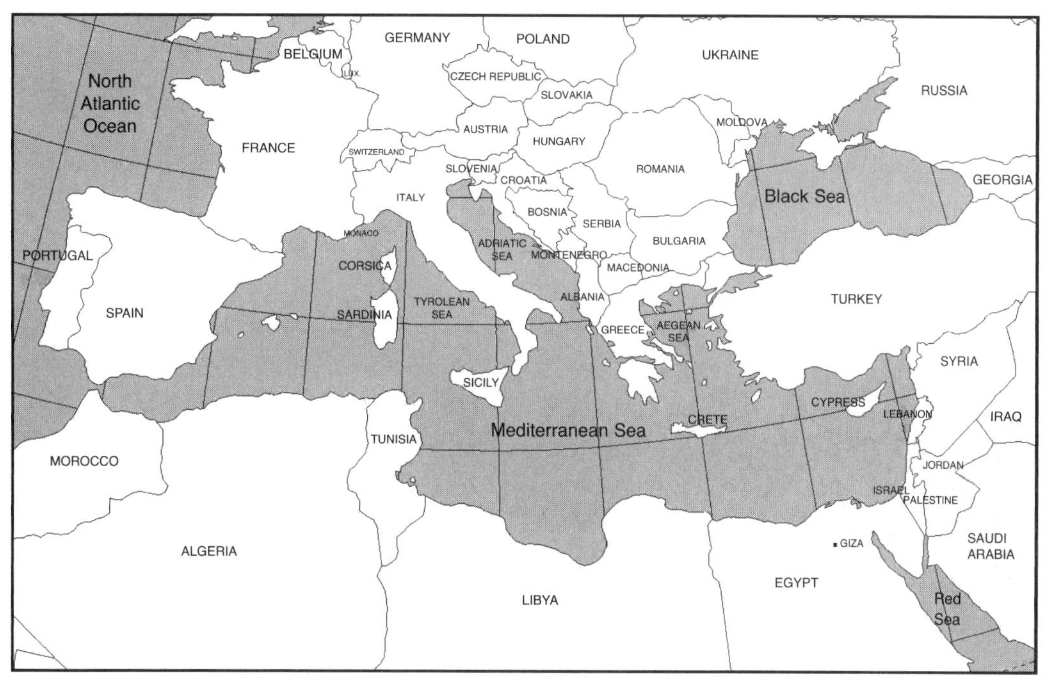

Appendix C - The Answers

NOTE: Some of the Study Questions ask for personal information about your own nutritional habits. The answers to such questions will obviously vary from person to person. For such questions I have provided sample answers, which may help you in coming up with your own.

Chapter One

1. God gave us fruits, nuts, seeds, and plants in the Garden of Eden, and all of these foods are available to us today. We in America have the additional benefit of foods that are imported to us directly from the Mediterranean region.
2. After the Flood, God allowed man to eat animal products such as meat, fish, and eggs. These foods were eaten on special occasions like weddings and feasts, and during special religious observances like Passover. I do my best to follow the Bible's example by eating small portions of meat only on special occasions like parties and weddings, or after church on Sundays.
3. An easy way to tell what to eat and when is to follow the Mediterranean food pyramid. This is a visual representation of the healthiest diet, which has been followed since Bible times in the Mediterranean region. We can also tell which foods to eat by reading about the foods that are mentioned in the Bible. Sometimes I eat ice cream more than once a week, mainly because I don't eat other sweets and really enjoy ice cream once in a while. When I do have ice cream, I get a brand that doesn't have any chemicals in it. I try to buy the kind of ice cream or sorbet that is made with natural sugars or with no sugar at all, and I always have fresh fruit with it.
4. The Mediterranean diet pyramid is a pictorial way of showing which foods are part of a healthy diet. The main groups are grains; fruits, beans, legumes, nuts, and vegetables; olive oil; cheese and yogurt; fish; followed by poultry; eggs; sweets; and red meat.
5. I eat mostly vegetables, nuts, beans, seeds, and whole grains. I eat fruit, dairy, and eggs frequently but not daily. I also have olive oil daily even if it is just in cooking. I have the other foods once or twice a week but not on the same days. If I have eggs for breakfast or lunch, I do not also have poultry or meat in the same day. Sometimes I have tuna fish and egg salad in a sandwich for lunch. When I have this, I have red peppers, olives, onions, garlic, and parsley or cilantro in with it, and lettuce on the sandwich, so that actually I get a very small amount of egg or tuna. I never eat pork unless it is hidden in foods that I eat when I'm out somewhere, but on occasion I do eat shrimp in a green salad. The Bible diet tells me to eat mostly vegetables and grains, so that's what I do!
6. We should have only small amounts of fatty foods like red meat, poultry, eggs, and sweets.

Chapter Two

1. Grains can be eaten at any time during the day. I like to eat them for breakfast, snacks, lunch, and dinner. I recommend three or four servings a day.
2. Grains provide fiber that can eliminate constipation and other problems with digestion. They also provide protein and vitamin E for the good health of arteries, skin, hair, and other mucous membranes. Grains provide energy-fuel for the body. They reduce your risk for many types of cancers and the kind of heart disease common to women after menopause.
3. Whole grains were eaten in Bible times. They ate wheat, spelt, millet, and barley. I try to eat only whole, unprocessed grains. I especially like to have brown rice, whole wheat, and spelt, and I often have barley crackers or barley soup. Millet is also great to put into soup or to eat for breakfast, and I often do that too.
4. Jesus and Elisha probably multiplied barley bread, as it was the bread of the common people. The

bread they had in Bible times was a heavier, coarser bread than we have today. Usually it was not baked in a loaf pan like we use today. Bible bread was round and flat, much like many European breads still are. They also had unleavened bread, which is something like crackers.

Chapter Three

1. Ezekiel's bread recipe contains several grains, beans, and legumes. This is unique, as most breads only contain one grain and no beans.
2. Ezekiel was told to eat Ezekiel Bread as punishment, but the remarkable thing is that Ezekiel Bread is really healthy stuff! Its mixture of grains, beans, and lentils gives us complete protein that could sustain us even if we ate nothing else. Of course, I would want to eat vegetables, but if I had to choose just one food, I would choose Ezekiel Bread.
3. Amino acids are the building blocks, the smallest components of protein. There are a great many of them and some can only be obtained from food. We need them to rebuild our bodies, keep us healthy, and give us strength.
4. Beans and lentils are great because they are inexpensive, can be stored without refrigeration, cook easily, and are very healthy. Beans are filled with fiber and carbohydrates for proper digestion and energy. They also contain protein. Beans can help reduce cholesterol and other fat levels in the body, reduce all kinds of cancers, heart disease, diabetes, and diverticulitis.
5. Soybeans are the most healthful bean because they contain complete protein, so they don't have to be complemented with a grain to be healthful. They also contain fiber and phytoestrogens. Soybeans can be made into many different products including tofu, tempeh, and soy milk.

Chapter Four

1. The king was looking for the best, brightest, most alert, most fit young men; Daniel and his friends were all that and more. The king found these Hebrew young men to be in better shape than his own men.
2. Daniel asked that he be allowed to eat the same food that he generally had been, which was much different from the food that the king provided for his regular men. Because Daniel was used to eating mainly vegetables, grains, beans, and no alcohol, the king's guards were suspicious of him. The king usually fed all his men rich meats, desserts, and lots of alcohol.
3. The largest percentage or portion of my diet should be vegetables. This means that I should eat as much of all the others foods combined as I do vegetables each day, even more than 5 half-cup servings. Vegetables are important in my diet because they contain fiber, vitamins, minerals, and other phytonutrients.
4. The color in vegetables makes a wonderful display of God's handiwork when arranged beautifully on a plate, serving dish, or buffet. God created the colored vegetables to show me easily which vegetables were best for me to eat. The darker or richer the color is, the more nutrients God put in the vegetable. This makes it easy for me to select the healthiest vegetables for me and my family.
5. Some vegetables are especially good for me because they contain the highest amounts of nutrients. Vegetables like carrots, winter squash, broccoli, kale, garlic, watercress, sweet potatoes, peas, brussels sprouts, and tomatoes are very important in my diet to keep me healthy from head to toe. Raw vegetables are also good for me because they are the highest in enzymes that can help to reverse aging, prevent cancer, and improve my digestion.
6. Many diseases might be prevented by eating a diet high in vegetables. The most common diseases that respond to better nutrition are: hypertension, diabetes, heart disease, cancers, constipation, diverticulitis, and cataracts.
7. Children love to eat vegetables when they have had some part in growing, shopping for, or preparing them. They also often prefer to eat raw vegetables as snacks—things like carrot sticks, baby carrots, peas in the pod, red and green pepper strips, and even baby lettuce.
8. Cucumbers, garlic, leeks, and onions were the vegetables that the Israelites longed for in the desert. Cucumbers are a good source of water. Garlic, onions, and leeks are useful in reducing high blood pressure and cholesterol, aiding digestion, and reducing allergies. This made them very important health foods.

Chapter Five

1. Nuts! Specifically walnuts and almonds, and fruits. Nuts contain fat—the good kind of fat called essential fatty acids. This is very important for healthy skin, hair, and eyes, as well as healthy mucous membranes in all parts of the body. They also contain some forms of protein that are also essential for health.
2. I have tried to follow a low-fat diet for several years, and I am having trouble with dry skin and fly-away, dry hair, so I'm going to start adding some walnuts, almonds, and pistachio nuts and

nut butters into my diet. I will also experiment with adding flaxseeds to cereals and breads. I realize that my cholesterol might be creeping up, and I want to work toward lowering it so the nuts and seeds will help.

3. Fruit is high in fiber, which is good for digestion. Raisins and grapes contain two nutrients that will help prevent cancer, ellagic acid and resveratrol. Many fruits are known to prevent cerebrovascular disease and atherosclerosis because of the fiber and other phytonutrients they contain.
4. Fruits can help to reverse or prevent central nervous system problems, bladder infections, and incontinence. Eating a wide variety of fruit every day will provide these heath benefits. I especially try to have cranberries in some form every few days to prevent bladder problems.
5. Tomatoes, olives, and avocados are really fruits even though we usually eat them as if they were vegetables. I am going to begin having ripe olives in fruit salads along with avocados. I think I'll experiment with making homemade tomato jam and jelly this summer just like my grandmother used to do. I understand that small pear tomatoes make great jam. I'm also going to incorporate more of these three fruits into salads, pasta salads especially, and sandwiches. I even think I'll make scrambled egg sandwiches for breakfast with whole wheat bread and sliced tomatoes. My mother gave me a really great recipe for mayonnaise, I'm going to try it with extra-virgin olive oil.
6. The bitter principle of olive leaves is called oleuropein and it is very useful in warding off E. coli and salmonella. This might be why there is more trouble with bacteria in North America than there is in places where olives and olive oil are used more liberally.

Chapter Six

1. Having dairy products daily is a good way to ensure that I am giving myself and my family enough calcium. My children do not want to drink milk but they will eat cheese, so we try to have some of the really natural cheeses for them, especially in their lunches each day so that they have enough calcium to keep relaxed at school and after they come home so they can concentrate on their schoolwork.
2. There has been a controversy over cow's milk for thousands of years. Sometimes I think it is foolish because cow's milk is so readily available. But then again, there is a child in our Sunday school class who is really allergic to milk and suffers even when she drinks just a little.
3. God gave mothers the ability to produce milk for their newborn children. This is a really natural way to keep infants healthy. I'm not surprised that the ingredients in mother's milk protect babies from a lot of diseases and bacteria; it's part of God's plan!
4. Yogurt was eaten in Bible times and it has many health-giving properties.
5. Fermented milk products are very helpful when taking antibiotics because they reintroduce the good bacteria that is essential for health that the antibiotics kill off. I really feel that eating yogurt and kefir on a daily basis keeps digestion and intestines functioning better than without it. Fermented dairy products help to build up immunity to all sorts of bacteria. I would never travel without yogurt tablets or some form of probiotic to keep from getting sick because of the higher bacteria count in places like Mexico, India, South America, and China.
6. In New Testament times milk was primarily for children.

Chapter Seven

1. Many of Jesus's disciples were fishermen. Fishing was a big industry in the Mediterranean region. This is often cited as the reason for why one of the symbols of Christianity is the fish. Common people ate fish, fishermen were common people, and Jesus walked among common people.
2. Fish has been a mainstay in the Mediterranean diet for thousands of years. Since this is considered to be one of the healthiest diets, it stands to reason that eating fish is also healthy. Fish have a lot of important nutrients in them like DHA and EPA.
3. The best fish to eat for health are the fatty and very fatty fish like sardines, salmon, tuna, catfish and orange roughy, to name a few. I often eat fish sandwiches for lunch. Sometimes I serve my family some really old-fashioned fish meals like tuna-and-noodle casserole or salmon patties from a recipe book that my grandmother gave me.
4. Medical research has shown that eating fish and fish oil helps the following conditions: heart disease, high triglycerides, pain and inflammation, asthma, and rheumatoid arthritis. These are the diseases that are now considered to be the most troubling for a large percentage of the population. We seem to hear more about these diseases nowadays I think, because fewer people are eating right and even fewer people are eating fish. When people do eat fish, they eat processed or deep-fried fish, and that is not as good for them.
5. Broiled, poached, and baked fish are the best

ways to cook and eat fish. They can often be dressed up with herbs and low-fat sauces. It's really easy to bake fish in a foil or parchment-paper packet with herbs. You can even do it outdoors on the barbecue.

Chapter Eight

1. Passover includes bitter herbs as a remembrance of the bitter tears the Israelites shed while they were slaves in Egypt. This is also a meal where fat is eaten and the bitter herbs help my body digest the fat and use it effectively. They are also important because they contain minerals and vitamin A or beta-carotene and can also help to remove toxins from my body like lead and mercury.
2. Dandelions grow almost everywhere. I think I'll get some from the baseball diamond in the park. It is fenced in and dogs are not allowed. We have planned a special Seder at my church this spring and we will have parsley and dandelion greens then. I'm even going to do a special project in Sunday school with the bitter herbs and let the kids try them. There are farm-grown dandelions in my local supermarket so I can include them in my salads.
3. Including dark green leafy vegetables in my diet or taking dark green algae can help reduce cancer, birth defects, macular degeneration, and vascular diseases. I'm going to start having only dark green leafy salads. I'm going to make sure that all sandwiches have dark green lettuce on them. I'm going to use fresh parsley in foods and as a garnish on cooked foods. I think I'll even start growing parsley on my windowsill, so I'll have some available at all times.
4. Parsley and cilantro are so plentiful in the supermarket that they can be added to everything. This might even help my family have fewer colds next winter. People just ate more of the foods that were inexpensive and readily available in Bible times, like greens, fish, and olive oil. I'm going to start doing that too.

Chapter Nine

1. In Leviticus the Bible talks about all the fat belonging to the Lord. They were also told to burn that same fat as an offering to God. God was pleased by the scent of the fat burning as an offering.
2. The prohibited fats are the ones found around the organs in most animals. In pigs this fat is called lard; in beef, suet or tallow; in chickens, chicken fat, although many Europeans call it Chicken Schmaltz.
3. Fat is not really bad if we eat the right kind of fat like olive oil, nut and seed oils, and flaxseeds. These fats contain the essential fatty acids that help keep nerves, skin, hair, and brain healthy. We really need these fats; that's why they are called essential!
4. The Bible diet says we should eat eggs and poultry a few times a week. That seems sensible to me because there are so many different proteins to choose from.
5. The following foods are to be eaten a few times per week: sweets, eggs, and poultry. I'm very careful about what I eat so I don't eat more of the foods than the amounts recommended in the Mediterranean/Bible diet.
6. Even though I try to stay away from pork and pork products, I often end up eating bacon in salads or breakfast burritos. I don't make a really big deal about it though, because I know that the New Testament says all foods are clean. I don't like to eat food with chemicals and preservatives so I stay away from bacon, ham, and lard for health reasons, not because they are unclean. It is more important for me to have a nice meal with great fellowship than to make a scene about eating bacon.

Chapter Ten

1. Honey was made from fruits like dates, from carob pods; and honey was made by bees too. Milk and honey were always mentioned together because they always ate them together and because they were symbols of wealth and privilege. They generally ate milk products with honey and other sweets so that the protein in the milk balanced the sweetness of the honey.
2. We should not eat sweets every day; they can be eaten a few times a week if I'm watching my health and following the Bible diet. The really best forms of sweets are natural fruits. However, if I want to have a muffin, cake, or cookies, I will make them myself out of natural sweeteners and whole wheat flour so they will be healthier.
3. Heart disease and high blood pressure are generally related to high salt consumption. Cutting down on salt or cutting it out completely can help people who have these problems, but they should talk to their doctor first. People ate more salt as preservatives in foods during Bible times. I think it didn't affect them as much because they didn't eat a lot salt otherwise, as we do today in our many processed foods.
4. Water. I drink it frequently during the day and even have a glass as soon as I get up in the morning. I think there is more emphasis on drinking water lately because we keep our houses hotter,

therefore dryer, and we need more water.

5. There is never an important time to drink wine as far as I'm concerned! If I drink wine I have the kind with no alcohol in it. My church never talks against drinking wine specifically, but they don't encourage it either. I'm glad there is a place that doesn't encourage drinking that I can go to for fun and fellowship.
6. The healthful properties in wine can be obtained by drinking grape or other fruit juices and eating grapes whole, including the seeds and skins. This can help prevent many kinds of cancers and prevent aging, which I'm all for preventing.

Chapter Eleven

1. Clean animals were beef, chickens, fish with scales, and lambs. Unclean animals were pigs, horses, shrimp, and lobster. Many people have gotten into the habit of eating a lot of pork products, and the pork producers say they are cleaner because they aren't fed garbage as much, but I still read that parasites are being found in many of the unclean foods mentioned in the Bible. That keeps me from eating them.
2. Peter was told in a vision to eat a lot of different foods and some of them were considered unclean. He was shocked because he had never eaten any of them and couldn't imagine God telling him to eat them. He later learned that Jesus had been preaching that people were not made unclean by the foods they ate but by the things they said.
3. God instituted the cleanliness rules of washing hands and feet and burying excrement, and they are still being followed today.
4. Food should always be fresh and free of mold and bruises. Before preparing any food the surface of the preparation area should be clean. If meat will be cut, the cutting board should be cleaned with chlorine bleach before and after. Everything should be clean including your hands, knives, other utensils, board, and anything that is going to touch the food being prepared. All fruits and vegetables should be washed with soap and water before cooking or eating them.
5. Foods grown without pesticides or chemicals are called "organically grown." I think it is becoming more important because so many foods are being contaminated with harmful chemicals that many people have become chemically sensitive. There are so many chemicals that we can't keep away from in the air that I want to be included in keeping chemicals out of my body by using organically grown foods. This will also help the environment to become cleaner too.
6. God said to get rid of any mold in my house, and if I can't get rid of it, to tear the house down and throw away the materials. This seems radical, but in light of the many health problems due to mold and mildew, I'm going to get serious about mold and mildew.

Chapter Twelve

1. I think Elijah had depression, major depression. He is important to this chapter because I realize that many people suffer from depression, both average and great like Elijah. I'm not so critical of people with depression now.
2. The angel told Elijah to eat several times a day. This is really important to bring good health to anybody even if they don't have depression. Eating frequently can keep my blood-sugar levels stabilized, and this will give me constant energy.
3. Depression symptoms include poor self-image or self-esteem, lack of self-confidence, withdrawal from social activities, changes in appetite, loss of energy or fatigue, and difficulty in concentrating.
4. The most important things I can do if I think I have depression is to see my doctor; eat small frequent meals; avoid sugar, caffeine, and alcohol; and get enough sleep.
5. David helped Saul by playing music for him. I really find some classical music uplifting, especially Vivaldi's Four Seasons. I like a lot of the old hymns, and many of the chant records; they make me feel close to God, and this comfort prevents me from feeling down. Then again I don't have depression. I had a friend in college who was diagnosed with depression, and she used to sit in her dorm room and listen to really loud acid-rock music. It was very irritating. Her counselors made her stop playing the music, and she began to feel better, so I have been aware of this for many years.

Chapter Thirteen

1. Eve was tempted by the devil to eat the forbidden fruit and she got Adam involved. Jesus was also tempted by the devil to turn stones into bread when he was fasting in the desert. The devil figured that Jesus would be so hungry that he would go for it and turn stones into bread. Jesus resisted. Adam and Eve did not. It is important to know about them so that we can pattern our lives on Jesus—ask God for help when we are tempted and not give in to the temptations of other humans. They might be doing the work of the devil, as Eve was.
2. Hypoglycemia is low blood sugar and it happens when the body doesn't get enough food.

Hyperglycemia is high blood sugar, which happens to people who have trouble handling sugar for one reason or another. These two conditions can be avoided by eating small, frequent meals of whole foods, and avoiding large amounts of sugar, caffeine, and nicotine.

3. Jesus gave the disciples fish for breakfast mainly because they were fishermen. It was also the custom to eat fish for breakfast.
4. White flour pretzels and crackers have been my snacks for a long time and I always feel tired later. Now I am going to start eating whole grain pretzels and crackers. Even though God created all things, he did not create junk food.
5. Hannah was barren and also had an eating disorder. She refused to eat for a long time because her rival, Peninnah, was picking on her for her barrenness.
6. Compulsive overeating, anorexia nervosa, and bulimia nervosa. Compulsive overeating is a common eating disorder that affects men and women. Anorexia nervosa and bulimia nervosa are two common eating disorders that mainly affect women, although more and more young men are exhibiting these disorders. Eating disorders can come from poor body image or self-image or from being teased or put down by peers or parents. There are also indications that these disorders are often displays of power or control. There are a lot of new ideas being published now that show that often these disorders are the result of mineral deficiencies, food allergies, or brain chemical imbalances.

Chapter Fourteen

1. God cursed the Israelites with wasting diseases, blight, mold and mildew, among other things, because they had been disobedient.
2. People around the world are refusing to follow the laws of God. Even Jews and Christians are not following God's laws. This is causing a lot of problems with health, sanitation, and diseases. Candida seems like a real plague since so many people that I know seem to have it in varying degrees. Many people are too busy to pay attention to their children. The children feel this lack of love, and this suppresses their immune systems and allows candida to take hold. Eating processed foods can also be part of the problem since processed food also suppresses the immune system and allows candida to take hold.
3. They could not have bread, fermented foods, and wine, which encourage various yeasts to grow. The common element is disobedience to God and disregard for God's laws, especially not honoring your father and mother and not forgiving one another. They sound very similar to the kinds of things that were going on in Bible times to the Hebrews.
4. Eat whole foods, no yeast or fermented food, and eat lots of parsley, garlic, yogurt, olive oil, and perhaps take some of the nutritional supplements that can either kill yeast or prevent it from living. Also, find a sympathetic doctor or nutritionist who can help to rid my body of this plague.

Chapter Fifteen

1. Paul taught that Christians were to be serious at all times about following Jesus and loving God and that our bodies were the church, a holy temple. Our bodies are the way God gets to be known on this earth. We must talk about him to others, after carrying him in our hearts, so that we are the church or temple.
2. God often chooses to heal people who ask for healing through prayer and/or crying out. God has also inspired men to develop medicines that can also heal diseases. Many of the current medicines are designed from the herbs and other organic materials that God created.
3. We don't really know why Jesus was so adamant about forgiving, but he preached about forgiving all the time. From his words in the Bible we can deduce that forgiveness and forgiving were very important for healing to take place.
4. Many of the emotions that belong to what New Testament Christians called "earthly way" can cause damage to various organs in our bodies. Such emotions as anger and rage have been shown to actually cause heart problems, encourage high blood pressure, and even bring on a stroke. Negative emotions, stress, rage, and tension can shut off the blood circulation, causing lack of oxygen to many parts of the body. They can also use up the minerals that are necessary for relaxation, thereby causing contractions of the heart and blood vessel muscles.

Chapter Sixteen

1. Jesus and his disciples walked everywhere because they had no other transportation besides donkeys! Even donkey carts took the same amount of time as walking, so people generally walked beside their donkeys.
2. The best way to start exercising is to start with walking, move on to power walking, and escalate to speed walking. There are a lot of things that I do in the normal course of my day that could be made into better exercise. Instead of using the dryer, I could hang the clothes outside; that would be more exercise.

3. Actually, I am more active than when I was a child. Now I ride a mountain bike, hike, and play several games at the gym plus lift weights. I try to walk everywhere possible. Recently we got a dog and that creates more exercise just chasing after her and taking her for walks. I do a lot more activities now than when I was a child because I didn't like competitive sports. I did take tap-dancing lessons for a while, and that was a lot of exercise.
4. Often when I am at the gym on the treadmill or bike, I listen to Christian praise audiotapes specifically for exercising. I have often gotten a lot of comments when I lost track of what I was doing and began to sing, loudly I might add, while listening to a tape and jogging on the treadmill.

Chapter Seventeen

1. The seven feasts are Passover, the Feast of Unleavened Bread, First Fruits, Pentecost, Trumpets, Atonement, and Tabernacles. These were given as times to remember God, read from Scriptures, and attend services.
2. They didn't feast at all! Yom Kippur was also called the Day of Atonement, when people were to deny themselves pleasures, including eating.
3. There was always the danger of eating too much food, eating over a long period of time, and eating a lot of fatty foods. I work at eating a small amount when I am at a feast or potluck dinner. I take small amounts and never go back for seconds.
4. Being overweight has always been associated with overindulgence in food. We can develop digestive problems from eating too much food, and syndrome X is often associated with too much food at one time. Eating a little before going to a feast can help us from becoming so hungry that we lose control and eat too much.
5. God appointed feasts for the Israelites to set aside time to remember him. God should be the center of all feasts.

Chapter Eighteen

1. The Bible assigned fasts for the Israelites to follow including the fasts of the fourth, fifth, seventh, and tenth months. Fasts were generally done to commemorate historical occurrences.
2. There are the major and minor fasts. The major fast was to take no food or drink from sundown to sundown. The minor fast was to take no food or drink from sunup to sundown. Many cultures still practice one day of major fasting for the purpose of seeking God.
3. Christians often fast from one food for a period of time, generally over Lent. Many Christians are renewing the practice of fasting for one full twenty-four-hour period, often every week. This kind of fast, when approached correctly, can be of spiritual and physical benefit.
4. Ease into a fast by reducing foods in a slow and methodical way and ending up on just juice, broth, or water for a period of time. No one should just stop eating food and go immediately to liquids, particularly one like coffee.
5. Fasting to seek God is between each person and God and is not to be discussed with anyone. In Jesus's day, many religious sects bragged about how they were fasting and even did things to themselves so everyone could see that they were fasting. This is not seeking God, but making a public show of fasting.

Appendix D - The Experts

Bennet, Rita—Founder of The Emotionally Free Course for Prayer Counselors. She is the author of *How to Pray for Inner Healing*, *Making Peace with Your Inner Child*, and *Emotionally Free*. Her ministry, Christian Renewal Association, which she began with her late husband, Dennis, is located in Edmonds, Washington.

Cherry, Reginald, M.D.—Practices diagnostic and preventive medicine in Houston, Texas, and can be seen on the television show *The Doctor and the Word*. He is the author of *The Doctor and the Word* and *The Bible Cure*.

Colbert, Don, M.D.—A board-certified family practice doctor and speaker who has also extensively studied nutrition. Don is the author of many books on health, including the thirty-book series The Bible Cure as well as *What Would Jesus Eat?* Dr. Colbert lives in Orlando, Florida, where he also runs the Divine Health Wellness Center.

Contreras, Francisco, M.D.—Specializes in improving the physical, mental, and spiritual lives of people with cancer using conventional and alternative therapies. He is the general director of the Oasis of Hope Hospital in Baja California, Mexico. He is the author of *Health in the 21st Century: Will Doctors Survive?* He is a frequent contributor to the *Eternally Fit* television show.

Cook, Suzan Johnson, Ph.D.—Is a senior pastor at the Believers Christian Fellowship in New York City and was described by the *New York Times* as Billy Graham and Oprah rolled into one.

Cooper, Kenneth H., M.D., M.P.H.—Often called the Father of Modern Aerobics since he was the person who coined the term "aerobics." He is the author of *Aerobics*, *Controlling Cholesterol*, *Dr. Kenneth H. Cooper's Antioxidant Revolution*, *Dr. Kenneth H. Cooper's Advanced Nutritional Therapies*, *Faith-Based Fitness*, and *It's Better to Believe*. He is also the founder of the Cooper Institute for Aerobics Research in Dallas, Texas.

Crook, William G., M.D.—Practicing physician, medical writer, and lecturer. He has written *The Yeast Connection*, *The Yeast Connection Cookbook*, *Chronic Fatigue Syndrome and The Yeast Connection*, and *The Yeast Connection and the Woman*. The late Dr. Crook lived in Jackson, Tennessee.

Frähm, Anne and David—Founders of HealthQuarters, a nonprofit educational organization aimed at helping people with cancer. The late Anne spent much of her time helping others recover from cancer. They are the authors of *A Cancer Battle Plan* and *Healthy Habits*.

Hager, David W., M.D., and Linda Carruth Hager—Authors of *Stress and the Woman's Body*. Dr. Hager was named by *Good Housekeeping* as one of America's top doctors for women.

Hartman, Jack and Judy—Authors of more than ten books on Bible study and faith as well as *Increased Energy and Vitality*. Through Lamplight Ministries in Dunedin, Florida, they encourage people to have faith and to eat the foods God provided for us to eat.

Jakes, T. D.—Founder and senior pastor of the Potter's House church in Dallas, Texas. He is the author of several books and has a weekly television show. Bishop Jakes is best known for his massive crusades and conferences across the country.

Littauer, Florence—Internationally known speaker and author with over twenty books to her credit. She is the founder of CLASS (Christian Leaders, Authors, and Speakers Services) and encourages Christians to become the best speakers and presenters they can be. She lives with her husband, Fred, in San Marcos, California.

McIlhaney, Joe S., M.D.—OB/GYN and the author of *1,001 Health-Care Questions Women Ask*. He is often heard on the *Focus on the Family* radio show.

McMillan, S. I., M.D.—Author of the Christian classics: *None of the Diseases* and *Discern These Times*, and is currently working on another book, *You Can Be Sure.*

Mercola, Joseph, D.O.—An osteopathic physician in private practice in Schaumburg, Illinois, Dr. Mercola is the author of *Dr. Mercola's Total Health Program.*

Meyer, Joyce—Has been in full-time ministry since 1980 and can be seen and heard around the world on her radio and television program *Enjoying Everyday Life.* Joyce is the bestselling author of more than seventy inspirational books and lives with her husband in St. Louis, Missouri.

Pearson, Mark—Author of *Christian Healing* and president of the Institute for Christian Renewal in Plaistow, New Hampshire.

Rubin, Jordan—The author of *The Maker's Diet*, which sold nearly 2 million copies as a *New York Times* bestseller. Jordan is the founder of the Biblical Health Institute and lives with his family in Palm Beach Gardens, Florida.

Russell, Rex, M.D.—Radiologist in practice in Fort Smith, Arkansas, and the author of *What the Bible Says About Healthy Living.*

Salaman, Maureen Kennedy—Speaker and health writer. She is the author of *Nutrition: The Cancer Answer, Foods That Heal, Foods That Heal Companion Cookbook, The Diet Bible: The Bible for Dieters*, and *All Your Health Questions Answered, Naturally.*

Shriner, Jim—Fitness expert, the host of his own national television show, *Eternally Fit*, and the author of a fitness book also called *Eternally Fit.* He lives in Ormond Beach, Florida.

Smith, Pamela, R.D.—Author of *Eat Well-Live Well, Healthy Expectations*, and *When Your Hormones Go Haywire.* She is frequently heard on the *Focus on the Family* radio show.

Swope, Mary Ruth, Ph.D.—Nutritionist, author, speaker, and seminar leader. She is the author of *Nutrition for Christians, Are You Sick and Tired of Feeling Sick and Tired?, The Spiritual Roots of Barley, Listening Prayer, Green Leaves of Barley*, and *Of These Ye May Freely Eat.* She also is involved with Nutrition with a Mission in Melbourne, Florida.

Townsley, Cheryl—Author of *Food Smart!* a seminar leader, cooking instructor, and the owner of Lifestyles for Health.

Wagemaker, Herbert, M.D.—Christian psychiatrist in Jacksonville, Florida. He is the author of *How Can I Understand My Kids?, Parents and Discipline*, and *The Surprising Truth About Depression.*

Whitaker, Julian, M.D.—Medical director of the Whitaker Wellness Institute. He is the author of many books, including *Shed Ten Years in Ten Weeks*, and *The Pain Relief Breakthrough*, co-authored with Brenda Adderly, M.H.A.

Endnotes

Chapter 1

1. Billy Graham, *Angels,* 149.
2. L. Serra-Majem, et al., "Scientific evidence of interventions using the Mediterranean diet: a systematic review. *Nutrition Review* 2006 February; 64(2 Pt 2):S27-47.
3. A. Trichopoulou et al., "Cancer and Mediterranean dietary traditions," *Cancer Epidemiology, Biomarkers, and Prevention,* September 2000; 9(9):869–73.
4. N. Scarmeas et al. "Mediterranean diet risk for Alzheimer's disease," *Annals of Neurology,* April 18, 2006.
5. Reginald Cherry, M.D., *The Bible Cure,* 69.
6. Kathleen Baldinger, *The World's Oldest Health Plan,* 44.
7. Don Colbert, M.D. *What Would Jesus Eat?* 28.
8. K. J. Joshipura et al., "The effect of fruit and vegetable intake on risk for coronary heart disease," *Annals of Internal Medicine,* June 19, 2001; 134(12):1106–14
9. M. Adams et al., "A diet rich in green and yellow vegetables inhibits atherosclerosis in mice," *Journal of Nutrition.* July 2006; 136(7): 1886–9.
10. Kenneth Cooper, M.D., *Advanced Nutritional Therapies,* 292.
11. Julian Whitaker, M.D., *Medical Memory Boosters and Brain Enhancers,* 3.
12. U.S. Department of Agriculture Human Nutrition Service, *Home and Garden Bulletin,* #252. Note: This and other government information can be obtained by calling the Consumer Information Department (toll-free) at 1-888-878-3256. Or contact them through their Internet site, www.pueblo.csa.gov.
13. F. J. He et al., "Fruit and vegetable consumption and stroke: meta-analysis of cohort studies," *Lancet* 2006, Jan 28; 367(9507):32.
14. Cooper, *Advanced Nutritional Therapies,* 294.
15. Pamela Smith, *Healthy Expectations,* 18.
16. Jordan Rubin, *The Great Physician's Rx,* 27.
17. Maureen Salaman, *The Diet Bible: The Bible for Dieters,* 59.
18. Dr. Mary Ruth Swope, *Are You Sick and Tired of Feeling Sick and Tired?* 116.
19. C. A. Gonzalez et al., "Meat intake and risk of stomach and esophageal adenocarcinoma within the European Prospective Investigation into Cancer and Nutrition (EPIC)," *Journal of the National Cancer Institute,* March 1, 2006 98(5):345–54.
20. C. Rodriguez et al., "Meat consumption among Black and White men and risk of prostate cancer in the Cancer Prevention Study II Nutrition Cohort," *Cancer Epidemiology, Biomarkers, and Prevention,* February 2006; 15(2):211–6.
21. Swope, *Are You Sick and Tired of Feeling Sick and Tired?* 116.

Chapter 2

1. Don Colbert, M.D., *What Would Jesus Eat?* 29.
2. B. J. Venn and J. L. Mann, "Cereal grains, legumes and diabetes," *European Journal of Clinical Nutrition,* November 2004; 58(11):1443–61.
3. J. A. Nettleton et al., "Dietary patterns are associated with biochemical markers of inflammation and endothelial activation in the Multi-Ethnic Study of Atherosclerosis (MESA)," *American Journal of Clinical Nutrition,* June 2006; 83(6):1369–79.
4. Don Colbert, M.D., *What Would Jesus Eat?* 33
5. Cheryl Townsley, *Food Smart,* 116.
6. L. U. Thompson, "Antioxidants and Hormone-Mediated Health Benefits of Whole Grains," *Critical Reviews in Food Science and*

Nutrition, 1994, 473–97.

7. J. Slavin, D. Jacobs, and L. Marquart, "Whole-Grain Consumption and Chronic Disease: Protective Mechanisms," *Nutrition and Cancer,* 1997, 14–21.
8. Jordan Rubin, *The Great Physician's Rx,* 26.
9. Purity Foods Internet Home Page (purityfoods.com).
10. Dr. Mary Ruth Swope, *The Spiritual Roots of Barley,* 87.
11. Colbert, *What Would Jesus Eat?* 28.
12. Reginald Cherry, M.D., *The Bible Cure,* 89.
13. Maureen Salaman, *The Diet Bible: The Bible for Dieters,* 227.

Chapter 3

1. Rex Russell, M.D., *What the Bible Says About Healthy Living,* 104.
2. Maureen Salaman, *The Diet Bible: The Bible for Dieters,* 226.
3. Cheryl Townsley, *Food Smart,* 120.
4. Pamela Smith, R.D., *When Your Hormones Go Haywire,* 186.
5. D. J. A. Jenkins et al., "Assessment of the longerterm effects of a dietary portfolio of cholesterol-lowering foods in hypercholesterolemia," *American Journal of Clinical Nutriton,* March 2006; 83(3):582–91.
6. Russell, *What the Bible Says About Healthy Living,* 104.
7. Reginald Cherry, M.D.,*The Bible Cure,* 106.
8. Townsley, *Food Smart,* 120.
9. V. S. Haak et al. "Increasing Amounts of Dietary Fiber Provided by Foods Normalizes Physiologic Response of Large Bowel Without Altering Calcium Balance or Fecal Steroid Excretion," *American Journal of Clinical Nutrition,* September 1998, 615–22.
10. C. L. Williams, "Importance of Dietary Fiber in Childhood," *Journal of the American Dietetic Association,* October 1995, 1140–46.
11. J. W. Anderson et al. "Bakery Products Lower Serum Cholesterol Concentrations in Hypercholesterolemic Men," *American Journal of Clinical Nutrition,* November 1991, 836–40.
12. "Soy Protein in Adult Human Nutrition: A Review with New Data," in *Soy Protein and Human Nutrition,* H. Wilcke, D. Hopkins, D. Waggle, eds., Academic Press, 1979.
13. Francisco Contreras, M.D., *Health in the 21st Century,* 278.
14. A. Dalu et al., "Genistein, a Component of Soy, Inhibits the Expression of the Egf and Erbb2/Neu Receptors in the Rat Dorsolateral Prostate," *Prostate,* September 1998, 36–43.
15. Smith, *When Your Hormones Go Haywire,* 186.
16. S. A. Bingham et al., "Phytoestrogens: Where Are We Now?" *British Journal of Nutrition,* May 1998, 393–406.
17. A. Berger et al., "Plant sterols: factors affecting their efficacy and safety as functional food ingredients," *Lipids in Health and Disease,* April 2004, 3:5.
18. F. Blotman et al., "Efficacy and Safety of Avocado/Soybean Unsaponifiables in the Treatment of Symptomatic Osteoarthritis of the Knee and Hip: A Prospective, Multicenter, Three-Month, Randomized, Double-Blind, Placebo-Controlled Trial," *Revue du Rhumatisme,"* English ed., December 1997, 825–34.

Chapter 4

1. Jack and Judy Hartman, *Increased Energy and Vitality,* 132.
2. Mark A. Pearson, *Christian Healing,* 288.
3. Hartman, *Increased Energy and Vitality,* 131.
4. A. Favero, M. Parpinel, S. Franceschi, "Diet and Risk of Breast Cancer: Major Findings from an Italian Case-Control Study," *Biomedicine and Pharmacotherapy,* 1998, 109–15.
5. K. Lock et al., "The global burden of disease attributable to low consumption of fruit and vegetables: implications for the global strategy on diet," *Bulletin of the World Health Organization,* February 2005; 83(2):100–108.
6. T. M. Wolever and D. J. Jenkins, "What Is a High Fiber Diet?" *Advances in Experimental Medicine and Biology,* 1997, 35–42.
7. M. J. Hill, "Nutrition and Human Cancer," *Annals of the New York Academy of Sciences,* December 29, 1997, 68–78.
8. W. J. Craig, "Phytochemicals: Guardians of Our Health," *Journal of the American Dietetic Association,* October 1997, S199–S204.
9. Kenneth H. Cooper, M.D., *Advanced Nutritional Therapies,* 191.
10. J. H. O'Keefe, C. J. Lavie Jr., B. D. McCallister, "Insights into the Pathogenesis and Prevention of Coronary Artery Disease," *Mayo Clinic Proceedings,* January 1995, 69–79.
11. E. Gonzaez de Mejia, A. Quintanar-Hernandez, G. Loarca-Pina, "Antimutagenic

Activity of Carotenoids in Green Peppers Against Some Nitroarenes," *Mutation Research*, August 7, 1998, 11–19.

12. Cooper, *Advanced Nutritional Therapies*, 68.
13. Julian Whitaker, M.D., *Whitaker's Guide to Natural Healing*, 1995, 41.
14. A. Guenegou et al., "Serum carotenoids, vitamins A and E, and 8 year lung function decline in a general population," *Thorax*, April 2006; 61(4):320–26.
15. M. Mozaffarieh et al., "The role of the carotenoids, lutein and zeaxanthin, in protecting against age-related macular degeneration: a review based on controversial evidence," *Nutrition Journal*, December 11, 2003; 2:20.
16. C. W. Chang et al., "Current use of dietary supplementation in patients with age-related macular degeneration," *Canadian Journal of Ophthalmology*. February 2003; 38(1):27–32.
17. Francisco Contreras, M.D., *Health in the 21st Century*, 303.
18. Rex Russell, M.D., *What the Bible Says About Healthy Living*, 196.
19. M. Kumar and J. S. Berwal, "Sensitivity of Food Pathogens to Garlic," *Journal of Applied Microbiology*, February 1998, 213–15.
20. H. K. Berthold, T. Sudhop, K. von Bergmann, "Effect of a Garlic Oil Preparation on Serum Lipoproteins and Cholesterol Metabolism: A Randomized Controlled Trial," *Journal of the American Medical Association*, June 17, 1998, 1900–1902.
21. A. Bordia, S. K. Verma, K. C. Srivastava, "Effect of Garlic on Blood Lipids, Blood Sugar, Fibrinogen and Fibrinolytic Activity in Patients with Coronary Artery Disease," *Prostaglandins, Leukotrienes, and Essential Fatty Acids*, April 1998, 257–63.
22. M. Steiner and R. S. Lin, "Changes to Platelet Function and Susceptibility of Lipoproteins to Oxidation Associated with Administration of Aged Garlic Extract," *Journal of Cardiovascular Pharmacology*, June 1998, 904–8.
23. J. L. Efendy, D. L. Simmons, G. R. Campbell, J. H. Campbell, "The Effect of Aged Garlic Extract, 'Kyolic,' on the Development of Experimental Atherosclerosis," *Atherosclerosis*, July 1997, 37–42.

Chapter 5

1. A. Chisholm et al., "A Diet Rich in Walnuts Favourably Influences Plasma Fatty Acid Profile in Moderately Hyperlipidaemic Subjects," *European Journal of Clinical Nutrition*, January 1998, 12–16.
2. M. Abbey, M. Noakes, G. B. Belling, and P. J. Nestel, "Partial Replacement of Saturated Fatty Acids with Almonds or Walnuts Lowers Total Plasma Cholesterol and Low-Density-Lipoprotein Cholesterol," *American Journal of Clinical Nutrition*, May 1994, 995–999; G. A. Spiller et al., "Nuts and Plasma Lipids: An Almond-Based Diet Lowers Ldl-C While Preserving Hdl-C," *Journal of the American College of Nutrition*, June 1998, 285–290.
3. Reginald Cherry, M.D., *The Bible Cure*, 73.
4. M. J. Zibaeenezhad et al., "Walnut consumption in hyperlipidemic patients," *Angiology*, September-October 2005; 56(5):581–83.
5. J. B. Gray and A. M. Martinovic, "Eicosanoids and Essential Fatty Acid Modulation in Chronic Disease and the Chronic Fatigue Syndrome," *Medical Hypothesis*, July 1994, 31–42.
6. G. Hornstra et al., "Essential Fatty Acids in Pregnancy and Early Human Development," *European Journal of Obstetrics, Gynecology, and Reproductive Biology*, July 1995, 57–62.
7. E. N. Siguel and R. H. Lerman, "Prevalence of Essential Fatty Acid Deficiency in Patients with Chronic Gastrointestinal Disorders," *Metabolism: Clinical and Experimental*, January 1996, 12–23.
8. M. C. Kruger and D. F. Horrobin, "Calcium Metabolism, Osteoporosis and Essential Fatty Acids: A Review," *Progress in Lipid Research*, September 1997, 131–51.
9. K. Sieja, "Selenium Deficiency in Women with Ovarian Cancer Undergoing Chemotherapy and the Influence of Supplementation with This Micro-Element on Biochemical Parameters," *Pharmazie*, July 1998, 473–76.
10. Cheryl Townsley, *Food Smart*, 119.
11. Joyce Meyer, *Look Great, Feel Great*, 74.
12. A. R. Harper et al., "Flaxseed oil increases the plasma concentrations of cardioprotective (omega-3) fatty acids in humans," *Journal of Nutrition*, Jan 2006; 136(1):83–87.
13. Pamela Smith, R.D., *When Your Hormones Go Haywire*, 114.
14. Jim Shriner, *Eternally Fit*, 39.
15. Artalejo F. Rodriguez et al., "Consumption of Fruit and Wine and the Decline in Cerebrovascular Disease Mortality in Spain, Stroke," *Stroke*, August 29, 1998, 1556–1561.

16. Cherry, *The Bible Cure,* 112.

17. M. V. Clement et al., "Chemopreventive Agent Resveratrol," *Blood,* August 1, 1998, 996–1002.

18. F. Levi et al., "Food Groups and Risk of Oral and Pharyngeal Cancer," *International Journal of Cancer,* August 31, 1998, 705–9.

19. A. V. de Whalley et al., "Flavonoids Inhibit the Oxidative Modification of Low Density Lipoproteins by Macrophages," *Biochemical Pharmacology,* June 1, 1990, 1743–50.

20. K. Fujoika et al., "The effects of grapefruit on weight and insulin resistance: relationship to the metabolic syndrome," *Journal of Medicinal Food,* spring 2006; 9(1):49–54.

21. H. Hu and Y. M. Qin, "Grape seed proanthocyanidin extract induced mitochondria-associated apoptosis in human acute myeloid leukaemia 14.3D10 cells," *Chinese Medical Journal,* March 5, 2006; 119(5):417–21.

22. A. Shukitt-Hale et al., "Effects of Concord grape juice on cognitive and motor deficits in aging," *Nutrition,* March 2006; 22(3):295–302.

23. F. C. Lau, B. Shukitt-Hale, and J. A. Joseph, "The beneficial effects of fruit polyphenols on brain aging." *Neurobiology of Aging,* December 2005; 26 Suppl 1:128–32.

24. W. Yi et al., "Phenolic compounds from blueberries can inhibit colon cancer cell proliferation and induce apoptosis," *Journal of Agriculture and Food Chemistry,* 2005 September 7; 53(18):7320–29.

25. S. R. McAnulty et al., "Effect of daily fruit ingestion on angiotensin converting enzyme activity, blood pressure, and oxidative stress in chronic smokers," *Free Radical Research,* 2005 November; 39(11):1241–48.

26. G. D. Stoner et al., "Protection against esophageal cancer in rodents with lyophilized berries: potential mechanisms," *Nutrition and Cancer,* 2006; 54(1):33–46.

27. K. A. Rodrigo et al., "Suppression of the tumorigenic phenotype in human oral squamous cell carcinoma cells by an ethanol extract derived from freeze-dried black berries," *Nutrition and Cancer,* 2006; 54(1):58–68.

28. L. J. Nohynek et al., "Berry phenolics: antimicrobial properties and mechanisms of action against severe human pathogens," *Nutrition and Cancer,* 2006; 54(1):18–32.

29. Ibid.

30. T. Pajk et al., "Efficiency of apples, strawberries, and tomatoes for reduction of oxidative stress in pigs as a model for humans," *Nutrition,* 2006 April; 22(4):376–84.

31. A. Naemura et al., "Anti-thrombotic effect of strawberries," *Blood Coagulation and Fibrinolysis,* October 2005; 16(7):501–9.

32. A. Malik and H. Mukhtar, "Prostate cancer prevention through pomegranate fruit," *Cell Cycle,* 2006 February; 5(4):371–73.

33. L. S. Adams et al., "Pomegranate juice, total pomegranate ellagitannins, and punicalagin suppress inflammatory cell signaling in colon cancer cells," *Journal of Agricultural and Food Chemistry,* February 8, 2006; 54(3):980–85.

34. F. Visioli and C. Galli, "Oleuropein Protects Low Density Lipoprotein From Oxidation," *Life Sciences,* 1994, 1965–71.

35. Rex Russell, M.D., *What the Bible Says About Healthy Living,* 134.

36. N. H. Aziz et al., "Comparative Antibacterial and Antifungal Effects of Some Phenolic Compounds," *Microbios,* 1998, 43–54; *Biology,* June 1998, 981–87.

37. H. S. Tranter, S. C. Tassou, G33 Nychas, K. Koutsoumanis, et al., "Modelling the Effectiveness of a Natural Antimicrobial on Salmonella Enteritidis," *Journal of Applied Microbiology;* "The Effect of the Olive Phenolic Compound, Oleuropein, on the Growth of Enterotoxin B Production by Staphyloccus Aureus," *Journal of Applied Microbiology,* March 1993, 253–59; J. W. Austin et al., "Growth and Toxin Production by Clostridium Botulinum," *Journal of Good Protection,* March 1998, 324–28.

38. H. K. Hamdi and R. Castellon, "Oleuropein, a non-toxic olive iridoid, is an anti-tumor agent and cytoskeleton disruptor," *Biochemical and Biophysical Research Communications,* September 2, 2005; 334(3):769–78.

39. R. Fabiani et al., "Virgin olive oil phenols inhibit proliferation of human promyelocytic leukemia cells (HL60) by inducing apoptosis and differentiation," *Journal of Nutrition,* March 2006; 136(3):614–19.

40. M. I. Covas et al., "Postpriandial LDL phenolic content and LDL oxidation are modulated by olive oil phenolic compounds in humans," *Free Radical Biology and Medicine,* February 15, 2006; 40(4):608–16.

41. S. Salvini et al., "Daily consumption of a high-phenol extra-virgin olive oil reduces oxidative DNA damage in postmenopausal women," *British Journal of Nutrition,* April 2006; 95(4):742–51.

42. Smith, *When Your Hormones Go Haywire,* 211.
43. Kathleen O'Bannon Baldinger, "Olive Leaf Extract: Ancient Solution to Modern Ailments," *Nature's Impact,* December/ January 1999.

Chapter 6

1. Kathleen O'Bannon Baldinger, *The World's Oldest Health Plan,* 166.
2. L. H. Kushi, E. B. Lenart, W. C. Willett, "Health Implications of Mediterranean Diets in Light of Contemporary Knowledge," *American Journal of Clinical Nutrition,* June 1995, 1407S–1415S.
3. Don Colbert, M.D., *What Would Jesus Eat?* 202.
4. George Schwartz, *Food Power,* 96.
5. Strehlow Wighard, *Hildegard of Bingen's Medicine,* 32.
6. Jean Carper, *Food Your Miracle Medicine,* 18.
7. A. M. Albertson, R. C. Tobelmann, L. Marquart, "Estimated Dietary Calcium Intake and Food Sources," *Journal of Adolescent Health,* January 1997, 20–26.
8. Pamela Smith, R.D., *When Your Hormones Go Haywire,* 111.
9. Jim Shriner, *Eternally Fit,* 28.
10. L. K. Massey and S. A. Kynast-Gales, "Substituting Milk for Apple Juice Does Not Increase Kidney Stone Risk," *Journal of the American Dietetic Association,* March 1998, 303–8.
11. Joe S. McIlhaney, M.D., *1001 Health-Care Questions Women Ask,* 310.
12. F. F. Rubaltelli et al., "Intestinal Flora in Breast- and Bottle-Fed Infants," *Journal of Perinatal Medicine,* 1998, 186–91.
13. M. Olivares et al., "Antimocrobial potential of four Lactobacillus strains isolated from breast milk," *Journal of Applied Microbiology,* July 2006; 101(1):72–79.
14. Murray Michael, *Encyclopedia of Natural Medicine,* 157.
15. Erasmus Udo, *The Complete Guide to Fats and Oils in Health and Nutrition,* 218.
16. J. G. Barone et al., "Breastfeeding during infancy may protect against bedwetting during childhood," *Peadiatrics,* July 2006; 118(1):254–59.
17. U. Birberg-Thornberg et al., "Nutrition and theory of mind: The role of polyunsaturated fatty acids (PUFA) in the development of theory of mind," *Prostaglandins Leukotrienes and Essential Fatty Acids,* May 31, 2006.
18. Rex Russell, M.D., *What the Bible Says About Healthy Living,* 216.
19. Leonid Ber and Karolyn Gazella, *Activate Your Immune System,* 41.
20. Rona Zoltan, *The Colostrum Option: All the Natural Anti-Aging Growth Hormones and Immune Immune Enhancers Provided by Mother Nature!* 3.
21. Y. Yamada, S. Saito, H. Morikawa, "Hepatocyte Growth Factor in Human Breast Milk," *American Journal of Reproductive Immunology,* August 1998, 112–20.
22. Maureen Salaman, *The Diet Bible: The Bible for Dieters,* 228.
23. G. Schaafsma et al., "Effects of Milk Products, Fermented by Lactobacillus Acidophilus," *European Journal of Clinical Nutrition,* June 1998, 436–40.
24. E. Shalev et al., "Ingestion Of Yogurt Containing Lactobacillus Acidophilus," *Archives of Family Medicine,* November/ December 1996, 593–96.
25. Pamela Smith, *Healthy Expectations,* 87.
26. Shriner, *Eternally Fit,* 39.
27. A. S. Yalcin, "Emergin therapeutic potential of whey proteins and peptides." *Current Pharmaceutical Design,* 2006; 12(13):1637–43.
28. P. W. Parodi, "Dairy product consumption and the risk of breast cancer," *Journal of the American College of Nutrition,* December 2005; 24(6 Supplement):556S–68S.
29. Dr. Mary Ruth Swope, *Are You Sick and Tired of Feeling Sick and Tired?* 86.

Chapter 7

1. Kathleen O'Bannon Baldinger, *The World's Oldest Health Plan,* 281.
2. Kenneth Barker, ed., *The NIV Study Bible,* 1602.
3. Jordan Rubin, *The Maker's Diet,* 145.
4. Kenneth Cooper, M.D., *Advanced Nutritional Therapies,* 167.
5. J. A. Nettleton and R. Katz, "n-3 long-chain polyunsaturated fatty acids in type 2 diabetes: a review," *Journal of the American Dietetics Association,* March 2005; 105(3):428–40.
6. B. Miljanovic et al., "Relation between dietary n-3 and n-6 fatty acids and clinically diagnosed dry eye syndrome in women," *American Journal of Clinical Nutrition,* October 2005; 82(4):887–93.

7. B. A. Watkins, Y. Li, and M. F. Seifert, "Dietary ratio of n-6/n-3 PUFAs and docosahexaenoic acid: actions on bone mineral and serum biomarkers in ovariectomized rats," *Journal of Nutritional Biochemistry,* April 2006; 17(4):282–89.

8. J. Dry and D. Vincent, "Effect of fish oil diet on asthma," *International Archives of Allergy and Applied Immunology,* 1991, 156–57.

9. P. C. Calder, "Immunoregulatory and Inti-Inflammatory Effects of N-3 Polyunsaturated Fatty Acids," *Brazilian Journal of Medical and Biological Research,* April 1998, 467–90.

10. Julian Whitaker, M.D., *The Pain Relief Breakthrough,* 153.

11. G. Hansen et al., "Nutritional Status of Danish Patients with Rheumatoid Arthritis and Effects of a Diet Adjusted in Energy Intake, Fish Content, and Antioxidants," *Ugeskrift for Laeger,* May 18, 1998, 3074–78.

12. Dry and Vincent, "Effect of fish oil diet on asthma," 156–57.

13. T. Bjorkkjaer et al., "Short-term duodenal seal oil administration normalized n-6 to n-3 fatty acid ratio in rectal mucosa and ameliorated bodily pain in patients with inflammatory bowel disease," *Lipids in Health and Disease,* March 20, 2006; 5:6.

14. J. C. Maroon and J. W. Bost, "Omega-3 fatty acids (fish oil) as an anti-inflammatory: an alternative to nonsteroidal anti-inflammatory drugs for discogenic pain," *Surgical Neurology,* April 2006; 65(4):326–31.

15. W. Matsuyama et al., "Effects of omega-3 polyunsaturated fatty acids on inflammatory markers in COPD," *Chest,* December 2005; 128(6):3817–27.

16. A. M. Issa et al., "The effect of omega-3 fatty acids on cognitive function in aging and dementia: a systematic review," *Dementia and Geriatric Cognitive Disorders,* 2006; 21(2):88–96.

17. R. Uauy and A. D. Dangour, "Nutrition and brain development and aging: role of essential fatty acids," *Nutrition Review,* 2006 May; 64(5 Pt 2):S24–33.

18. A. J. Richardson, "Omega-3 fatty acids in ADHD and related neurodevelopmental disorders," *International Review of Psychiatry,* April 2006; 18(2):155–72.

19. J. M. Bourre, "Dietary omega-3 fatty acids and psychiatry: mood, behaviour, stress, depression, dementia, and aging," *The Journal of Nutrition, Health, and Aging,* 2005; 9(1):31–38.

20. H. Nemets et al., "Omega-3 treatment of childhood depression: a controlled, double-blind pilot study," *American Journal of Psychiatry,* June 2006; 163(6):1098–1100.

21. Kenneth H. Cooper, M.D., *Advanced Nutritional Therapies,* 220.

22. N. F. Sheard, "Fish Consumption and Risk of Sudden Cardiac Death," *Nutrition Reviews,* June 1998, 177–79; K. Landmark, "Fish, Fish Oils, Arrhythmias and Sudden Death," *Tidsskrift for den Norske Laegeforening,* June 1998, 2328–81.

23. D. Q. Bao et al., "Effects of Dietary Fish and Weight Reduction on Ambulatory Blood Pressure in Overweight Hypertensives," *Hypertension,* 710–17.

24. D. R. Morgan et al., "Effects of dietary omega-3 fatty acid supplementation on endothelium-dependent vasodilation in patients with chronic heart failure," *American Journal of Cardiology,* February 15, 2006; 97(4):547–51.

25. I. Romieu et al., "Omega-3 fatty acid prevents heart rate variability reductions associated with particulate matter," *American Journal of Respiratory and Critical Care Medicine,* December 15, 2005; 172(12):1534–40.

Chapter 8

1. Jordan Rubin, *The Great Physician's Rx,* 87.

2. T. Negishi, H. Rai, H. Hayatsu, "Antigenotoxic Activity Of Natural Chlorophylls," *Mutation Research,* May 1997, 97–100.

3. U. Harttig and G. S. Bailey, "Chemoprotection by Natural Chlorophylls in Vivo," *Carcinogenesis,* July 1998, 1323–26.

4. James F. Balch and A. Phyllis, *Prescription for Nutritional Healing,* 75.

5. Don Colbert, M.D., *What Would Jesus Eat?* 107.

6. James B. Balch and A. Phyllis, *Prescription for Nutritional Healing,* 69.

7. Y. Omura et al., "Significant Mercury Deposits in Internal Organs Following the Removal of Dental Amalgam," *Acupuncture and Electro-Therapeutics Research,* April 1996, 133–60.

8. Francisco Contreras, M.D., *Health in the 21st Century,* 273.

9. Rubin, *The Great Physician's Rx,* 54, 58.

10. K. Tanaka et al., "Oral Administration of a Unicellular Green Algae, Chlorella Vulgaris, Prevents Stress-Induced Ulcer," *Planta Medica,* October 1997, 465–66.

11. K. Noda et al., "A Water-Soluble Antitumor Glycoprotein from Chlorella Vulgaris," *Planta Medica,* October 1996, 423–26.

12. H. M. Kim et al., "Inhibitory Effect of Mast Cell-Mediated Immediate-Type Allergic Reactions in Rats by Spirulina," *Biochamical Pharmacology,* April 1998, 1071–76.

13. B. A. Buletsa et al., "The Prevalence, Structure and Clinical Problems of Multiple Sclerosis," *Likarska Sprava,* October/December 1996, 163–65.

14. Kathleen O'Bannon Baldinger, *The World's Oldest Health Plan*, 1994, 160.

15. Joseph Dommers Vehling, ed. and trans., *Apicius, Cookery and Dining in Imperial Rome,* (New York, Dover Publications,) 1977.

16. Colbert, *What Would Jesus Eat?* 97.

17. J. M. Seddon et al., "Dietary Carotenoids, Vitamins A, C, E, and Advanced Age-Related Macular Degeneration," *Journal of the American Medical Association,* November 9, 1994, 1413–20.

18. J. M. Seddon et al., "A Prospective Study of Cigarette Smoking and Age-Related Macular Degeneration in Women," *Journal of the American Medical Association,* October 9, 1996, 1141–46.

19. Colbert, *What Would Jesus Eat?* 96.

20. E. Jennings, "Folic Acid as a Cancer-Preventing Agent," *Medical Hypotheses,* September 1995, 297–303.

21. T. K. Eskes, "Open or Closed? A World of Difference: A History of Homocysteine Research," *Nutrition Reviews,* August 1998, 236–44.

Chapter 9

1. Jordan Rubin, *The Great Physician's Rx,* 29.

2. L. H. Kushi, E. B. Lenart, W. C. Willett, "Health Implications of Mediterranean Diets in Light of Contemporary Knowledge," *American Journal of Clinical Nutrition,* June 1995, 1416s–1427s.

3. Julian Whitaker, M.D., *The Pain Relief Breakthrough,* 153.

4. Maureen Salaman, *The Diet Bible: The Bible for Dieters,* 57.

5. Jim Shriner, *Eternally Fit,* 29.

6. D. M. DeMarini, "Dietary Interventions of Human Carcinogenesis," *Mutation Research,* May 1998, 457–65.

7. Salaman, *The Diet Bible,* 59.

8. Ibid., 63.

Chapter 10

1. Nigel F. Hepper, *Baker Encyclopedia of Bible Plants,* 118.

2. Don Colbert, M.D., *What Would Jesus Eat?* 159.

3. Joyce Meyer, *Look Great, Feel Great,* 37.

4. D. J. Chisholm, L. V. Campbell, and E. W. Kraegen, "Pathogenesis of the Insulin Resistance Syndrome (Syndrome X)," *Clinical and Experimental Pharmacology and Physiology,* September 1997, 782–84.

5. R. J. Barnard et al., "Diet-Induced Insulin Resistance Precedes Other Aspects of the Metabolic Syndrome," *Journal of Applied Physiology,* April 1998, 1311–15.

6. J. Yip, F. S. Facchini, G. M. Reaven, "Resistance to Insulin-Mediated Glucose Disposal as a Predictor of Cardiovascular Disease," *Journal of Clinical Endocrinology and Metabolism,* August 1998, 2773–76.

7. G. M. Baillie et al., "Insulin and Coronary Artery Disease," *Annals of Pharmacotherapy,* February 1998, 233–47.

8. D. S. Hardin et al., "Treatment of Childhood Syndrome X," *Pediatrics,* August 1997, E5.

9. Reginald Cherry, M.D., *The Bible Cure,* 106.

10. Jordan Rubin, *The Great Physician's Rx,* 54, 60.

11. F. P. Cappuccio et al., "Double-Blind Randomised Trial of Modest Salt Restriction in Older People," *Lancet,* September 1997, 850–54.

12. Pamela Smith, *When Your Hormones Go Haywire,* 200.

13. Kenneth H. Cooper, M.D., *Advanced Nutritional Therapies,* 324.

14. N. Fuenmayor et al., "Salt Sensitivity Is Associated with Insulin Resistance in Essential Hypertension," *American Journal of Hypertension,* April 1998, 397–402.

15. Rubin, *The Great Physician's Rx,* 45.

16. Colbert, *What Would Jesus Eat?* 143.

17. C. C. Cook, "B Vitamin Deficiency and Neuropsychiatric Syndromes in Alcohol Misuse," *Alcohol and Alcoholism,* July 1998, 317–36.

Chapter 11

1. Dr. Mary Ruth Swope, *Are You Sick and Tired of Feeling Sick and Tired?* 77.

2. Anne E. and J. David Frähm, *Healthy Habits,* 46.
3. Jordan Rubin, *The Great Physician's Rx,* 33.
4. Ibid. 33.
5. S. I. McMillen, M.D., *None of These Diseases,* 25.
6. "Food Safety in the Kitchen: A 'HACCP' Approach," Food Safety and Inspection Service, United States Department of Agriculture, Consumer Education, and Information booklet.
7. McMillen, *None of These Diseases,* 23.
8. Ibid., 15.
9. S. W. Huang and J. W. Kimborough, "Mold Allergy Is a Risk Factor for Persistent Cold-Like Symptoms in Children," *Clinical Pediatrics,* December 1997, 695–99.
10. M. Halonen et al., "Alternaria as a Major Allergen for Asthma in Children Raised in a Desert Environment," *American Journal of Respiratory and Critical Care Medicine,* April 1997, 1356–61.
11. C. S. Li, C. W. Hsu, and M. L. Tai, "Indoor Pollution and Sick Building Syndrome Symptoms Among Workers in Day-Care Centers," *Archives of Environmental Health,* May-June 1997, 200–207.
12. Francisco Contreras, M.D., *Health in the 21st Century,* 86.
13. F. Fung, R. Clark, and S. Williams, "Stachybotrys, a Mycotoxin-Producing Fungus of Increasing Toxicologic Importance," *Journal of Toxicology, Clinical Toxicology,* 1998, 79–86.
14. M. C. Yin and W. S. Cheung, "Inhibition of Aspergillus Niger and Aspergillus Flavus by Some Herbs and Spices," *Journal of Food Protection,* January 1998, 123–25.

Chapter 12

1. Dr. Suzan Johnson Cook, *Live Like You're Blessed,* 119.
2. Ibid., 129.
3. D. R. Blumenthal, J. Neeman, and C. M. Murphy, "Lifetime Exposure to Interparental Physical and Verbal Aggression and Symptom Expression in College Students," *Violence and Victims,* 1998, 175–96.
4. W. R. Beardslee, E. M. Versage, and T. R. Gladstone, "Children of Affectively Ill Parents: A Review of the Past 10 Years," *Journal of the American Academy of Child Adolescent Psychiatry,* November 1998, 1134–41.
5. Y. Miyake et al., "Dietary folate and vitamins B (12), B (6), and B (2) intake and the risk of postpartum depression in Japan: The Osaka Maternal and Child Health Study," *Journal of Affective Disorder,* June 29, 2006.
6. P. J. Lustman and R. E. Clouse, "Depression in diabetic patients: the relationship between mood and glycemic control," *Journal of Diabetes Complications,* March-April 2005; 19(2):113–22.
7. C. R. Markus et al., "Does Carbohydrate-Rich, Protein-Poor Food Prevent a Deterioration of Mood and Cognitive Performance of Stress-Prone Subjects When Subjected to a Stressful Task?," *Appetite,* August 1998, 49–65.
8. R. Edwards, M. Peet, J. Shay, and D. Horrobin, "Omega-3 Polyunsaturated Fatty Acid Levels in the Diet and in Red Blood Cell Membranes of Depressed Patients," *Journal of Affective Disorders,* March 1998, 149–55.
9. Jim Shriner, *Eternally Fit,* 25–26.
10. W. David Hager, M.D., and Linda Carruth Hager, *Stress and the Woman's Body,* 207.
11. A. S. Wells et al., "Alterations in Mood After Changing to a Low-Fat Diet," *British Journal of Nutrition,* January 1998, 23–30.
12. John Diamond, M.D., *Your Body Doesn't Lie* 159–67.
13. Jordan Rubin, *The Great Physician's Rx,* 159.
14. Rita Bennett, *How to Pray for Inner Healing,* 77.
15. N. Grisaru et al., "Transcranial Magnetic Stimulation in Mania," *American Journal of Psychiatry,* November 1998, 1608–10.
16. Julian Whitaker, M.D., *The Pain Relief Breakthrough,* 68.

Chapter 13

1. T. D. Jakes, *Lay Aside the Weight,* 68.
2. Joseph Mercola, M.D., *Mercola's Total Health Program,* 10.
3. Dr. Mary Ruth Swope, *Are You Sick and Tired of Being Sick and Tired?* 118.
4. Mercola, *Mercola's Total Health Program,* 10.
5. Jim Shriner, *Eternally Fit,* 38–39.
6. Pamela Smith, *When Your Hormones Go Haywire,* 162.
7. Jakes, *Lay Aside the Weight,* 125.
8. Herbert Wagemaker, M.D., *The Surprising Truth About Depression,* 42.
9. H. Leighton Steward, C. Bethea Morrison,

S. Andrew Samuel, and Luis Balart, *Sugar Busters!* 35.

10. A.J. Siegel, "The Biblical Diagnostician and the Anorexic Bride," *Fertility and Sterility,* January 1998, 8–10.
11. Joe McIlhaney, M.D., *1001 Health-Care Questions Women Ask,* 80.
12. D. C. Jimerson et al., "Decreased Serotonin Function in Bulimia Nervosa," *Archives of General Psychiatry,* June 1997, 529–34.
13. Florence Littauer, *Your Personality Tree,* 203.

Also of Interest:

Mary Pipher, Ph.D., *Reviving Ophelia* (G. P. Putnam, 1994).

Cheryl Boone O'Neill, *Starving for Attention* (Continuum, 1982).

Frank Minirth, M.D., Paul Meier, M.D., Robert Hemfelt, M.D., and Sharon Sneed, M.D., *Love Hunger* (Thomas Nelson, 1990).

Fred and Florence Littauer, *Freeing Your Mind from Memories That Bind* (Thomas Nelson, 1992).

Chapter 14

1. William Crook, M.D., *The Yeast Connection,* Preface, i.
2. S. W. Huang and J. W. Kimbrough, "Mold Allergy Is a Risk Factor for Persistent Cold-like Symptoms in Children," *Clinical Pediatrics,* December 1997, 695–99.
3. P. Kurnatowski et al., "The fungal infections in patients hospitalized in an intensive care unit," *Wiadomosci Parazytologiczne,* 2005; 51(1):23–27.
4. E. M. Missoni et al., "Role of yeasts in diabetic foot ulcer infection," *Acta Medica Croatica,* 2006; 60(1):43–50.
5. B. J. Noble and A. P. Mitchell, "Genetics and genomics of Candida albican biofilm formation," *Cell Microbiology,* July 11, 2006.
6. Crook, *The Yeast Connection and the Woman,* 56.
7. Ibid., 40–43.
8. Don Colbert, M.D., *The Bible Cure for Candida and Yeast Infections,* 19.
9. J. M. Concha, L. S. Moore, and W. J. Holloway, "Antifungal Activity of Melaleuca Alternifolia (Tea-Tree) Oil Against Various Pathogenic Organisms," *Journal of the American Podiatric Medical Association,* October 1998, 489–92.
10. Colbert, *The Bible Cure for Candida and Yeast Infections,* 35.

Chapter 15

1. Don Colbert, M.D. *The Bible Cure for Candida and Yeast Infections,* 62.
2. Jordan Rubin, *The Great Physician's Rx,* 62.
3. M. L. Nurminen, R. Korpela, and H. Vapaatola, "Dietary Factors in the Pathogenesis and Treatment of Hypertension," *Annals of Medicine,* April 1998, 143–50.
4. K. Breithaupt-Grogler et al., "Protective Effect of Chronic Garlic Intake on Elastic Properties of Aorta in the Elderly," *Circulation,* October 1997, 2649–55.
5. E. M. Lau and J. Woo, "Nutrition and Osteoporosis," *Current Opinion in Rheumatology,* July 1998, 368–72.
6. Rubin, *The Great Physician's Rx,* 204.
7. Mark Pearson, *Christian Healing,* 120–1.
8. Kenneth H. Cooper, M.D., *It's Better to Believe,* 183.
9. Pearson, *Christian Healing,* 58.

Chapter 16

1. R. Gosselink and M. Decramer, "Peripheral Skeletal Muscles and Exercise Performance in Patients with COPD," *Monaldi Archives for Chest Disease,* August 1998, 419–23.
2. E. A. Platz et al., "Physical Activity and Benign Prostatic Hyperplasia," *Archives of Internal Medicine,* November 1998, 2349–56.
3. B. Zerahn et al., "Bone Loss After Hip Fracture Is Correlated to the Postoperative Degree of Mobilisation," *Archives of Orthopaedic and Trauma Surgery,* 1998, 453–56.
4. Don Colbert, M.D., *What Would Jesus Eat?* 173.
5. W. A. Smith, "Fibromyalgia Syndrome," *Nursing Clinics of North America,* December 1998, 653–69.
6. H. Tanaka, M. J. Reiling, and D. R. Seals, "Regular Walking Increases Peak Limb Vasodilatory Capacity of Older Hypertensive Humans," *Journal of Hypertension,* April 1998, 423–28.
7. J. Iwamoto et al., "Effect of Increased Physical Activity on Bone Mineral Density in Postmenopausal Osteoporotic Women," *Keio Journal of Medicine,* September 1998, 157–61.

8. T. M. Manini et al., "Daily activity energy expenditure and mortality among older adults," *Journal of the American Medical Association,* July 12, 2006:296(2):216–18.

9. T. M. Asikainen et al., "Effect of brisk walking in 1 or 2 daily bouts and moderate resistance training on lower-extremity muscle strength, balance, and walking performance in women who recently went through menopause: a randomized, controlled trial," *Physical Therapy,* July 2006; 86(7):912–23.

10. Julian Whitaker, M.D., and Brenda Adderly, M.H.A., *The Pain Relief Breakthrough,* 39.

Chapter 17

1. Don Colbert, M.D., *The Bible Cure for Candida and Yeast Infections,* 77.
2. Ibid., 34.
3. J. R. Petrie, S. J. Cleland, and M. Small, "The Metabolic Syndrome: Overeating, Inactivity, Poor Compliance or 'Dud' Advice?" *Diabetic Medicine,* November 1998, S29–S31.
4. A. G. Christen and J. A. Christen, "Horace Fletcher (1849–1919): 'The Great Masticator,'" *Journal of the History of Dentistry,* November 1997, 95–100.
5. Jordan Rubin, *The Maker's Diet,* 195.
6. T. D. Jakes, *Lay Aside the Weight,* 109.

Chapter 18

1. Michael Strassfeld, *The Jewish Holidays,* 85.
2. T. D. Jakes, *Lay Aside the Weight,* 93.
3. Cheryl Townsley, *Food Smart,* 182–83.
4. Rex Russell, M.D., *What the Bible Says About Healthy Living,* 89.
5. Ibid., 93.
6. R. Kradin, "The placebo response complex," *Journal of the Annals of Psychology,* 2004 November; 49(5):617–34.

Index

B

C

D

E

F

G

H

I

N

O

S

T

U

V

W

X

Y

Z